# THE BIG FEMINIST BUT

Comics about Women, Men and
the IFs, ANDs & BUTs of Feminism

Edited by Shannon O'Leary & Joan Reilly

This book is dedicated to the 4th Wave.

Second edition published by
Alternative Comics
21607B Stevens Creek Blvd.
Cupertino, CA 95014
IndyWorld.com

Editors: Shannon O'Leary & Joan Reilly
Consulting Editors: Rob Clough & Suzanne Kleid
Design Consultant: Levon Jihanian
Cover Design and Illustration: Joan Reilly
Book Layout Design: Joan Reilly

Second Printing, December, 2014. PRINTED IN CANADA

# Table of Contents

# Acknowledgments

**This book would not exist without the generous support and encouragement of:** Sultan Saeed Al Darmaki, Jeanne A. Heaton, Tom Neely, Emily Nilsson, Tracy Sane, Anina Moore, Linda Sciuto, Brooke Devine, Anna Livia Cardin Gomart, David Heaton, Charles Brownstein, Rebecca Eisenberg, Annie Koyama, Amanda Marcotte, Kent Osborne, Laura Hudson, Lorraine Almeida, Brett Schenker, Matt Patterson, Eli Bishop, Julie Eliza Cardenas, The Brown/Holroyd Family, Lora Bartlett, Mission: Comics & Art, Jeanne Block, Maya Sinclair, Jared Gardner, , Sarah Wood, Michael Volovar, Marsha Webb, Aaron L. Nuttall, Maria Annichia Riolo, Cathy Stevens, Lisa Ullmann, Tyler & Wendy Chin-Tanner, Sabrina Yoong, Katie Gillum, Steven desJardins, ione nomiki, Ben Whittenbury, Robert Fish, Dave McCullough, Terry of Wexford, Robert Reilly, Sthefan Turque Schultz, Pippa Bianco, Ean Murphy, Patricia H. Erb, Arlen Schumer, Dan Sharber, Chris Glazier, Prema "Big But" Behan, Vesa-Matti Ollila, Radhika Natarajan, Retta Thompson Clews, Allegheny College, SARO, CONSIDER THE TROUBLE, Barry Perlman, Josh Marowitz, Heather Shaughnessy, Jeff Stevenson, Nathan X McDyer, Mira Prinz Arey, David johnson, Rebecca Jane Weinstein, Clare Haggarty, Dominique Rolin, Chris Sarnowski, Maggie Scott, John S Costello, Laura Singley, Margaret McCarthy, Liz Walsh, Nicole Rudick, Earnest Racket, Ann Adkinson, Chance Press, Kamikaze Truths, Marianne Falck Orby, James Lehr, Gwen Clay, Lyla Warren, University of Chicago Library, Mo Morelli, Kate Stewart, Liene Verzemnieks, Kevin J. "Womzilla" Maroney, Elliott Sawyer, Raphaël, H F Biggs, Kris McNyset, Mark Arsenault, Jay Jordan, MBeck, Lujo Records, Ria, Alejandra Quintas, Jeff Pollet, Tony Breed, ra-φ, Ross Macpherson, Adalyn Mae Montero, Paul Braidford, Dalia T., Kay Starr, Anna Weiss, Liz Nugent, James Gary, Teresa Wall, Yuval Sivan, William Burns, Becky Kershman, Mark Katzoff, Allegra Stout, @WebGuyShy, Jesse Barnes, Stina Hansson, Delaine Derry Green, Janna Solis, Emily Willson, Pauline Zaldonis, Jery, Lars Ingebrigtsen, Kyle Coffey, Sadie Denver, Diana E. Williams, Christopher Capozzoli, Shannan, Christie Theys, Janice M. Eisen, Jah Furry, jamie jamie, Santiago Sanabria, Amanda Ackerman, Shanna Maurizi, Nika Vagner, Dee Morgan, Danielle Schulman, Erica Friedman, Ryan Suits, Lety R-Z, Hope Larson, AV, DB, HS, NM, Kelli Pax Phillips, Michael Handler, Levon Jihanian, N. Saphra, David Golbitz, Alexis Siemon, The Rev. Rafer Roberts, Jo Dawson, Steve Stormoen, James Daily, Song Hia, Heloise Lanoix, Adam Staffaroni, Rev. Kellie Rupard-Schorr, Ali Grotkowski, Deva Kyle, Kimberly Egolf, Molly Scaison, Erica Irk Bercegeay, Jeremy Baum, Olivia Desormeaux, Tim Hamilton, Karley Johnston, Big Feminist Marnie Galloway, Stephen Kupiec, S.E. Andres, Johanna Draper Carlson, Kevin Moore, Marie Stewart, Greg Norwood, The Sequential Artists Workshop, Angela Paman, Karen Green, Christine Davitt, Kathryn Gilmore, Toby Deutsch, L Worsh, Duffi McDermott, Andrew Farago, Lawrence McClurkin, Shauna Gordon-McKeon, Lynn & Roger OLeary-Archer, Kara Moore O'Leary & Kevin Moore-O'Leary, Jordan Johnson, Jenn Frederick, Hilary SK, Melanie W, Wendy Peters, Michelle Kreutzer, James Masente, Melanie Stevens, Amy Finkel, Moms Read Comics, John Gallagher, Isaac Cates, Jacob Haller, Nice-Ass Allison, Joy Decena, Sarah Elsewhere, Dean Haspiel, Brendan Tihane, Jason Grey, Jessi Jordan, Nikki Porter, mardou, Donna Mabry, Lindsey Briggs, Mandy Fehlbaum, Ursula Murray Husted and Bryan Bornmueller, James Specht, Veronica, Julie and Luke Casson, Amanda Tveidt, Heidi Butler, Alex Dahm, David Bitterbaum, Mia MacHatton Pryputniewicz, Laura Moore, Lynda Underwood, Ed Luce, Derek & Amelia R, Nick Kuntz, Lynne Hughes Maloney, Ben McKenzie (@labcoatman), Laura Krier, MAD, Wood, Joe Andrieu, Erika Moen, Joe Keatinge, Joshua 'Myca' Clark, Timothy Franklin, Simon Gärdenfors, Cj Reay, Jessica Abel and Matt Madden, elizabeth, Gwen [BDZoom.com], Tove Bonnedal, Julia Michalsky, Peter Sodja, Elizabeth B, Jason Viola, Stephen Hines, Caitlin M. Taylor, Jessica Beuthe, Maria Sandmo, Jenna Goodall, Lindsey Donovan, Alan O'Leary, A.j. Michel, Alison Ziesel, The Strumpet, Kate Hanley, David Nyer, Lizz Lunney, Damian Gordon, Kirt Dankmyer, Emma Vossen, Jack Baur, Teen Services Librarian, Sarah Wardlaw, Judy Lee, Amy E. Cohen, Tyler Cohen, Gerard Cronin, Felicity Kusinitz, Glynnis Fawkes, Justin Tokarski, Ashley E. Hurst, Timothy Eklund, Niki La Teer, Beth Dean, Jeff Gibbons, Kristofer K Loukas, Popi Charalambous, Andi Zeisler, Kjerstin Johnson, Kurt Anderson, Erin Subramanian, Alison Hallett, Helen Collins, Melissa Nappi, Lauren Burke, MariNaomi, Vanessa Satone, Amos Turner, Lori A. Smith, Jonathan Korman, Taylor Wells, Jessalyn Miyashiro, David Lasky, Esq., Brianne McMillan, Amy F Huziak, Holly Rushing, Kate Drwecka, Sarra Bankston, Gina Curtice, Adam "Sundog" Pasion, Kelly Berger, Bess Williamson, Jeanine Schaefer, Bradford Chatterjee, Bailey SR, Nóirín Plunkett, Daniel Pittman & Melissa Craig, Chris Rosa, Mary Dore, Brian Gardes, Dana Jeri Maier, Naomi Oliver, Marion Allard, Yunn Wei Yee, Blanca G. Valdivia, Camilla Stacey, Liz Argall, Stefan Lindberg, Alexa Dickman, j wallace, Robert J. Ontell, Esq., raighne, Greg Lieberknecht, Comics Bulletin, Martin Cendreda, Shane Wegner, Lisa Derrick, Andy Ristaino, Penny Penniston, A. Ho, Rhiannon Brock, Karen Williams, Heather Nunnelly, Naomi Clark, Tina Chronopoulos, Sarah Gilbert, Alice Quinn, Gabrielle Gamboa, Monica Neddi, A. M. Vargas-Machuca, Rinu, Sarah Bostwick, Rachael O'Rourke, Sheila Ashdown, Chris Schoen, Erin LaPooks Alvarez, Katie Goodrich, Adam Nelson, Charlotte Dye, Jason Rodriguez, Vince Averello, James McShane, Meg & The Pug of Darkness, Ryan Bayne, Martin Torstensson, Alison Wilgus, Aaron Kashtan, Leah Kunz, Christopher Daley, Jackie Lealess, Nicole Maunsell, Mike Ramsey, Shadowcthuhlu, May-Ling Gonzales, Tara Brannigan, Jennifer Wolf, Barry Deutsch, flussberg, Elizabeth Lower-Basch, Lauren Davis, Tim Marsh, Kayla Cagan, Oddy-Knocky, Jim Higgins, Carrie S Trimble, Minty Lewis, Simon Linder, Janet Hong Yam, Emily & Grat, Amanda Bennett, A Friend, Coral Peterson, erina chablis, Catherine James, Cathya J. Leiser, Elizabeth M., Sarah Louise Smith, Dawnalee, Tony Ridgway, Heidi MacDonald, Ross A. Lincoln, B Arnold, Janna O'Shea, Anastasia Warzinski, Diana Swartz, Adam Pruett, Olivia Jeffes and Chad Mccamlie, E Cummings, Suzie Kotzer-Fischer, C Cassano, Aaron Dellutri, Stephanie Bao, Bob Doherty, Marcin J. Wolynski, Burning Wood Media, Sammi Guidera, Elizabeth S., Brandon Geurts, Zoe Witzeling, Ann, Rickard Eriksson, Weiss Hall, Robynne Blumë, Dorothy Ford, Jordan Carp, Louise Larsen, Andrew Storey, Sarah Eileen, Susanna, Kelly Froh, Sally East, Lindsey Erin Babe Sterrett, Kawai Shen (Cute Juice Comics), Lostwhilecaching, Kaloian Doganov, Dan Spiegel, Zack Soto.

# An Introduction to The Big Feminist BUT

by Shannon O'Leary
Illustrations by Joan Reilly

What follows are the ideas, experiences and impressions of individual cartoonists and writers at a very specific moment in time: the end of the first decade of the 21st century. As a whole, however, *The Big Feminist BUT* should be considered in two contexts: that of its collective message and that of its medium.

*The Big Feminist BUT*'s collective message is more provocative and playful than it is polemic and is perhaps best considered through the lens of the disclaimers, "I'm not a feminist BUT..." or "I am a feminist BUT..." as in, "I am a total feminist but I'm going to be a stay-at-home mom for now" or "I'm not a feminist but I don't think you should be making decisions about my birth control." We are living in an era of unprecedented freedom and choice, but feminism—a large part of why we've arrived at this particular point in history—is a touchy, loaded word that suffers from a serious image problem. And if feminism is currently suffering from an image problem, does that mean it should just go away? Is it passé? Is there nothing left to fight for? Is there a discernable feminist movement? And if there is, what are its aims? What does it mean to be a feminist today? Who are today's feminists?

We asked our contributors to consider themselves on the much more level but still contradictory playing field both sexes are struggling to find their footing on today. What we got was a collection of distinctive, personal stories about the current state of gender equality that is in no way meant to be representative of all women and men's feelings and attitudes about feminism. But before we get to their comics and start thinking about where we are, it might help to briefly consider where we've been.

Let's start with the Seneca Falls convention of 1848, which marked the birthplace of the modern feminist movement. It was there that proto-suffragette Elizabeth Cady Stanton drafted and presented The Declaration of Sentiments. Based on the Declaration of Independence, The Declaration of Sentiments outlined a movement to attain the rights of

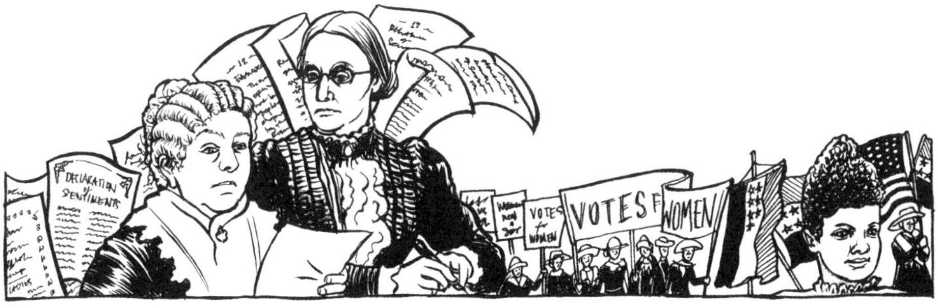
DECLARATION OF SENTIMENTS
VOTES for WOMEN
VOTES F
WOMEN

From Left to Right: Elizabeth Cady Stanton, Susan B. Anthony, suffragettes and Ida B. Wells

women in secular, political and religious spheres. Seventy-two years after that notion was first put forth by Stanton and her fellow First Wave Feminists; The United States ratified the 19th Amendment, which granted women the right to vote.

For the next twenty-five years or so, women made impressive strides both culturally and politically. They put on pants, flew planes and the new mediums of motion pictures and photographs often captured them jumping in and out of fountains full of champagne. While many obvious social and civic inequities still existed, images of independent women and "career gals" flourished in the popular films, books and magazines of the day. But that all came to a virtual standstill around 1946 – 1947 when the feminist movement experienced its first significant cultural and political backlash of the 20th Century.

As outlined by Betty Friedan in *The Feminine Mystique*, which celebrates its 50th Anniversary this year, the feminist movement stopped moving forward, and when it did, the word feminism became a dirty one. Feminists and their aims were characterized as destabilizing, pathological and unnatural. Women were instead encouraged to embrace the occupation of "Housewife" and to pursue self-actualization through waxing floors, baking cupcakes and making babies as the icon of the smiling 50's housewife cemented itself in popular culture.

It wasn't until the Food and Drug Administration approved the use of oral contraception (AKA "The Pill") in 1960 that issues of gender equality became prominent in American public discourse again. The Pill's availability ushered in The Sexual Revolution. Women, and men along with them, gained the freedom to choose when and when not to have

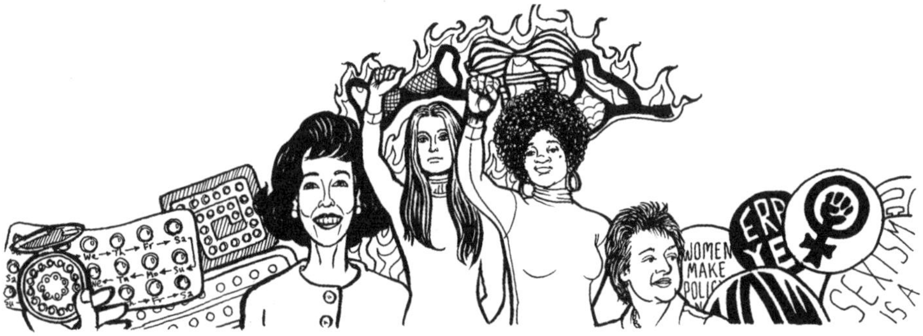
WOMEN
MAKE
From Left to Right: Helen Gurley Brown, Gloria Steinem, Dorothy Pitman Hughes and Betty Friedan

kids. Soon after, two of the most influential books of the 20th Century were published: Helen Gurley Brown's *Sex and The Single Girl* in 1962 and the aforementioned, *The Feminine Mystique* by Betty Friedan, one year later in 1963. Often overlooked as a frivolous, dated advice book, Gurley Brown's *Sex and the Single Girl* encouraged women to seek economic independence and have a sex life, whether they were married or not. While Friedan's meticulously researched and intellectual yet accessible *Feminine Mystique* challenged women to examine what she referred to as "the problem that has no name" to describe the emptiness they felt in the absence of the pursuit of work outside the home.

Both books became instant, international bestsellers and helped define the aims of Second Wave Feminism. By 1972, the landmark Supreme Court decision, *Roe vs. Wade*, legalized abortion, further guaranteeing a women's right to choose when and when not to start a family. That same year, feminists, led by Friedan and others, sought to ratify the Equal Rights Amendment to guarantee women equal rights to men under the United States Constitution. In 1982, after failing to obtain the requisite number of state ratifications, the ERA expired.

As Susan Faludi asserts in her 1991 book, *Backlash: The Undeclared War on American Women*, it was around that time that the 20th Century's second backlash against modern feminism emerged. The election of Ronald Reagan in 1981 ushered in a new era of populist conservatism. Feminism once again became a dirty word and images of desperate and neurotic nouveau-spinster careerists thrived at the box office in films like *Fatal Attraction* and in widely read publications, such as *Newsweek*, which famously published an article in 1986 that presented as fact a speciously researched statistic that women over the age of 40 were more likely to be shot by a terrorist than they were to get married.

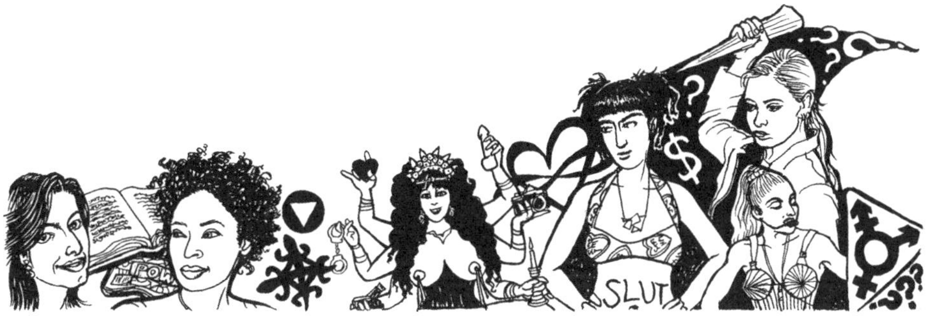
SLUT

From Left to Right: Susan Faludi, Rebecca Walker, Annie Sprinkle, Kathleen Hanna, Madonna and Buffy the Vampire Slayer

If historical patterns are to repeat as they did in the 20th Century, it's about time for the Third Wave Feminist Movement, which is thought to have emerged sometime around the publication of *Backlash*, to mobilize for something… But, what? While Third Wave Feminism might be responsible for The Lily Ledbetter Fair Pay Act and the empowering but somewhat schizophrenic cultural icons of Courtney Love, Buffy the Vampire Slayer and Hilary Clinton, its overall aims are unclear.

This book does not seek to define those aims. These stories are essentially dispatches from the shadows of that second backlash. The average age of the contributors and editors to *The Big Feminist BUT* rounds out to about 31 – 37 years old, with overlaps in either direction of approximately 7 years. As such, most of us came of age in the 1980s and 1990s. We fall generally under the demographics of Generations X, Y and Millennial and, much like our generations as a whole, have no collective assertion about where feminism should or is going as a social and political movement.

Which brings us to the medium of this book: comics, or as Will Eisner was the first to define it in his 1985 book, *Comics and Sequential Art*, sequential art. Similar to feminism, comics have pretty much always endured periods of being maligned and misunderstood. Two years prior to the Seneca Falls Convention, in 1846, the legendary English poet William Wordsworth authored a sonnet entitled "Illustrated Books and Newspapers" that demonized comics and pictorial narratives as the lowest form of entertainment. It contained the memorable verse:

> From manhood—back to childhood; for the age—
> Back towards caverned life's first rude career.
> Avaunt this vile abuse of pictured page!

Over a century later, in 1954, comics were made out to be the arbiters of juvenile delinquency with the implementation of the Comics Code Authority by the Comics Magazine Association of America, which established a code of ethics to prohibit lurid depictions of sex and violence in comic books. Then, in 2005, just as comics were starting to get a little respect, the Danish newspaper, *Jyllands-Posten*, published cartoons of the Islamic prophet, Muhammad, that were subsequently deemed a human rights violation by The United Nations.

Yet while they have been infantilized and subject to unnecessary censure due to the perception that they are both childish entertainment as well as a corrupting influence on children, there is no denying that comics, as an art form, have arrived. Also in 2005, *Time* magazine named the graphic novel *Watchmen* (DC Comics, 1986) by Alan Moore and Tony Gibbons as one of the 100 greatest novels of the Twentieth Century. Then in 2006, Alison Bechdel's *Fun Home*, a graphic novel memoir about coming out as a gay woman in a dysfunctional family, spent two weeks on the *New York Times* best-seller list, proving that comics can tackle serious issues such as gender politics and sexual identity.

It is the editors' intention for these comics to similarly inspire readers to consider their own attitudes towards feminism. We might, after all, just be on the verge of another revolution. In fact, comics, a medium that was forced early on to become notoriously insular to protect itself from those who sought to marginalize it, might learn something in the immediate from self-proclaimed radical feminist, bell hooks, who famously declared in 2000 with the publication of her book, *Feminism is for Everybody: Passionate Politics*, that, feminism is, indeed, for everyone.

For that matter, so are comics. There is now little doubt that comics can take on dry, sobering and complicated subjects with a depth of nuance and feeling that is difficult for straight prose to convey alone. Perhaps comics can likewise edify feminism by giving it the opportunity to be understood in a way that mere words are unable to. Apart from not taking itself so seriously, the comics medium might also remind the feminist movement of another invaluable truth that has served it well for years; no matter what indignities you may suffer for your cause, when no one takes you seriously while dismissing your efforts as unfunny and childish – you still need to get back to the drawing board and finish that damn comic.

We sincerely hope you enjoy these.

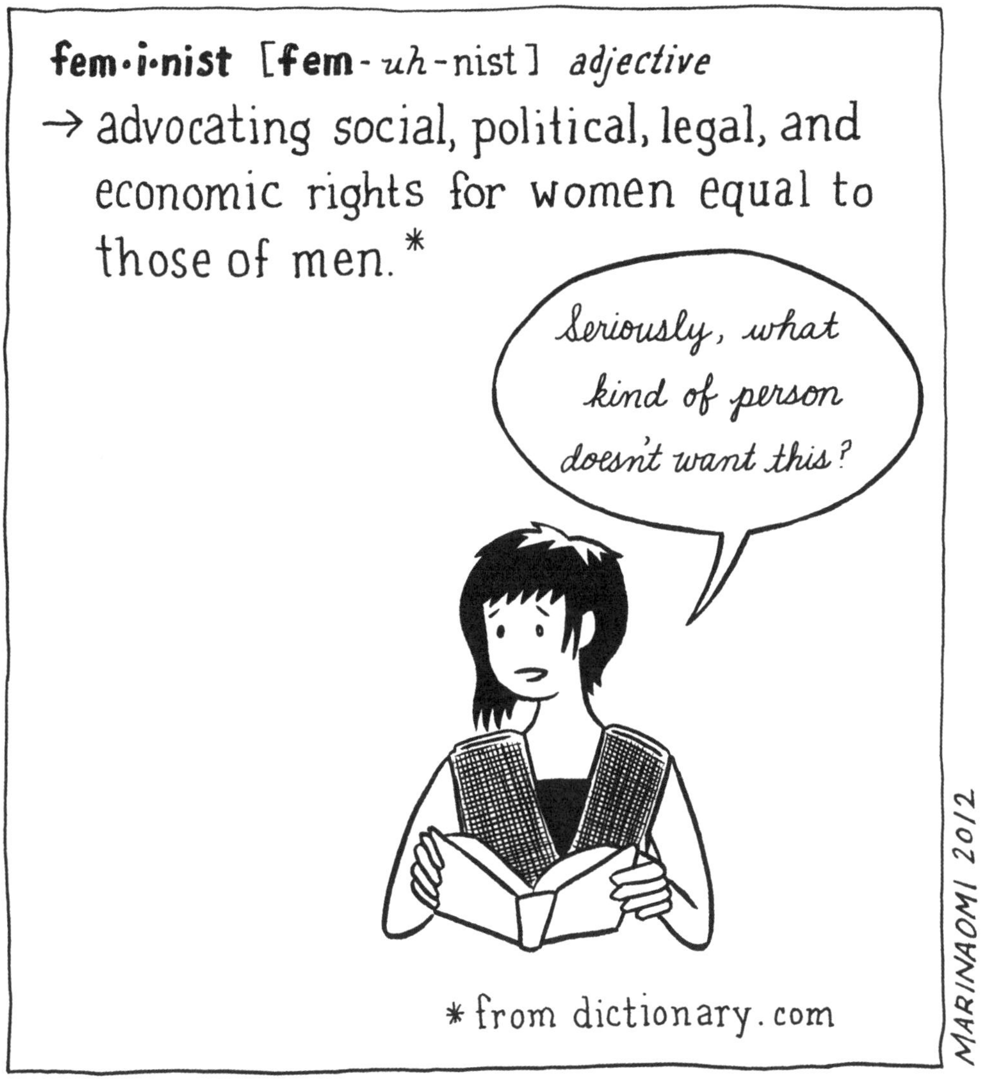
fem·i·nist [fem-uh-nist] adjective
→ advocating social, political, legal, and economic rights for women equal to those of men.*
Seriously, what kind of person doesn't want this?
* from dictionary.com
MARINAOMI 2012

When anyone claims they aren't a feminist, I assume they don't know what they're talking about.

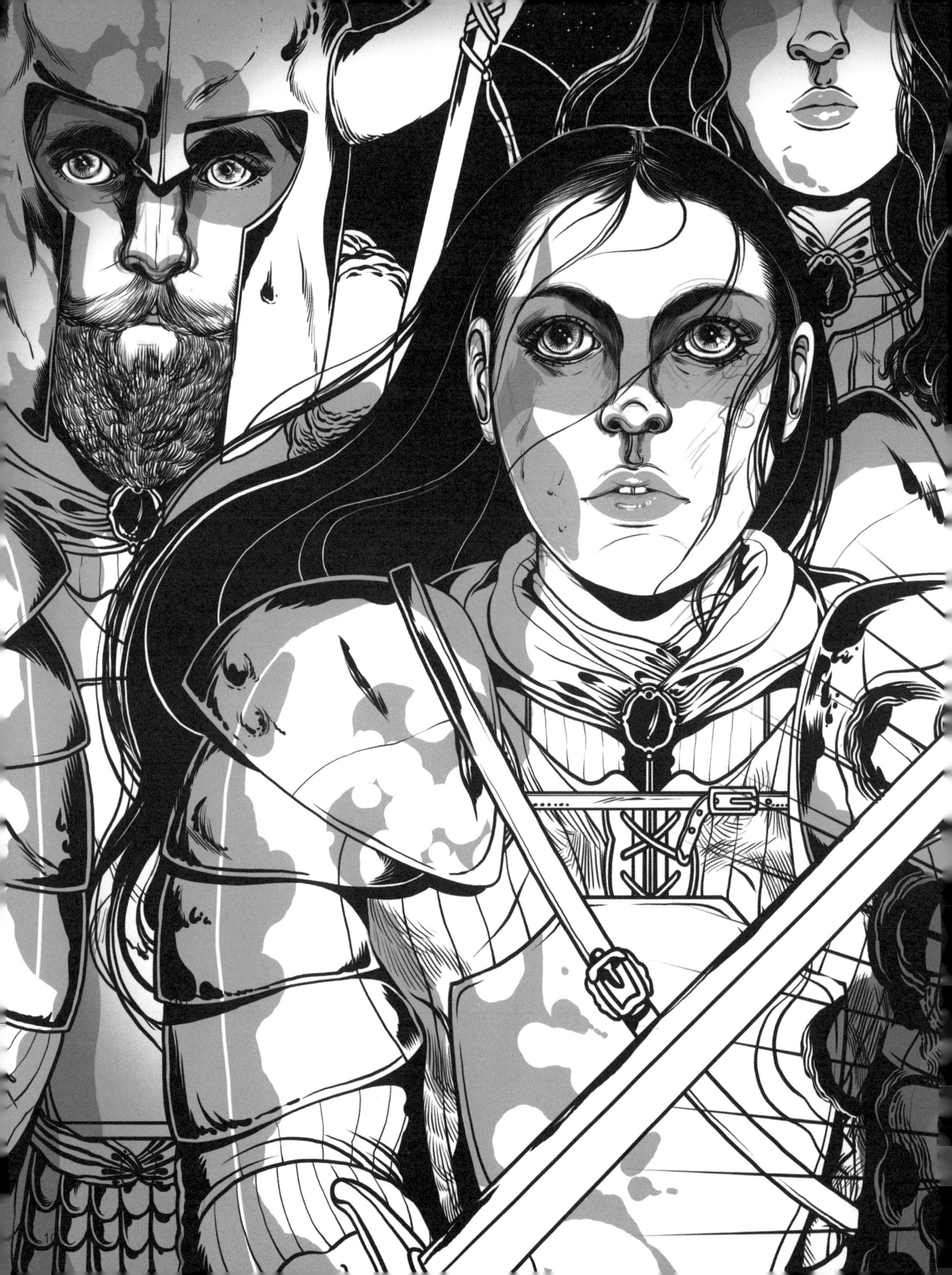

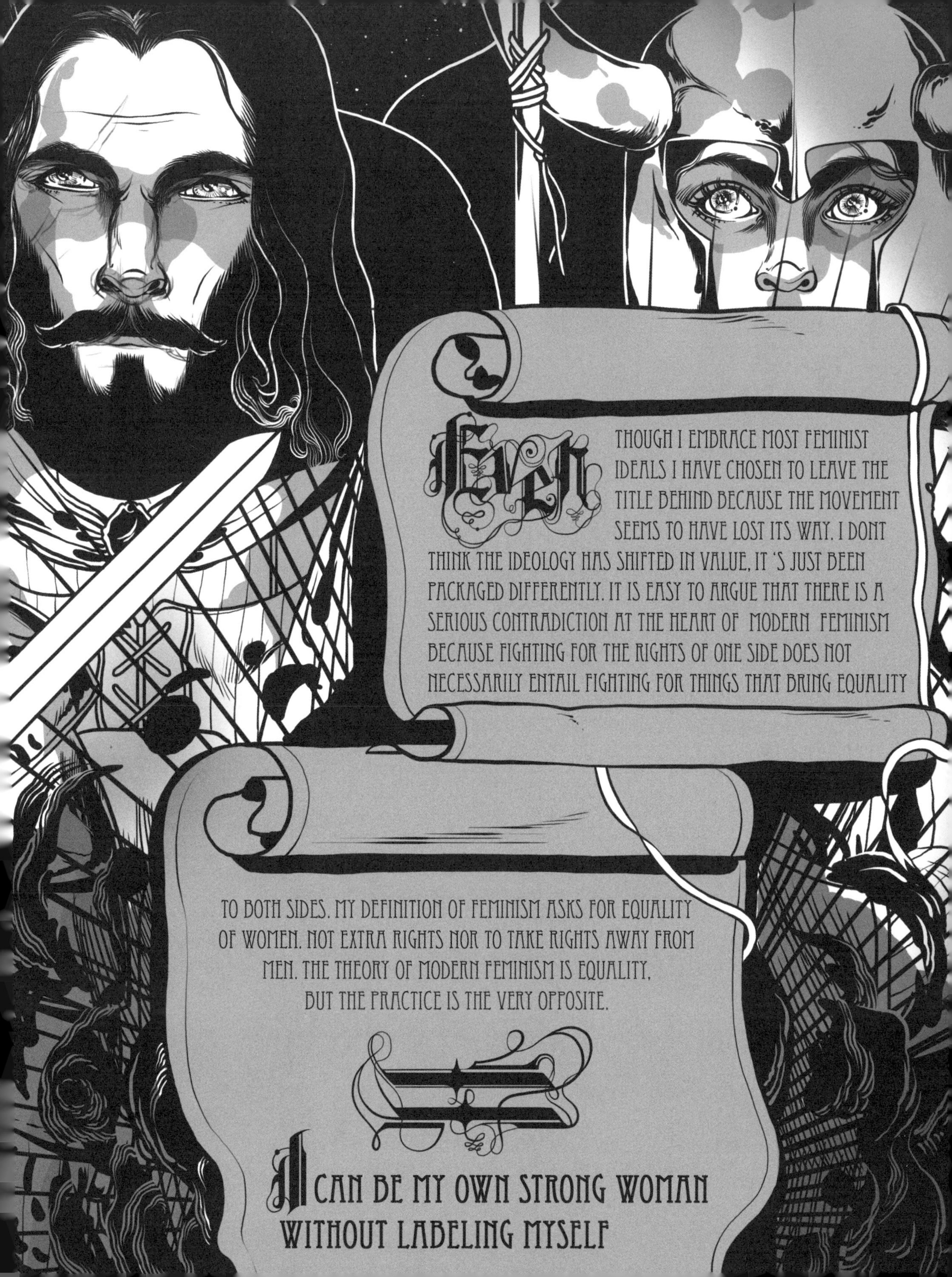
Even though I embrace most feminist ideals I have chosen to leave the title behind because the movement seems to have lost its way. I dont think the ideology has shifted in value, it 's just been packaged differently. It is easy to argue that there is a serious contradiction at the heart of modern feminism because fighting for the rights of one side does not necessarily entail fighting for things that bring equality
to both sides. My definition of feminism asks for equality of women, not extra rights nor to take rights away from men. The theory of modern feminism is equality, but the practice is the very opposite.
I can be my own strong woman without labeling myself

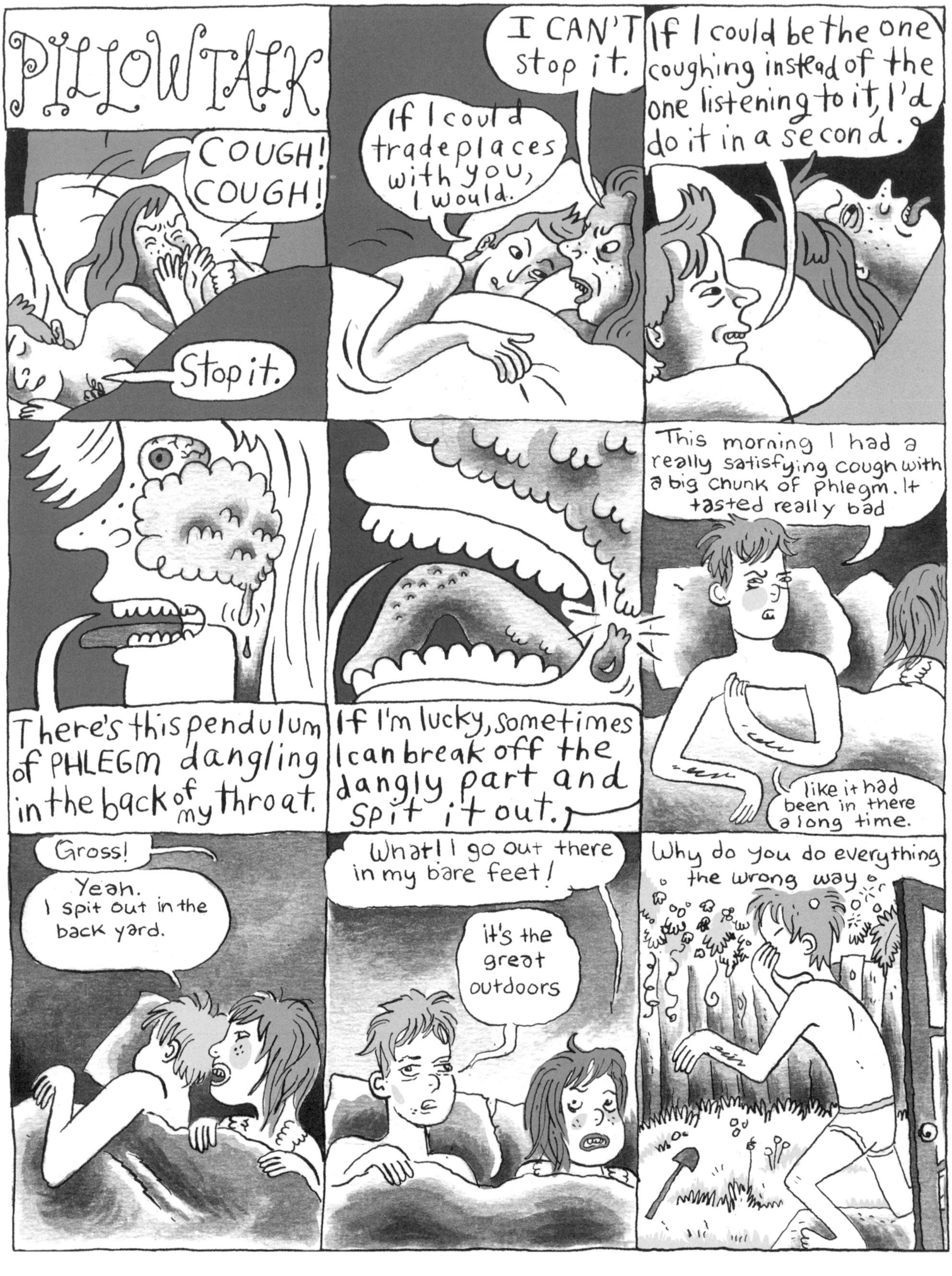
PILLOWTALK
COUGH! COUGH!
Stop it.
I CAN'T stop it.
If I could tradeplaces with you, I would.
If I could be the one coughing instead of the one listening to it, I'd do it in a second.
There's this pendulum of PHLEGM dangling in the back of my throat.
If I'm lucky, sometimes I can break off the dangly part and spit it out.
This morning I had a really satisfying cough with a big chunk of phlegm. It tasted really bad
like it had been in there a long time.
Gross!
Yeah. I spit out in the back yard.
What! I go out there in my bare feet!
it's the great outdoors
Why do you do everything the wrong way

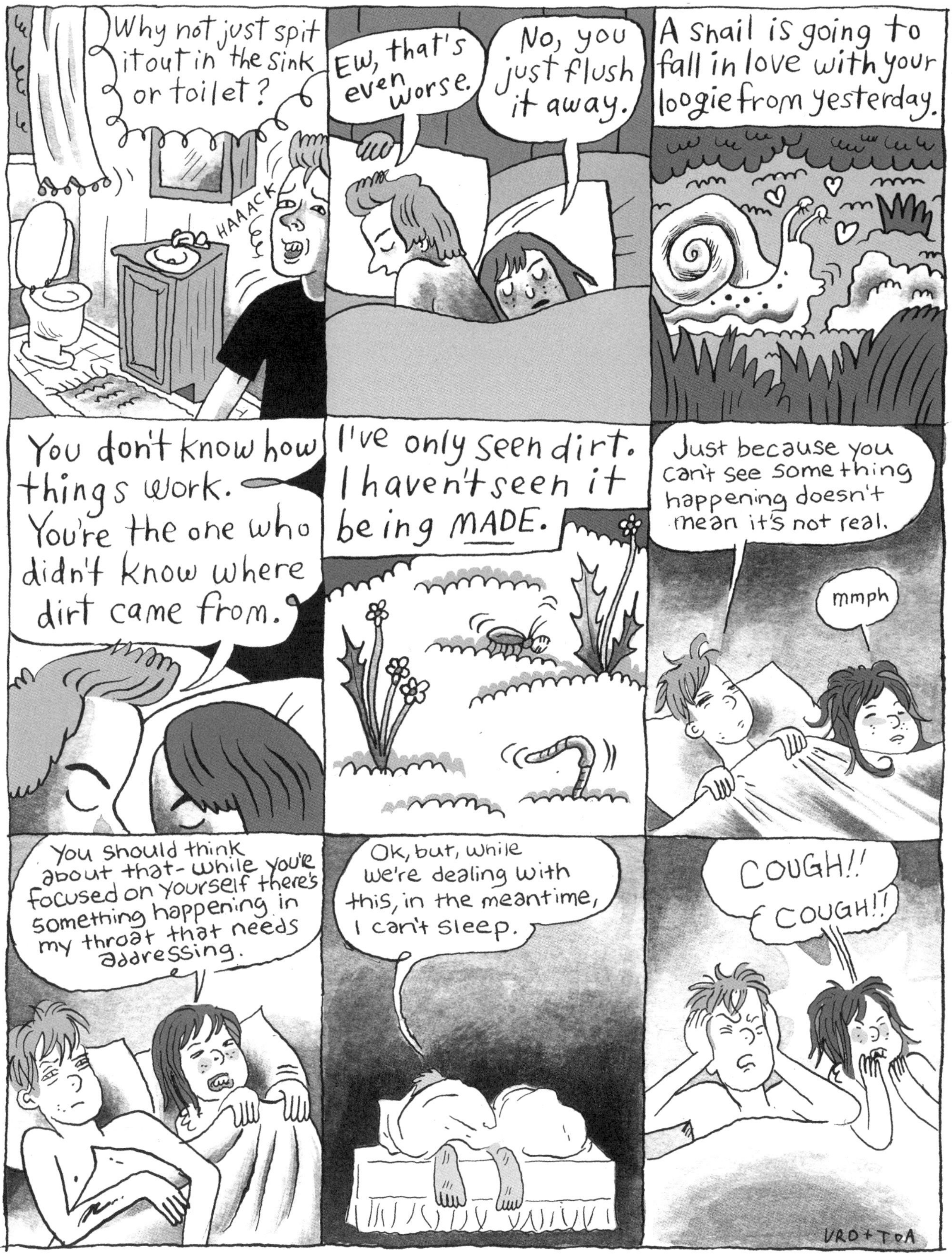
Why not just spit it out in the sink or toilet?
HAAACK
Ew, that's even worse.
No, you just flush it away.
A snail is going to fall in love with your loogie from yesterday.
You don't know how things work.
You're the one who didn't know where dirt came from.
I've only seen dirt. I haven't seen it being MADE.
Just because you can't see something happening doesn't mean it's not real.
mmph
You should think about that- while you're focused on yourself there's something happening in my throat that needs addressing.
Ok, but, while we're dealing with this, in the meantime, I can't sleep.
COUGH!!
COUGH!!
VRO+TOA

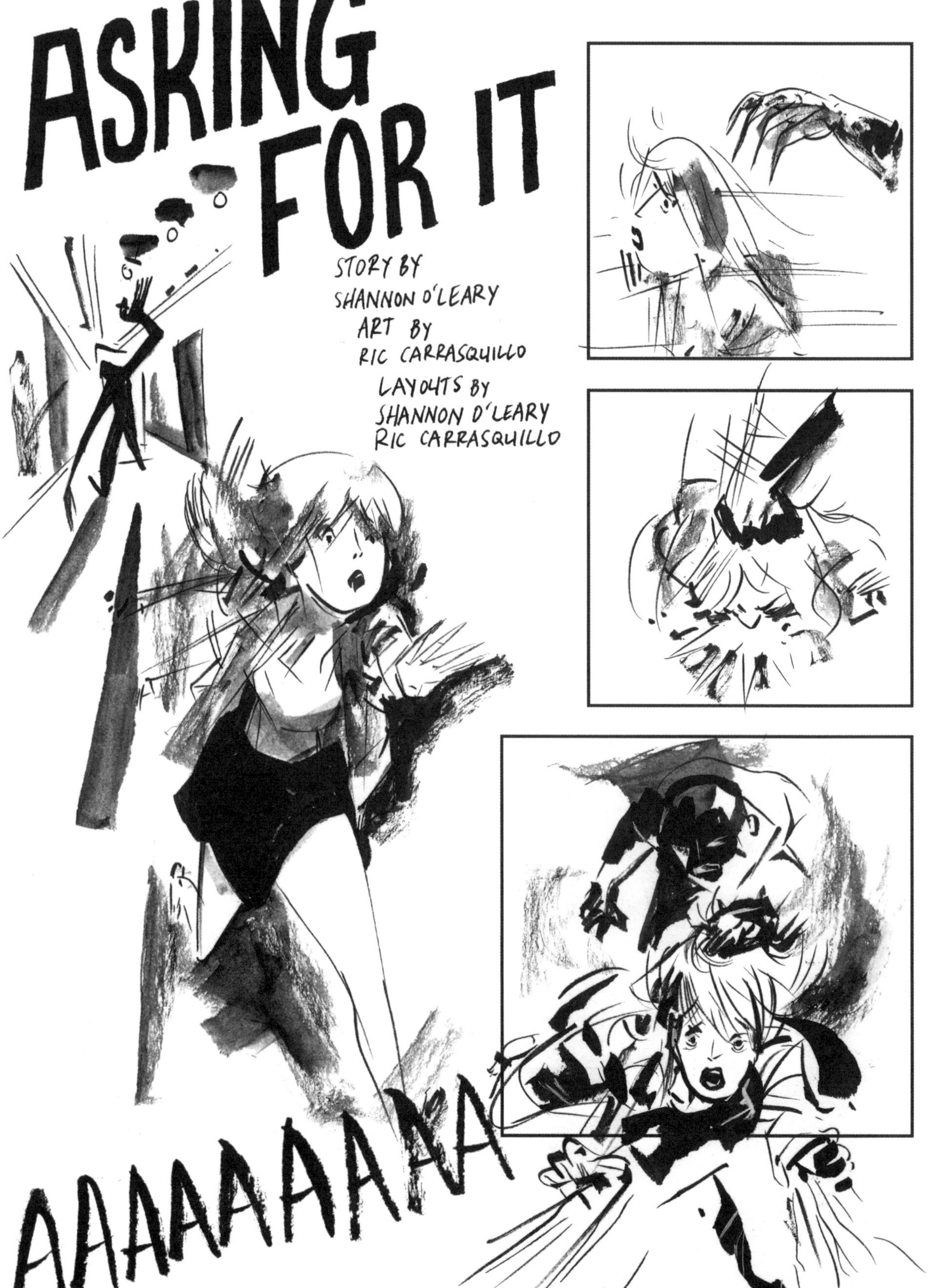
ASKING FOR IT
STORY BY SHANNON O'LEARY
ART BY RIC CARRASQUILLO
LAYOUTS BY SHANNON O'LEARY RIC CARRASQUILLO
AAAAAAAAA

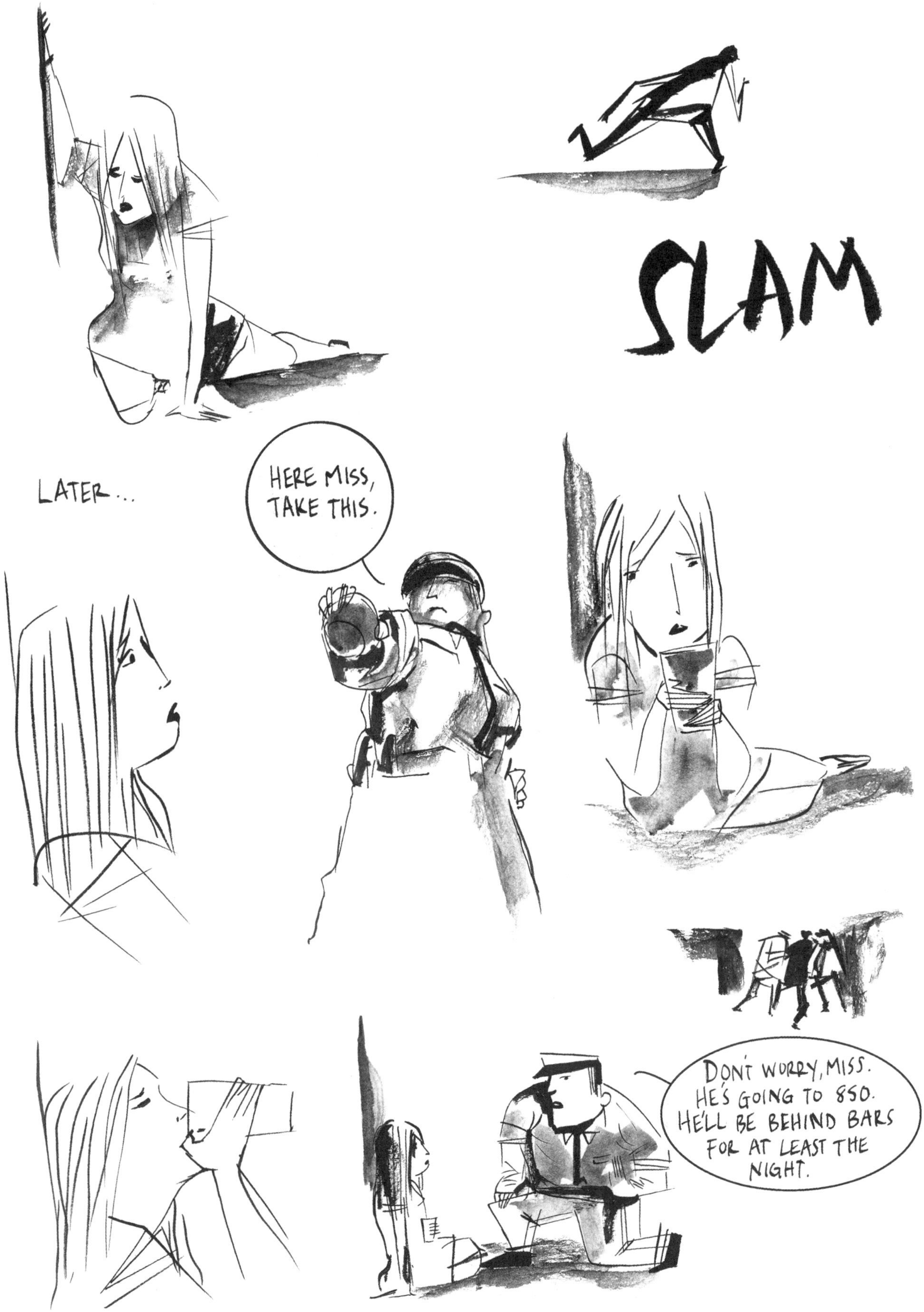
SLAM
LATER...
HERE MISS, TAKE THIS.
DON'T WORRY, MISS. HE'S GOING TO 850. HE'LL BE BEHIND BARS FOR AT LEAST THE NIGHT.

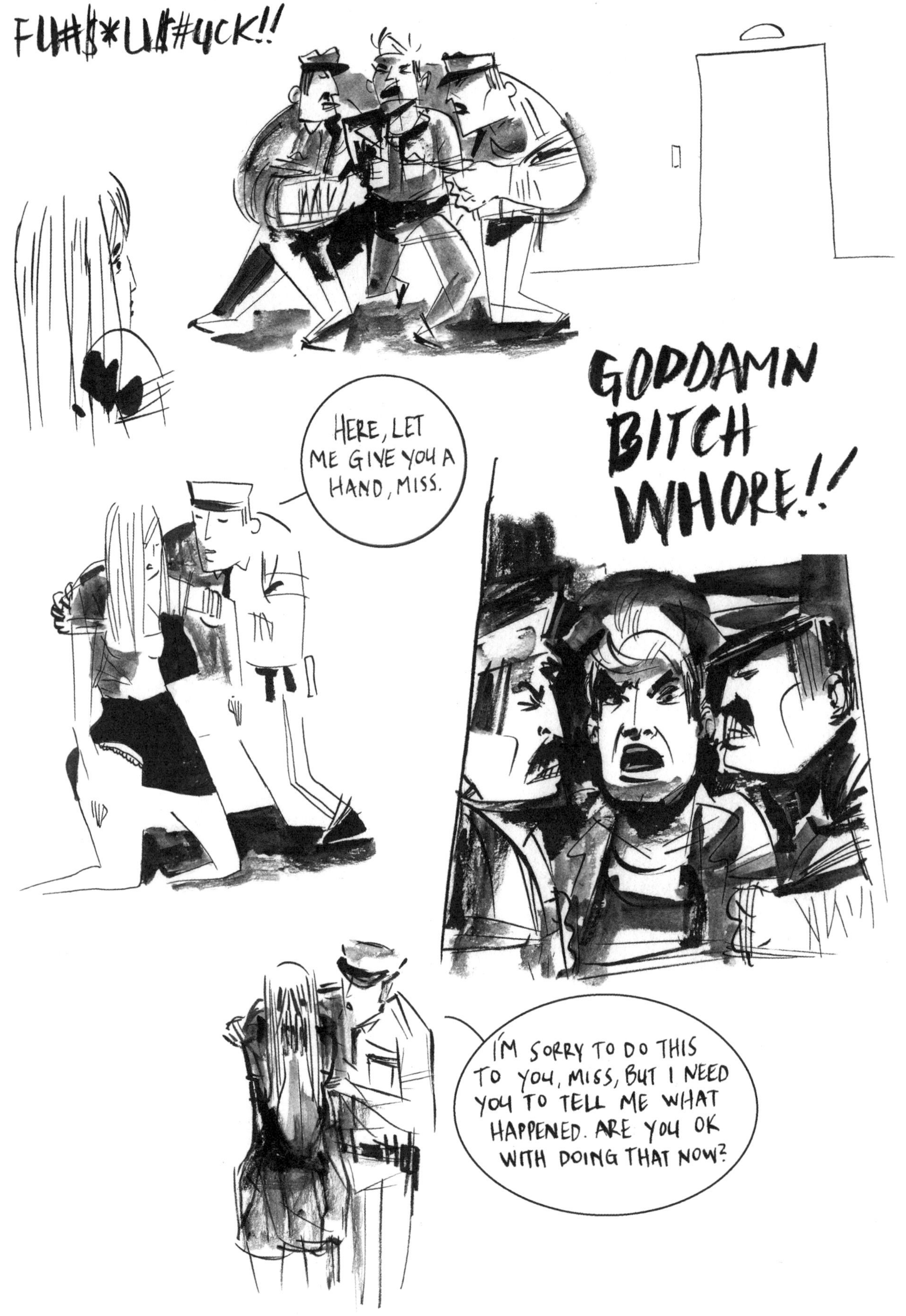
FU#$*U#UCK!!
HERE, LET ME GIVE YOU A HAND, MISS.
GODDAMN BITCH WHORE!!
I'M SORRY TO DO THIS TO YOU, MISS, BUT I NEED YOU TO TELL ME WHAT HAPPENED. ARE YOU OK WITH DOING THAT NOW?

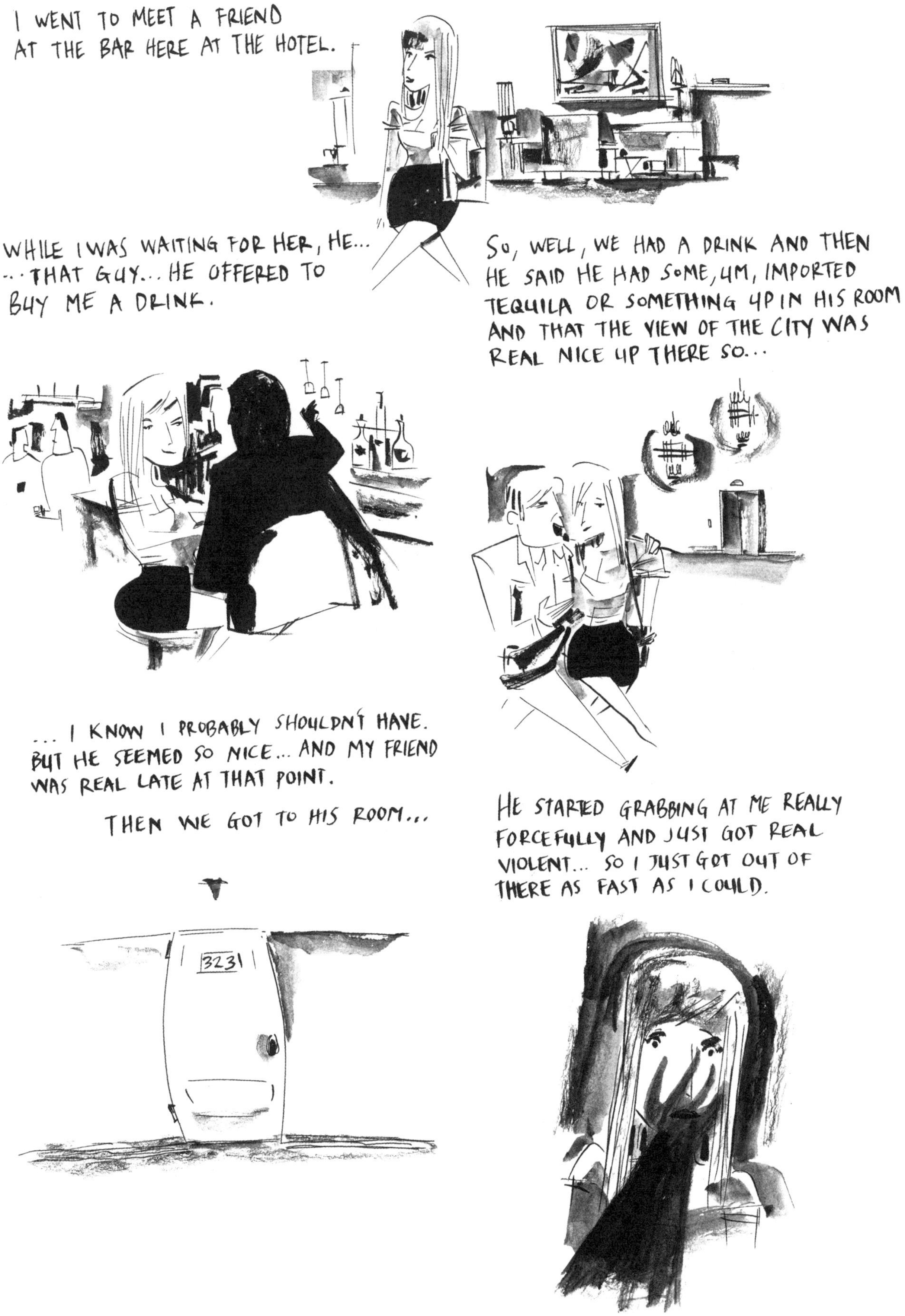
I WENT TO MEET A FRIEND AT THE BAR HERE AT THE HOTEL.
WHILE I WAS WAITING FOR HER, HE... ...THAT GUY... HE OFFERED TO BUY ME A DRINK.
SO, WELL, WE HAD A DRINK AND THEN HE SAID HE HAD SOME, UM, IMPORTED TEQUILA OR SOMETHING UP IN HIS ROOM AND THAT THE VIEW OF THE CITY WAS REAL NICE UP THERE SO...
... I KNOW I PROBABLY SHOULDN'T HAVE. BUT HE SEEMED SO NICE... AND MY FRIEND WAS REAL LATE AT THAT POINT.
THEN WE GOT TO HIS ROOM...
HE STARTED GRABBING AT ME REALLY FORCEFULLY AND JUST GOT REAL VIOLENT... SO I JUST GOT OUT OF THERE AS FAST AS I COULD.
3231

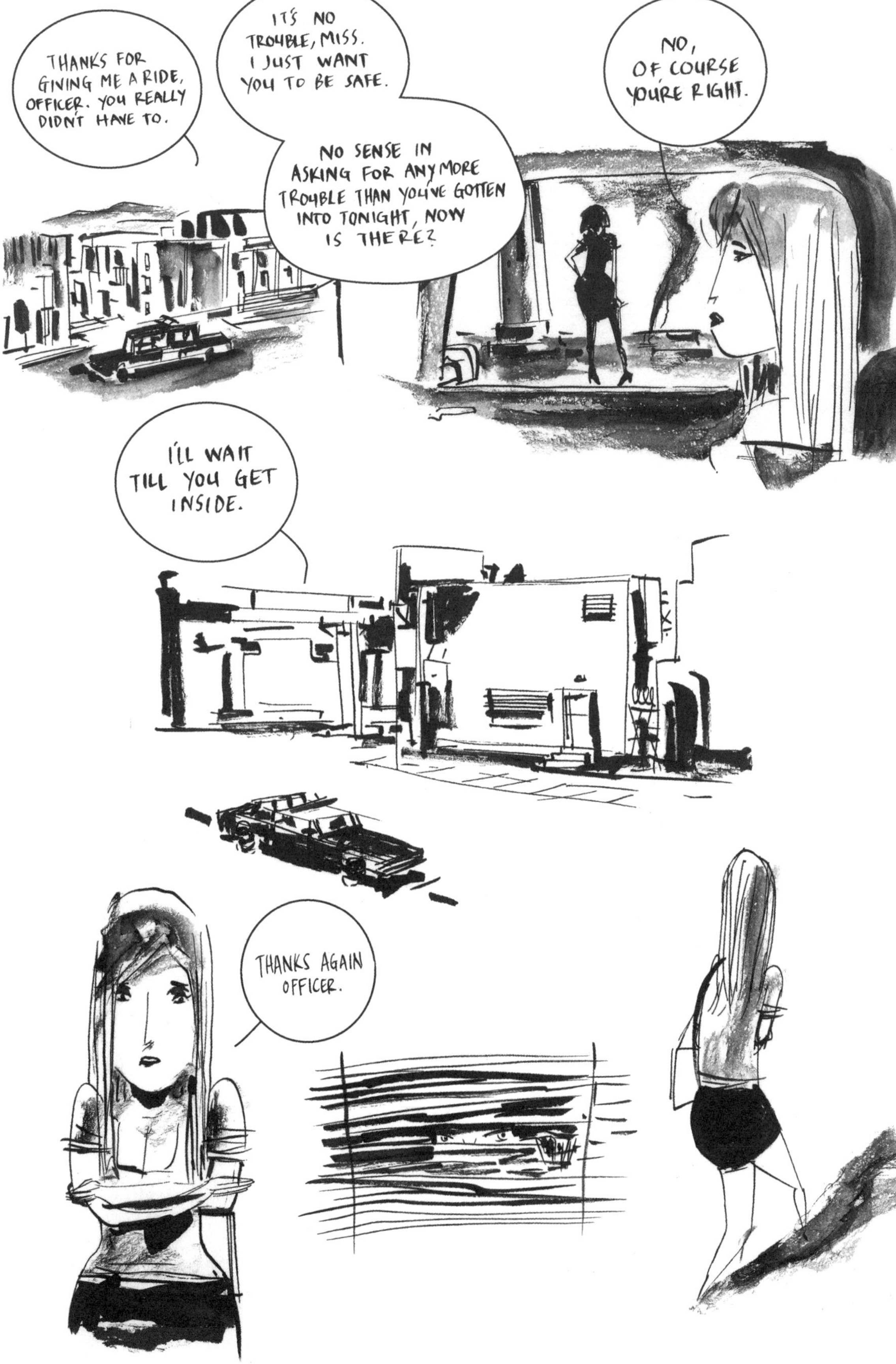
THANKS FOR GIVING ME A RIDE, OFFICER. YOU REALLY DIDN'T HAVE TO.
IT'S NO TROUBLE, MISS. I JUST WANT YOU TO BE SAFE.
NO SENSE IN ASKING FOR ANYMORE TROUBLE THAN YOU'VE GOTTEN INTO TONIGHT, NOW IS THERE?
NO, OF COURSE YOU'RE RIGHT.
I'LL WAIT TILL YOU GET INSIDE.
THANKS AGAIN OFFICER.

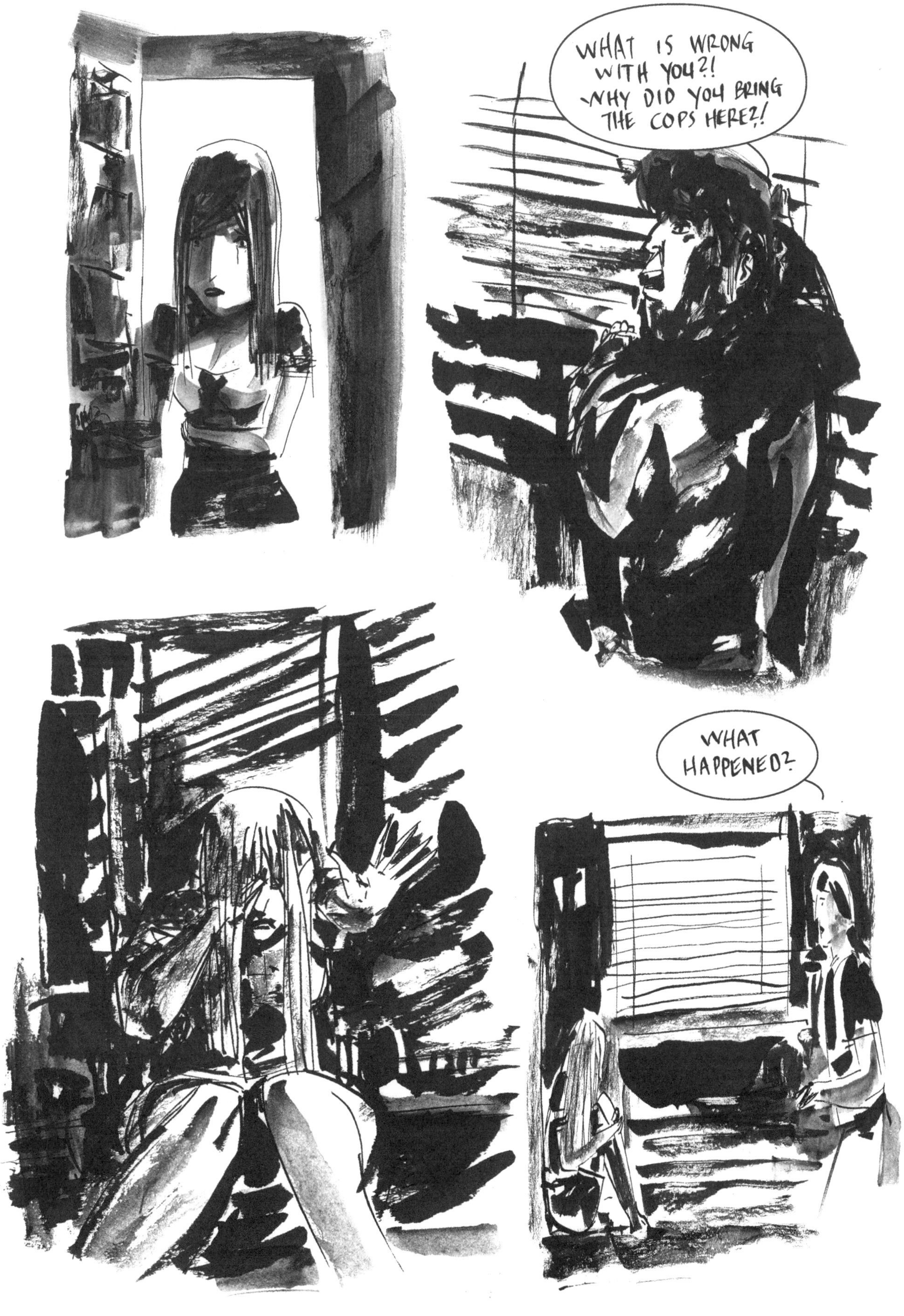
WHAT IS WRONG WITH YOU?! -WHY DID YOU BRING THE COPS HERE?!
WHAT HAPPENED?

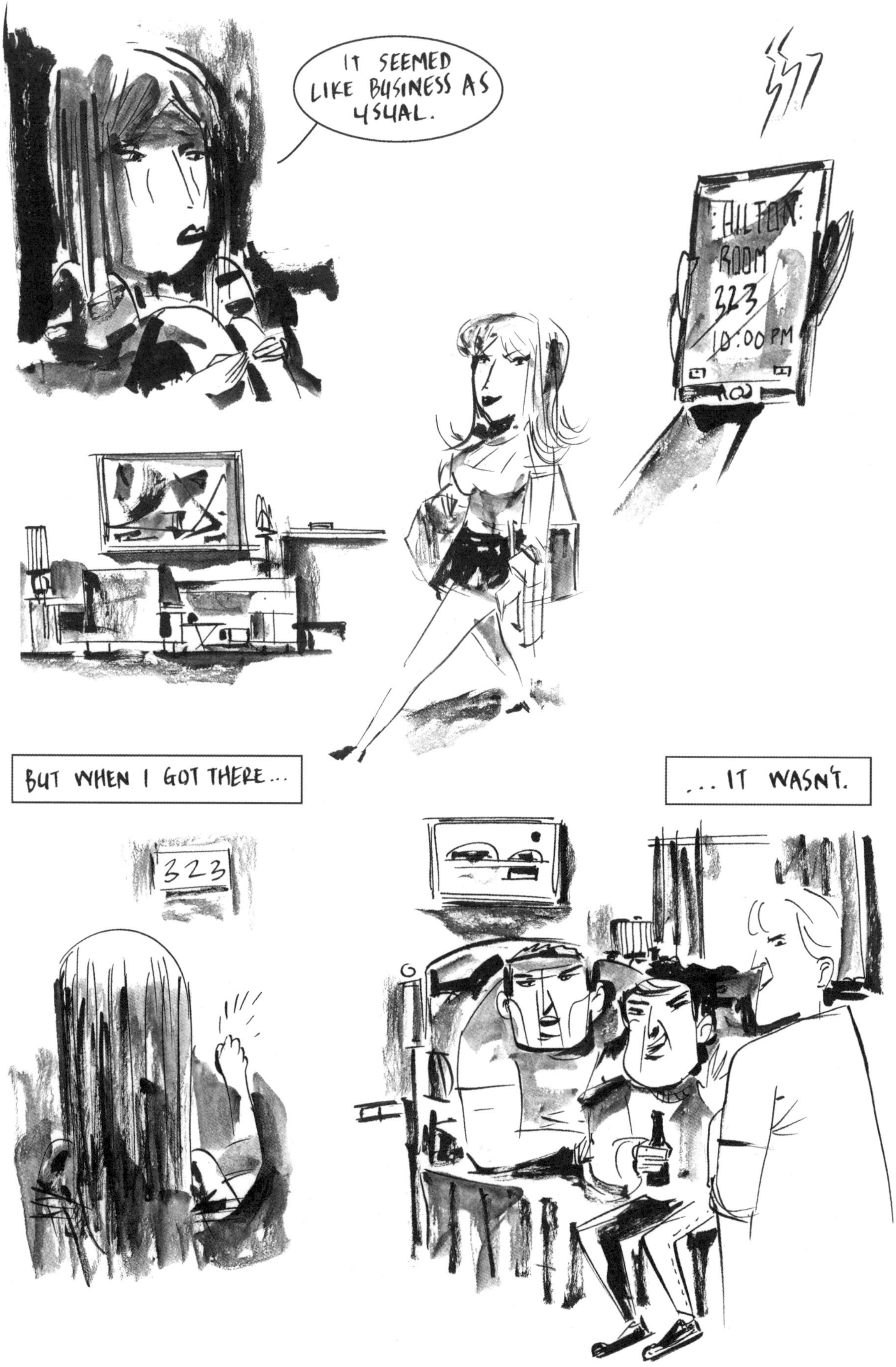
IT SEEMED LIKE BUSINESS AS USUAL.
HILTON ROOM 323 10:00 PM
BUT WHEN I GOT THERE...
...IT WASN'T.
323

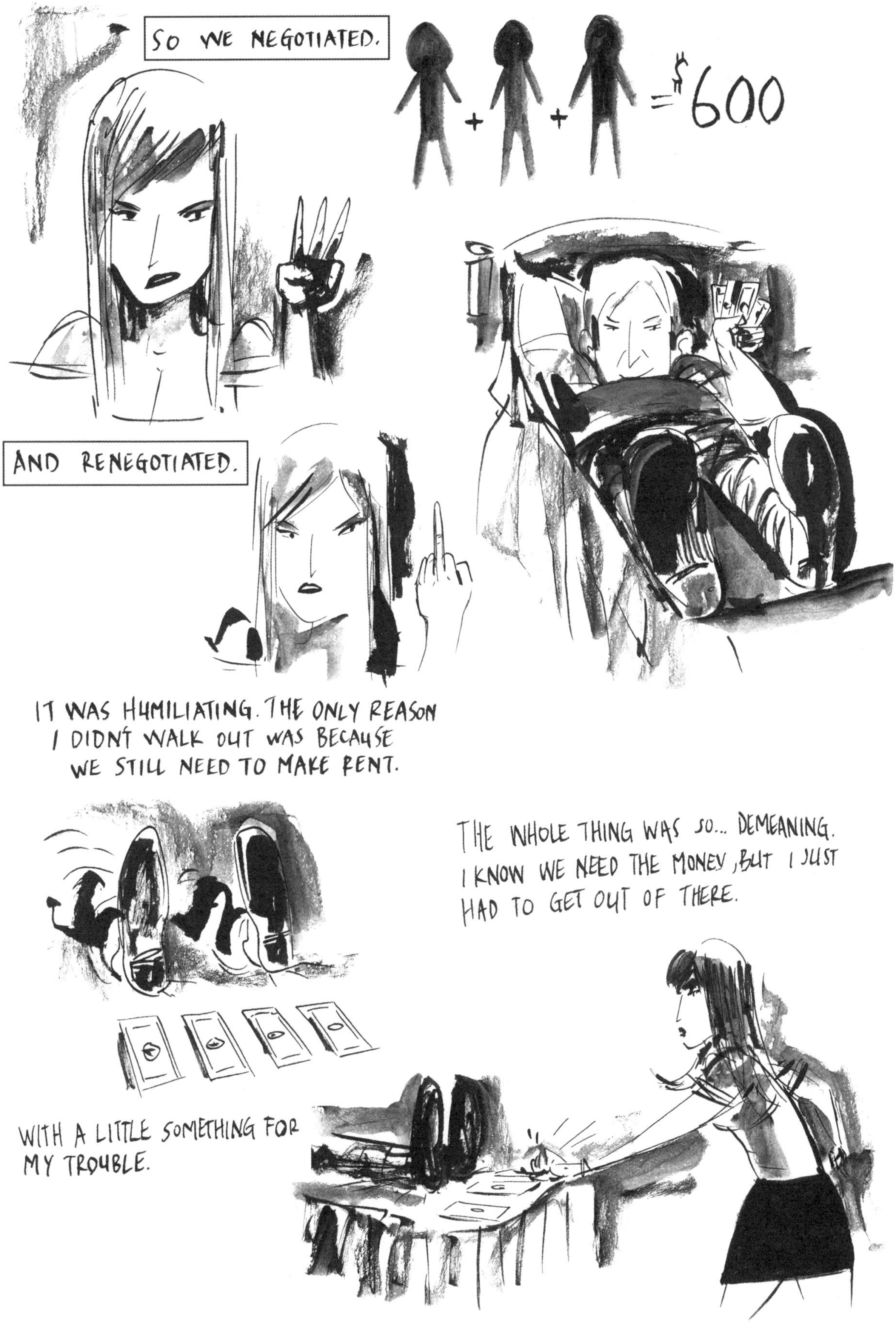
SO WE NEGOTIATED.
$600
AND RENEGOTIATED.
IT WAS HUMILIATING. THE ONLY REASON I DIDN'T WALK OUT WAS BECAUSE WE STILL NEED TO MAKE RENT.
THE WHOLE THING WAS SO... DEMEANING. I KNOW WE NEED THE MONEY, BUT I JUST HAD TO GET OUT OF THERE.
WITH A LITTLE SOMETHING FOR MY TROUBLE.

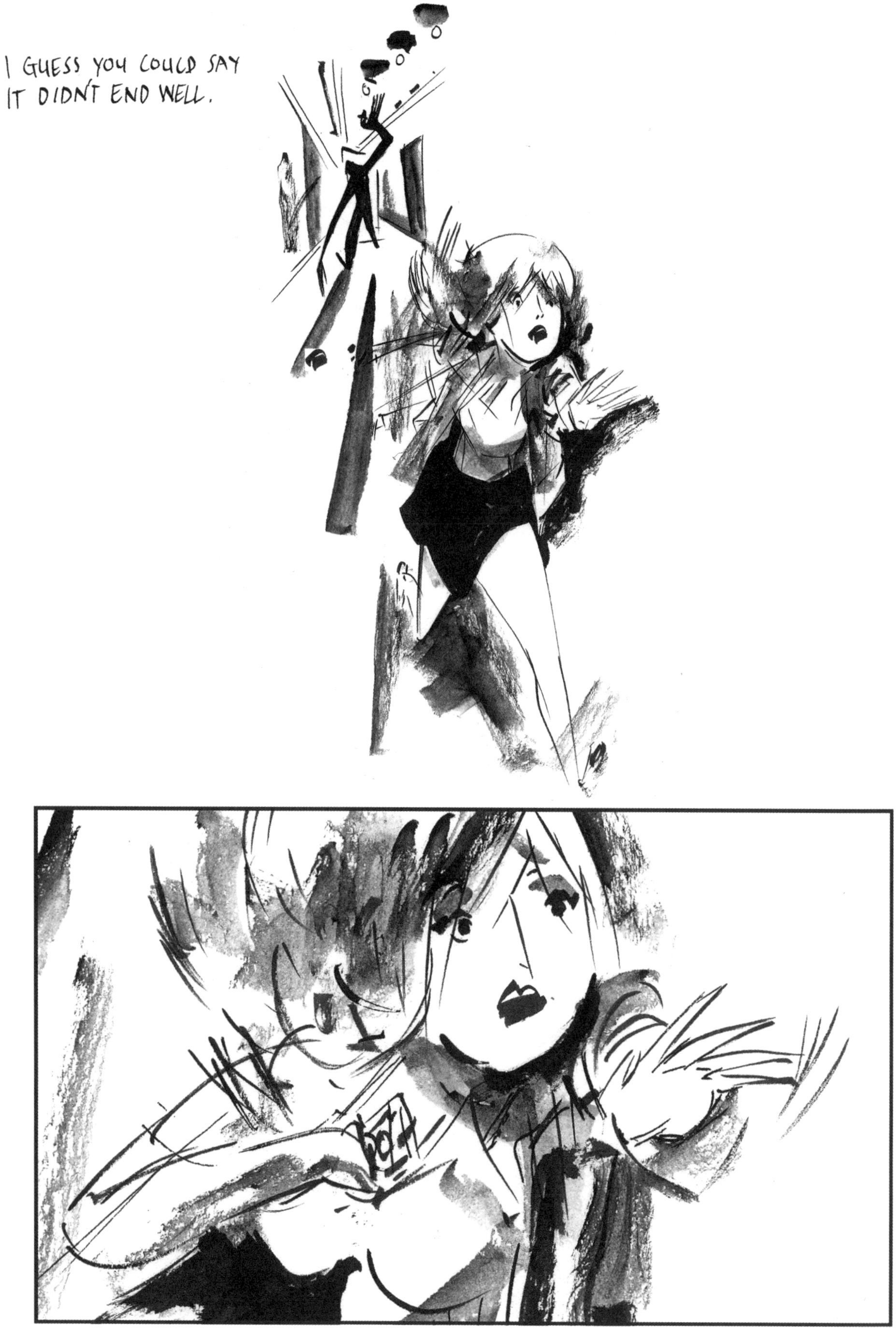
I GUESS YOU COULD SAY IT DIDN'T END WELL.

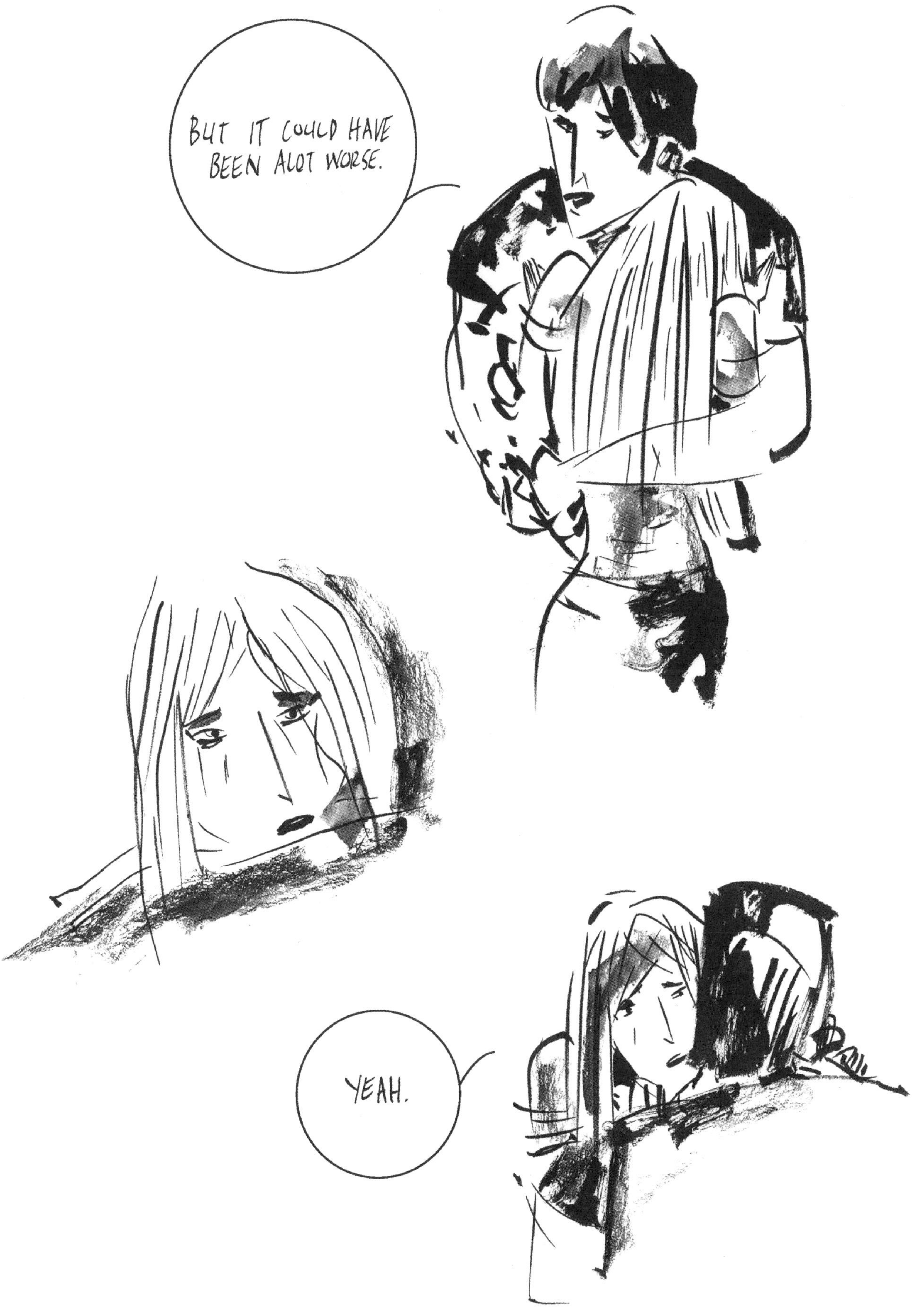
BUT IT COULD HAVE BEEN ALOT WORSE.
YEAH.

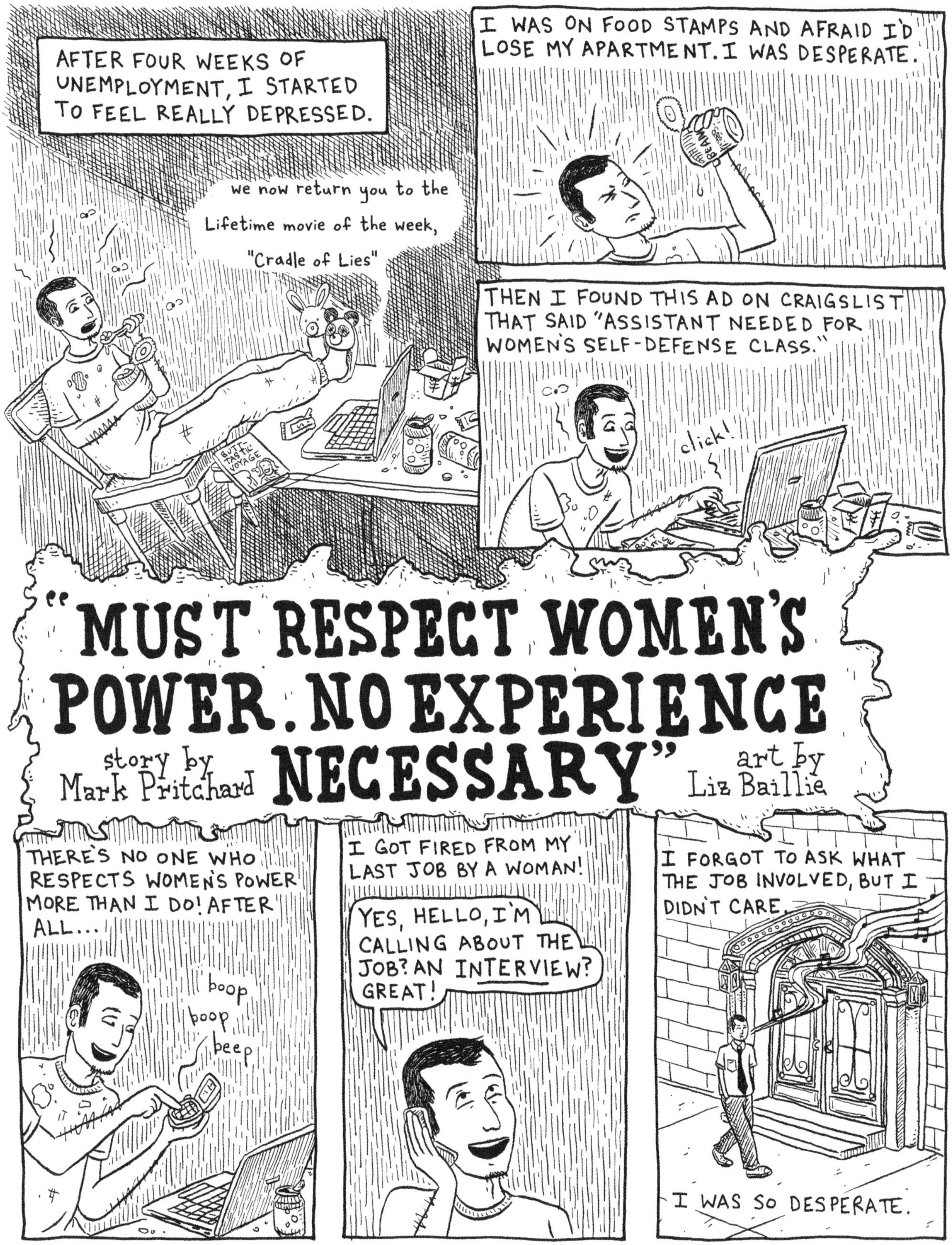

AFTER FOUR WEEKS OF UNEMPLOYMENT, I STARTED TO FEEL REALLY DEPRESSED.
we now return you to the Lifetime movie of the week, "Cradle of Lies"
BUTT-TASTIC VOYAGE
I WAS ON FOOD STAMPS AND AFRAID I'D LOSE MY APARTMENT. I WAS DESPERATE.
THEN I FOUND THIS AD ON CRAIGSLIST THAT SAID "ASSISTANT NEEDED FOR WOMEN'S SELF-DEFENSE CLASS."
click!
"MUST RESPECT WOMEN'S POWER. NO EXPERIENCE NECESSARY"
story by Mark Pritchard
art by Liz Baillie
THERE'S NO ONE WHO RESPECTS WOMEN'S POWER MORE THAN I DO! AFTER ALL...
boop
boop
beep
I GOT FIRED FROM MY LAST JOB BY A WOMAN!
YES, HELLO, I'M CALLING ABOUT THE JOB? AN INTERVIEW? GREAT!
I FORGOT TO ASK WHAT THE JOB INVOLVED, BUT I DIDN'T CARE.
I WAS SO DESPERATE.

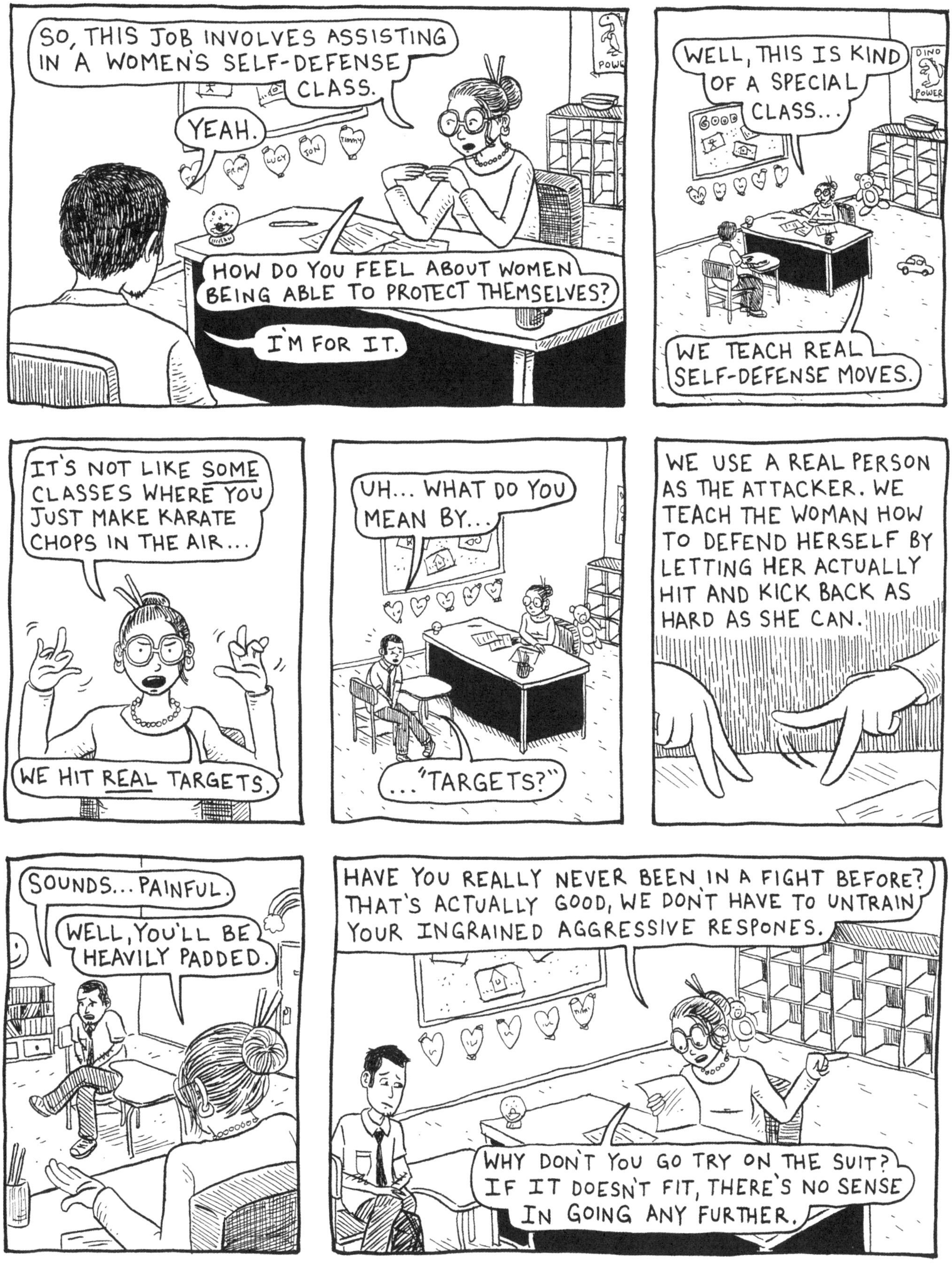
SO, THIS JOB INVOLVES ASSISTING IN A WOMEN'S SELF-DEFENSE CLASS.
YEAH.
HOW DO YOU FEEL ABOUT WOMEN BEING ABLE TO PROTECT THEMSELVES?
I'M FOR IT.
WELL, THIS IS KIND OF A SPECIAL CLASS...
DINO POWER
GOOD
WE TEACH REAL SELF-DEFENSE MOVES.
IT'S NOT LIKE SOME CLASSES WHERE YOU JUST MAKE KARATE CHOPS IN THE AIR...
WE HIT REAL TARGETS.
UH... WHAT DO YOU MEAN BY...
..."TARGETS?"
WE USE A REAL PERSON AS THE ATTACKER. WE TEACH THE WOMAN HOW TO DEFEND HERSELF BY LETTING HER ACTUALLY HIT AND KICK BACK AS HARD AS SHE CAN.
SOUNDS... PAINFUL.
WELL, YOU'LL BE HEAVILY PADDED.
HAVE YOU REALLY NEVER BEEN IN A FIGHT BEFORE? THAT'S ACTUALLY GOOD, WE DON'T HAVE TO UNTRAIN YOUR INGRAINED AGGRESSIVE RESPONES.
WHY DON'T YOU GO TRY ON THE SUIT? IF IT DOESN'T FIT, THERE'S NO SENSE IN GOING ANY FURTHER.

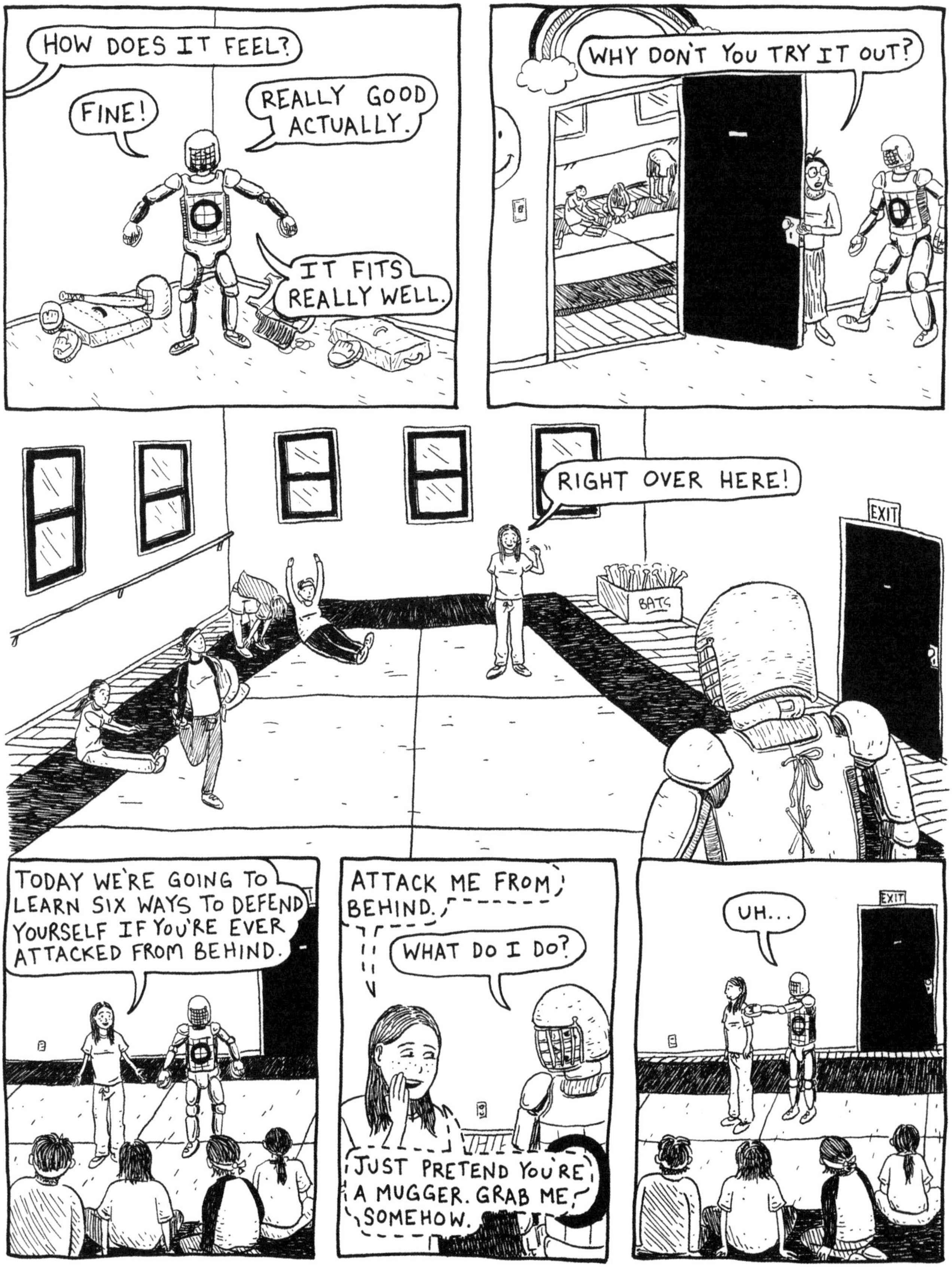
HOW DOES IT FEEL?
FINE!
REALLY GOOD ACTUALLY.
IT FITS REALLY WELL.
WHY DON'T YOU TRY IT OUT?
RIGHT OVER HERE!
EXIT
BATS
TODAY WE'RE GOING TO LEARN SIX WAYS TO DEFEND YOURSELF IF YOU'RE EVER ATTACKED FROM BEHIND.
ATTACK ME FROM BEHIND.
WHAT DO I DO?
JUST PRETEND YOU'RE A MUGGER. GRAB ME SOMEHOW.
UH...
EXIT

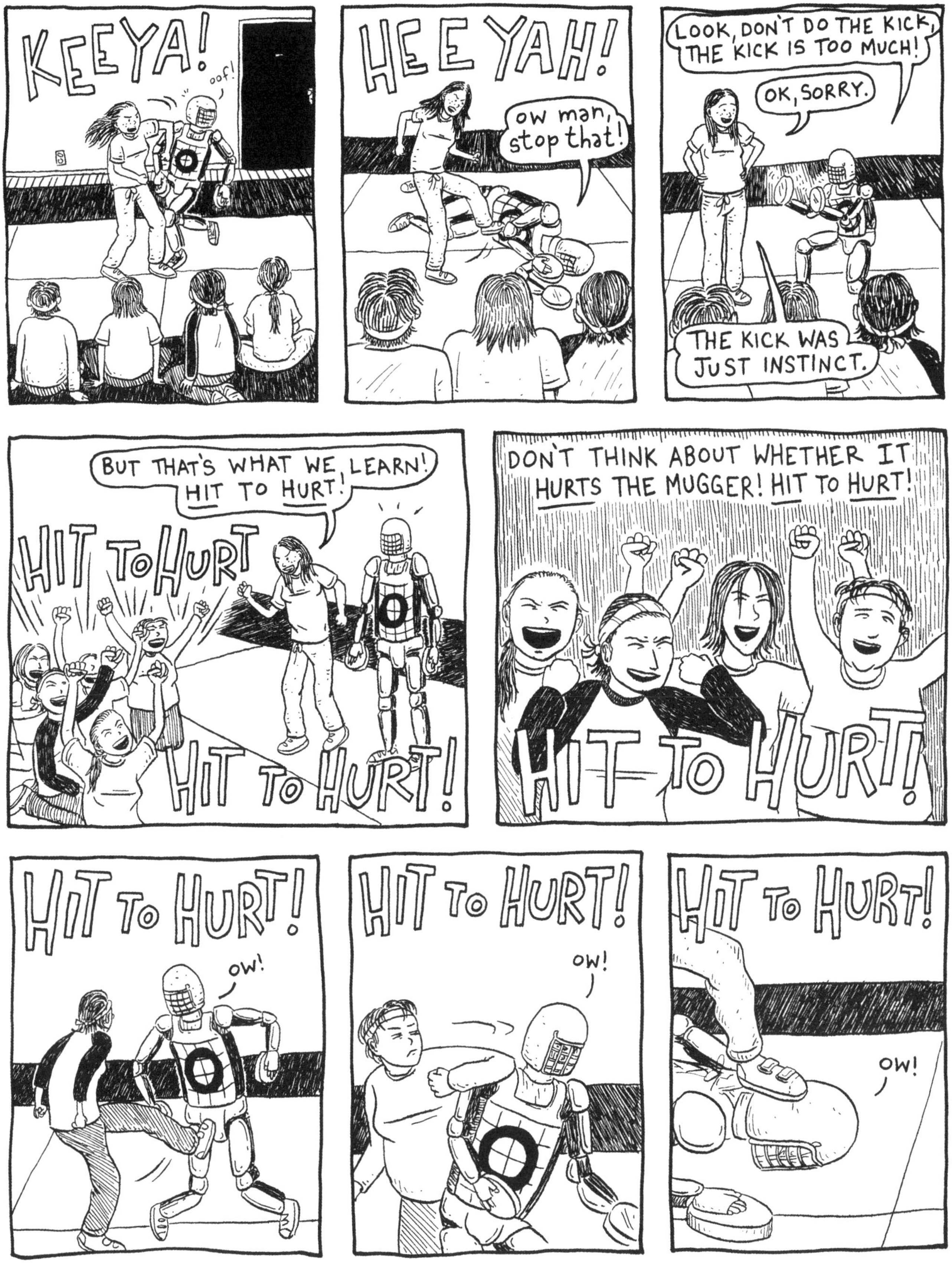

KEEYA!
oof!
HEE YAH!
ow man, stop that!
LOOK, DON'T DO THE KICK, THE KICK IS TOO MUCH!
OK, SORRY.
THE KICK WAS JUST INSTINCT.
BUT THAT'S WHAT WE LEARN! HIT TO HURT!
HIT TO HURT
HIT TO HURT!
DON'T THINK ABOUT WHETHER IT HURTS THE MUGGER! HIT TO HURT!
HIT TO HURT!
HIT TO HURT!
OW!
HIT TO HURT!
OW!
HIT TO HURT!
OW!

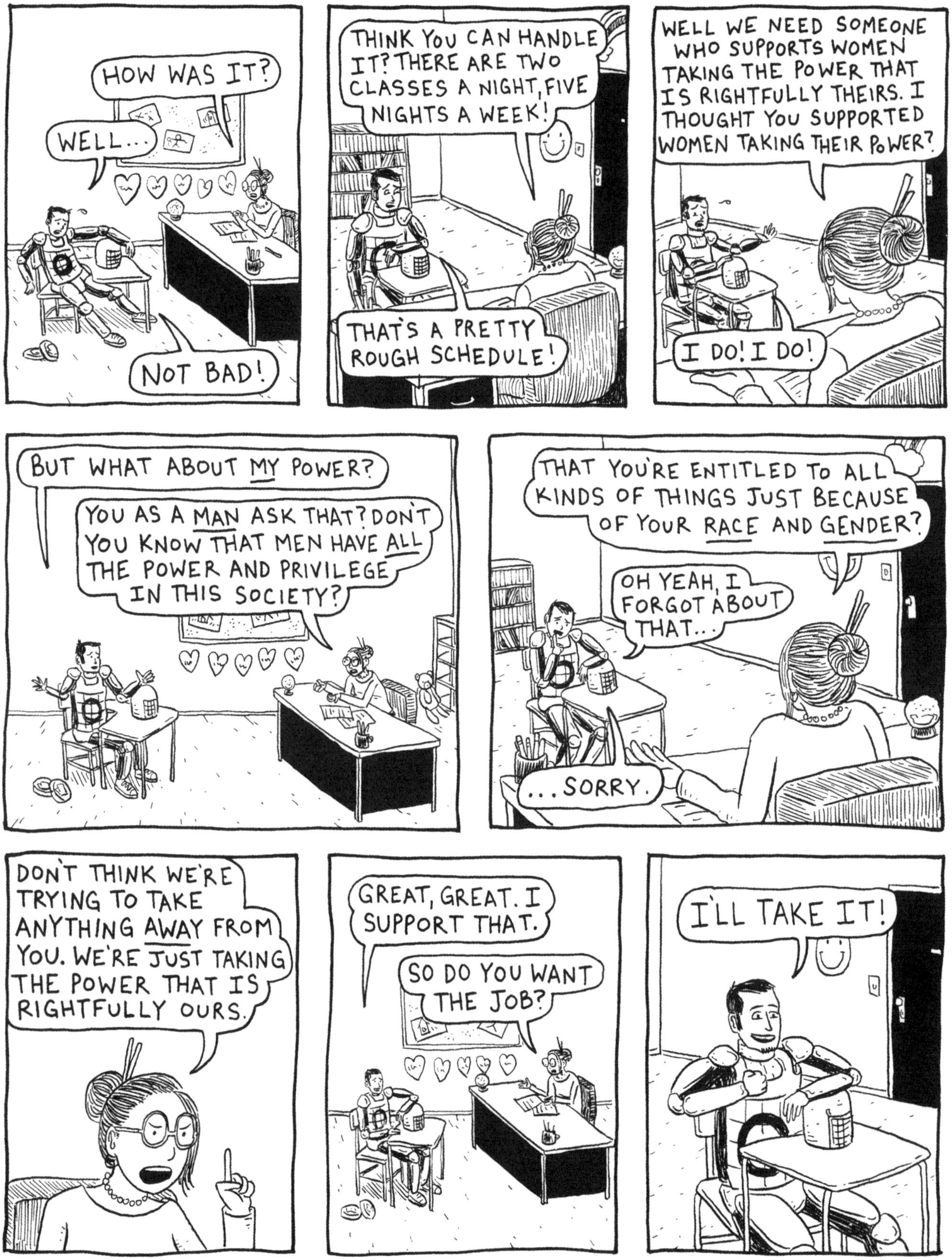
HOW WAS IT?
WELL...
NOT BAD!
THINK YOU CAN HANDLE IT? THERE ARE TWO CLASSES A NIGHT, FIVE NIGHTS A WEEK!
THAT'S A PRETTY ROUGH SCHEDULE!
WELL WE NEED SOMEONE WHO SUPPORTS WOMEN TAKING THE POWER THAT IS RIGHTFULLY THEIRS. I THOUGHT YOU SUPPORTED WOMEN TAKING THEIR POWER?
I DO! I DO!
BUT WHAT ABOUT MY POWER?
YOU AS A MAN ASK THAT? DON'T YOU KNOW THAT MEN HAVE ALL THE POWER AND PRIVILEGE IN THIS SOCIETY?
THAT YOU'RE ENTITLED TO ALL KINDS OF THINGS JUST BECAUSE OF YOUR RACE AND GENDER?
OH YEAH, I FORGOT ABOUT THAT...
...SORRY.
DON'T THINK WE'RE TRYING TO TAKE ANYTHING AWAY FROM YOU. WE'RE JUST TAKING THE POWER THAT IS RIGHTFULLY OURS.
GREAT, GREAT. I SUPPORT THAT.
SO DO YOU WANT THE JOB?
I'LL TAKE IT!

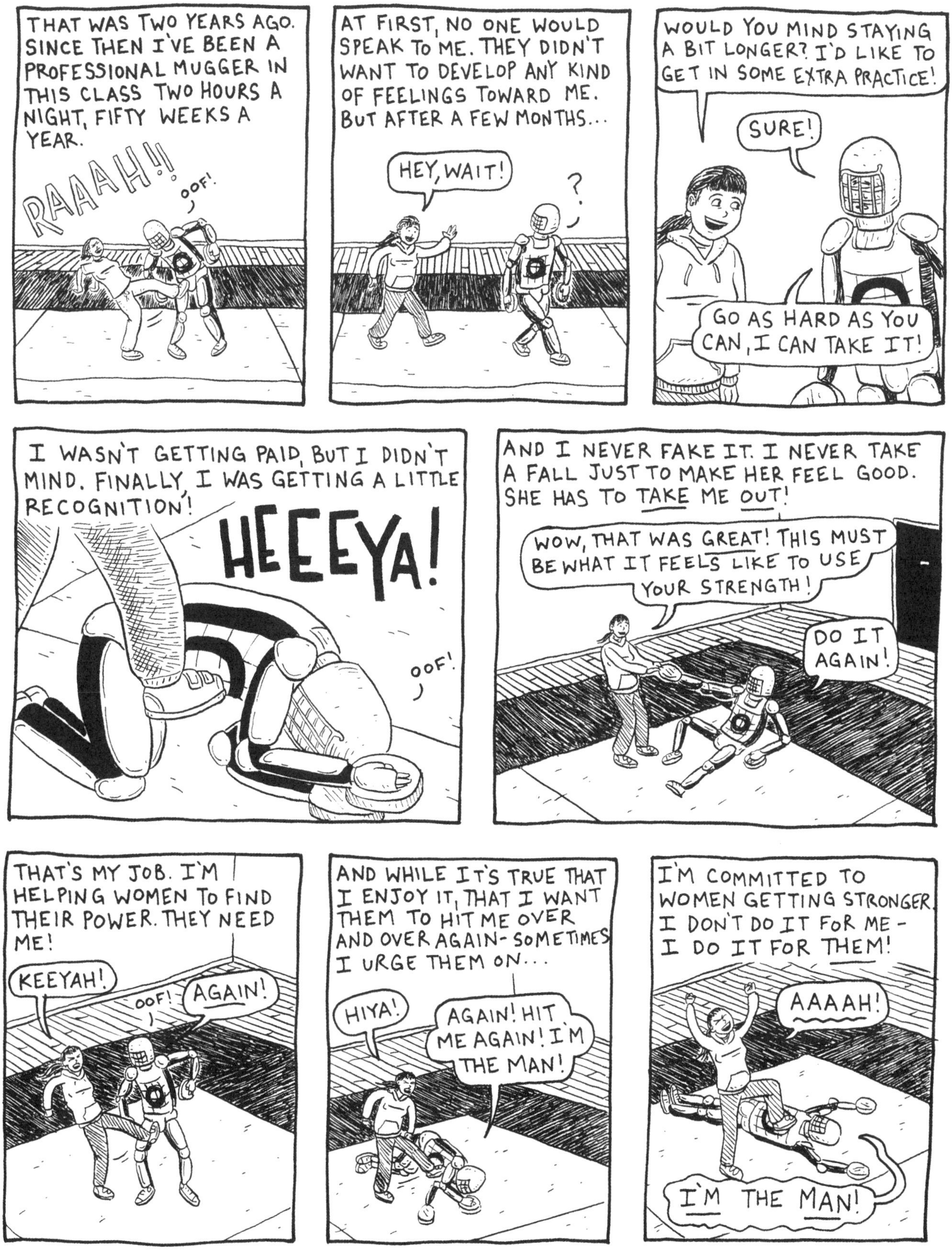

THAT WAS TWO YEARS AGO. SINCE THEN I'VE BEEN A PROFESSIONAL MUGGER IN THIS CLASS TWO HOURS A NIGHT, FIFTY WEEKS A YEAR.
RAAAH!!
OOF!
AT FIRST, NO ONE WOULD SPEAK TO ME. THEY DIDN'T WANT TO DEVELOP ANY KIND OF FEELINGS TOWARD ME. BUT AFTER A FEW MONTHS...
HEY, WAIT!
?
WOULD YOU MIND STAYING A BIT LONGER? I'D LIKE TO GET IN SOME EXTRA PRACTICE!
SURE!
GO AS HARD AS YOU CAN, I CAN TAKE IT!
I WASN'T GETTING PAID, BUT I DIDN'T MIND. FINALLY, I WAS GETTING A LITTLE RECOGNITION!
HEEEYA!
OOF!
AND I NEVER FAKE IT. I NEVER TAKE A FALL JUST TO MAKE HER FEEL GOOD. SHE HAS TO TAKE ME OUT!
WOW, THAT WAS GREAT! THIS MUST BE WHAT IT FEELS LIKE TO USE YOUR STRENGTH!
DO IT AGAIN!
THAT'S MY JOB. I'M HELPING WOMEN TO FIND THEIR POWER. THEY NEED ME!
KEEYAH!
OOF!
AGAIN!
AND WHILE IT'S TRUE THAT I ENJOY IT, THAT I WANT THEM TO HIT ME OVER AND OVER AGAIN- SOMETIMES I URGE THEM ON...
HIYA!
AGAIN! HIT ME AGAIN! I'M THE MAN!
I'M COMMITTED TO WOMEN GETTING STRONGER. I DON'T DO IT FOR ME - I DO IT FOR THEM!
AAAAH!
I'M THE MAN!

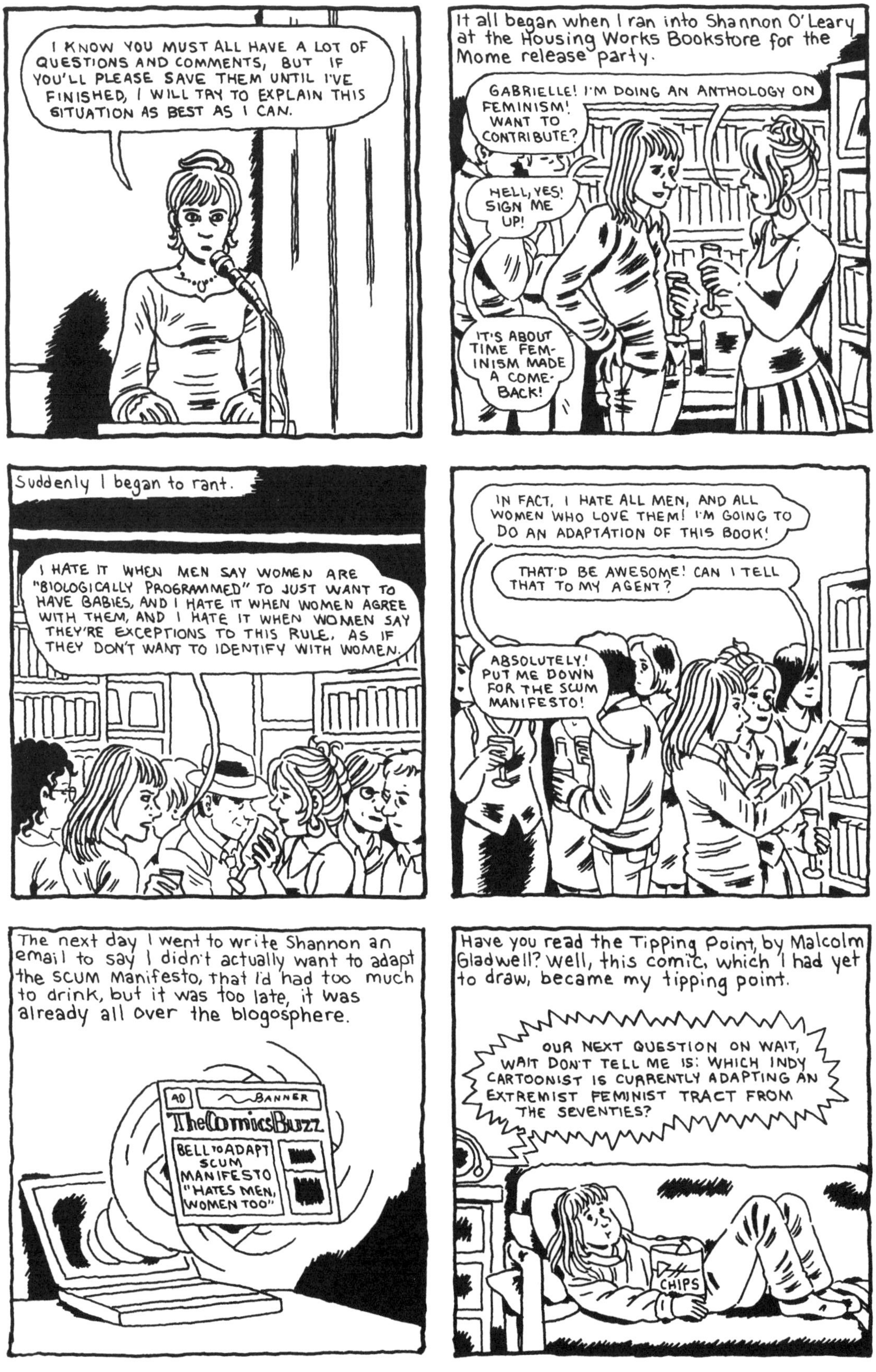
I KNOW YOU MUST ALL HAVE A LOT OF QUESTIONS AND COMMENTS, BUT IF YOU'LL PLEASE SAVE THEM UNTIL I'VE FINISHED, I WILL TRY TO EXPLAIN THIS SITUATION AS BEST AS I CAN.
It all began when I ran into Shannon O'Leary at the Housing Works Bookstore for the Mome release party.
GABRIELLE! I'M DOING AN ANTHOLOGY ON FEMINISM! WANT TO CONTRIBUTE?
HELL, YES! SIGN ME UP!
IT'S ABOUT TIME FEMINISM MADE A COME-BACK!
Suddenly I began to rant.
I HATE IT WHEN MEN SAY WOMEN ARE "BIOLOGICALLY PROGRAMMED" TO JUST WANT TO HAVE BABIES, AND I HATE IT WHEN WOMEN AGREE WITH THEM, AND I HATE IT WHEN WOMEN SAY THEY'RE EXCEPTIONS TO THIS RULE, AS IF THEY DON'T WANT TO IDENTIFY WITH WOMEN.
IN FACT, I HATE ALL MEN, AND ALL WOMEN WHO LOVE THEM! I'M GOING TO DO AN ADAPTATION OF THIS BOOK!
THAT'D BE AWESOME! CAN I TELL THAT TO MY AGENT?
ABSOLUTELY! PUT ME DOWN FOR THE SCUM MANIFESTO!
The next day I went to write Shannon an email to say I didn't actually want to adapt the SCUM Manifesto, that I'd had too much to drink, but it was too late, it was already all over the blogosphere.
AD
BANNER
The Comics Buzz
BELL TO ADAPT SCUM MANIFESTO "HATES MEN, WOMEN TOO"
Have you read the Tipping Point, by Malcolm Gladwell? Well, this comic, which I had yet to draw, became my tipping point.
OUR NEXT QUESTION ON WAIT, WAIT DON'T TELL ME IS: WHICH INDY CARTOONIST IS CURRENTLY ADAPTING AN EXTREMIST FEMINIST TRACT FROM THE SEVENTIES?
CHIPS

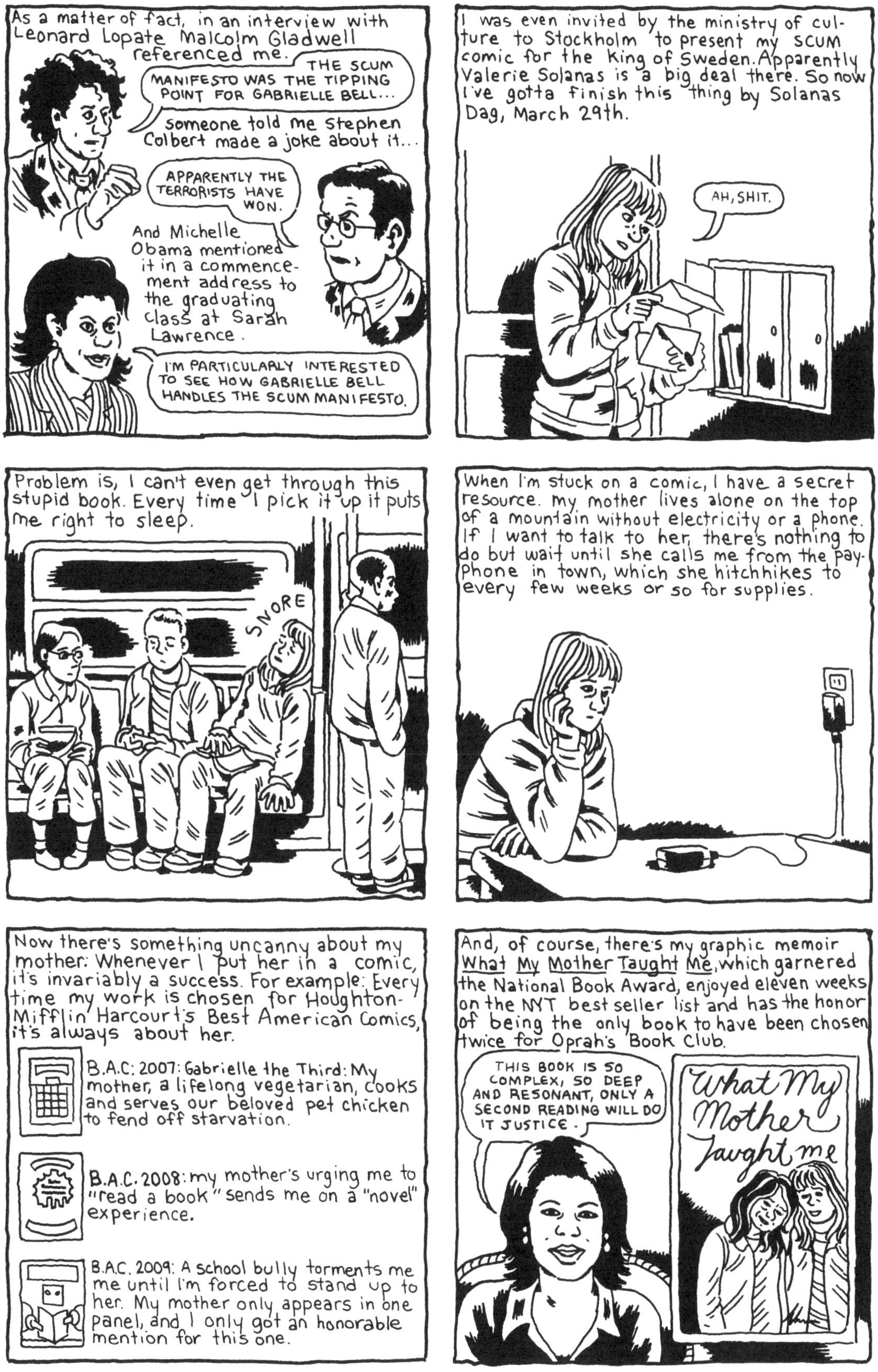
As a matter of fact, in an interview with Leonard Lopate Malcolm Gladwell referenced me.
THE SCUM MANIFESTO WAS THE TIPPING POINT FOR GABRIELLE BELL...
Someone told me Stephen Colbert made a joke about it...
APPARENTLY THE TERRORISTS HAVE WON.
And Michelle Obama mentioned it in a commencement address to the graduating class at Sarah Lawrence.
I'M PARTICULARLY INTERESTED TO SEE HOW GABRIELLE BELL HANDLES THE SCUM MANIFESTO.
I was even invited by the ministry of culture to Stockholm to present my SCUM comic for the King of Sweden. Apparently Valerie Solanas is a big deal there. So now I've gotta finish this thing by Solanas Dag, March 29th.
AH, SHIT.
Problem is, I can't even get through this stupid book. Every time I pick it up it puts me right to sleep.
SNORE
When I'm stuck on a comic, I have a secret resource. My mother lives alone on the top of a mountain without electricity or a phone. If I want to talk to her, there's nothing to do but wait until she calls me from the payphone in town, which she hitchhikes to every few weeks or so for supplies.
Now there's something uncanny about my mother: Whenever I put her in a comic, it's invariably a success. For example: Every time my work is chosen for Houghton-Mifflin Harcourt's Best American Comics, it's always about her.
B.A.C: 2007: Gabrielle the Third: My mother, a lifelong vegetarian, cooks and serves our beloved pet chicken to fend off starvation.
B.A.C. 2008: my mother's urging me to "read a book" sends me on a "novel" experience.
B.A.C. 2009: A school bully torments me me until I'm forced to stand up to her. My mother only appears in one panel, and I only got an honorable mention for this one.
And, of course, there's my graphic memoir What My Mother Taught Me, which garnered the National Book Award, enjoyed eleven weeks on the NYT best seller list and has the honor of being the only book to have been chosen twice for Oprah's Book Club.
THIS BOOK IS SO COMPLEX, SO DEEP AND RESONANT, ONLY A SECOND READING WILL DO IT JUSTICE.
What My Mother Taught me

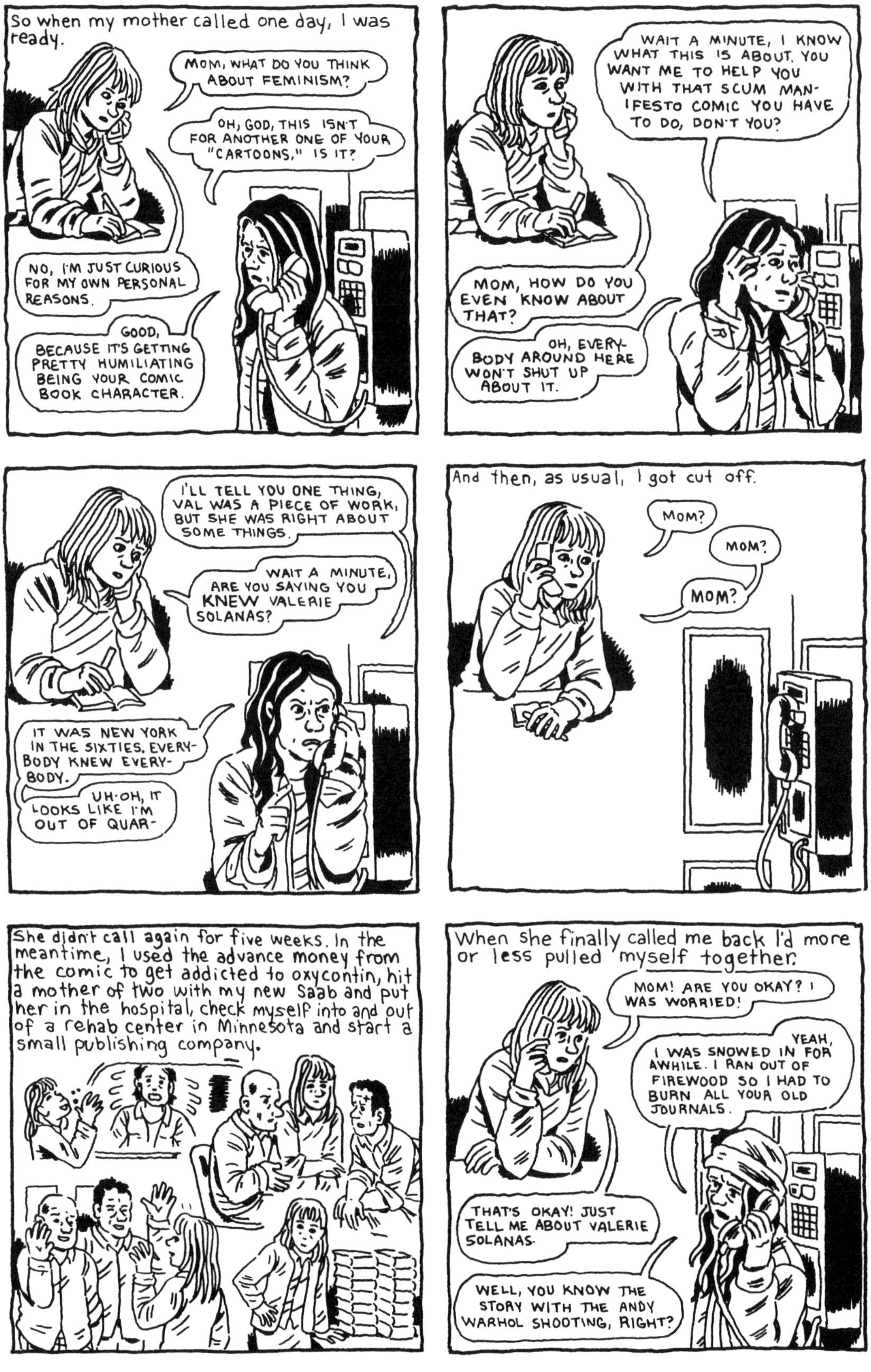
So when my mother called one day, I was ready.
MOM, WHAT DO YOU THINK ABOUT FEMINISM?
OH, GOD, THIS ISN'T FOR ANOTHER ONE OF YOUR "CARTOONS," IS IT?
NO, I'M JUST CURIOUS FOR MY OWN PERSONAL REASONS.
GOOD, BECAUSE IT'S GETTING PRETTY HUMILIATING BEING YOUR COMIC BOOK CHARACTER.
WAIT A MINUTE, I KNOW WHAT THIS IS ABOUT. YOU WANT ME TO HELP YOU WITH THAT SCUM MANIFESTO COMIC YOU HAVE TO DO, DON'T YOU?
MOM, HOW DO YOU EVEN KNOW ABOUT THAT?
OH, EVERYBODY AROUND HERE WON'T SHUT UP ABOUT IT.
I'LL TELL YOU ONE THING, VAL WAS A PIECE OF WORK, BUT SHE WAS RIGHT ABOUT SOME THINGS.
WAIT A MINUTE, ARE YOU SAYING YOU KNEW VALERIE SOLANAS?
IT WAS NEW YORK IN THE SIXTIES. EVERYBODY KNEW EVERYBODY.
UH-OH, IT LOOKS LIKE I'M OUT OF QUAR-
And then, as usual, I got cut off.
MOM?
MOM?
MOM?
She didn't call again for five weeks. In the meantime, I used the advance money from the comic to get addicted to oxycontin, hit a mother of two with my new Saab and put her in the hospital, check myself into and out of a rehab center in Minnesota and start a small publishing company.
When she finally called me back I'd more or less pulled myself together.
MOM! ARE YOU OKAY? I WAS WORRIED!
YEAH, I WAS SNOWED IN FOR AWHILE. I RAN OUT OF FIREWOOD SO I HAD TO BURN ALL YOUR OLD JOURNALS.
THAT'S OKAY! JUST TELL ME ABOUT VALERIE SOLANAS.
WELL, YOU KNOW THE STORY WITH THE ANDY WARHOL SHOOTING, RIGHT?

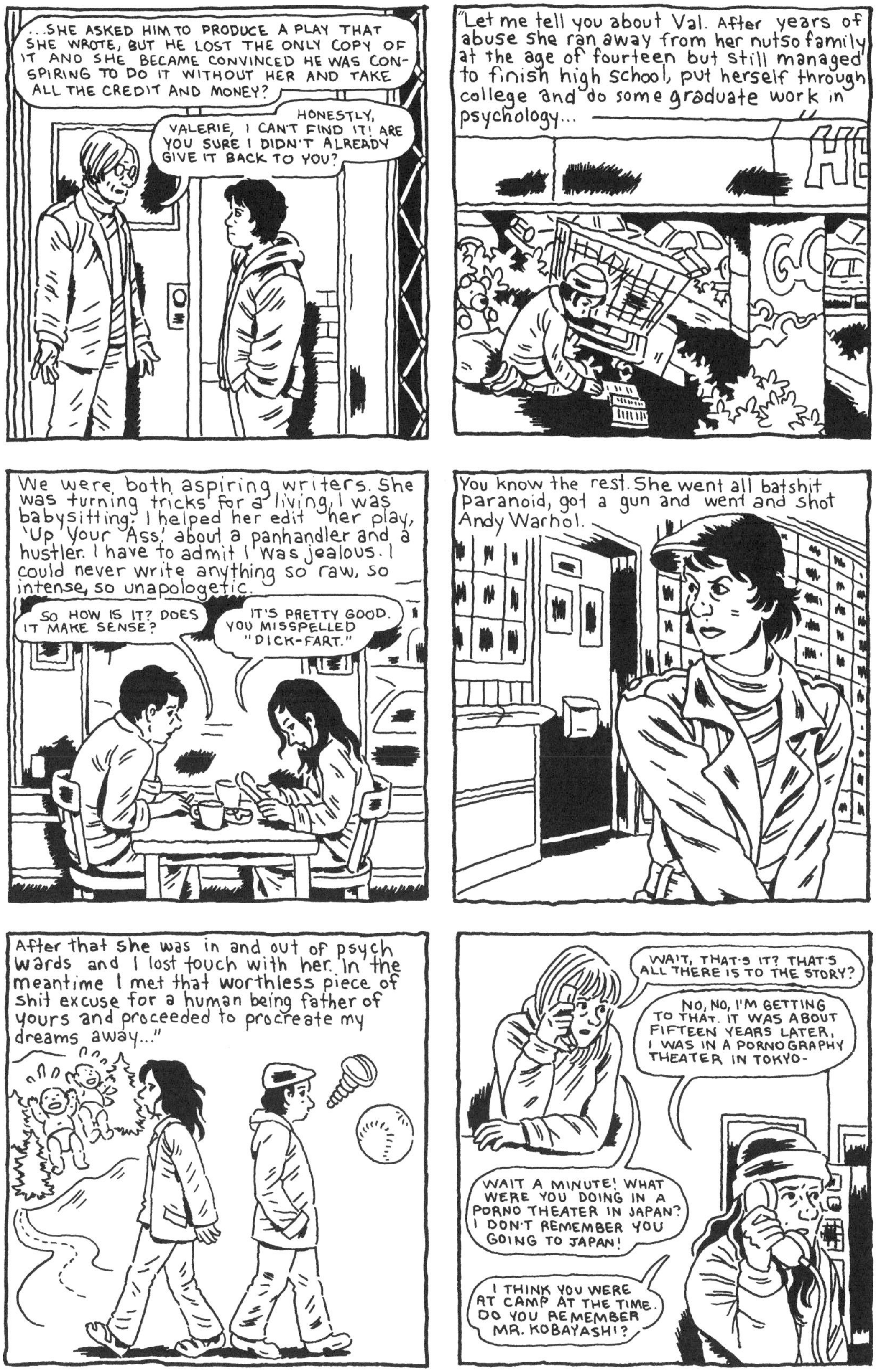
...SHE ASKED HIM TO PRODUCE A PLAY THAT SHE WROTE, BUT HE LOST THE ONLY COPY OF IT AND SHE BECAME CONVINCED HE WAS CONSPIRING TO DO IT WITHOUT HER AND TAKE ALL THE CREDIT AND MONEY?
HONESTLY, VALERIE, I CAN'T FIND IT! ARE YOU SURE I DIDN'T ALREADY GIVE IT BACK TO YOU?
"Let me tell you about Val. After years of abuse she ran away from her nutso family at the age of fourteen but still managed to finish high school, put herself through college and do some graduate work in psychology...
We were both aspiring writers. She was turning tricks for a living, I was babysitting. I helped her edit her play, 'Up Your Ass,' about a panhandler and a hustler. I have to admit I was jealous. I could never write anything so raw, so intense, so unapologetic.
SO HOW IS IT? DOES IT MAKE SENSE?
IT'S PRETTY GOOD. YOU MISSPELLED "DICK-FART."
You know the rest. She went all batshit paranoid, got a gun and went and shot Andy Warhol.
After that she was in and out of psych wards and I lost touch with her. In the meantime I met that worthless piece of shit excuse for a human being father of yours and proceeded to procreate my dreams away..."
WAIT, THAT'S IT? THAT'S ALL THERE IS TO THE STORY?
NO, NO, I'M GETTING TO THAT. IT WAS ABOUT FIFTEEN YEARS LATER, I WAS IN A PORNOGRAPHY THEATER IN TOKYO-
WAIT A MINUTE! WHAT WERE YOU DOING IN A PORNO THEATER IN JAPAN? I DON'T REMEMBER YOU GOING TO JAPAN!
I THINK YOU WERE AT CAMP AT THE TIME. DO YOU REMEMBER MR. KOBAYASHI?

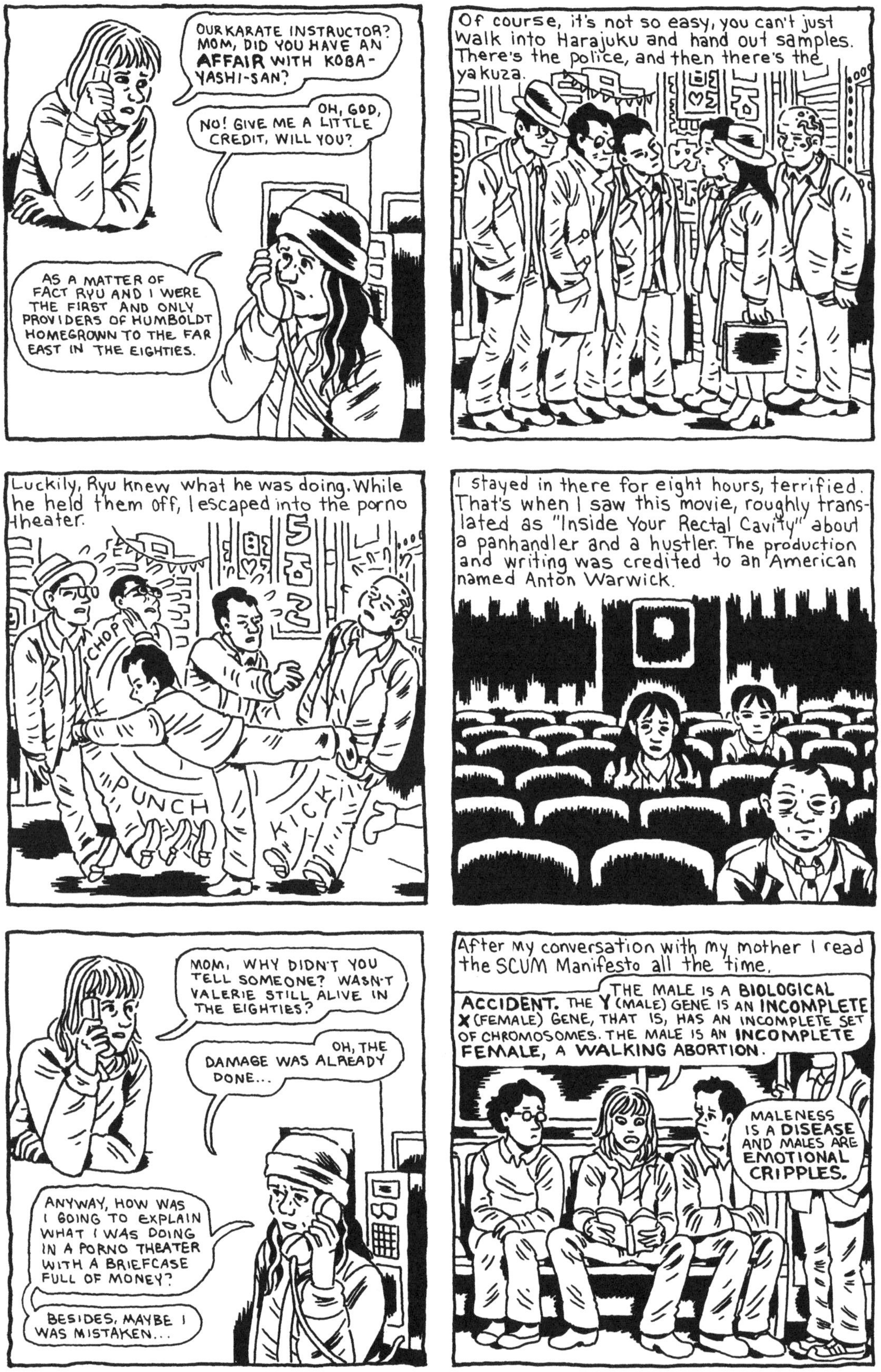

OUR KARATE INSTRUCTOR? MOM, DID YOU HAVE AN AFFAIR WITH KOBA-YASHI-SAN?
OH, GOD, NO! GIVE ME A LITTLE CREDIT, WILL YOU?
AS A MATTER OF FACT RYU AND I WERE THE FIRST AND ONLY PROVIDERS OF HUMBOLDT HOMEGROWN TO THE FAR EAST IN THE EIGHTIES.
Of course, it's not so easy, you can't just walk into Harajuku and hand out samples. There's the police, and then there's the yakuza.
Luckily, Ryu knew what he was doing. While he held them off, I escaped into the porno theater.
CHOP
PUNCH
KICK
I stayed in there for eight hours, terrified. That's when I saw this movie, roughly translated as "Inside Your Rectal Cavity" about a panhandler and a hustler. The production and writing was credited to an American named Anton Warwick.
MOM, WHY DIDN'T YOU TELL SOMEONE? WASN'T VALERIE STILL ALIVE IN THE EIGHTIES?
OH, THE DAMAGE WAS ALREADY DONE...
ANYWAY, HOW WAS I GOING TO EXPLAIN WHAT I WAS DOING IN A PORNO THEATER WITH A BRIEFCASE FULL OF MONEY?
BESIDES, MAYBE I WAS MISTAKEN...
After my conversation with my mother I read the SCUM Manifesto all the time.
THE MALE IS A BIOLOGICAL ACCIDENT. THE Y (MALE) GENE IS AN INCOMPLETE X (FEMALE) GENE, THAT IS, HAS AN INCOMPLETE SET OF CHROMOSOMES. THE MALE IS AN INCOMPLETE FEMALE, A WALKING ABORTION.
MALENESS IS A DISEASE AND MALES ARE EMOTIONAL CRIPPLES.

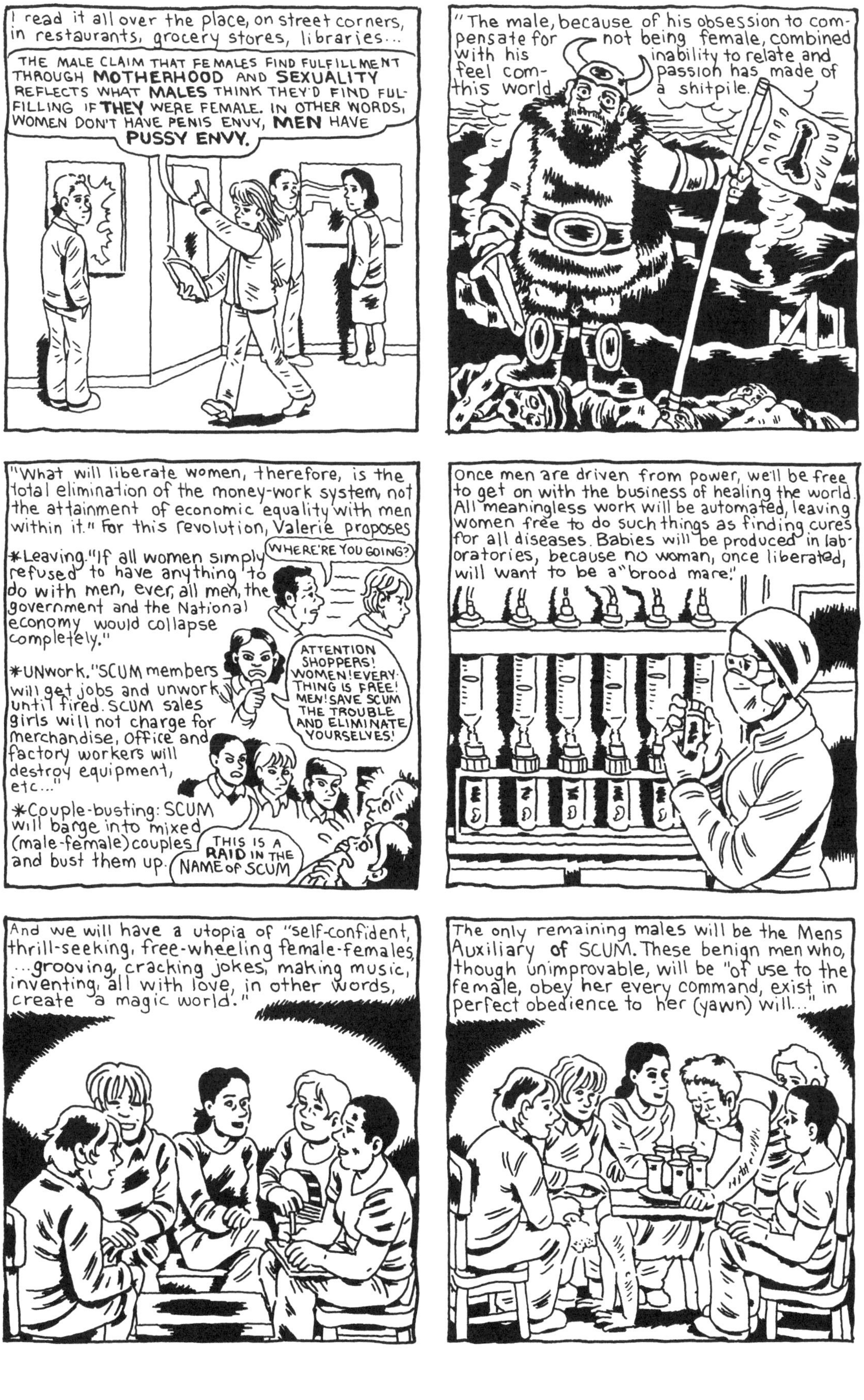
I read it all over the place, on street corners, in restaurants, grocery stores, libraries...
THE MALE CLAIM THAT FEMALES FIND FULFILLMENT THROUGH MOTHERHOOD AND SEXUALITY REFLECTS WHAT MALES THINK THEY'D FIND FULFILLING IF THEY WERE FEMALE. IN OTHER WORDS, WOMEN DON'T HAVE PENIS ENVY, MEN HAVE PUSSY ENVY.
"The male, because of his obsession to compensate for not being female, combined with his inability to relate and feel compassion has made of this world a shitpile.
"What will liberate women, therefore, is the total elimination of the money-work system, not the attainment of economic equality with men within it." For this revolution, Valerie proposes
*Leaving. "If all women simply refused to have anything to do with men, ever, all men, the government and the National economy would collapse completely."
WHERE'RE YOU GOING?
*UNwork. "SCUM members will get jobs and unwork until fired. SCUM sales girls will not charge for merchandise, office and factory workers will destroy equipment, etc..."
ATTENTION SHOPPERS! WOMEN! EVERYTHING IS FREE! MEN! SAVE SCUM THE TROUBLE AND ELIMINATE YOURSELVES!
*Couple-busting: SCUM will barge into mixed (male-female) couples and bust them up.
THIS IS A RAID IN THE NAME of SCUM
Once men are driven from power, we'll be free to get on with the business of healing the world. All meaningless work will be automated, leaving women free to do such things as finding cures for all diseases. Babies will be produced in laboratories, because no woman, once liberated, will want to be a "brood mare."
And we will have a utopia of "self-confident, thrill-seeking, free-wheeling female-females, ...grooving, cracking jokes, making music, inventing, all with love, in other words, create a magic world."
The only remaining males will be the Mens Auxiliary of SCUM. These benign men who, though unimprovable, will be "of use to the female, obey her every command, exist in perfect obedience to her (yawn) will..."

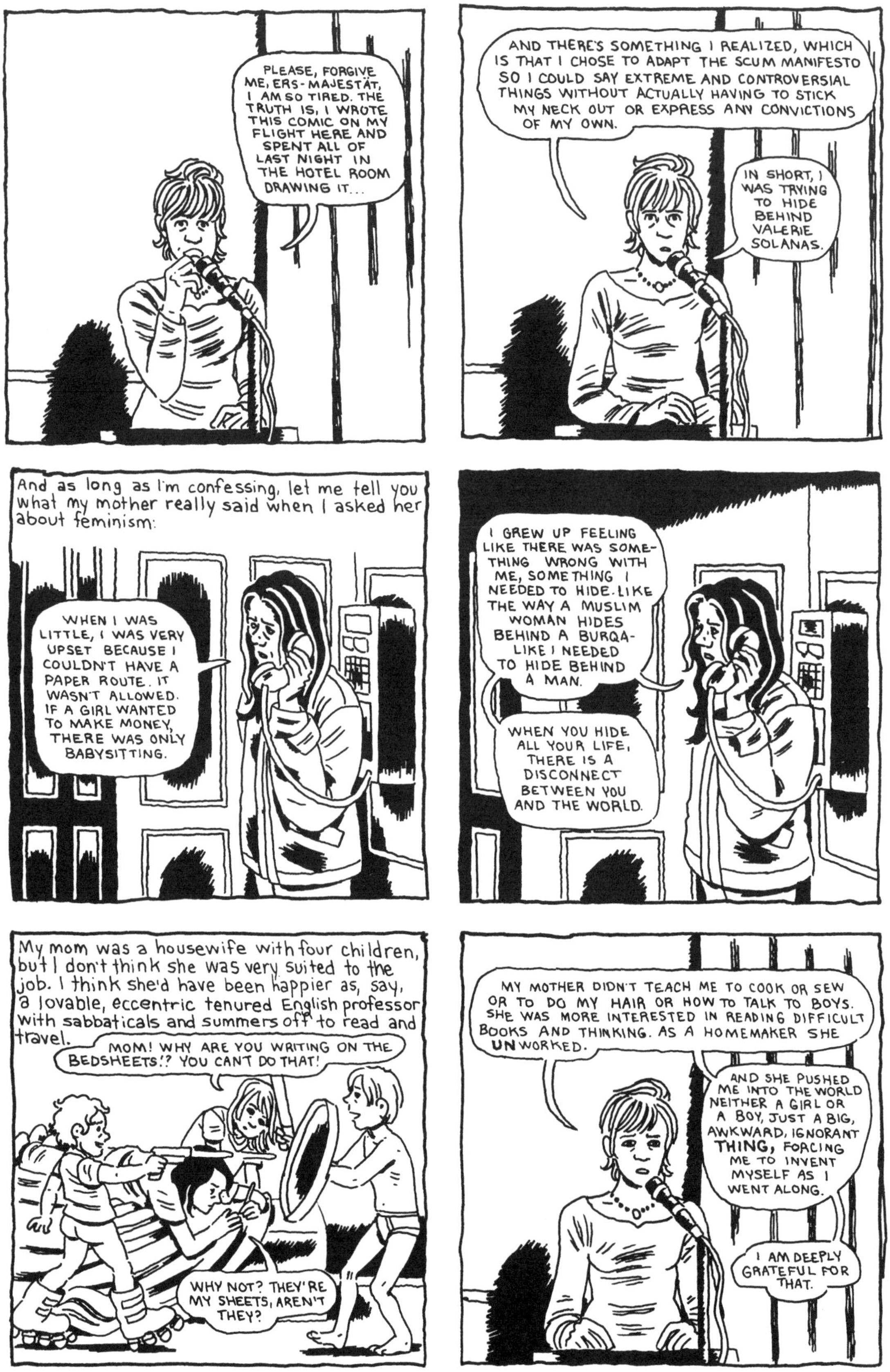

PLEASE, FORGIVE ME, ERS-MAJESTÄT, I AM SO TIRED. THE TRUTH IS, I WROTE THIS COMIC ON MY FLIGHT HERE AND SPENT ALL OF LAST NIGHT IN THE HOTEL ROOM DRAWING IT...
AND THERE'S SOMETHING I REALIZED, WHICH IS THAT I CHOSE TO ADAPT THE SCUM MANIFESTO SO I COULD SAY EXTREME AND CONTROVERSIAL THINGS WITHOUT ACTUALLY HAVING TO STICK MY NECK OUT OR EXPRESS ANY CONVICTIONS OF MY OWN.
IN SHORT, I WAS TRYING TO HIDE BEHIND VALERIE SOLANAS.
And as long as I'm confessing, let me tell you what my mother really said when I asked her about feminism:
WHEN I WAS LITTLE, I WAS VERY UPSET BECAUSE I COULDN'T HAVE A PAPER ROUTE. IT WASN'T ALLOWED. IF A GIRL WANTED TO MAKE MONEY, THERE WAS ONLY BABYSITTING.
I GREW UP FEELING LIKE THERE WAS SOMETHING WRONG WITH ME, SOMETHING I NEEDED TO HIDE. LIKE THE WAY A MUSLIM WOMAN HIDES BEHIND A BURQA- LIKE I NEEDED TO HIDE BEHIND A MAN.
WHEN YOU HIDE ALL YOUR LIFE, THERE IS A DISCONNECT BETWEEN YOU AND THE WORLD.
My mom was a housewife with four children, but I don't think she was very suited to the job. I think she'd have been happier as, say, a lovable, eccentric tenured English professor with sabbaticals and summers off to read and travel.
MOM! WHY ARE YOU WRITING ON THE BEDSHEETS!? YOU CAN'T DO THAT!
WHY NOT? THEY'RE MY SHEETS, AREN'T THEY?
MY MOTHER DIDN'T TEACH ME TO COOK OR SEW OR TO DO MY HAIR OR HOW TO TALK TO BOYS. SHE WAS MORE INTERESTED IN READING DIFFICULT BOOKS AND THINKING. AS A HOMEMAKER SHE UNWORKED.
AND SHE PUSHED ME INTO THE WORLD NEITHER A GIRL OR A BOY, JUST A BIG, AWKWARD, IGNORANT THING, FORCING ME TO INVENT MYSELF AS I WENT ALONG.
I AM DEEPLY GRATEFUL FOR THAT.

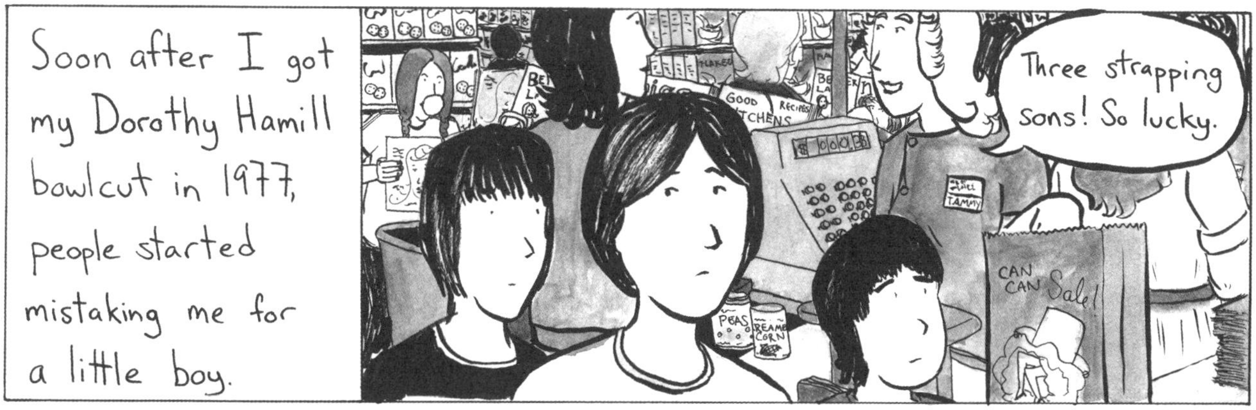
Soon after I got my Dorothy Hamill bowlcut in 1977, people started mistaking me for a little boy.
Three strapping sons! So lucky.
TAMMY
CAN CAN Sale!
PEAS
CREAMED CORN
GOOD KITCHENS
RECIPES

# TIMES I'VE BEEN MISTAKEN FOR A MAN

WRITTEN BY: BETH LISICK DRAWN BY: MK REED

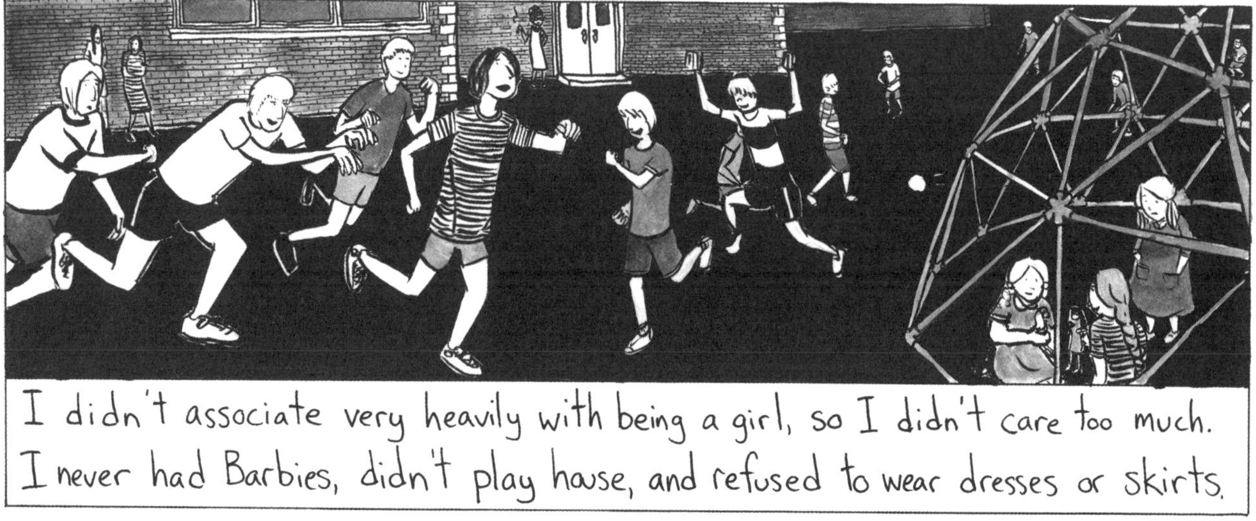
I didn't associate very heavily with being a girl, so I didn't care too much. I never had Barbies, didn't play house, and refused to wear dresses or skirts.

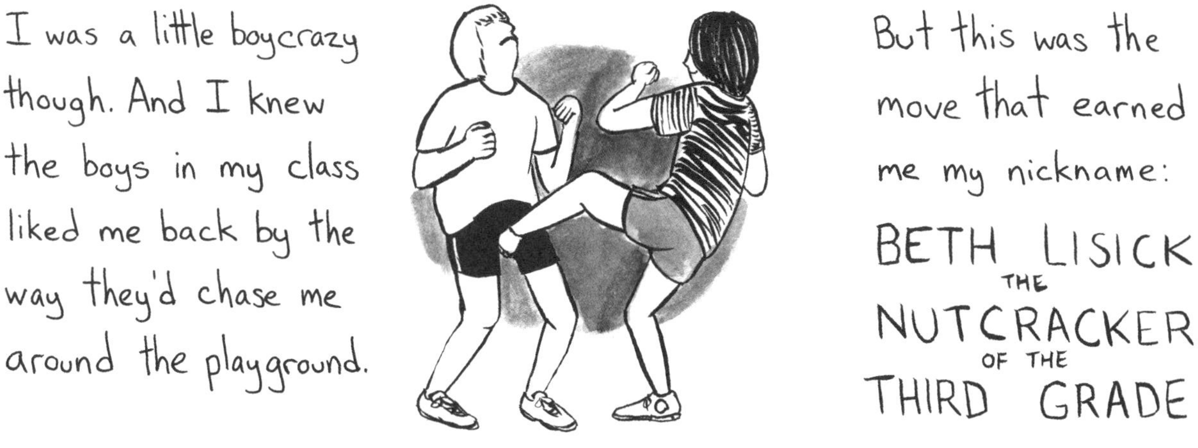
I was a little boycrazy though. And I knew the boys in my class liked me back by the way they'd chase me around the playground.
But this was the move that earned me my nickname:
BETH LISICK THE NUTCRACKER OF THE THIRD GRADE

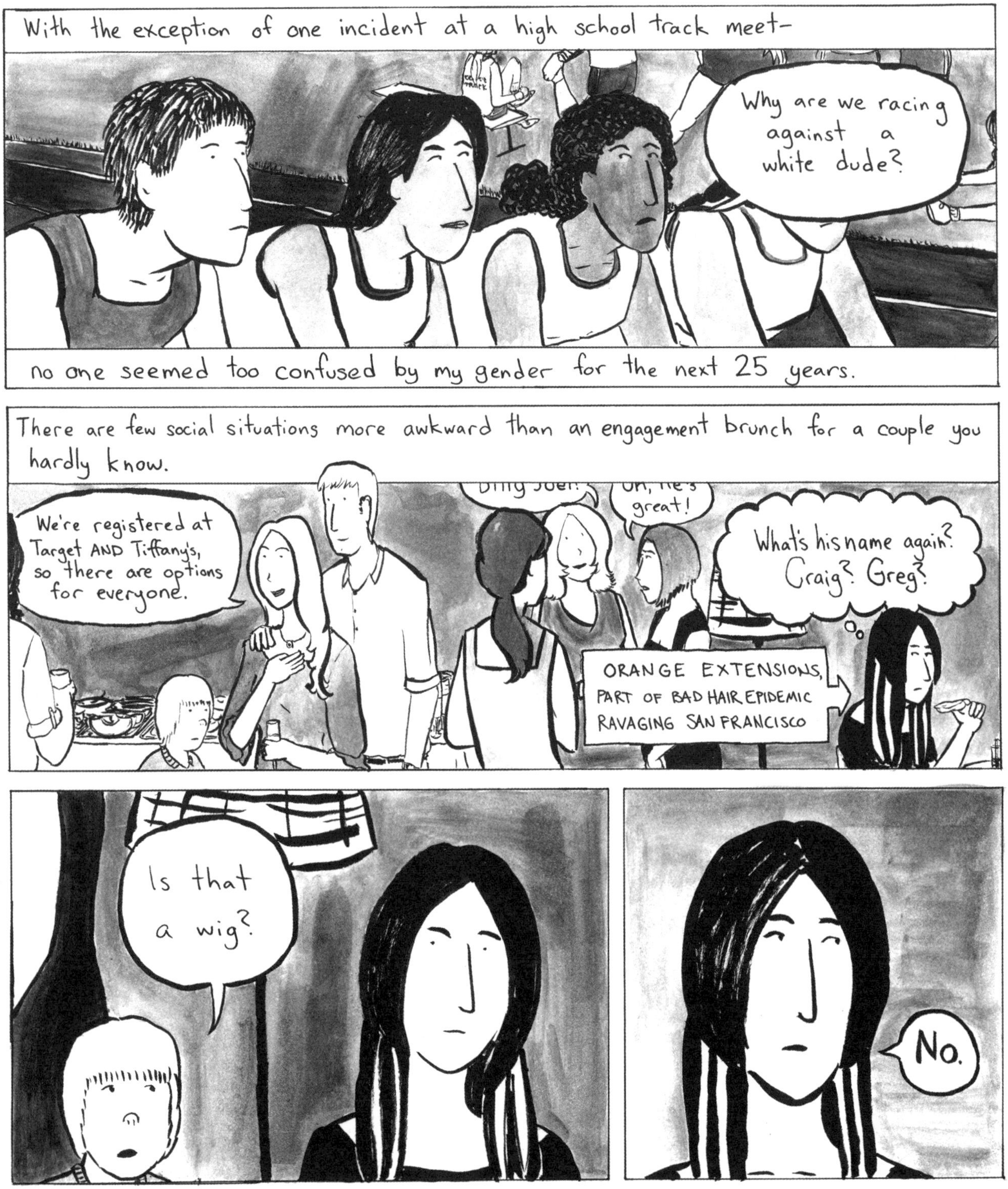
With the exception of one incident at a high school track meet-
Why are we racing against a white dude?
no one seemed too confused by my gender for the next 25 years.
There are few social situations more awkward than an engagement brunch for a couple you hardly know.
We're registered at Target AND Tiffany's, so there are options for everyone.
great!
What's his name again? Craig? Greg?
ORANGE EXTENSIONS, PART OF BAD HAIR EPIDEMIC RAVAGING SAN FRANCISCO
Is that a wig?
No.

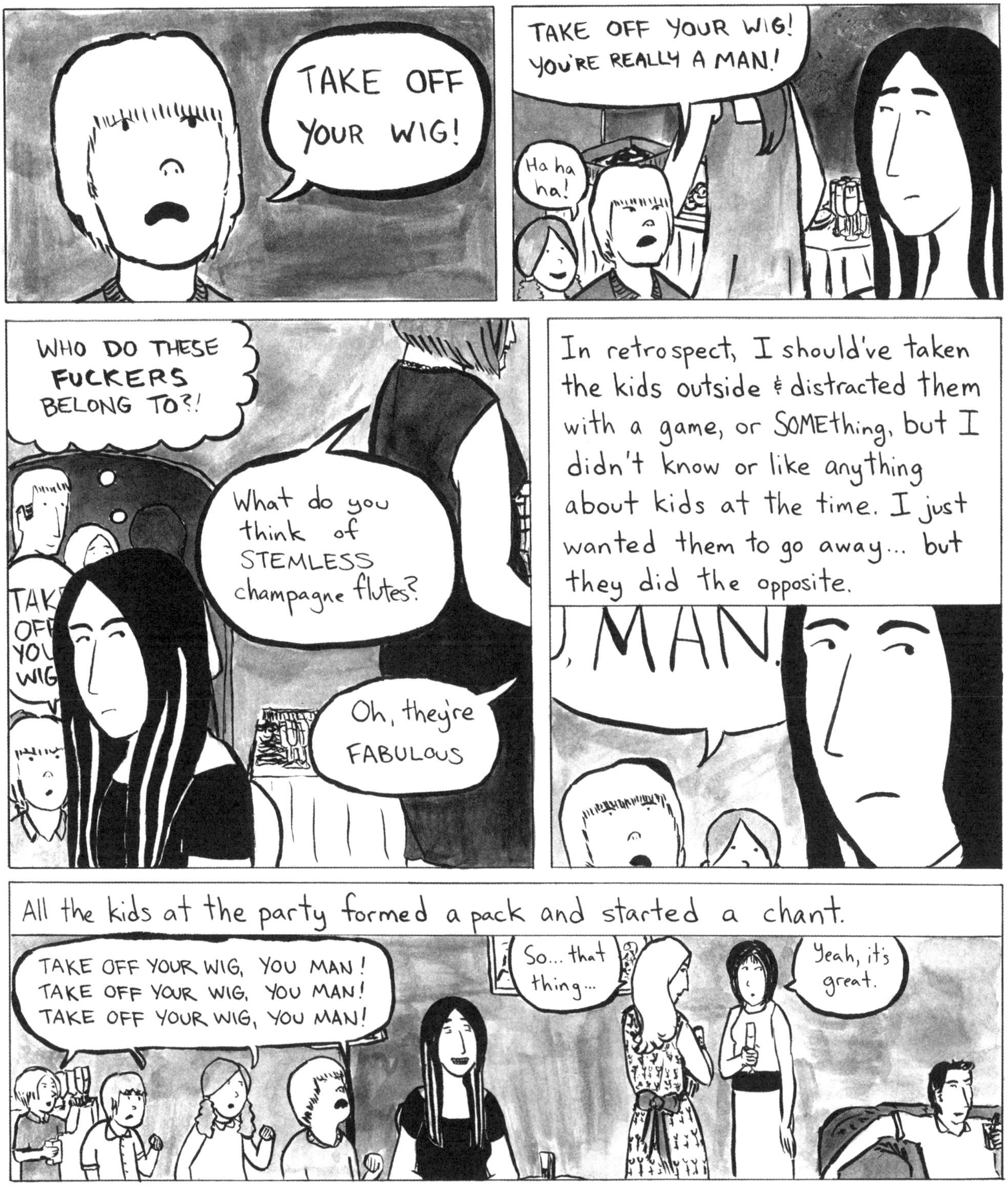
TAKE OFF YOUR WIG!
TAKE OFF YOUR WIG! YOU'RE REALLY A MAN!
Ha ha ha!
WHO DO THESE FUCKERS BELONG TO?!
What do you think of STEMLESS champagne flutes?
Oh, they're FABULOUS
In retrospect, I should've taken the kids outside & distracted them with a game, or SOMEthing, but I didn't know or like anything about kids at the time. I just wanted them to go away... but they did the opposite.
MAN!
All the kids at the party formed a pack and started a chant.
TAKE OFF YOUR WIG, YOU MAN! TAKE OFF YOUR WIG, YOU MAN! TAKE OFF YOUR WIG, YOU MAN!
So... that thing...
Yeah, it's great.

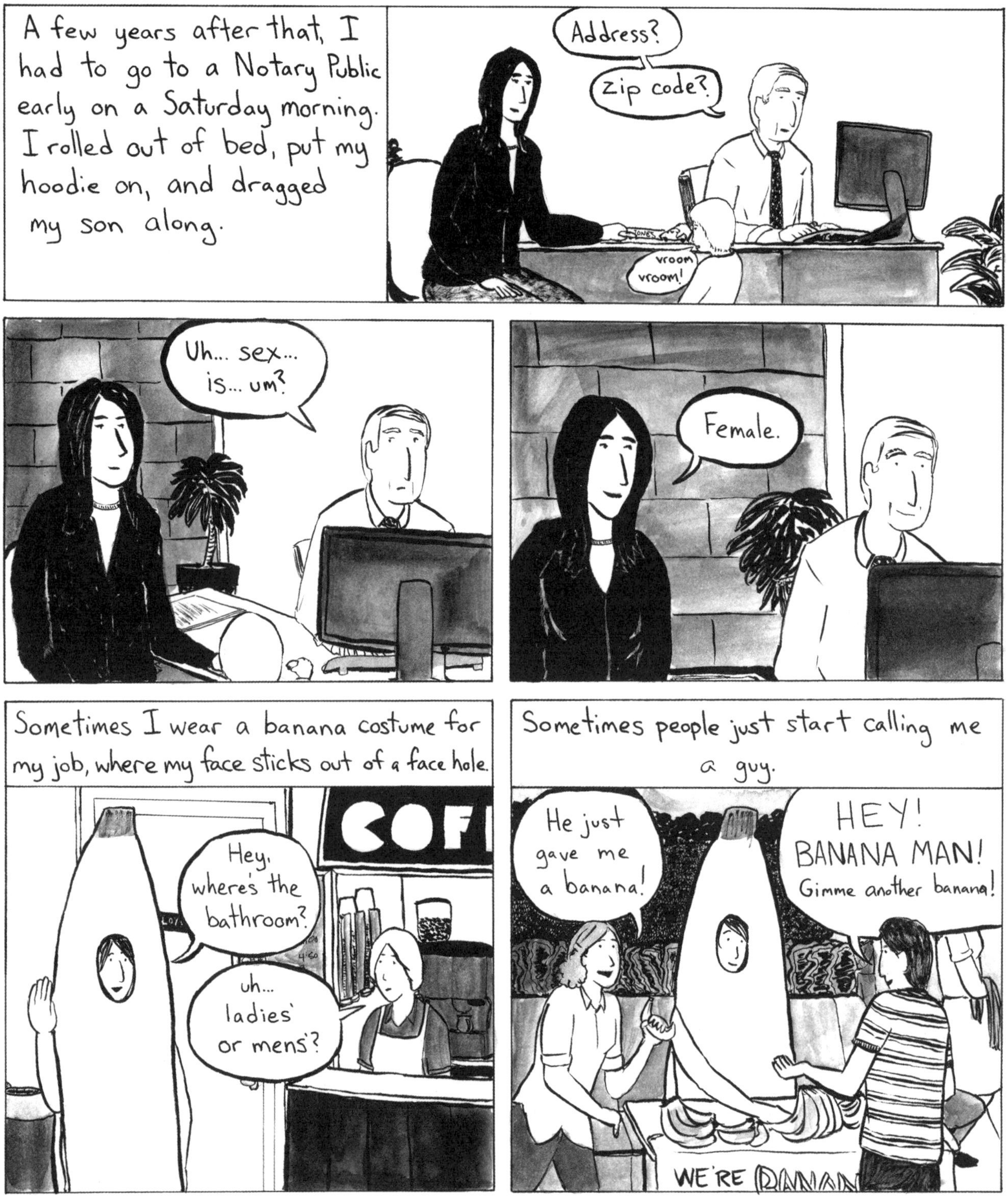
A few years after that, I had to go to a Notary Public early on a Saturday morning. I rolled out of bed, put my hoodie on, and dragged my son along.
Address?
zip code?
vroom vroom!
Uh... sex... is... um?
Female.
Sometimes I wear a banana costume for my job, where my face sticks out of a face hole.
Hey, where's the bathroom?
uh... ladies' or mens'?
Sometimes people just start calling me a guy.
He just gave me a banana!
HEY! BANANA MAN! Gimme another banana!
WE'RE

I don't think of myself as a particularly masculine looking person. I do have small boobs & kind of big hands - but also shoulder-length hair, bangs, & I usually wear lipstick. While those last three things don't necessarily make me a woman, it makes me wonder what part of me is giving off the manvibes.

My horrible secret theory is that I'm full of testosterone, and this makes me confident —

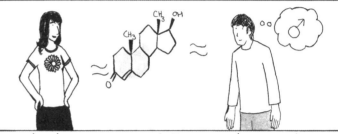

and strangers read this as male in a glance.

I told my theory to one of my best friends of fifteen years.

Do you think people are smelling my invisible manliness?

Oh yeah, totally!

She agreed so quickly that I knew she'd been thinking it for some time.

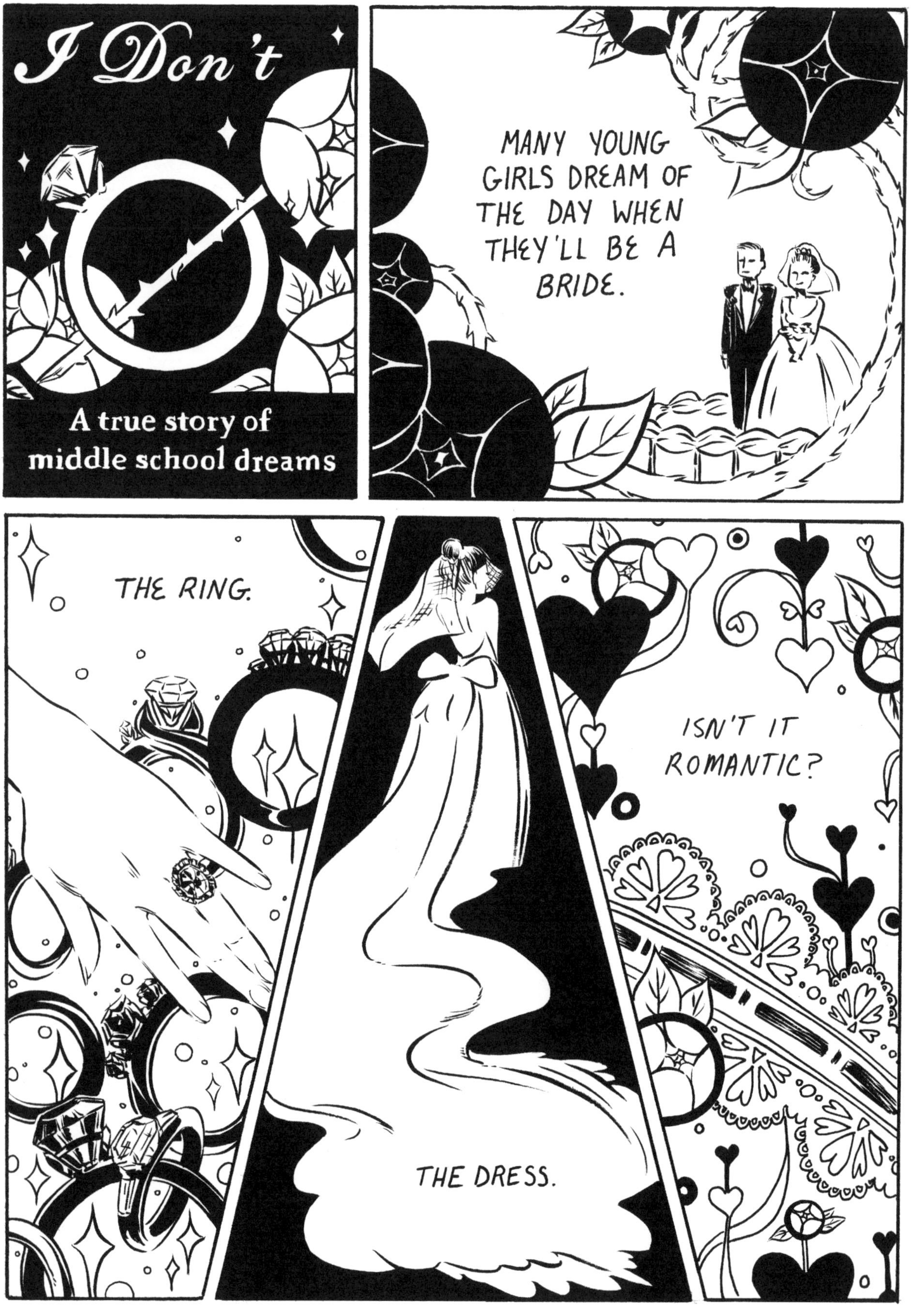
I Don't
A true story of middle school dreams
MANY YOUNG GIRLS DREAM OF THE DAY WHEN THEY'LL BE A BRIDE.
THE RING.
THE DRESS.
ISN'T IT ROMANTIC?

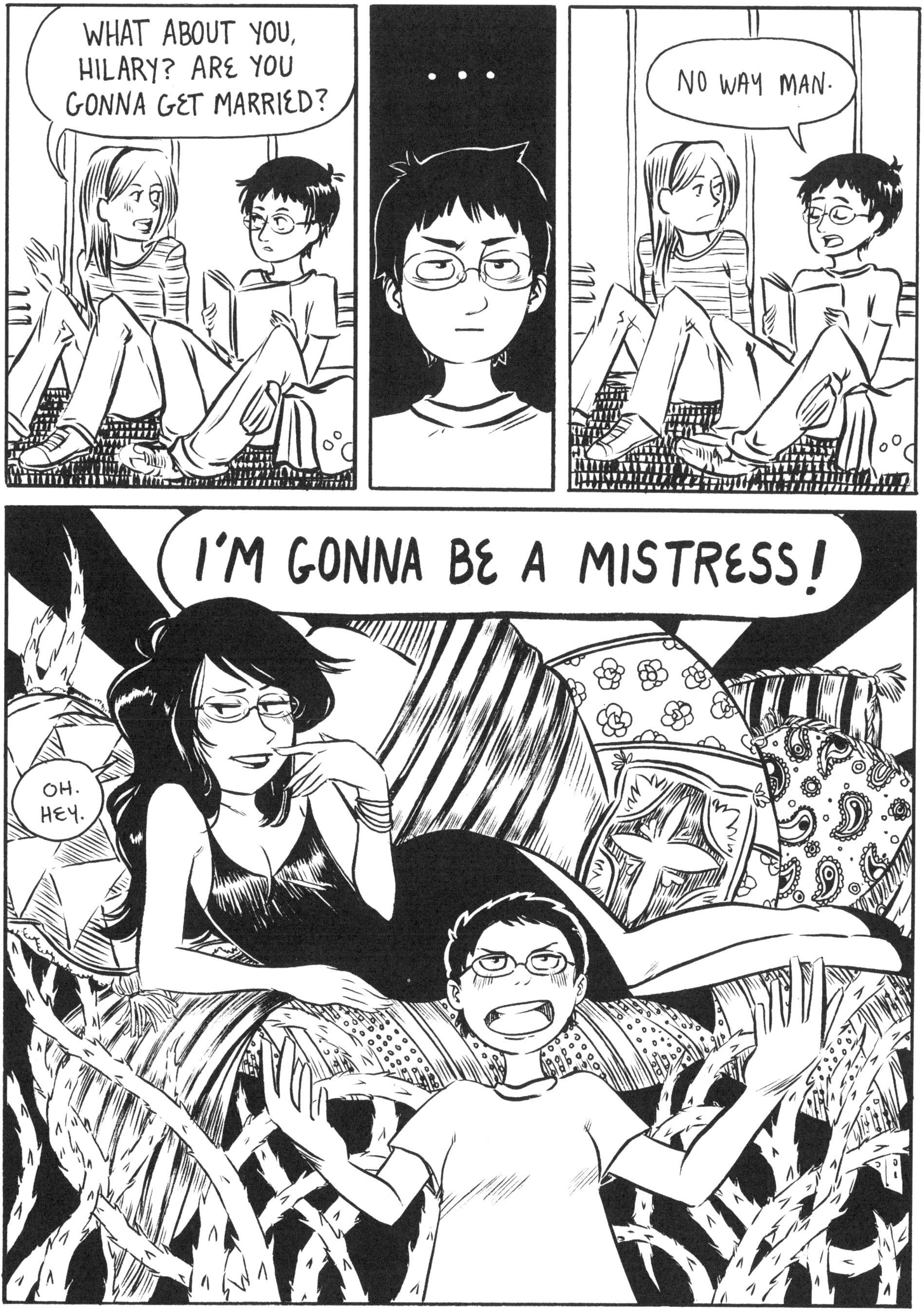
WHAT ABOUT YOU, HILARY? ARE YOU GONNA GET MARRIED?
. . .
NO WAY MAN.
I'M GONNA BE A MISTRESS!
OH. HEY.

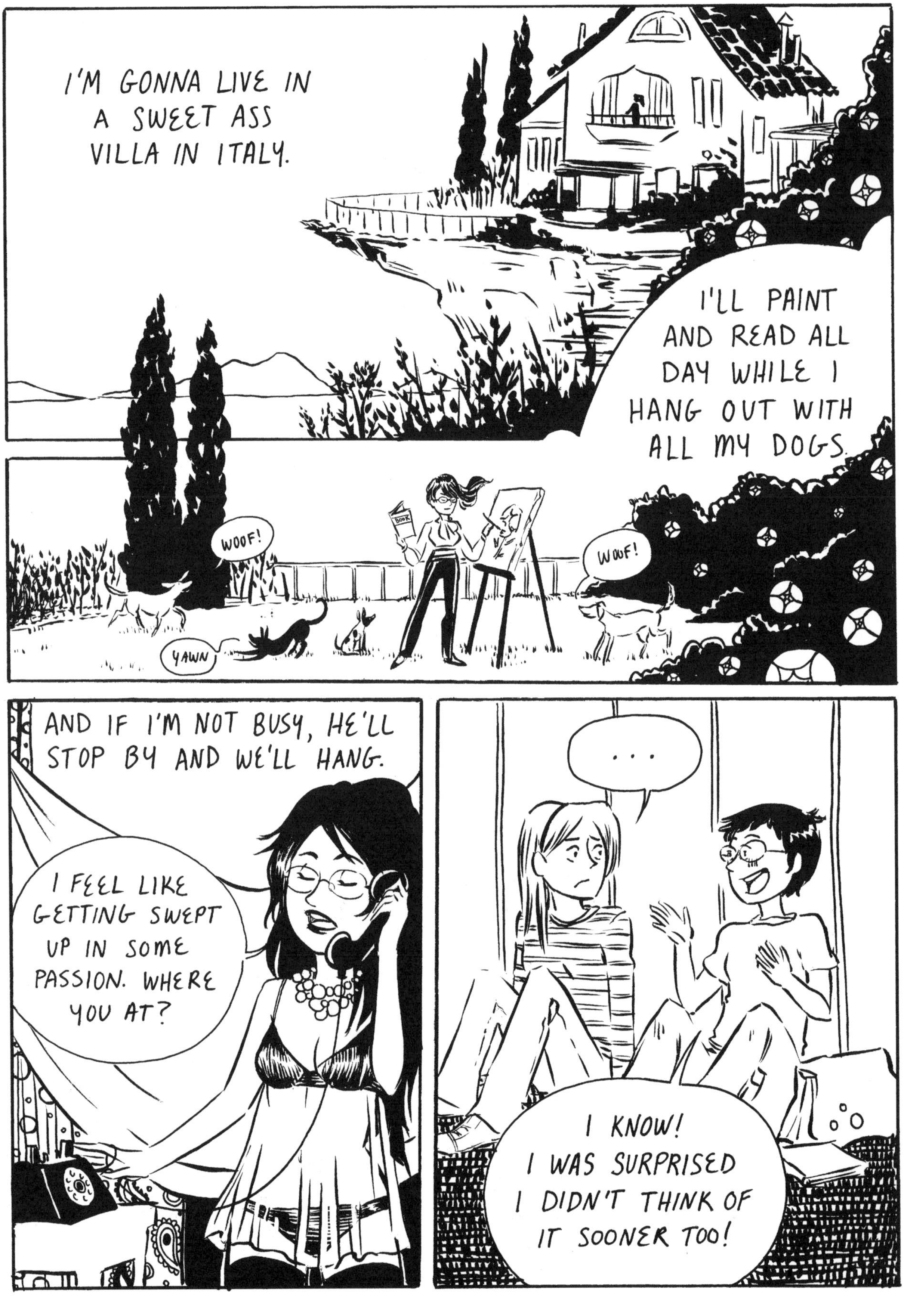
I'M GONNA LIVE IN A SWEET ASS VILLA IN ITALY.
I'LL PAINT AND READ ALL DAY WHILE I HANG OUT WITH ALL MY DOGS.
BOOK
WOOF!
WOOF!
YAWN
AND IF I'M NOT BUSY, HE'LL STOP BY AND WE'LL HANG.
I FEEL LIKE GETTING SWEPT UP IN SOME PASSION. WHERE YOU AT?
. . .
I KNOW! I WAS SURPRISED I DIDN'T THINK OF IT SOONER TOO!

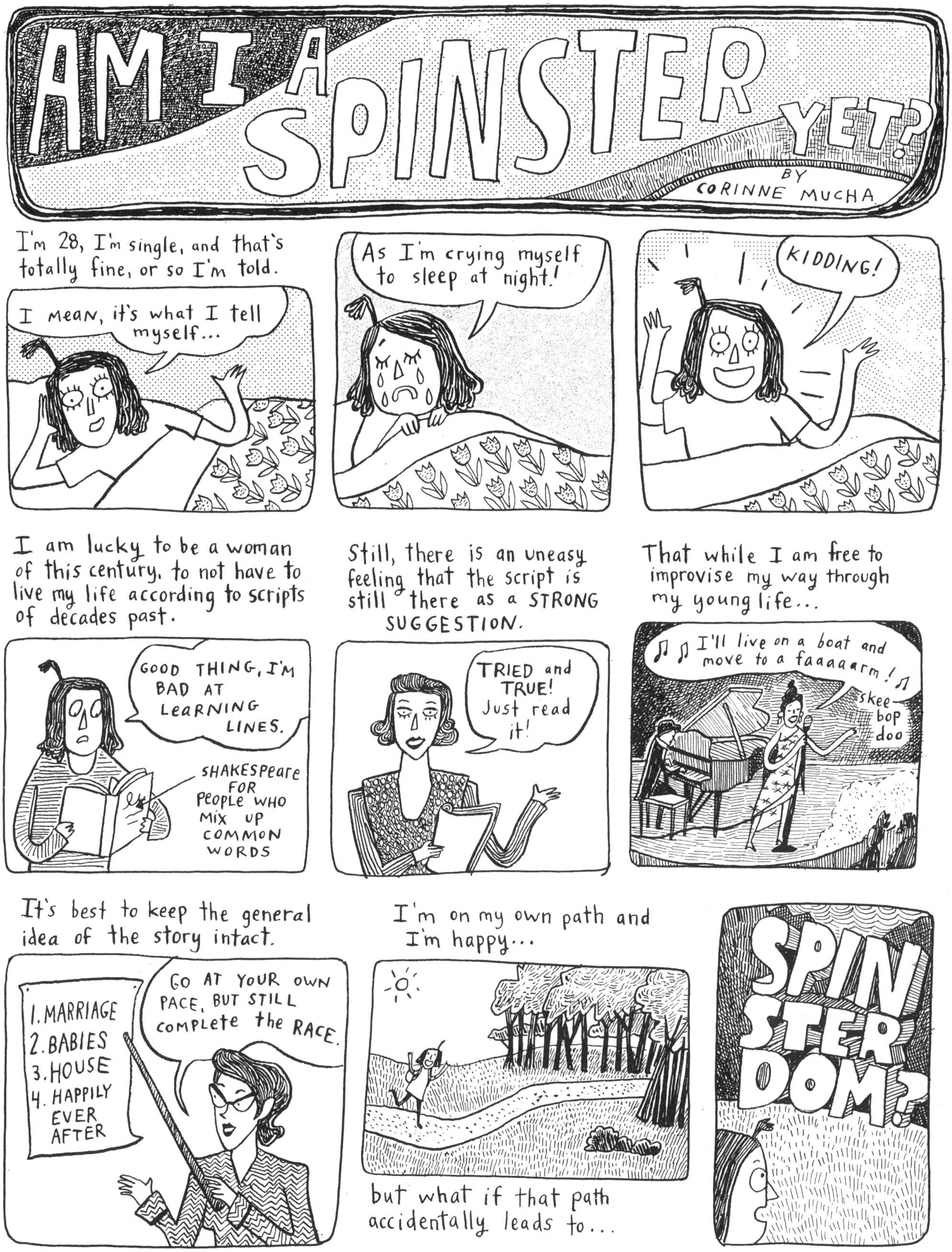
AM I A SPINSTER YET?
BY CORINNE MUCHA
I'm 28, I'm single, and that's totally fine, or so I'm told.
I MEAN, it's what I tell myself...
As I'm crying myself to sleep at night!
KIDDING!
I am lucky to be a woman of this century, to not have to live my life according to scripts of decades past.
GOOD THING, I'M BAD AT LEARNING LINES.
SHAKESPeare FOR PEOPLE WHO MIX UP COMMON WORDS
Still, there is an uneasy feeling that the script is still there as a STRONG SUGGESTION.
TRIED and TRUE! Just read it!
That while I am free to improvise my way through my young life...
♫ ♫ I'll live on a boat and move to a faaaaarm! ♫
skee-bop doo
It's best to keep the general idea of the story intact.
1. MARRIAGE
2. BABIES
3. HOUSE
4. HAPPILY EVER AFTER
GO AT YOUR OWN PACE, BUT STILL COMPLETE the RACE.
I'm on my own path and I'm happy...
but what if that path accidentally leads to...
SPINSTERDOM?

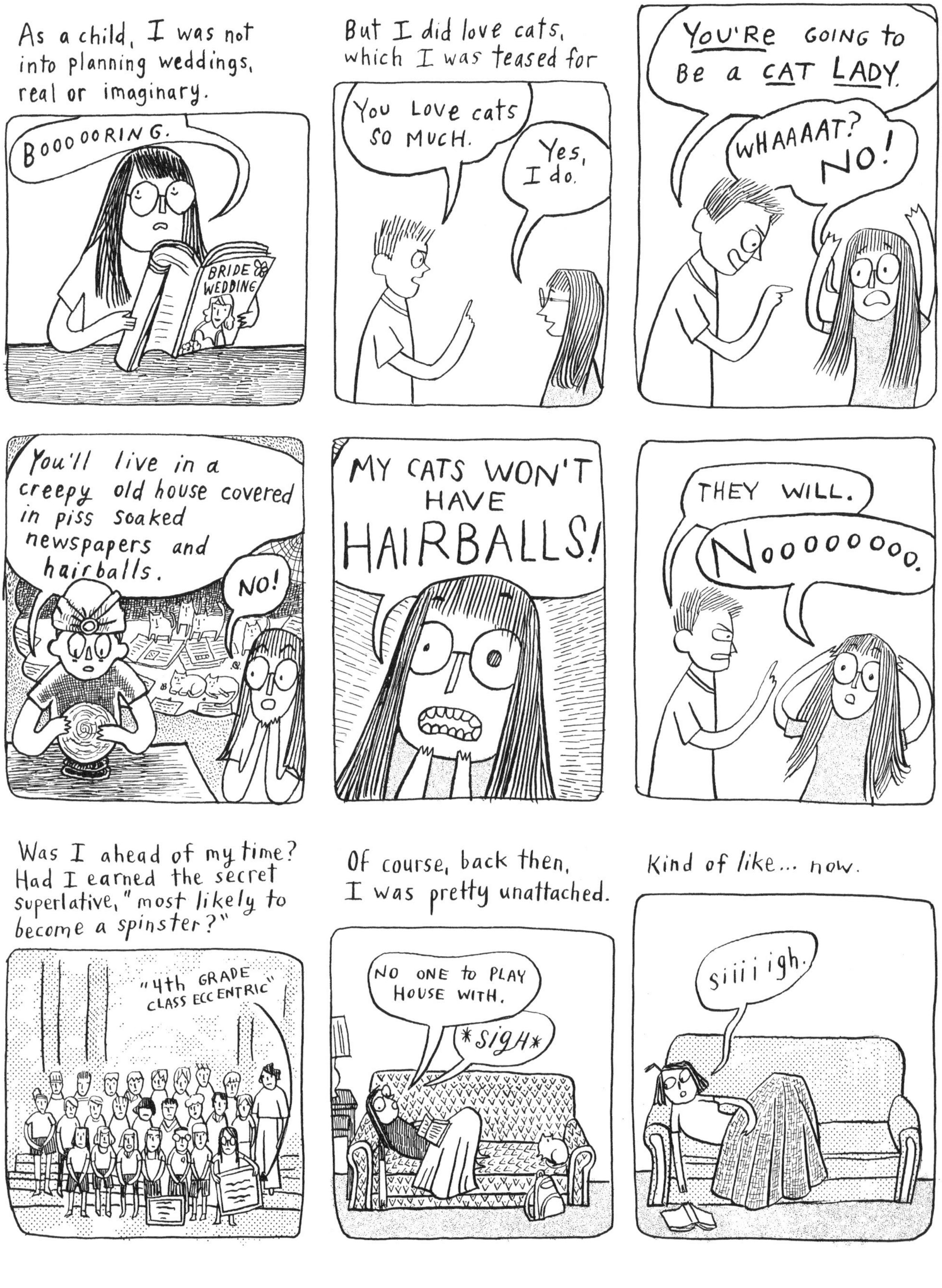
As a child, I was not into planning weddings, real or imaginary.
BOOOOORING.
BRIDE WEDDING
But I did love cats, which I was teased for
You love cats SO MUCH.
Yes, I do.
YOU'RE GOING to Be a CAT LADY.
WHAAAAT? NO!
You'll live in a creepy old house covered in piss soaked newspapers and hairballs.
NO!
MY CATS WON'T HAVE HAIRBALLS!
THEY WILL.
Nooooooo.
Was I ahead of my time? Had I earned the secret superlative, "most likely to become a spinster?"
"4th GRADE CLASS ECCENTRIC"
Of course, back then, I was pretty unattached.
NO ONE to PLAY HOUSE WITH.
*SIGH*
Kind of like... now.
siiiiigh.

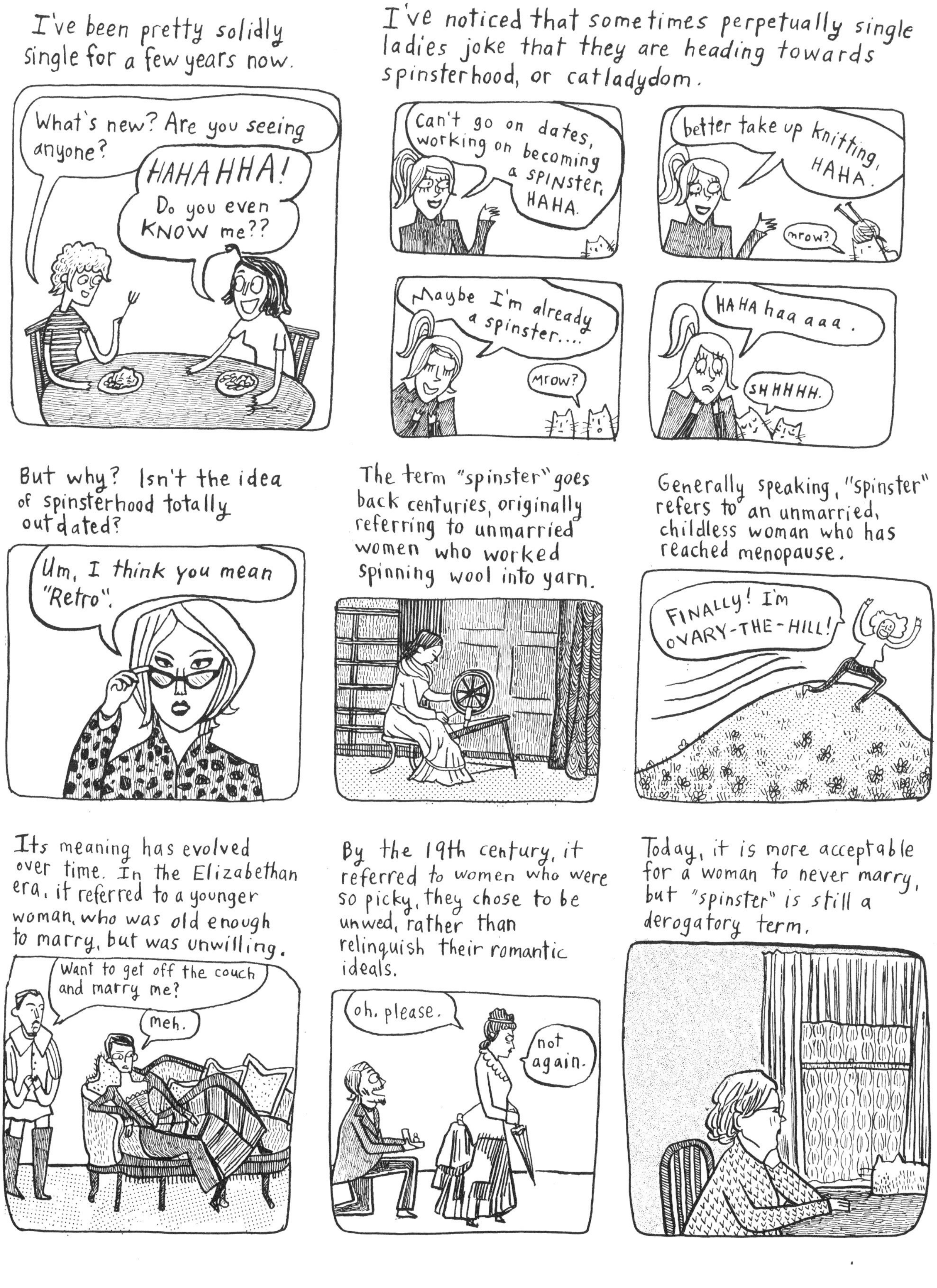
I've been pretty solidly single for a few years now.
What's new? Are you seeing anyone?
HAHAHHA! Do you even KNOW me??
I've noticed that sometimes perpetually single ladies joke that they are heading towards spinsterhood, or catladydom.
Can't go on dates, working on becoming a SPINster, HAHA.
better take up knitting, HAHA.
mrow?
Maybe I'm already a spinster....
mrow?
HAHA haa aaa.
SHHHHH.
But why? Isn't the idea of spinsterhood totally outdated?
Um, I think you mean "Retro".
The term "spinster" goes back centuries, originally referring to unmarried women who worked spinning wool into yarn.
Generally speaking, "spinster" refers to an unmarried, childless woman who has reached menopause.
FINALLY! I'm OVARY-THE-HILL!
Its meaning has evolved over time. In the Elizabethan era, it referred to a younger woman, who was old enough to marry, but was unwilling.
Want to get off the couch and marry me?
meh.
By the 19th century, it referred to women who were so picky, they chose to be unwed, rather than relinquish their romantic ideals.
oh, please.
not again.
Today, it is more acceptable for a woman to never marry, but "spinster" is still a derogatory term.

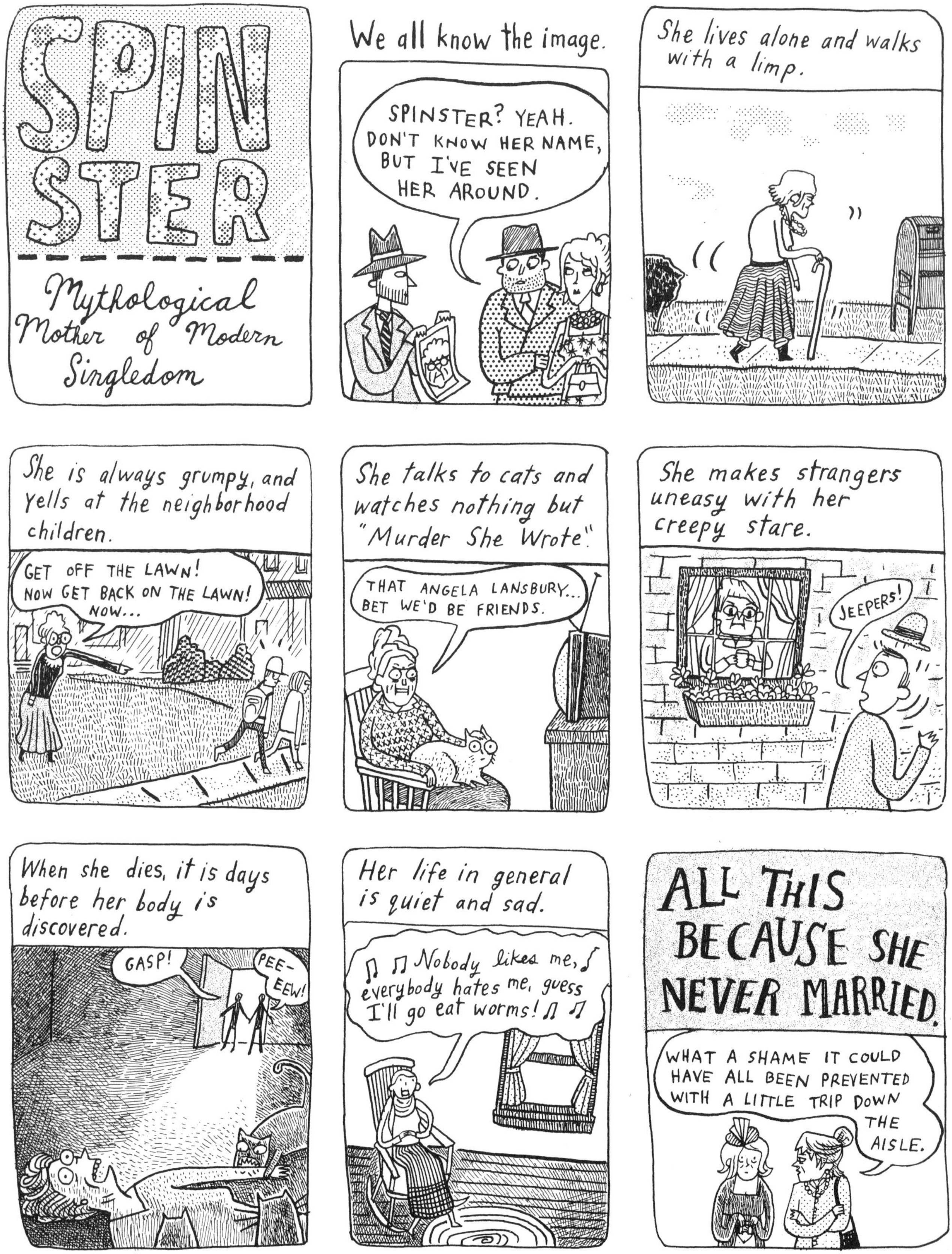
SPIN STER
Mythological Mother of Modern Singledom
We all know the image.
SPINSTER? YEAH. DON'T KNOW HER NAME, BUT I'VE SEEN HER AROUND.
She lives alone and walks with a limp.
She is always grumpy, and yells at the neighborhood children.
GET OFF THE LAWN! NOW GET BACK ON THE LAWN! NOW...
She talks to cats and watches nothing but "Murder She Wrote".
THAT ANGELA LANSBURY... BET WE'D BE FRIENDS.
She makes strangers uneasy with her creepy stare.
JEEPERS!
When she dies, it is days before her body is discovered.
GASP!
PEE-EEW!
Her life in general is quiet and sad.
♫ ♫ Nobody likes me, everybody hates me, guess I'll go eat worms! ♫ ♫
ALL THIS BECAUSE SHE NEVER MARRIED.
WHAT A SHAME IT COULD HAVE ALL BEEN PREVENTED WITH A LITTLE TRIP DOWN THE AISLE.

I'm a RATIONAL person. I know this Old Maid Myth is a sack of BULLSHIT. But I still get caught in worry. Because, you know, what if...

...I'm a PRE-SPINSTER?

WHAT IF I have EARLY ONSET SPINSTERHOOD?

I mean, I'm sure I have the sweaters for it.

Should I throw a party to fight for a cure?

you're invited!
SPINSTER PREVENTION GALA!
Ms. Mucha is in danger of becoming a cultural stereotype!
SEND YOUR ELIGIBLE BACHELORS!

What will happen if I FORGET to GET MARRIED?

I'VE ALWAYS BEEN A LATE BLOOMER. WHAT IF I DON'T GET MARRIED TILL AFTER I'M DEAD?

I'm gonna marry that ghost!

What _if_ I'm _meant_ to be alone? WHAT IF I WAS ALONE IN MY LAST LIFE, and I'll be alone in my NEXT LIFE because that's just what my SOUL is like, and the big joke is ALL "YOU wasted time on dating!"

THERE can be SO MUCH FEAR wrapped up in being SINGLE.

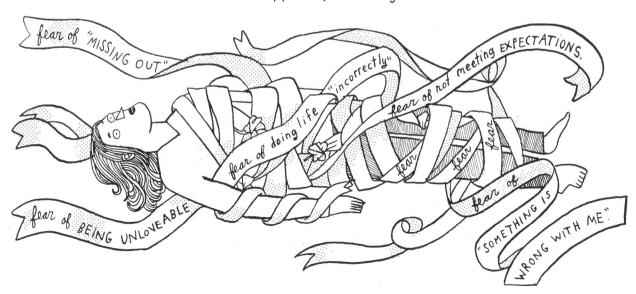

fear of "MISSING OUT"

fear of doing life "incorrectly"

fear of not meeting EXPECTATIONS.

fear

fear

fear of

fear of BEING UNLOVEABLE

"SOMETHING IS WRONG WITH ME."

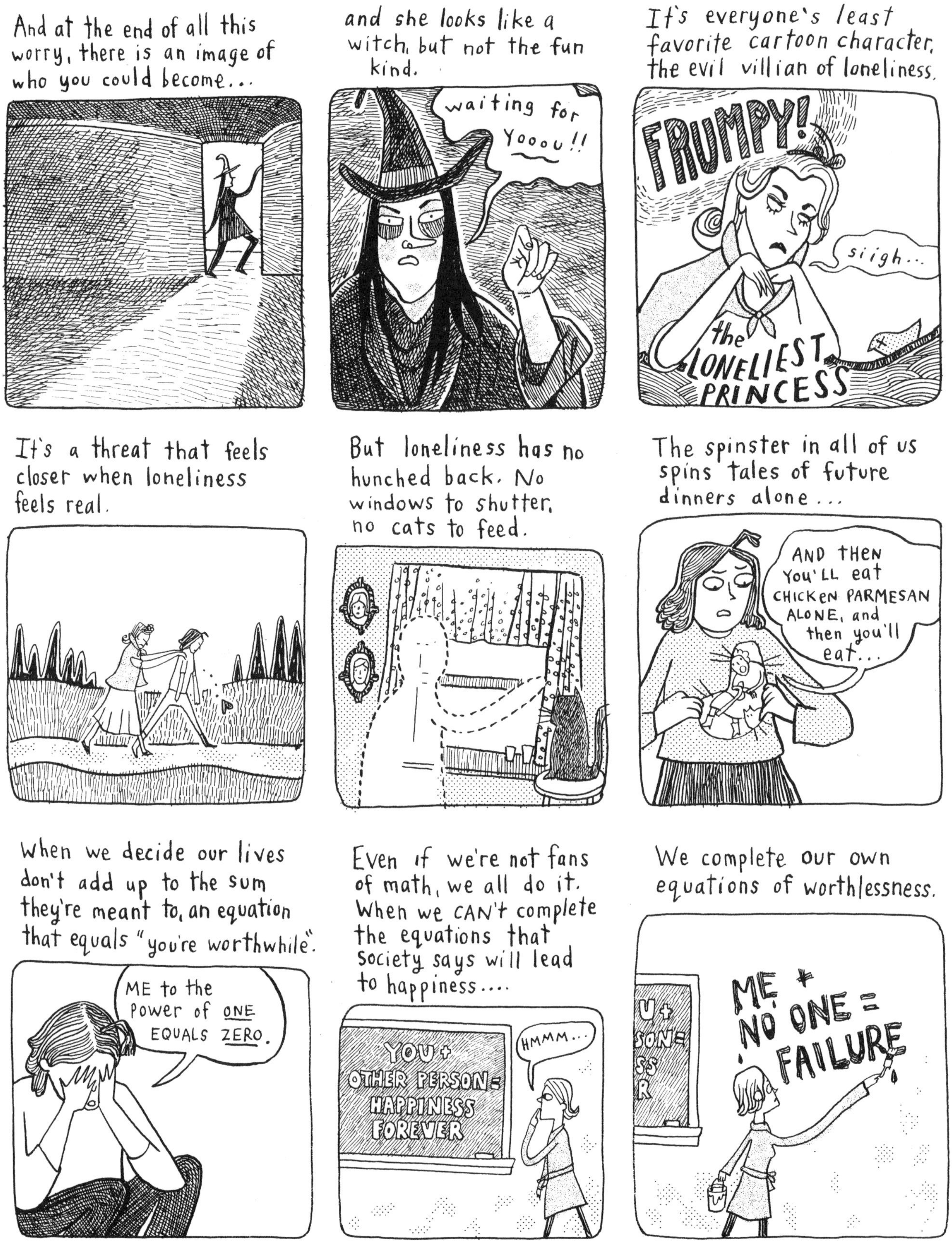
And at the end of all this worry, there is an image of who you could become...
and she looks like a witch, but not the fun kind.
waiting for Yooou!!
It's everyone's least favorite cartoon character, the evil villian of loneliness.
FRUMPY!
siigh...
the LONELIEST PRINCESS
It's a threat that feels closer when loneliness feels real.
But loneliness has no hunched back. No windows to shutter, no cats to feed.
The spinster in all of us spins tales of future dinners alone...
AND THEN YOU'LL eat CHICKEN PARMESAN ALONE, and then you'll eat...
When we decide our lives don't add up to the sum they're meant to, an equation that equals "you're worthwhile".
ME to the power of ONE EQUALS ZERO.
Even if we're not fans of math, we all do it. When we CAN'T complete the equations that society says will lead to happiness....
HMMM...
YOU + OTHER PERSON = HAPPINESS FOREVER
We complete our own equations of worthlessness.
ME + NO ONE = FAILURE

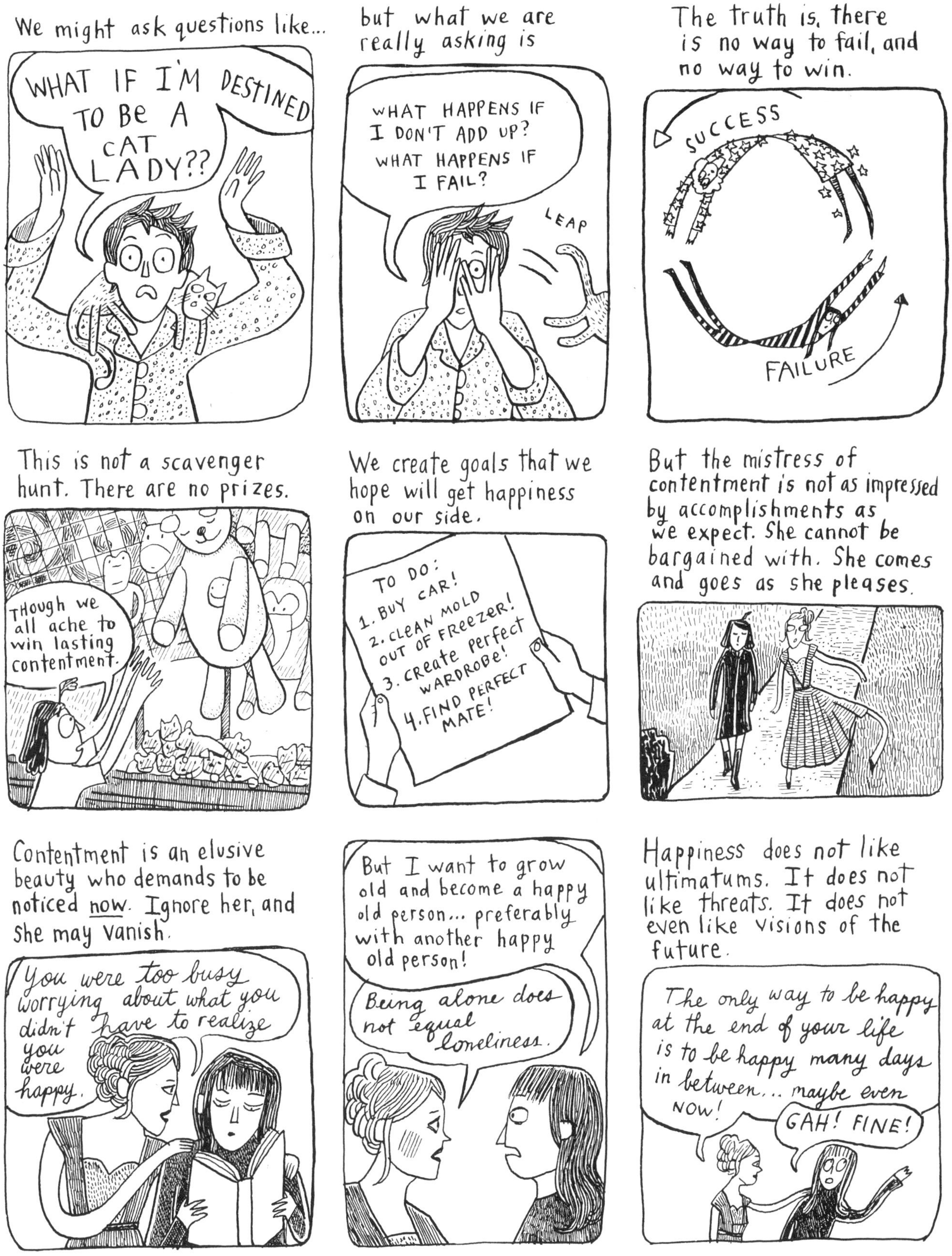
We might ask questions like...
WHAT IF I'M DESTINED TO BE A CAT LADY??
but what we are really asking is
WHAT HAPPENS IF I DON'T ADD UP? WHAT HAPPENS IF I FAIL?
LEAP
The truth is, there is no way to fail, and no way to win.
SUCCESS
FAILURE
This is not a scavenger hunt. There are no prizes.
Though we all ache to win lasting contentment.
We create goals that we hope will get happiness on our side.
TO DO: 1. BUY CAR! 2. CLEAN MOLD OUT OF FREEZER! 3. CREATE PERFECT WARDROBE! 4. FIND PERFECT MATE!
But the mistress of contentment is not as impressed by accomplishments as we expect. She cannot be bargained with. She comes and goes as she pleases.
Contentment is an elusive beauty who demands to be noticed now. Ignore her, and she may vanish.
You were too busy worrying about what you didn't have to realize you were happy.
But I want to grow old and become a happy old person... preferably with another happy old person!
Being alone does not equal loneliness.
Happiness does not like ultimatums. It does not like threats. It does not even like visions of the future.
The only way to be happy at the end of your life is to be happy many days in between... maybe even NOW!
GAH! FINE!

So am I destined for Spinsterdom? Who knows?

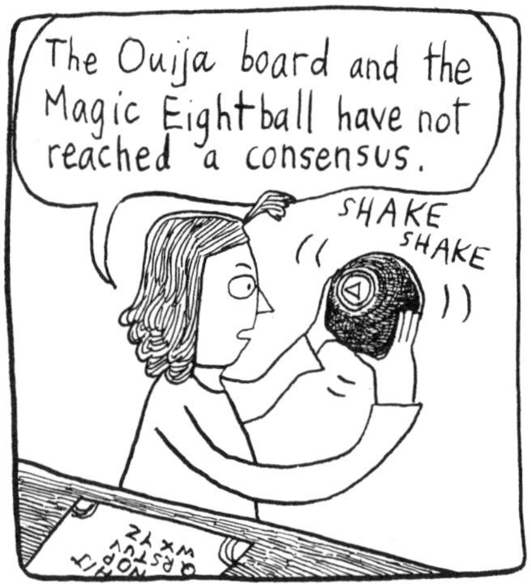
The Ouija board and the Magic Eightball have not reached a consensus.
SHAKE SHAKE

And really, who cares? Is it such a sorry fate?

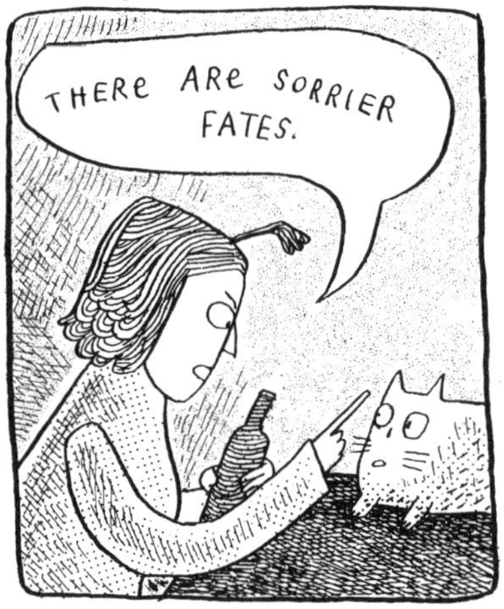
THERE ARE SORRIER FATES.

The word, taken literally, has no qualities shared with the bogeyman.

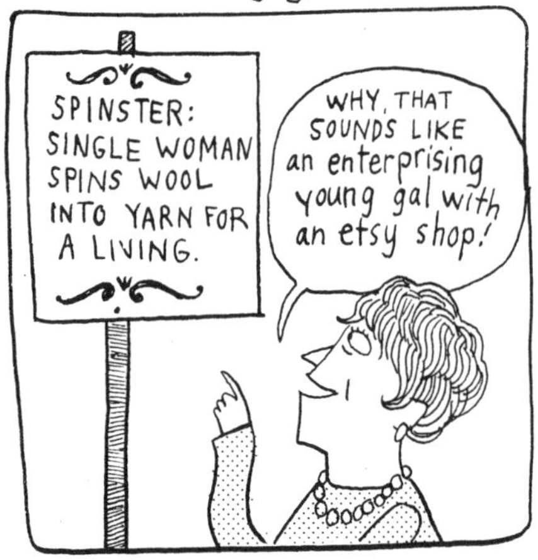
SPINSTER: SINGLE WOMAN SPINS WOOL INTO YARN FOR A LIVING.
WHY, THAT SOUNDS LIKE an enterprising young gal with an etsy shop!

I know a beautiful young spinster, actually. She even has the name of a Disney princess.

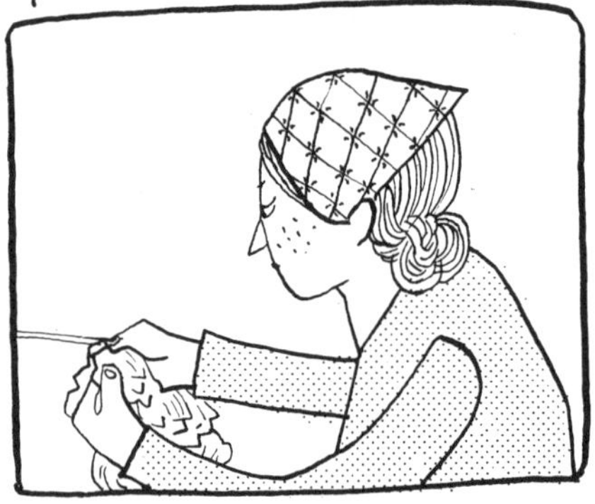

This woman has taken spinstering to a DIY extreme.

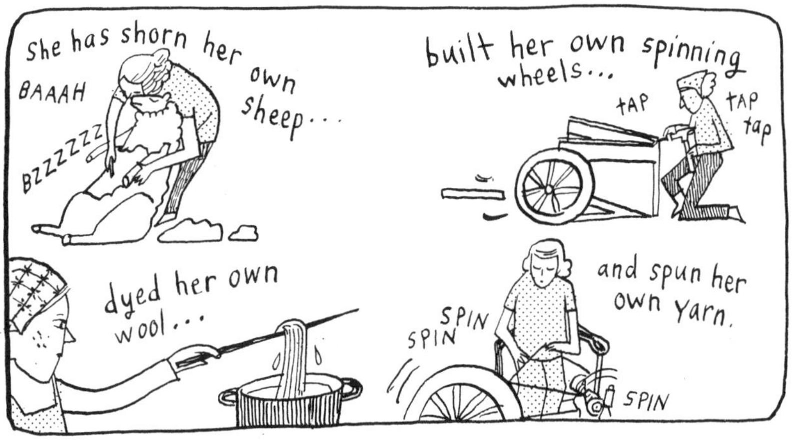
She has shorn her own sheep...
BAAAH
BZZZZZZ
built her own spinning wheels...
TAP
TAP
tap
dyed her own wool...
and spun her own yarn.
SPIN
SPIN
SPIN

She even sometimes carved her own buttons out of deer bone, from road-kill deer (that she had also butchered herself.)

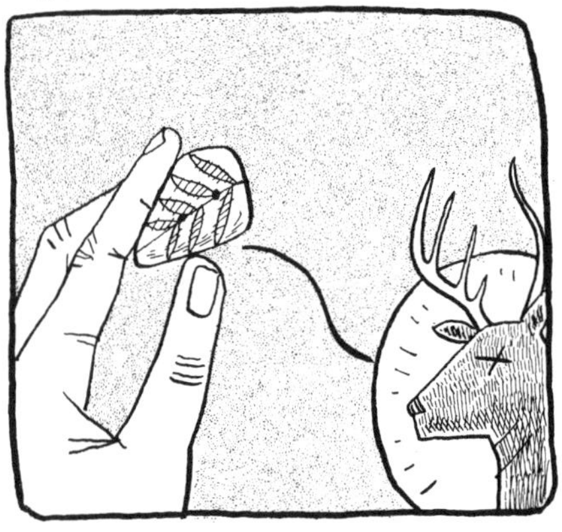

She is brave, and her hands make magic. She makes simple things that inspire awe, the kind of objects that remind you of your own potential.

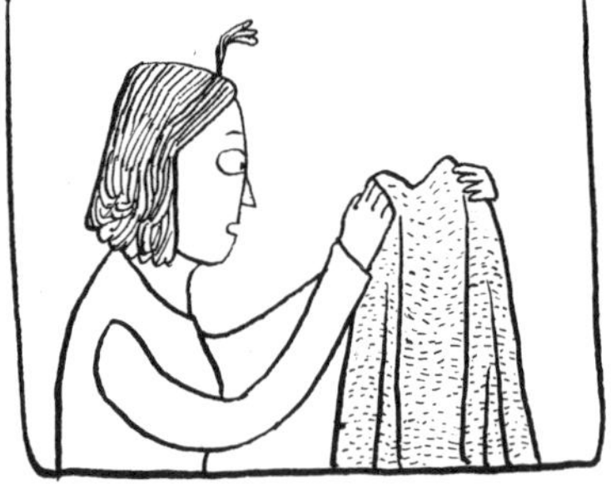

She is basically a total badass, which is everything that I hope to be.

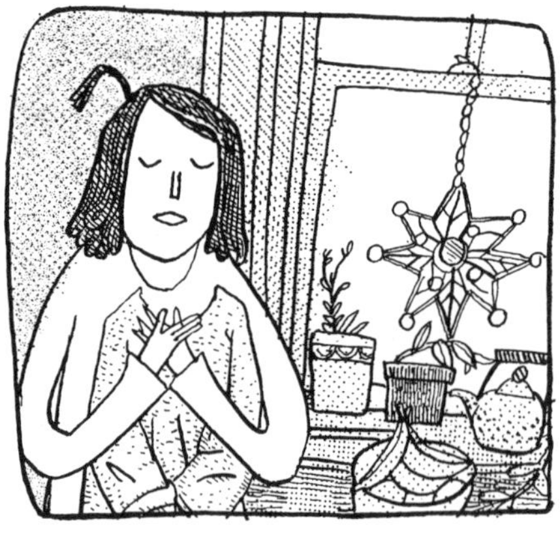

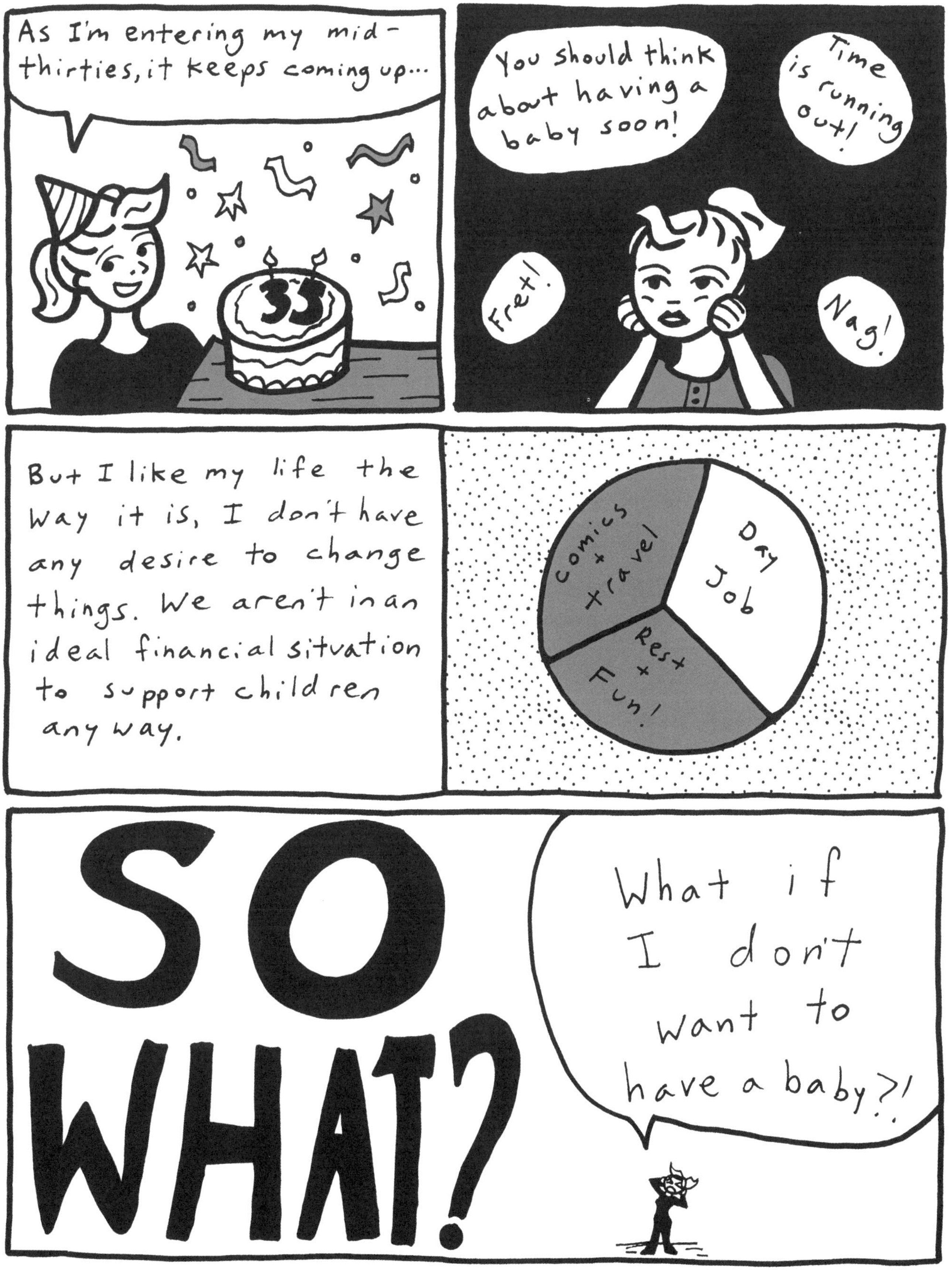
As I'm entering my mid-thirties, it keeps coming up...
33
You should think about having a baby soon!
Time is running out!
Fret!
Nag!
But I like my life the way it is, I don't have any desire to change things. We aren't in an ideal financial situation to support children anyway.
Comics + travel
Day Job
Rest + Fun!
SO WHAT?
What if I don't want to have a baby?!

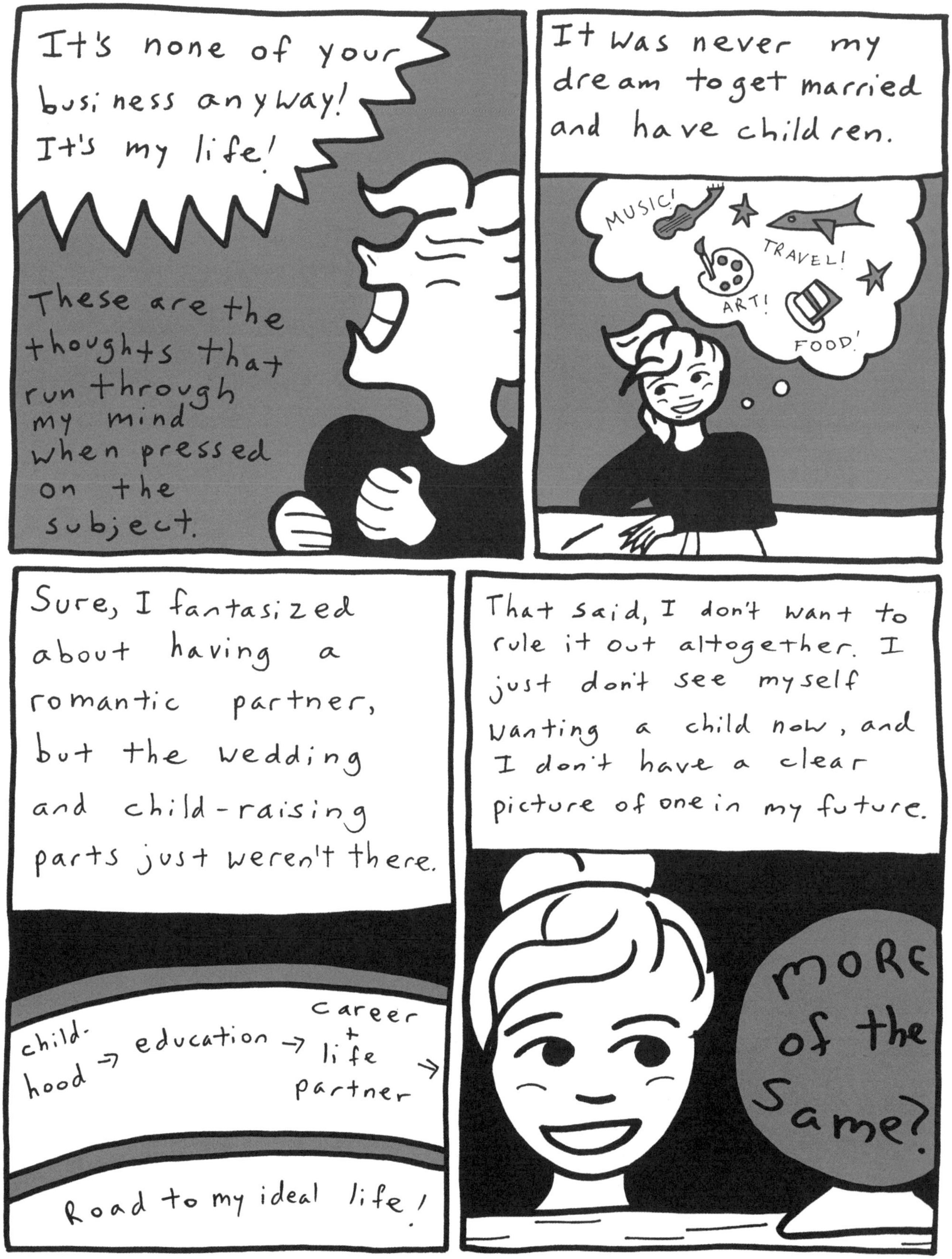
It's none of your business anyway! It's my life!
These are the thoughts that run through my mind when pressed on the subject.
It was never my dream to get married and have children.
MUSIC!
TRAVEL!
ART!
FOOD!
Sure, I fantasized about having a romantic partner, but the wedding and child-raising parts just weren't there.
child-hood → education → career + life partner →
Road to my ideal life!
That said, I don't want to rule it out altogether. I just don't see myself wanting a child now, and I don't have a clear picture of one in my future.
More of the Same?

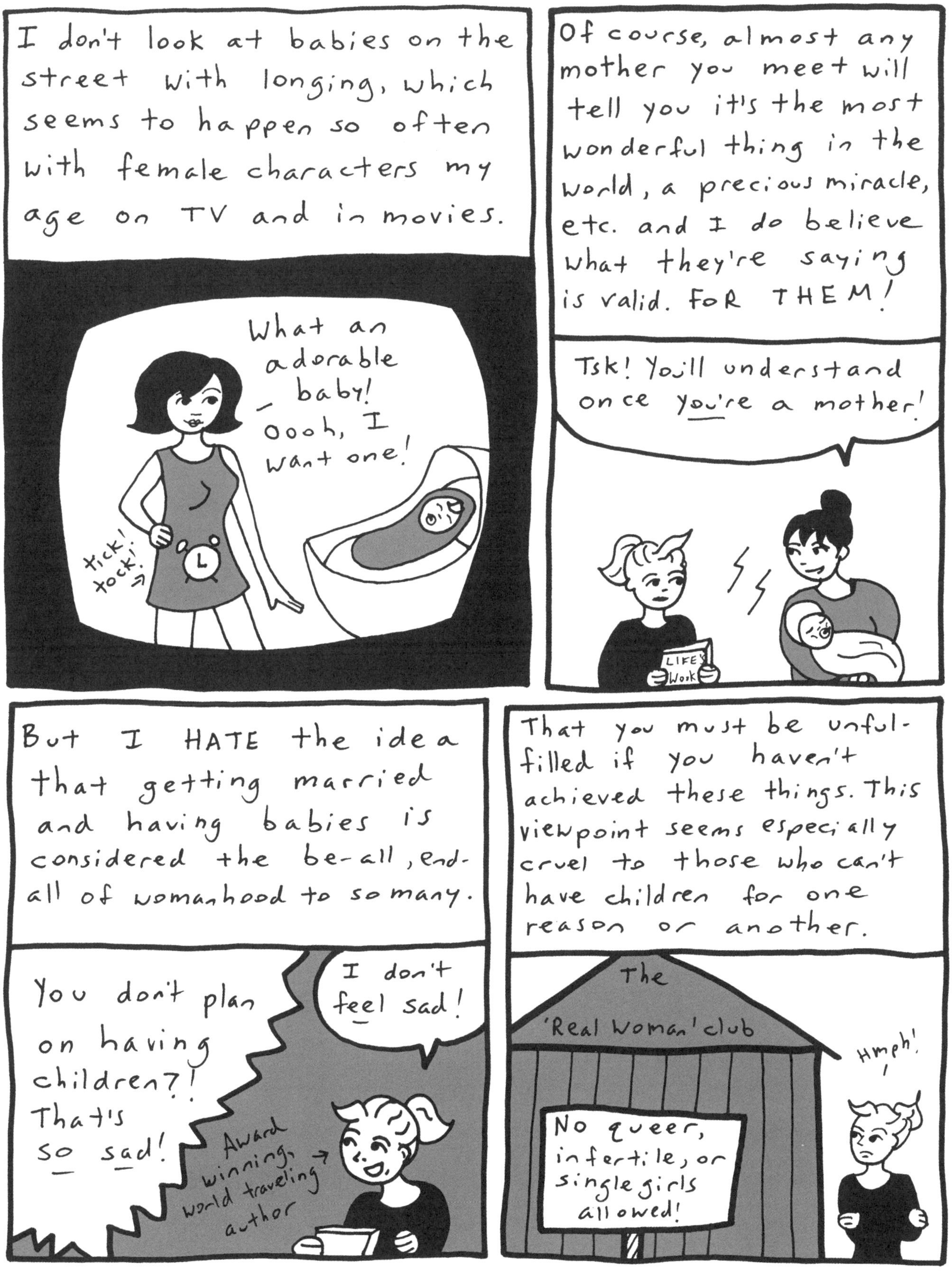
I don't look at babies on the street with longing, which seems to happen so often with female characters my age on TV and in movies.
What an adorable baby! Oooh, I want one!
tick! tock!
L
Of course, almost any mother you meet will tell you it's the most wonderful thing in the world, a precious miracle, etc. and I do believe what they're saying is valid. FOR THEM!
Tsk! You'll understand once you're a mother!
LIFE'S Work
But I HATE the idea that getting married and having babies is considered the be-all, end-all of womanhood to so many.
That you must be unfulfilled if you haven't achieved these things. This viewpoint seems especially cruel to those who can't have children for one reason or another.
You don't plan on having children?! That's so sad!
I don't feel sad!
Award winning, world traveling author
The 'Real Woman' club
No queer, infertile, or single girls allowed!
Hmph!

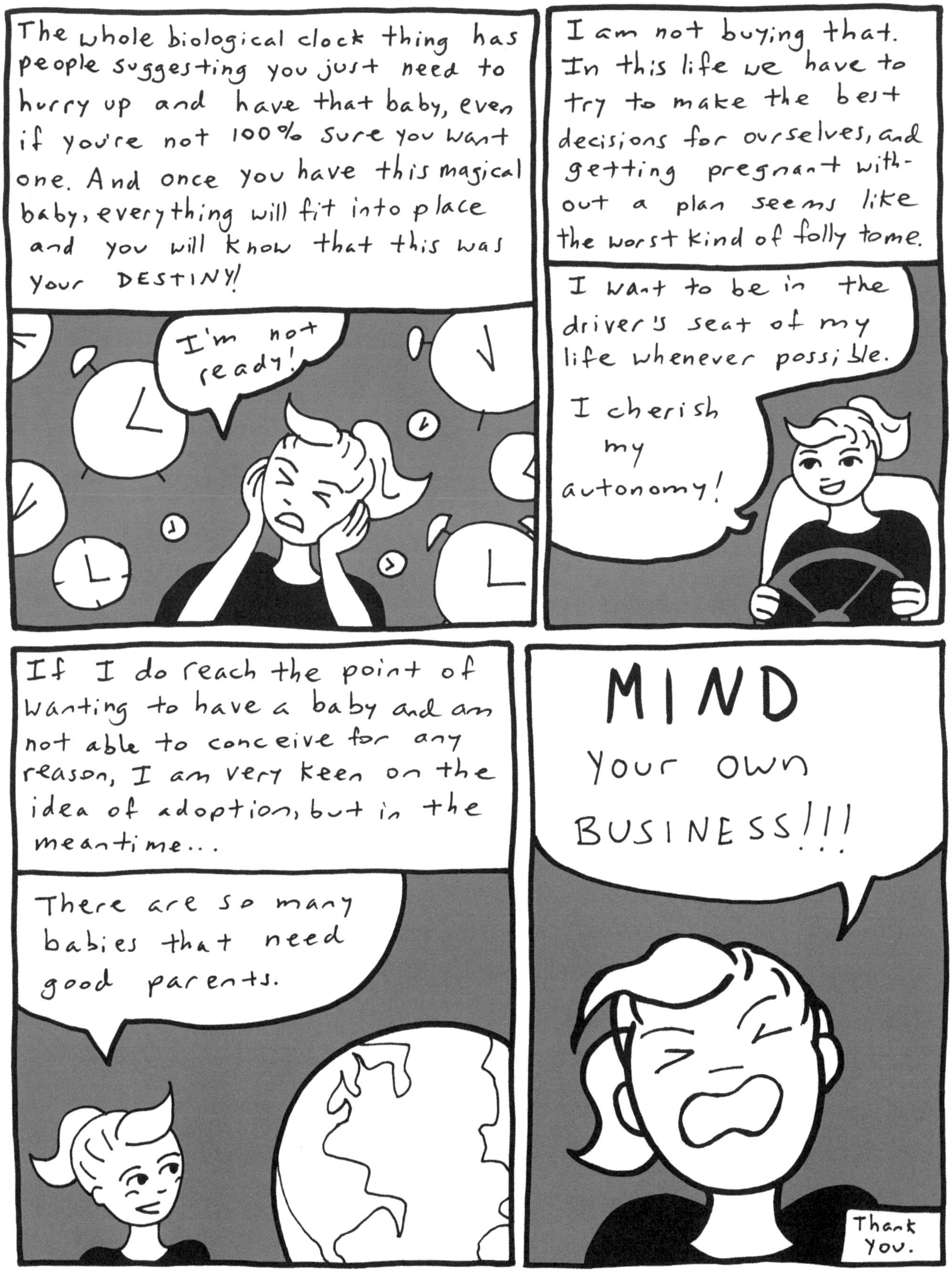
The whole biological clock thing has people suggesting you just need to hurry up and have that baby, even if you're not 100% sure you want one. And once you have this magical baby, everything will fit into place and you will know that this was your DESTINY!
I'm not ready!
I am not buying that. In this life we have to try to make the best decisions for ourselves, and getting pregnant without a plan seems like the worst kind of folly to me.
I want to be in the driver's seat of my life whenever possible.
I cherish my autonomy!
If I do reach the point of wanting to have a baby and am not able to conceive for any reason, I am very keen on the idea of adoption, but in the meantime...
There are so many babies that need good parents.
MIND your own BUSINESS!!!
Thank you.

Abby Denson 2011

# How to Make a Man out of Tin Foil

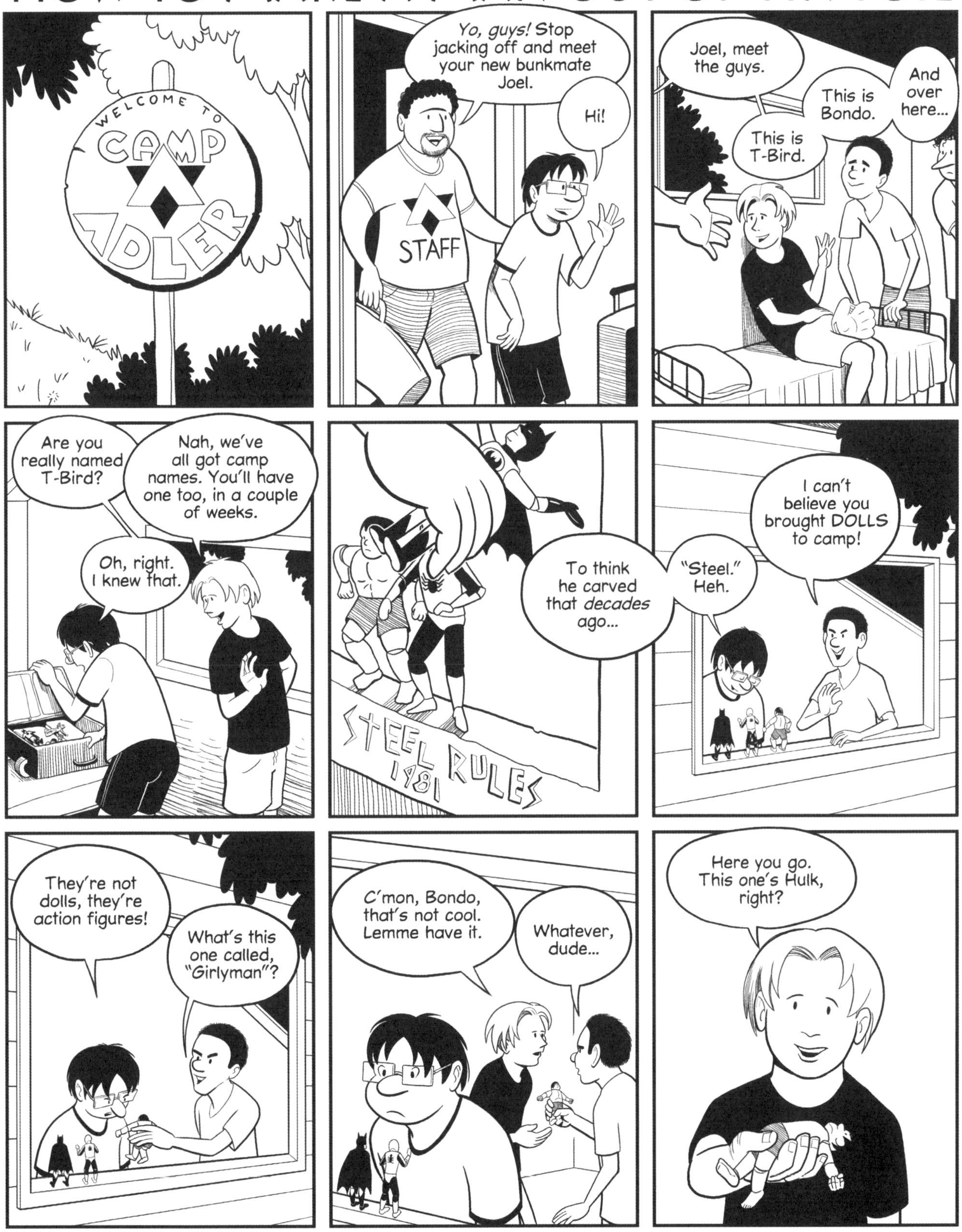

WELCOME TO
CAMP
ADLER
*Yo, guys!* Stop jacking off and meet your new bunkmate Joel.
STAFF
Hi!
Joel, meet the guys.
This is T-Bird.
This is Bondo.
And over here...
Are you really named T-Bird?
Nah, we've all got camp names. You'll have one too, in a couple of weeks.
Oh, right. I knew that.
STEEL RULES 1981
To think he carved that *decades* ago...
"Steel." Heh.
I can't believe you brought DOLLS to camp!
They're not dolls, they're action figures!
What's this one called, "Girlyman"?
C'mon, Bondo, that's not cool. Lemme have it.
Whatever, dude...
Here you go. This one's Hulk, right?

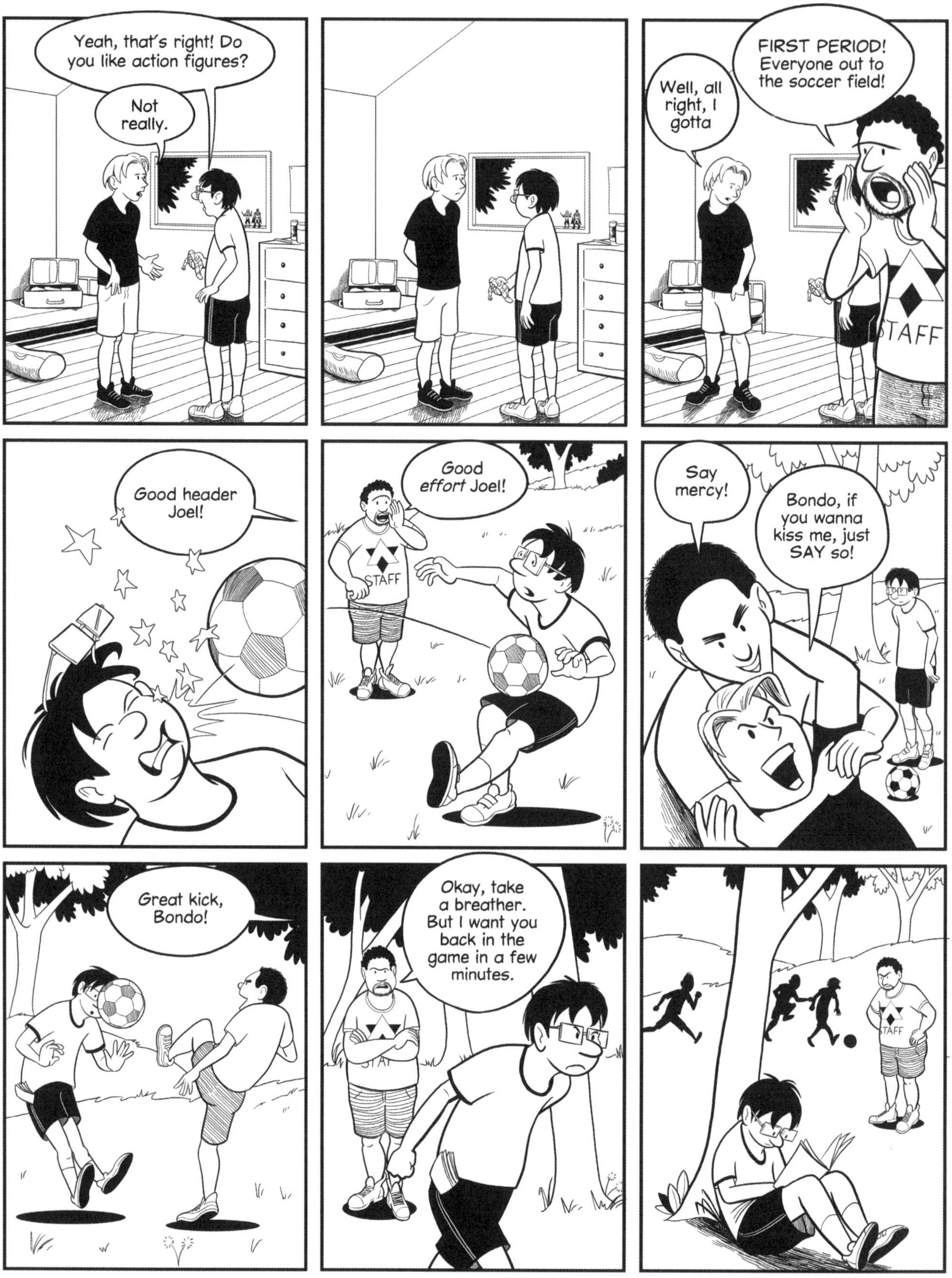
Yeah, that's right! Do you like action figures?
Not really.
Well, all right, I gotta
FIRST PERIOD! Everyone out to the soccer field!
STAFF
Good header Joel!
Good *effort* Joel!
STAFF
Say mercy!
Bondo, if you wanna kiss me, just SAY so!
Great kick, Bondo!
Okay, take a breather. But I want you back in the game in a few minutes.
STAFF

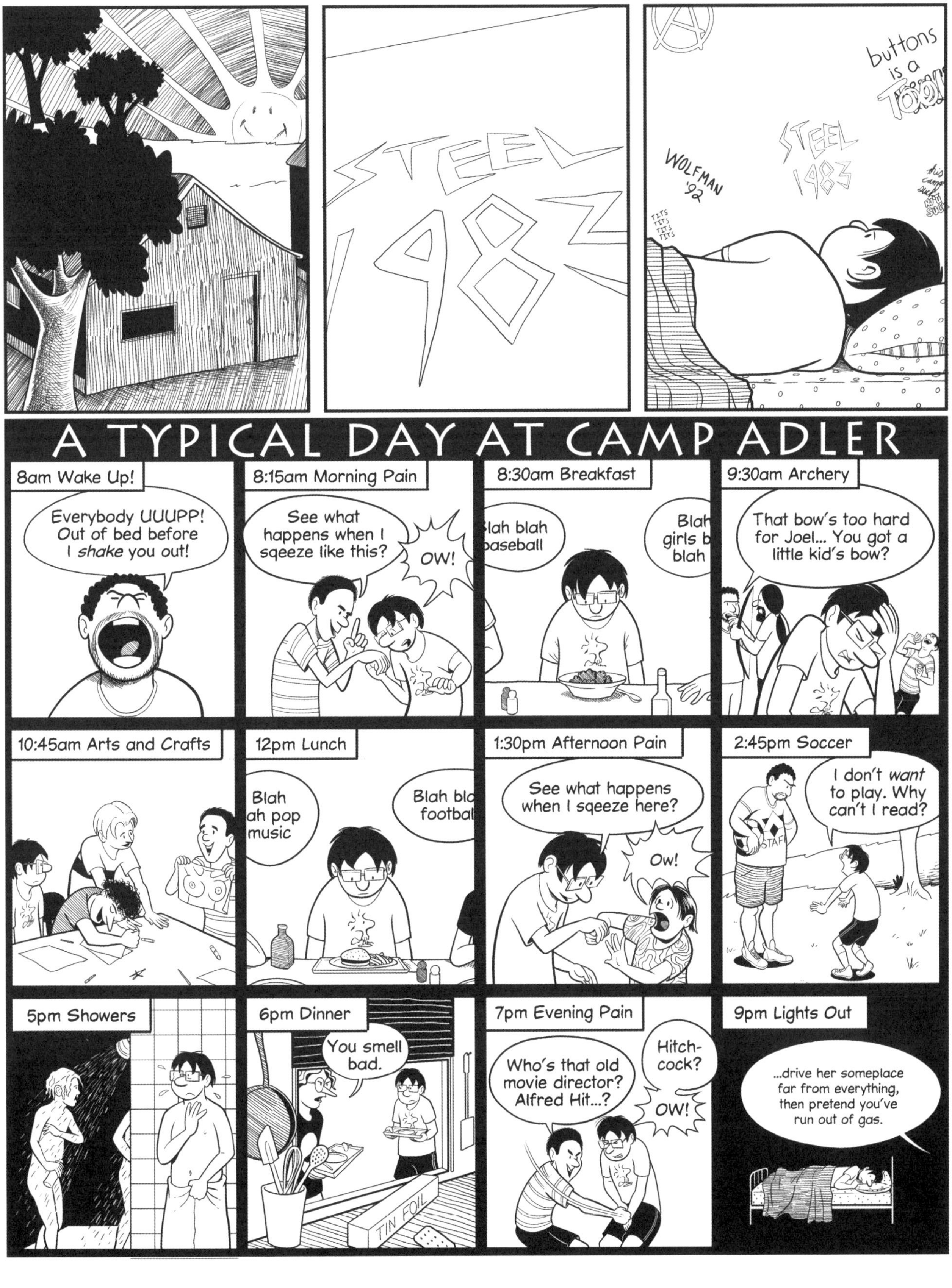

STEEL 1983
buttons is a
STEEL 1983
WOLFMAN '92
TITS TITS TITS TITS
A TYPICAL DAY AT CAMP ADLER
8am Wake Up!
Everybody UUUPP! Out of bed before I *shake* you out!
8:15am Morning Pain
See what happens when I sqeeze like this?
OW!
8:30am Breakfast
lah blah baseball
Blah girls b blah
9:30am Archery
That bow's too hard for Joel... You got a little kid's bow?
10:45am Arts and Crafts
12pm Lunch
Blah ah pop music
Blah bla footbal
1:30pm Afternoon Pain
See what happens when I sqeeze here?
Ow!
2:45pm Soccer
STAFF
I don't *want* to play. Why can't I read?
5pm Showers
6pm Dinner
You smell bad.
TIN FOIL
7pm Evening Pain
Who's that old movie director? Alfred Hit...?
Hitch-cock?
OW!
9pm Lights Out
...drive her someplace far from everything, then pretend you've run out of gas.

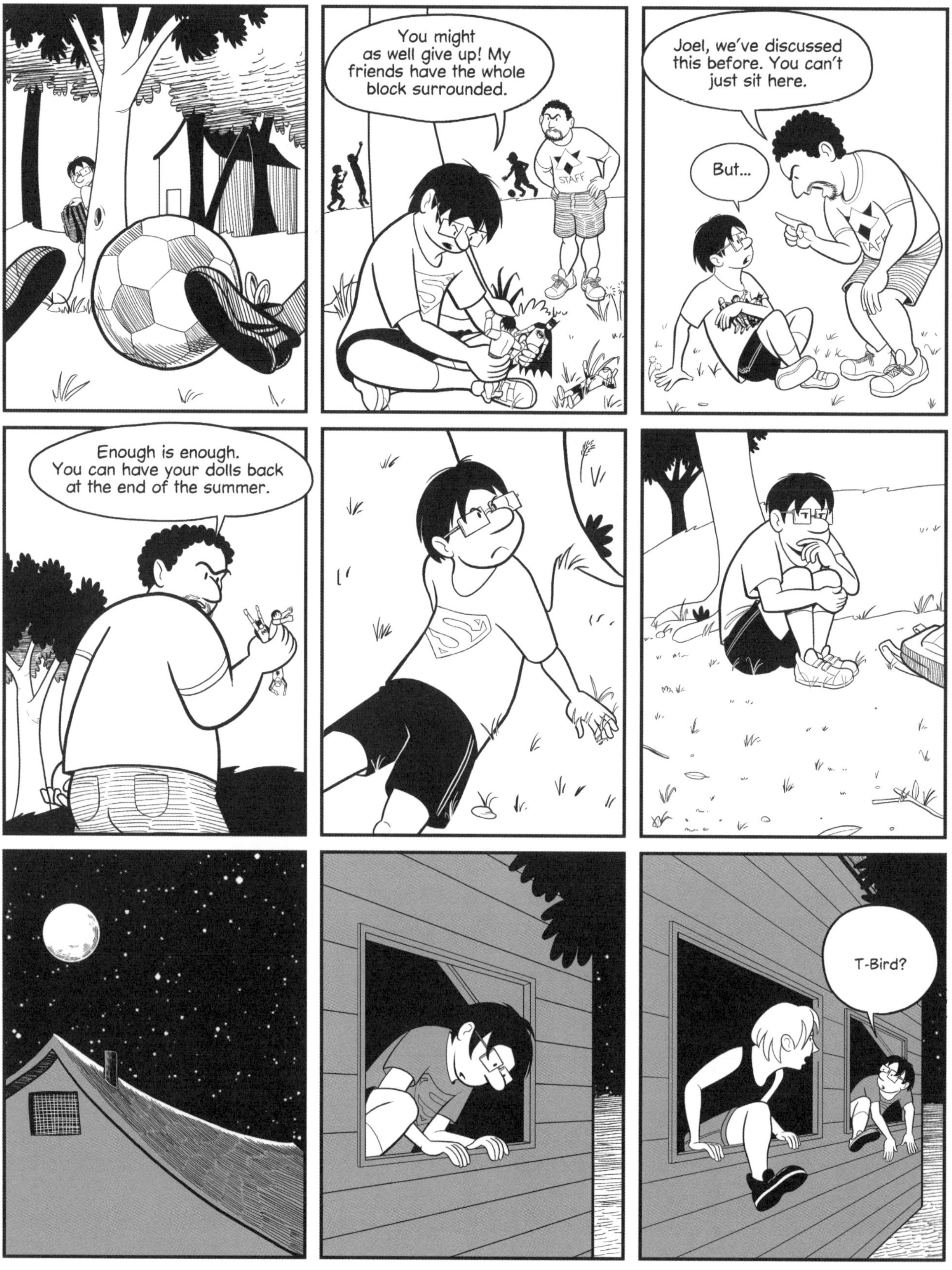
You might as well give up! My friends have the whole block surrounded.
STAFF
Joel, we've discussed this before. You can't just sit here.
But...
Enough is enough. You can have your dolls back at the end of the summer.
T-Bird?

What are you doing up?

Hey, Joel. Just visiting the girls' bunk.

Are you gonna, you know, have *sex*?

*What?* Nahh. I'm just gonna hang out, all right?

I'm, uh...

...have fun, T-Bird.

Why *should* he ask where I'm going? I barely even *exist*.

...can't let him do whatever he wants. Our job is to *mold* these boys, not just...

HEAD COUNSELOR'S OFFICE

DINING HALL

# HOW TO MAKE AN ACTION FIGURE OUT OF TIN FOIL

**1** Take a sheet of tin foil, taller than it's wide.

**2** Split it up the center, halfway up the sheet.

**3** Mold legs out of the split halves.

**4** Make a head. Squeeze under the chin to form the neck.

**5** Form arms out of the two unfolded corners.

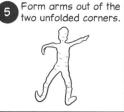

**6** Use more tin foil for capes, hammers, etc.

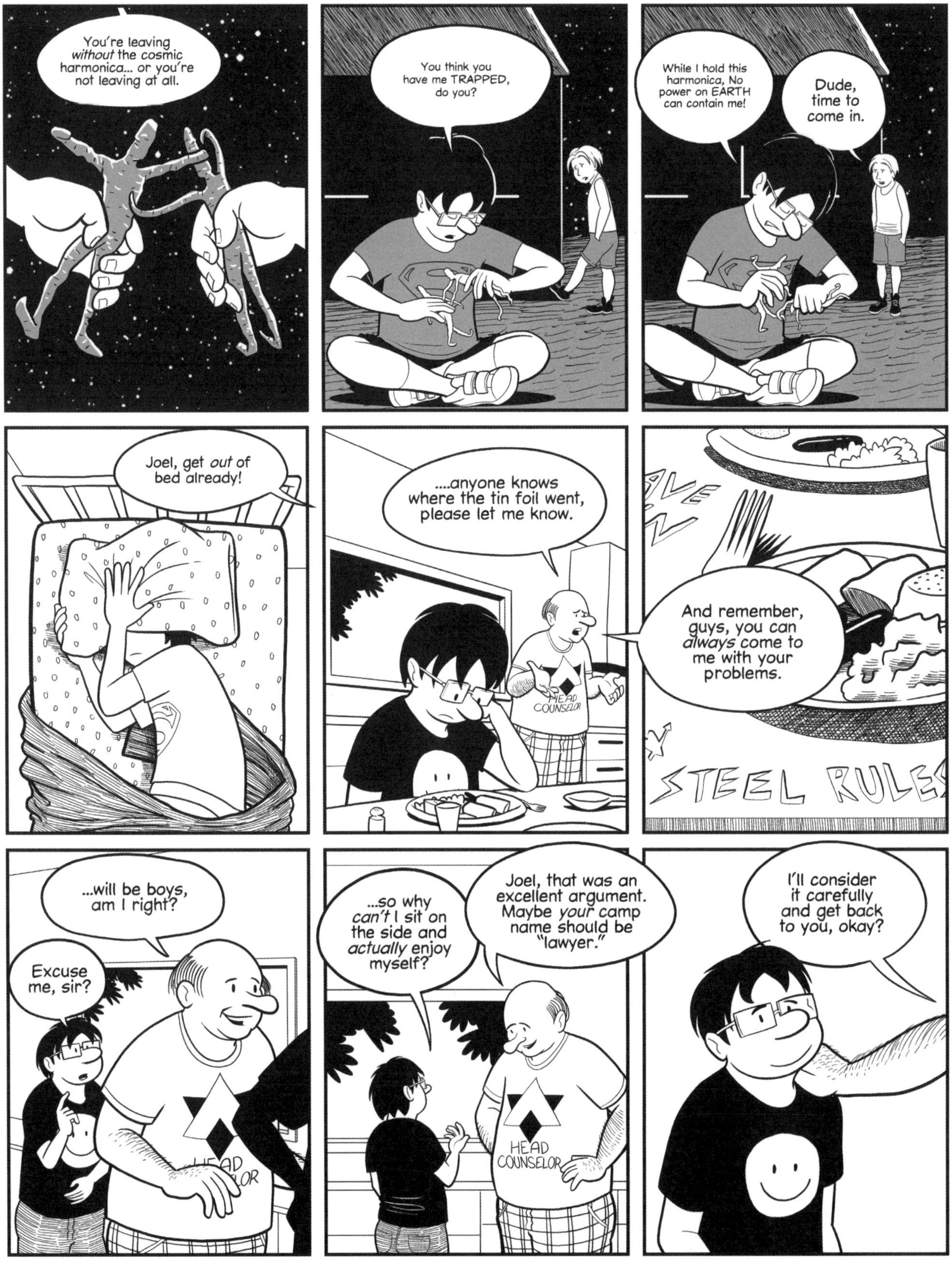
You're leaving *without* the cosmic harmonica... or you're not leaving at all.
You think you have me TRAPPED, do you?
While I hold this harmonica, No power on EARTH can contain me!
Dude, time to come in.
Joel, get *out* of bed already!
....anyone knows where the tin foil went, please let me know.
HEAD COUNSELOR
And remember, guys, you can *always* come to me with your problems.
STEEL RULES
...will be boys, am I right?
Excuse me, sir?
...so why *can't* I sit on the side and *actually* enjoy myself?
Joel, that was an excellent argument. Maybe *your* camp name should be "lawyer."
HEAD COUNSELOR
I'll consider it carefully and get back to you, okay?

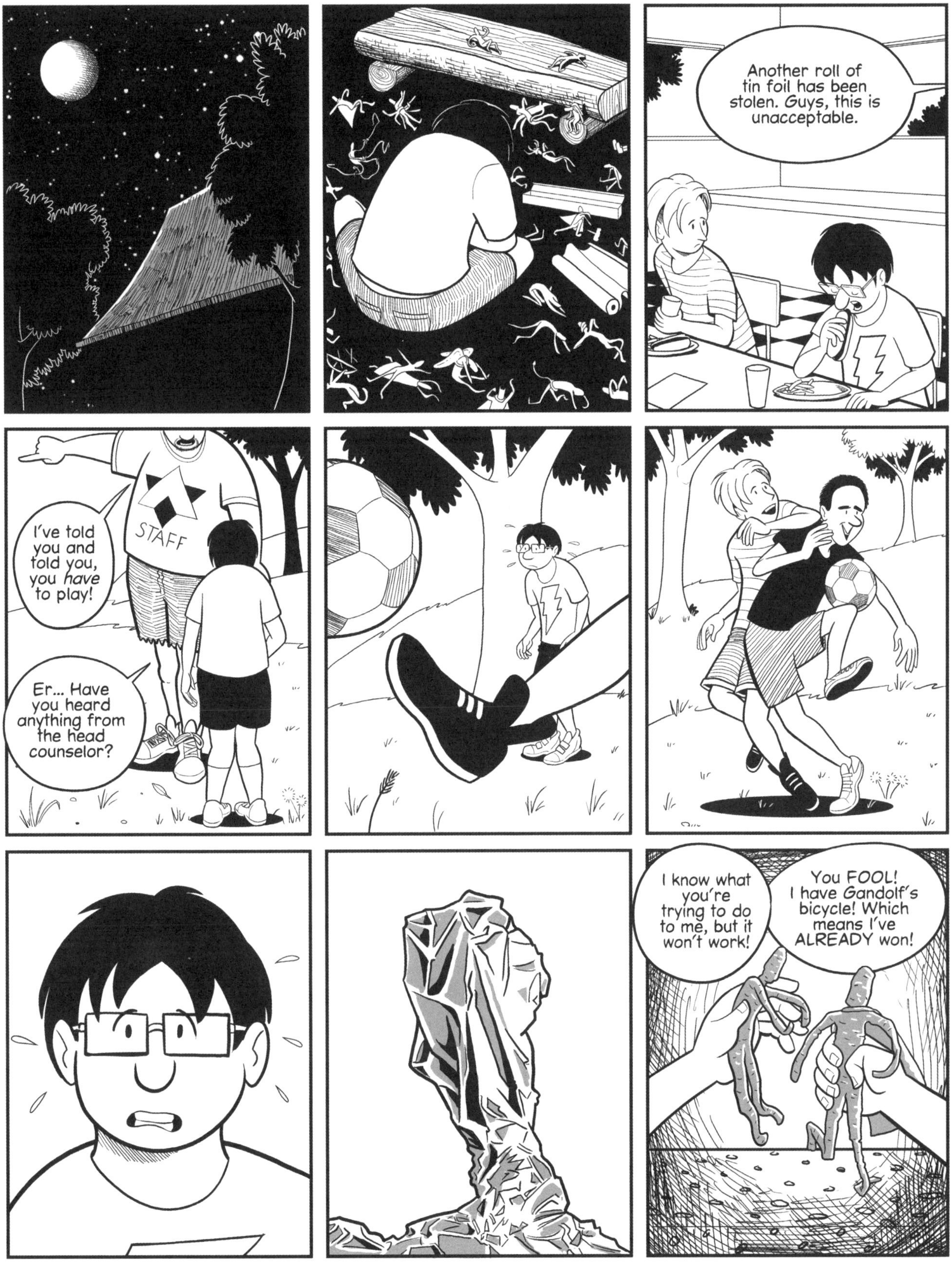
Another roll of tin foil has been stolen. Guys, this is unacceptable.
STAFF
I've told you and told you, you *have* to play!
Er... Have you heard anything from the head counselor?
I know what you're trying to do to me, but it won't work!
You FOOL! I have Gandolf's bicycle! Which means I've ALREADY won!

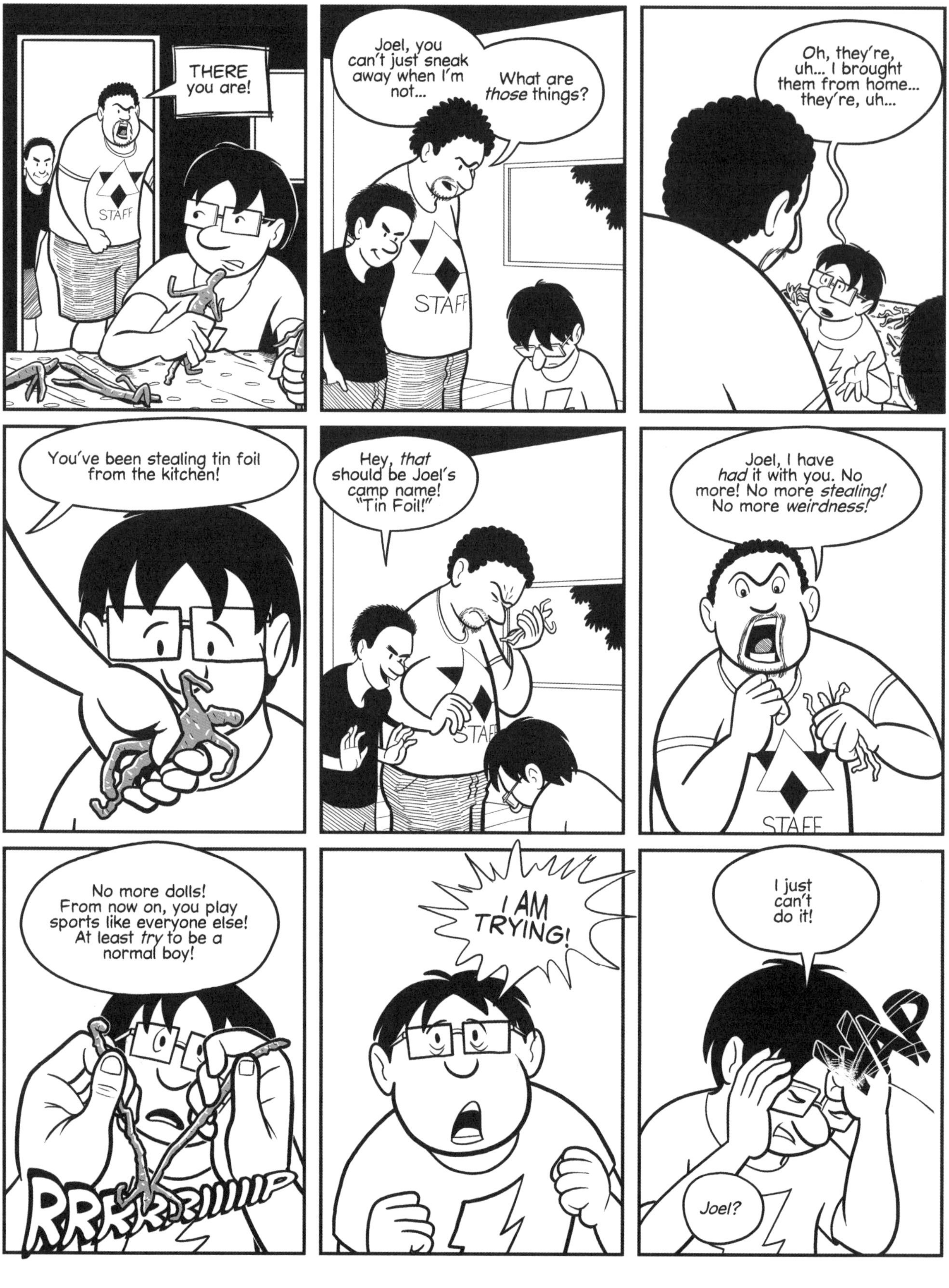
THERE you are!
Joel, you can't just sneak away when I'm not...
What are *those* things?
Oh, they're, uh... I brought them from home... they're, uh...
You've been stealing tin foil from the kitchen!
Hey, *that* should be Joel's camp name! "Tin Foil!"
Joel, I have *had* it with you. No more! No more *stealing!* No more *weirdness!*
No more dolls! From now on, you play sports like everyone else! At least *try* to be a normal boy!
RRRRRIIIIIP
I AM TRYING!
I just can't do it!
WAP
Joel?

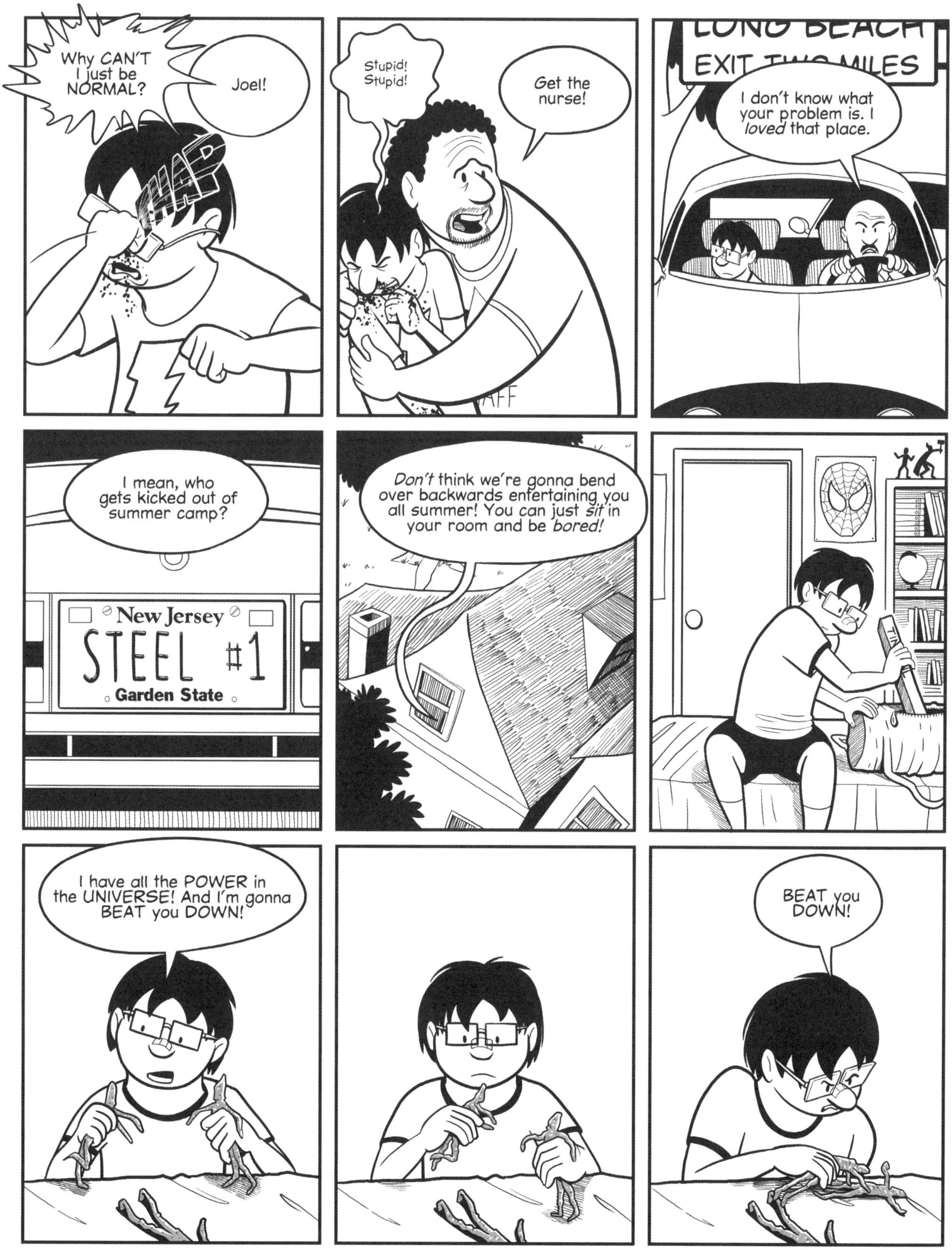

Why CAN'T I just be NORMAL?
Joel!
Stupid! Stupid!
Get the nurse!
I don't know what your problem is. I *loved* that place.
I mean, who gets kicked out of summer camp?
New Jersey
STEEL #1
Garden State
*Don't* think we're gonna bend over backwards entertaining you all summer! You can just *sit* in your room and be *bored!*
I have all the POWER in the UNIVERSE! And I'm gonna BEAT you DOWN!
BEAT you DOWN!

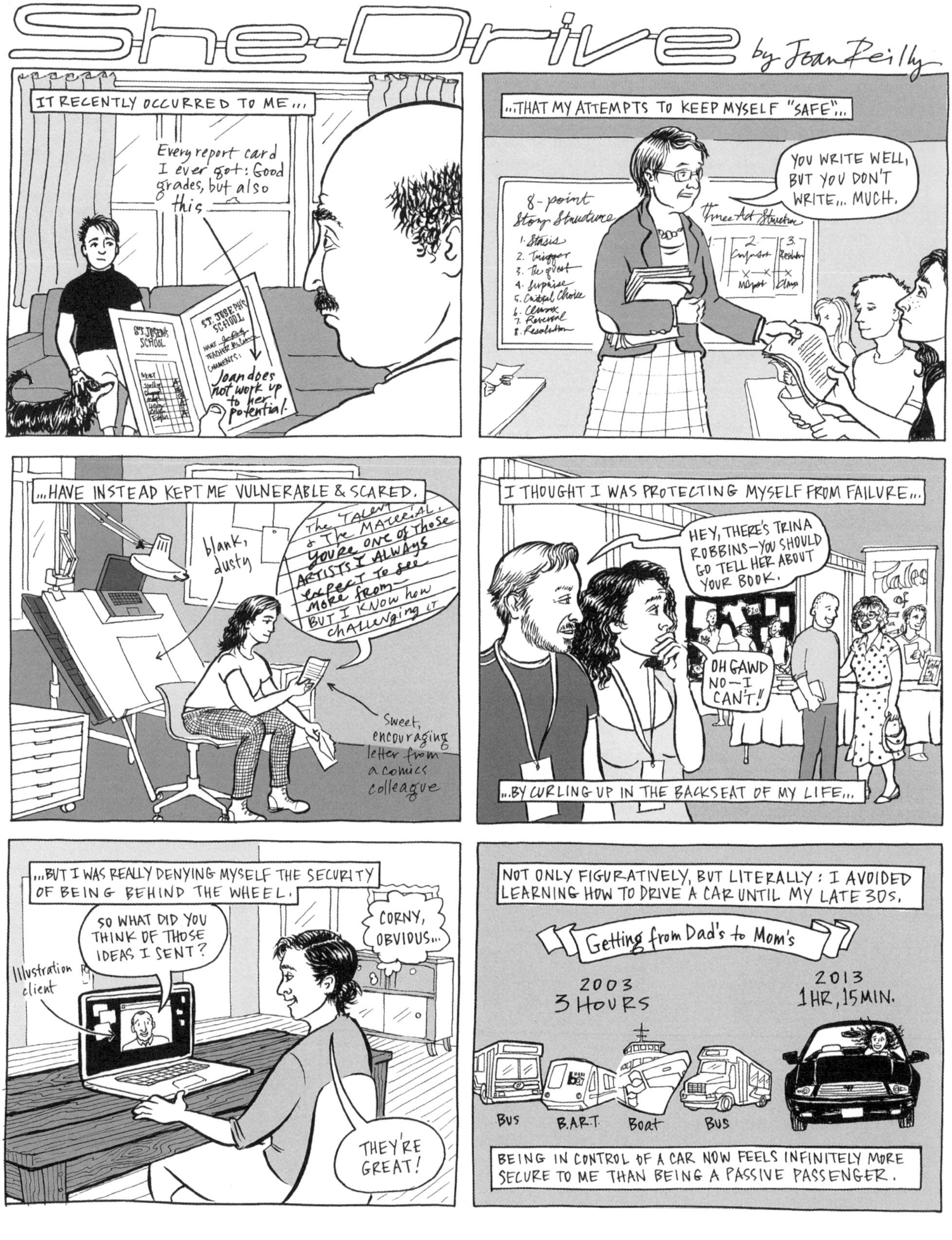

She-Drive
by Joan Reilly
IT RECENTLY OCCURRED TO ME...
Every report card I ever got: Good grades, but also this
ST. JOSEPH'S SCHOOL
ST. JOSEPH'S SCHOOL
NAME
TEACHER
COMMENTS:
Joan does not work up to her potential.
...THAT MY ATTEMPTS TO KEEP MYSELF "SAFE"...
8-point Story Structure
1. Stasis
2. Trigger
3. The quest
4. Surprise
5. Critical Choice
6. Climax
7. Reversal
8. Resolution
Three Act Structure
YOU WRITE WELL, BUT YOU DON'T WRITE... MUCH.
...HAVE INSTEAD KEPT ME VULNERABLE & SCARED.
blank, dusty
The TALENT & The MATERIAL. YOU'RE ONE OF THOSE ARTISTS I ALWAYS EXPECT TO SEE MORE FROM— BUT I KNOW how challenging it
Sweet, encouraging letter from a comics colleague
I THOUGHT I WAS PROTECTING MYSELF FROM FAILURE...
HEY, THERE'S TRINA ROBBINS—YOU SHOULD GO TELL HER ABOUT YOUR BOOK.
OH GAWD NO—I CAN'T!
...BY CURLING UP IN THE BACKSEAT OF MY LIFE...
...BUT I WAS REALLY DENYING MYSELF THE SECURITY OF BEING BEHIND THE WHEEL.
SO WHAT DID YOU THINK OF THOSE IDEAS I SENT?
CORNY, OBVIOUS...
Illustration client
THEY'RE GREAT!
NOT ONLY FIGURATIVELY, BUT LITERALLY: I AVOIDED LEARNING HOW TO DRIVE A CAR UNTIL MY LATE 30S.
Getting from Dad's to Mom's
2003 3 HOURS
2013 1 HR, 15 MIN.
Bus
B.A.R.T.
Boat
Bus
BEING IN CONTROL OF A CAR NOW FEELS INFINITELY MORE SECURE TO ME THAN BEING A PASSIVE PASSENGER.

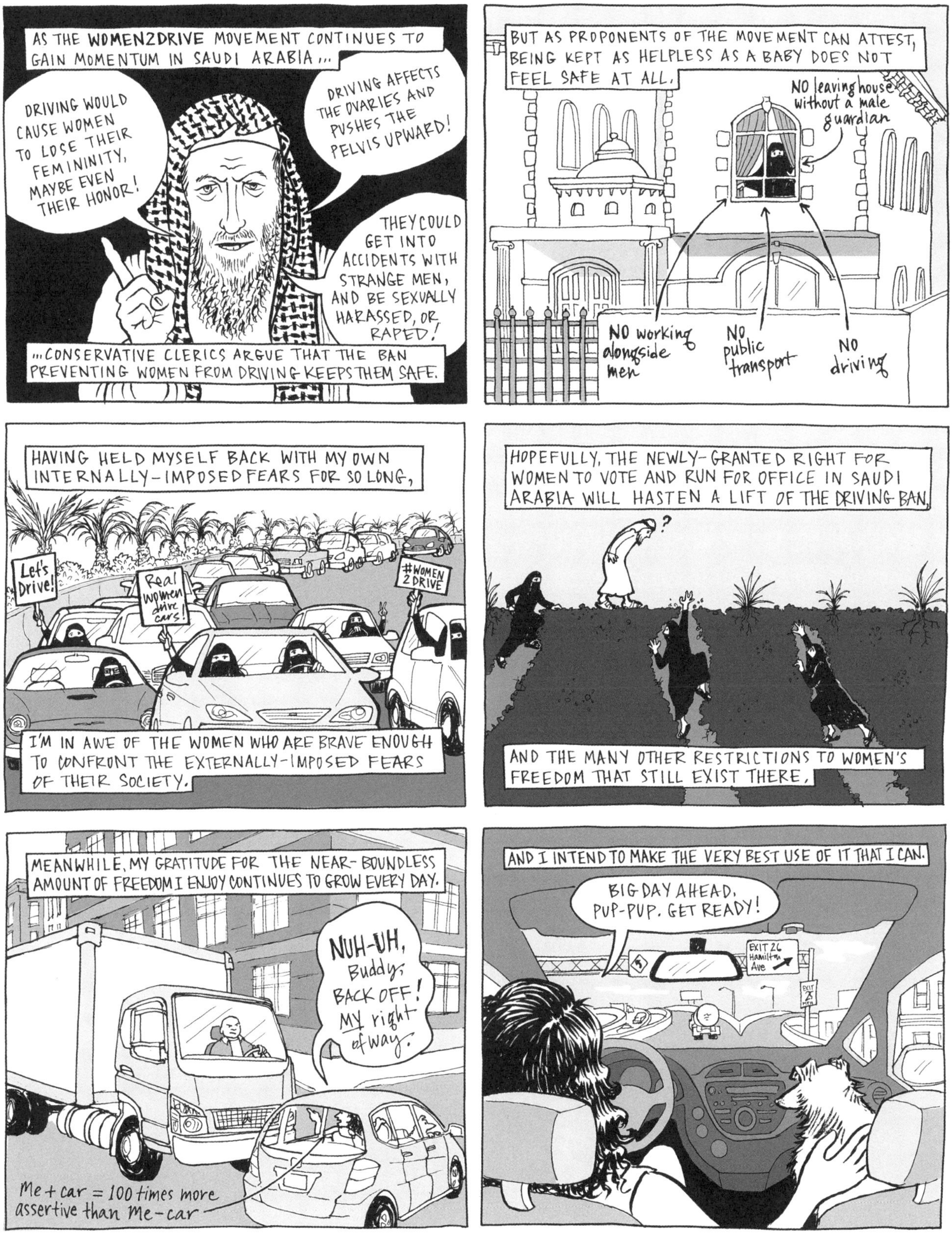
AS THE WOMEN2DRIVE MOVEMENT CONTINUES TO GAIN MOMENTUM IN SAUDI ARABIA...
DRIVING WOULD CAUSE WOMEN TO LOSE THEIR FEMININITY, MAYBE EVEN THEIR HONOR!
DRIVING AFFECTS THE OVARIES AND PUSHES THE PELVIS UPWARD!
THEY COULD GET INTO ACCIDENTS WITH STRANGE MEN, AND BE SEXUALLY HARASSED, OR RAPED!
...CONSERVATIVE CLERICS ARGUE THAT THE BAN PREVENTING WOMEN FROM DRIVING KEEPS THEM SAFE.
BUT AS PROPONENTS OF THE MOVEMENT CAN ATTEST, BEING KEPT AS HELPLESS AS A BABY DOES NOT FEEL SAFE AT ALL.
NO leaving house without a male guardian
NO working alongside men
No public transport
No driving
HAVING HELD MYSELF BACK WITH MY OWN INTERNALLY-IMPOSED FEARS FOR SO LONG,
Let's Drive!
Real women drive cars!
#WOMEN 2DRIVE
I'M IN AWE OF THE WOMEN WHO ARE BRAVE ENOUGH TO CONFRONT THE EXTERNALLY-IMPOSED FEARS OF THEIR SOCIETY.
HOPEFULLY, THE NEWLY-GRANTED RIGHT FOR WOMEN TO VOTE AND RUN FOR OFFICE IN SAUDI ARABIA WILL HASTEN A LIFT OF THE DRIVING BAN,
?
AND THE MANY OTHER RESTRICTIONS TO WOMEN'S FREEDOM THAT STILL EXIST THERE.
MEANWHILE, MY GRATITUDE FOR THE NEAR-BOUNDLESS AMOUNT OF FREEDOM I ENJOY CONTINUES TO GROW EVERY DAY.
NUH-UH, Buddy, BACK OFF! MY right of way.
Me + car = 100 times more assertive than Me - car
AND I INTEND TO MAKE THE VERY BEST USE OF IT THAT I CAN.
BIG DAY AHEAD, PUP-PUP. GET READY!
EXIT 26 Hamilton Ave

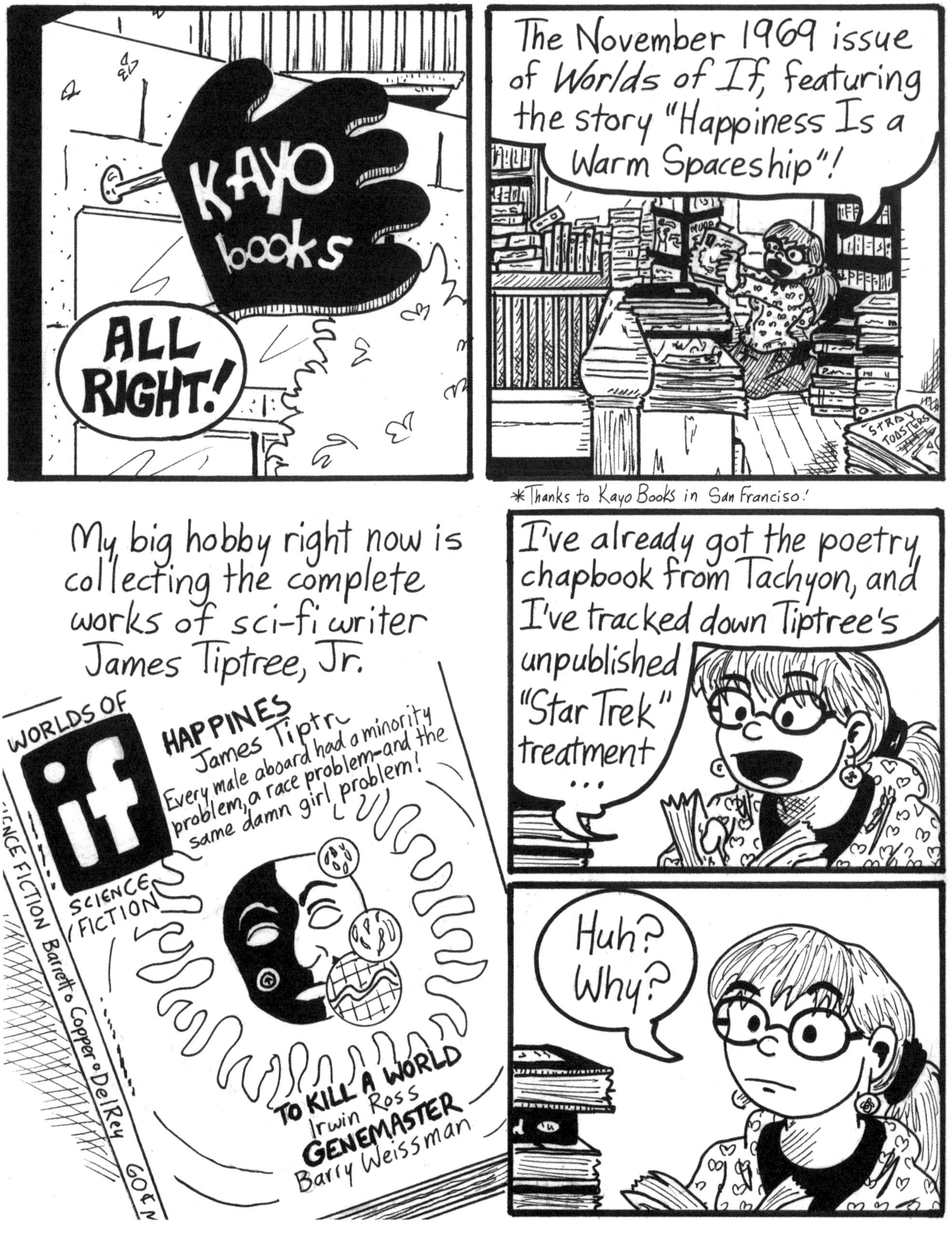
KAYO books
ALL RIGHT!
The November 1969 issue of *Worlds of If*, featuring the story "Happiness Is a Warm Spaceship"!
STRAY TOASTERS
*Thanks to Kayo Books in San Franciso!
My big hobby right now is collecting the complete works of sci-fi writer James Tiptree, Jr.
WORLDS OF if SCIENCE FICTION
HAPPINES
James Tiptr
Every male aboard had a minority problem, a race problem—and the same damn girl problem!
TO KILL A WORLD
Irwin Ross
GENEMASTER
Barry Weissman
Barrett • Copper • Del Rey
I've already got the poetry chapbook from Tachyon, and I've tracked down Tiptree's unpublished "Star Trek" treatment . . .
Huh? Why?

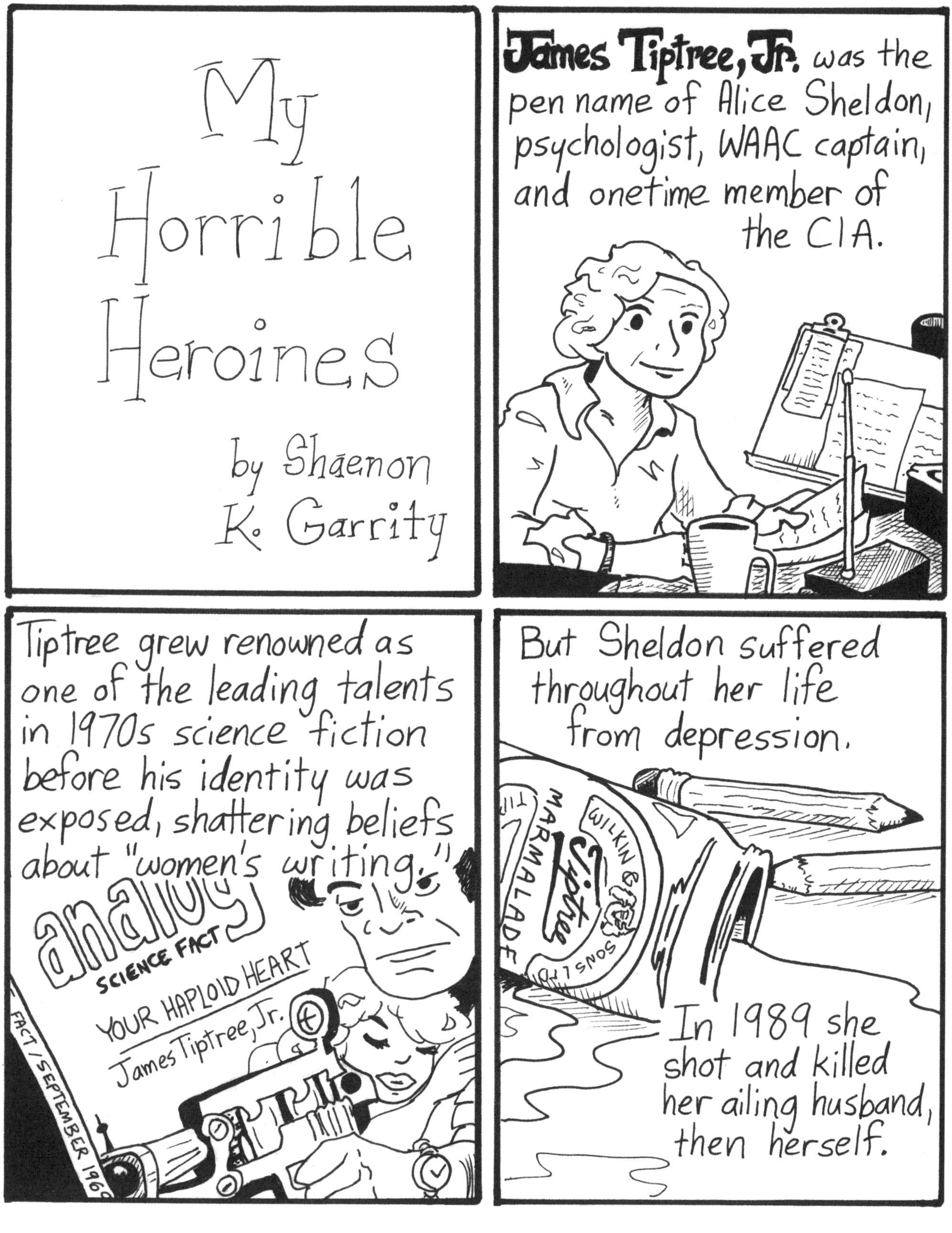
My Horrible Heroines
by Shaenon K. Garrity
James Tiptree, Jr. was the pen name of Alice Sheldon, psychologist, WAAC captain, and onetime member of the CIA.
Tiptree grew renowned as one of the leading talents in 1970s science fiction before his identity was exposed, shattering beliefs about "women's writing."
analog
SCIENCE FACT
YOUR HAPLOID HEART
James Tiptree, Jr.
FACT / SEPTEMBER 196
But Sheldon suffered throughout her life from depression.
WILKIN & SONS LTD
Tiptree
MARMALADE
In 1989 she shot and killed her ailing husband, then herself.

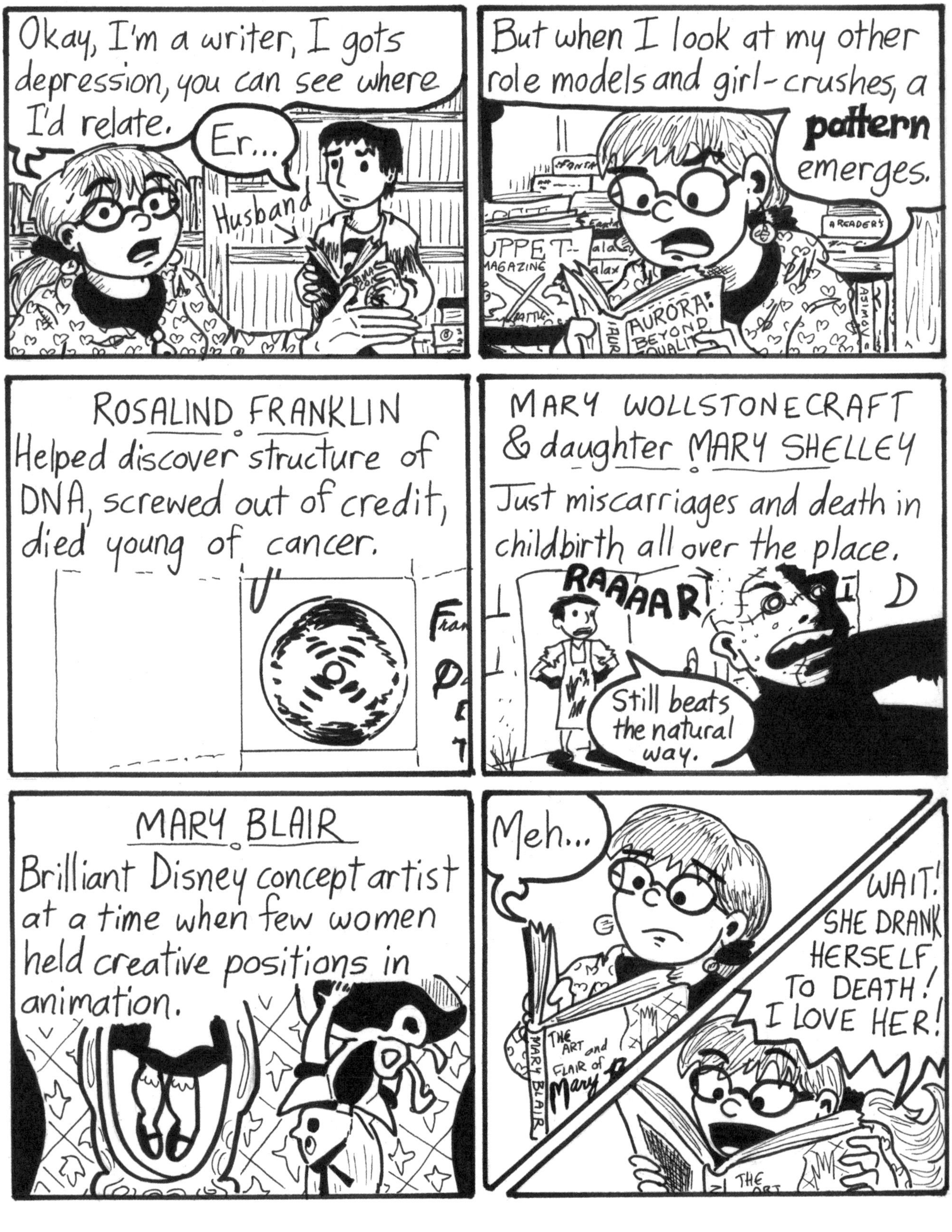
Okay, I'm a writer, I gots depression, you can see where I'd relate.
Er...
Husband
But when I look at my other role models and girl-crushes, a **pattern** emerges.
AURORA: BEYOND EQUALITY
ASIMOV
A READER'S
ROSALIND FRANKLIN
Helped discover structure of DNA, screwed out of credit, died young of cancer.
MARY WOLLSTONECRAFT & daughter MARY SHELLEY
Just miscarriages and death in childbirth all over the place.
RAAAAR!
Still beats the natural way.
MARY BLAIR
Brilliant Disney concept artist at a time when few women held creative positions in animation.
Meh...
THE ART and FLAIR of Mary B
MARY BLAIR
WAIT! SHE DRANK HERSELF TO DEATH! I LOVE HER!
THE ART

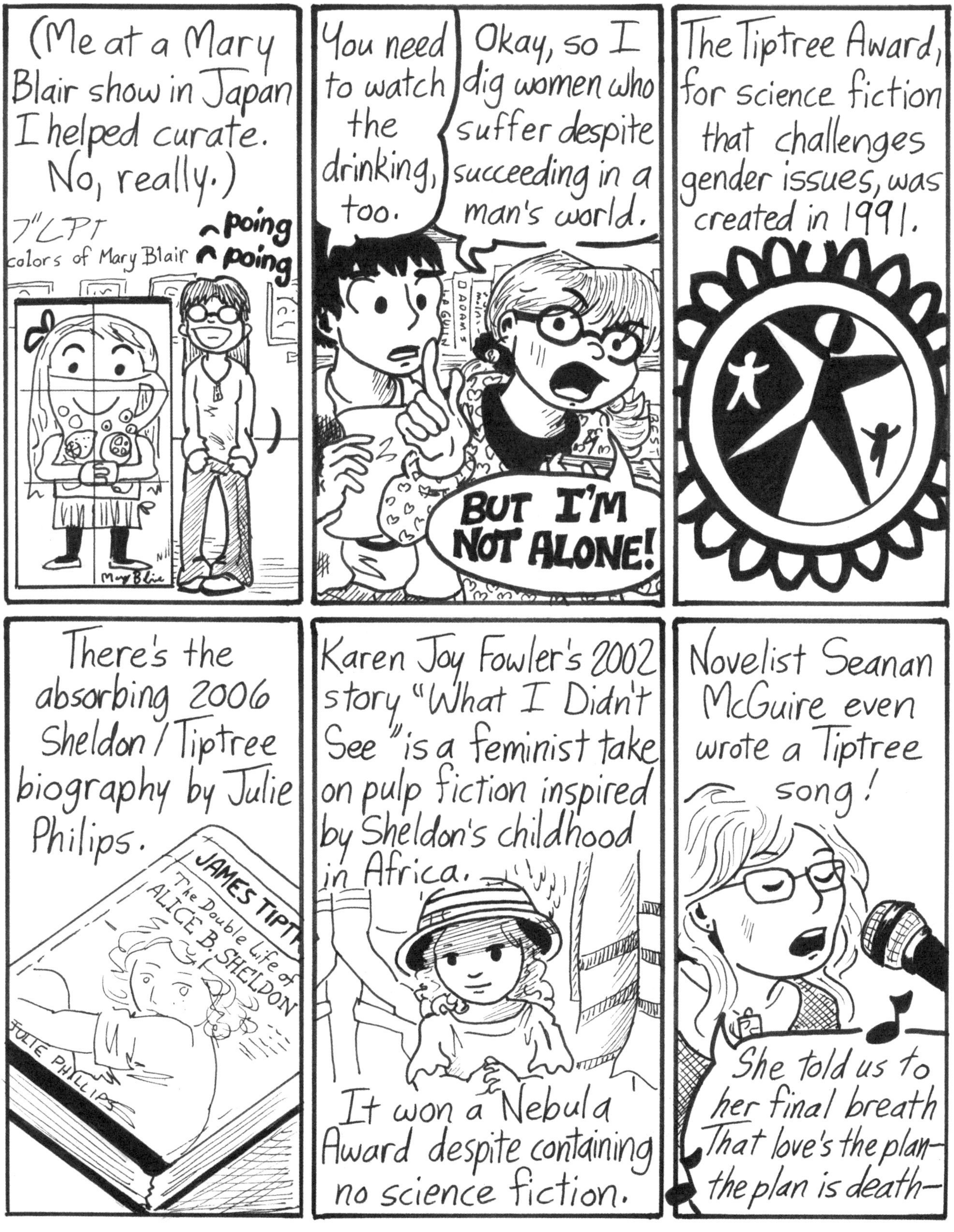
(Me at a Mary Blair show in Japan I helped curate. No, really.)
colors of Mary Blair
poing
poing
You need to watch the drinking, too.
Okay, so I dig women who suffer despite succeeding in a man's world.
BUT I'M NOT ALONE!
The Tiptree Award, for science fiction that challenges gender issues, was created in 1991.
There's the absorbing 2006 Sheldon / Tiptree biography by Julie Philips.
The Double Life of ALICE B. SHELDON
JULIE PHILLIPS
Karen Joy Fowler's 2002 story "What I Didn't See" is a feminist take on pulp fiction inspired by Sheldon's childhood in Africa.
It won a Nebula Award despite containing no science fiction.
Novelist Seanan McGuire even wrote a Tiptree song!
She told us to her final breath
That love's the plan–
the plan is death–

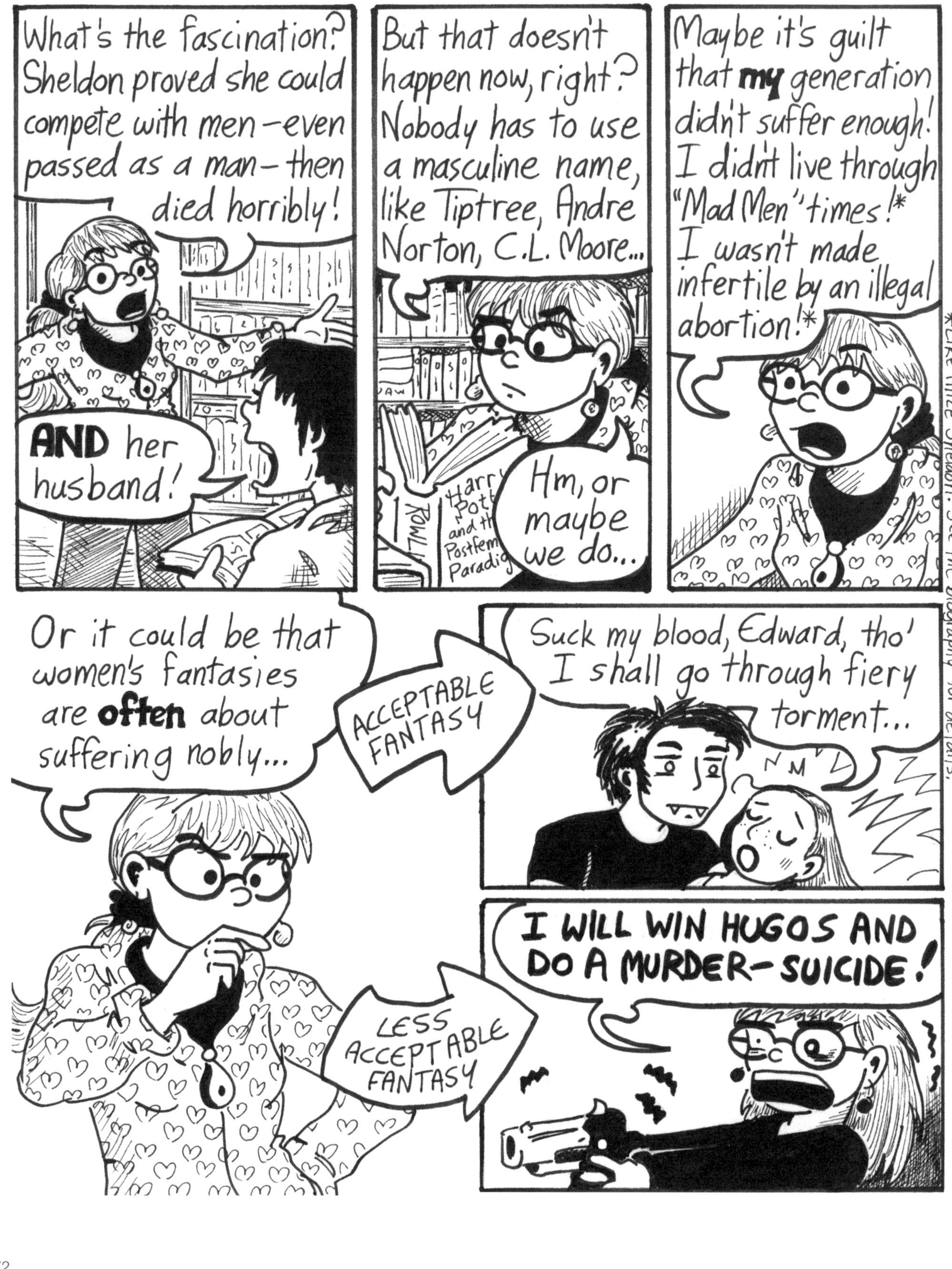
What's the fascination? Sheldon proved she could compete with men—even passed as a man—then died horribly!
AND her husband!
But that doesn't happen now, right? Nobody has to use a masculine name, like Tiptree, Andre Norton, C.L. Moore...
Harry Potter and the Postfem Paradig
Hm, or maybe we do...
Maybe it's guilt that my generation didn't suffer enough! I didn't live through "Mad Men" times!* I wasn't made infertile by an illegal abortion!*
*Like Alice Sheldon. See the biography for details!
Or it could be that women's fantasies are often about suffering nobly...
ACCEPTABLE FANTASY
Suck my blood, Edward, tho' I shall go through fiery torment...
LESS ACCEPTABLE FANTASY
I WILL WIN HUGOS AND DO A MURDER-SUICIDE!

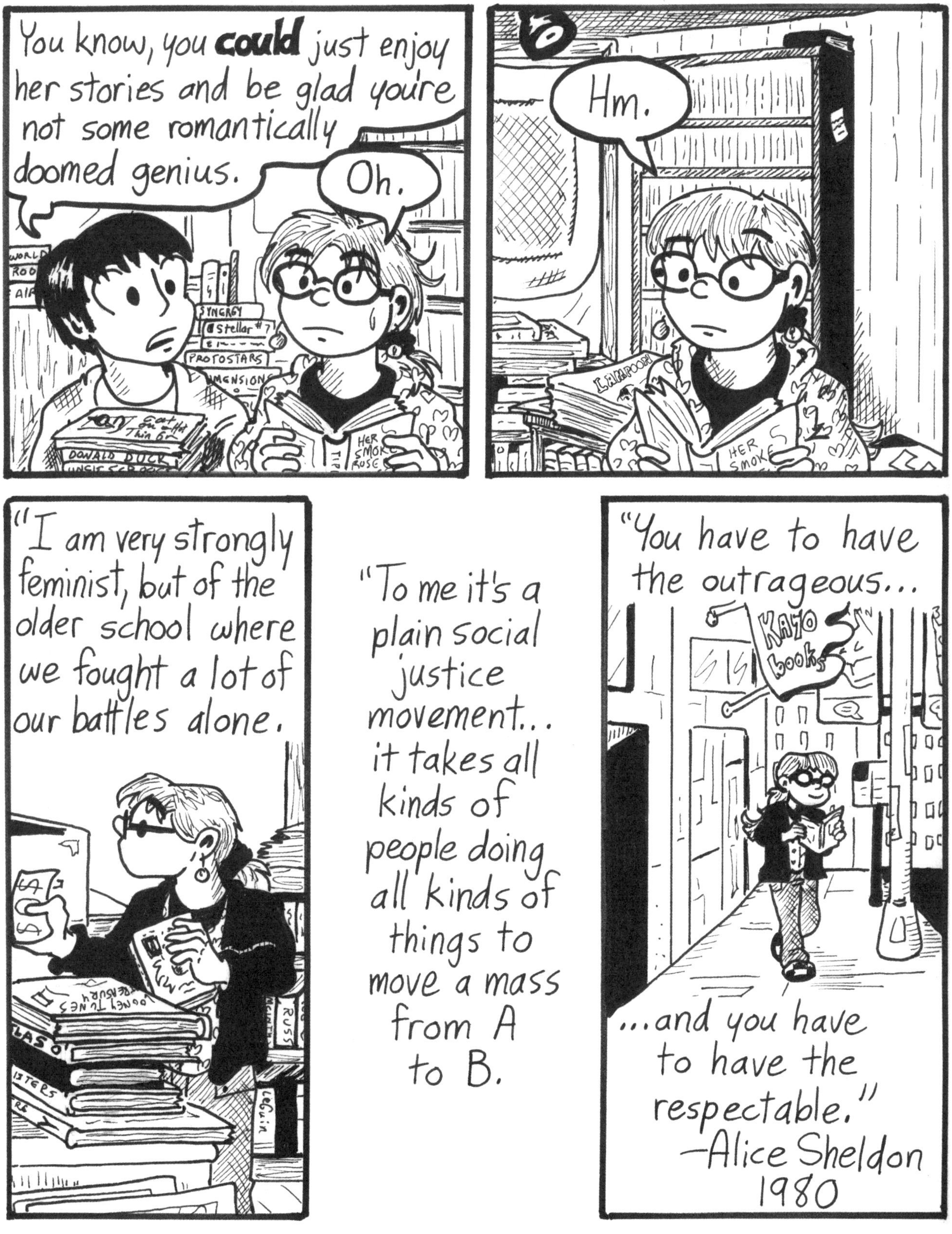

You know, you **could** just enjoy her stories and be glad you're not some romantically doomed genius.
Oh.
Hm.
"I am very strongly feminist, but of the older school where we fought a lot of our battles alone.
"To me it's a plain social justice movement... it takes all kinds of people doing all kinds of things to move a mass from A to B.
"You have to have the outrageous...
...and you have to have the respectable."
—Alice Sheldon 1980

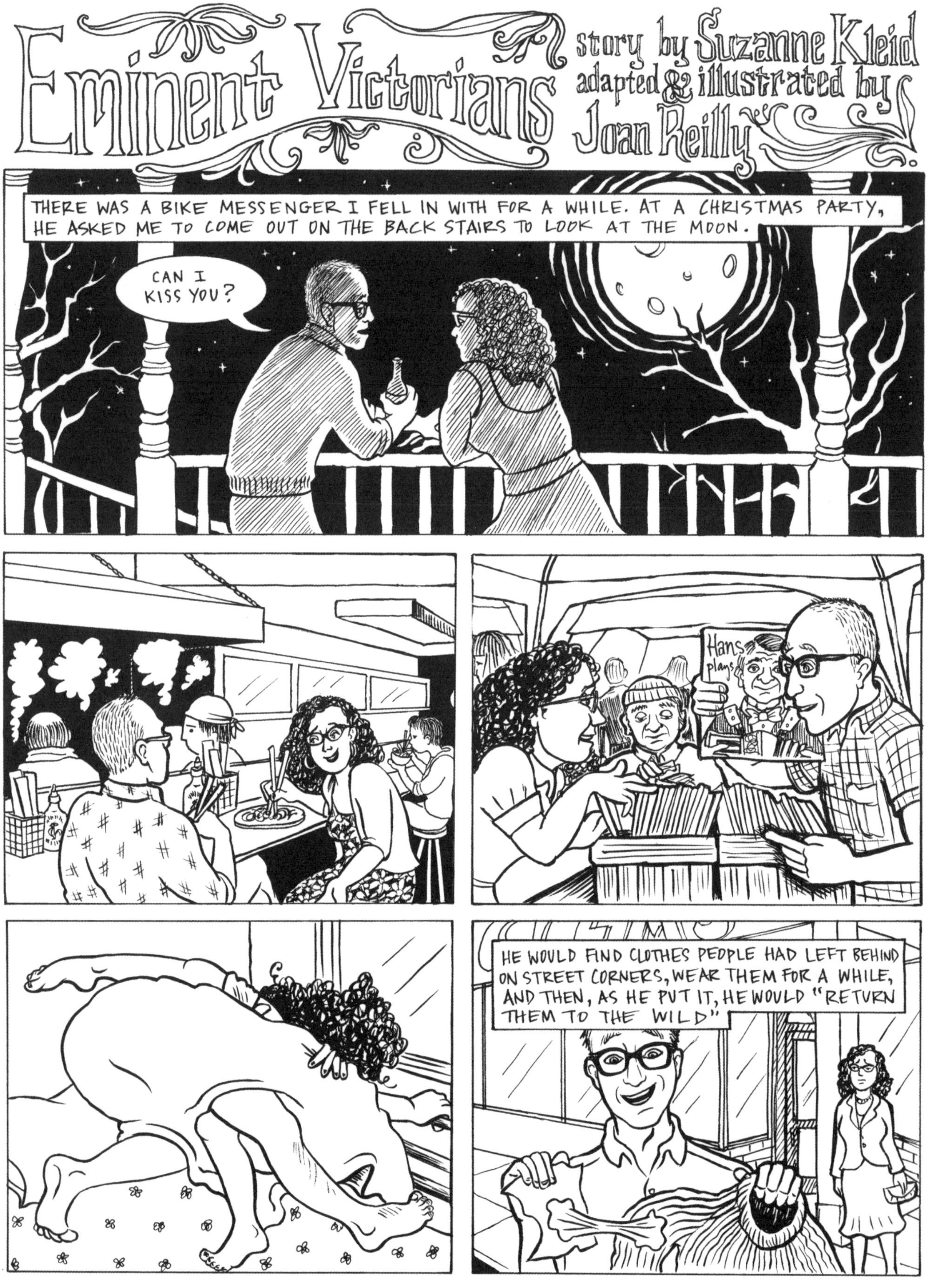
Eminent Victorians
story by Suzanne Kleid
adapted & illustrated by
Joan Reilly
THERE WAS A BIKE MESSENGER I FELL IN WITH FOR A WHILE. AT A CHRISTMAS PARTY, HE ASKED ME TO COME OUT ON THE BACK STAIRS TO LOOK AT THE MOON.
CAN I KISS YOU?
Hans plays
HE WOULD FIND CLOTHES PEOPLE HAD LEFT BEHIND ON STREET CORNERS, WEAR THEM FOR A WHILE, AND THEN, AS HE PUT IT, HE WOULD "RETURN THEM TO THE WILD"

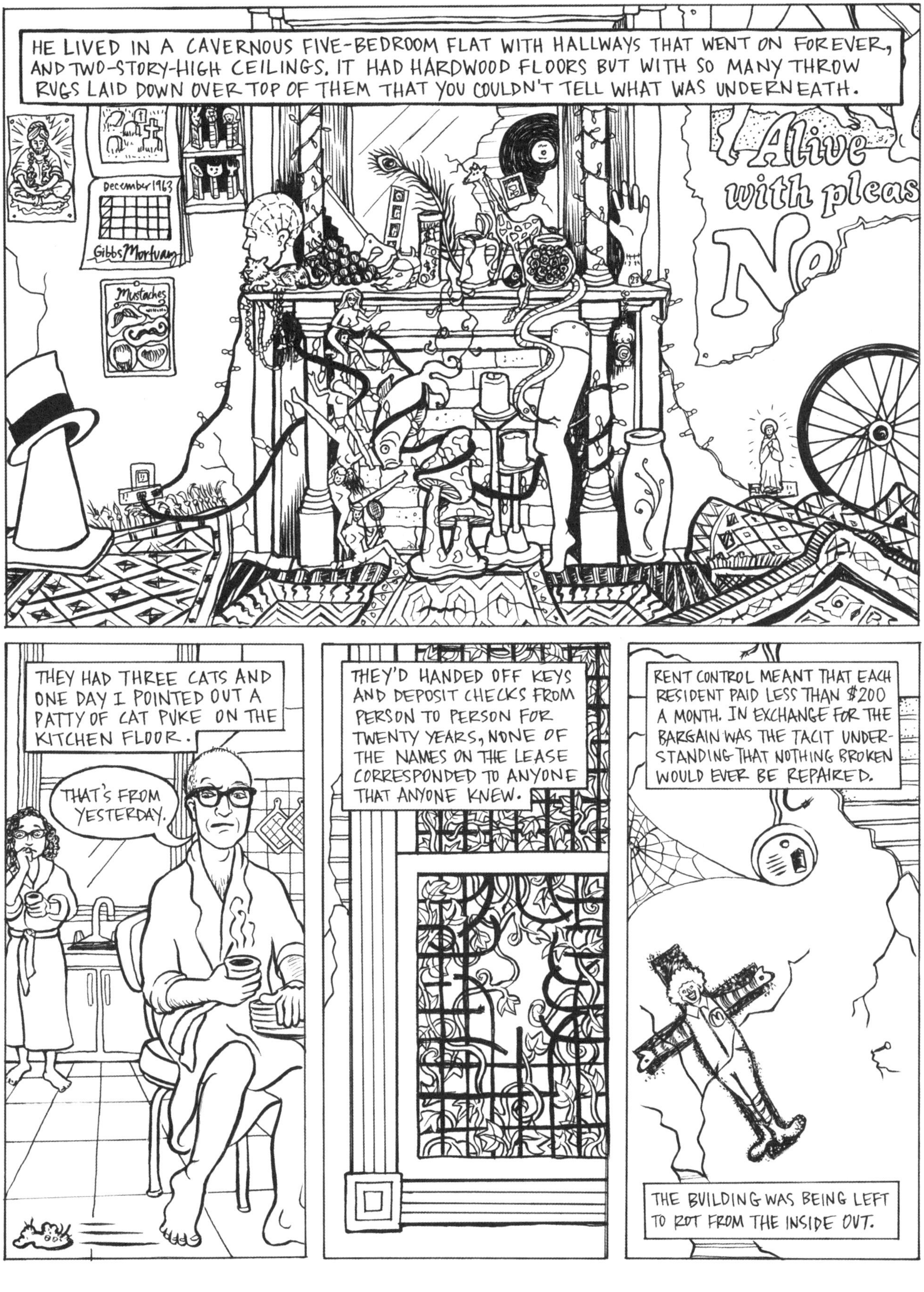

HE LIVED IN A CAVERNOUS FIVE-BEDROOM FLAT WITH HALLWAYS THAT WENT ON FOREVER, AND TWO-STORY-HIGH CEILINGS. IT HAD HARDWOOD FLOORS BUT WITH SO MANY THROW RUGS LAID DOWN OVER TOP OF THEM THAT YOU COULDN'T TELL WHAT WAS UNDERNEATH.
December 1963
Mustaches
Alive
with pleas
THEY HAD THREE CATS AND ONE DAY I POINTED OUT A PATTY OF CAT PUKE ON THE KITCHEN FLOOR.
THAT'S FROM YESTERDAY.
THEY'D HANDED OFF KEYS AND DEPOSIT CHECKS FROM PERSON TO PERSON FOR TWENTY YEARS, NONE OF THE NAMES ON THE LEASE CORRESPONDED TO ANYONE THAT ANYONE KNEW.
RENT CONTROL MEANT THAT EACH RESIDENT PAID LESS THAN $200 A MONTH. IN EXCHANGE FOR THE BARGAIN WAS THE TACIT UNDERSTANDING THAT NOTHING BROKEN WOULD EVER BE REPAIRED.
THE BUILDING WAS BEING LEFT TO ROT FROM THE INSIDE OUT.

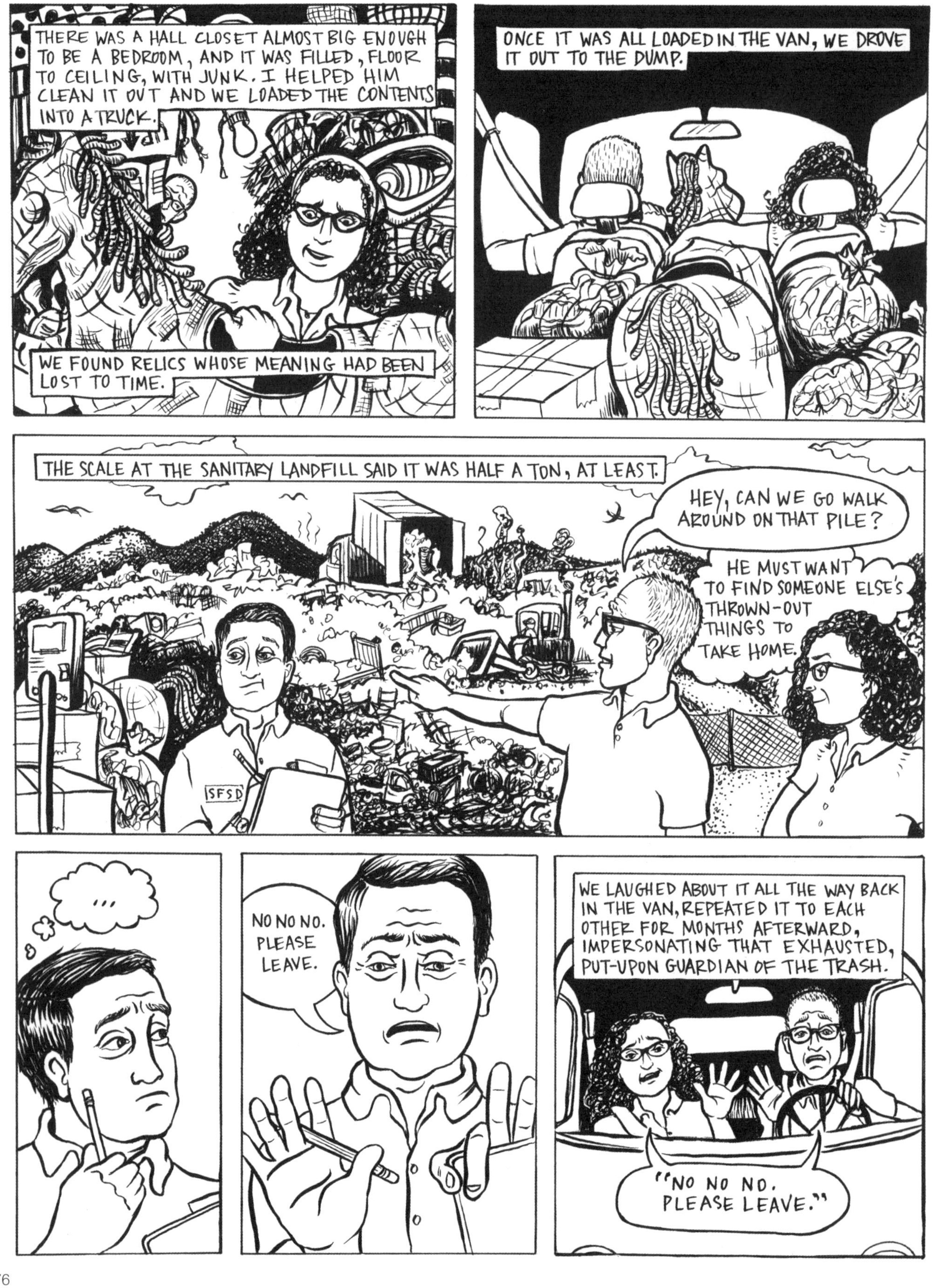
THERE WAS A HALL CLOSET ALMOST BIG ENOUGH TO BE A BEDROOM, AND IT WAS FILLED, FLOOR TO CEILING, WITH JUNK. I HELPED HIM CLEAN IT OUT AND WE LOADED THE CONTENTS INTO A TRUCK.
WE FOUND RELICS WHOSE MEANING HAD BEEN LOST TO TIME.
ONCE IT WAS ALL LOADED IN THE VAN, WE DROVE IT OUT TO THE DUMP.
THE SCALE AT THE SANITARY LANDFILL SAID IT WAS HALF A TON, AT LEAST.
HEY, CAN WE GO WALK AROUND ON THAT PILE?
HE MUST WANT TO FIND SOMEONE ELSE'S THROWN-OUT THINGS TO TAKE HOME.
SFSD
...
NO NO NO. PLEASE LEAVE.
WE LAUGHED ABOUT IT ALL THE WAY BACK IN THE VAN, REPEATED IT TO EACH OTHER FOR MONTHS AFTERWARD, IMPERSONATING THAT EXHAUSTED, PUT-UPON GUARDIAN OF THE TRASH.
"NO NO NO. PLEASE LEAVE."

I BOUGHT A DINING ROOM TABLE FROM A GUY OFF CRAIGSLIST. IT LOOKS LIKE IT'S NEVER BEEN USED. THE GUY HAS THIS JOB WHERE HE PUTS NEW FURNITURE IN HOUSES THAT ARE UP FOR SALE? AND THEN TAKES IT OUT AGAIN?

IT'S CALLED STAGING. HE'S A STAGER.

HOW THE HELL DO YOU EVEN KNOW WHAT THAT IS? I NEVER KNEW SOMETHING LIKE THAT EXISTED.

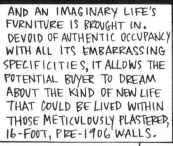

AN ENTIRE INDUSTRY EXISTS IN ORDER TO GIVE A HOUSE FOR SALE THE RIGHT FEEL INSIDE. THE OCCUPANT'S OWN BELONGINGS ARE PACKED INTO A CORNER OF THE BASEMENT, WITH THEIR ACCOMPANYING MIASMA OF DIVORCE & REGRET...

AND AN IMAGINARY LIFE'S FURNITURE IS BROUGHT IN. DEVOID OF AUTHENTIC OCCUPANCY WITH ALL ITS EMBARRASSING SPECIFICITIES, IT ALLOWS THE POTENTIAL BUYER TO DREAM ABOUT THE KIND OF NEW LIFE THAT COULD BE LIVED WITHIN THOSE METICULOUSLY PLASTERED, 16-FOOT, PRE-1906 WALLS.

I WALK BY THIS ONE HOUSE ON 22ND ST. EVERY DAY. THIS IS HOW IT LOOKED LAST YEAR:

A FEW MONTHS LATER:

A FEW MONTHS AFTER THAT:

Who ever steals my flowers you have some REAL BAD KARMA coming to you!!!!!

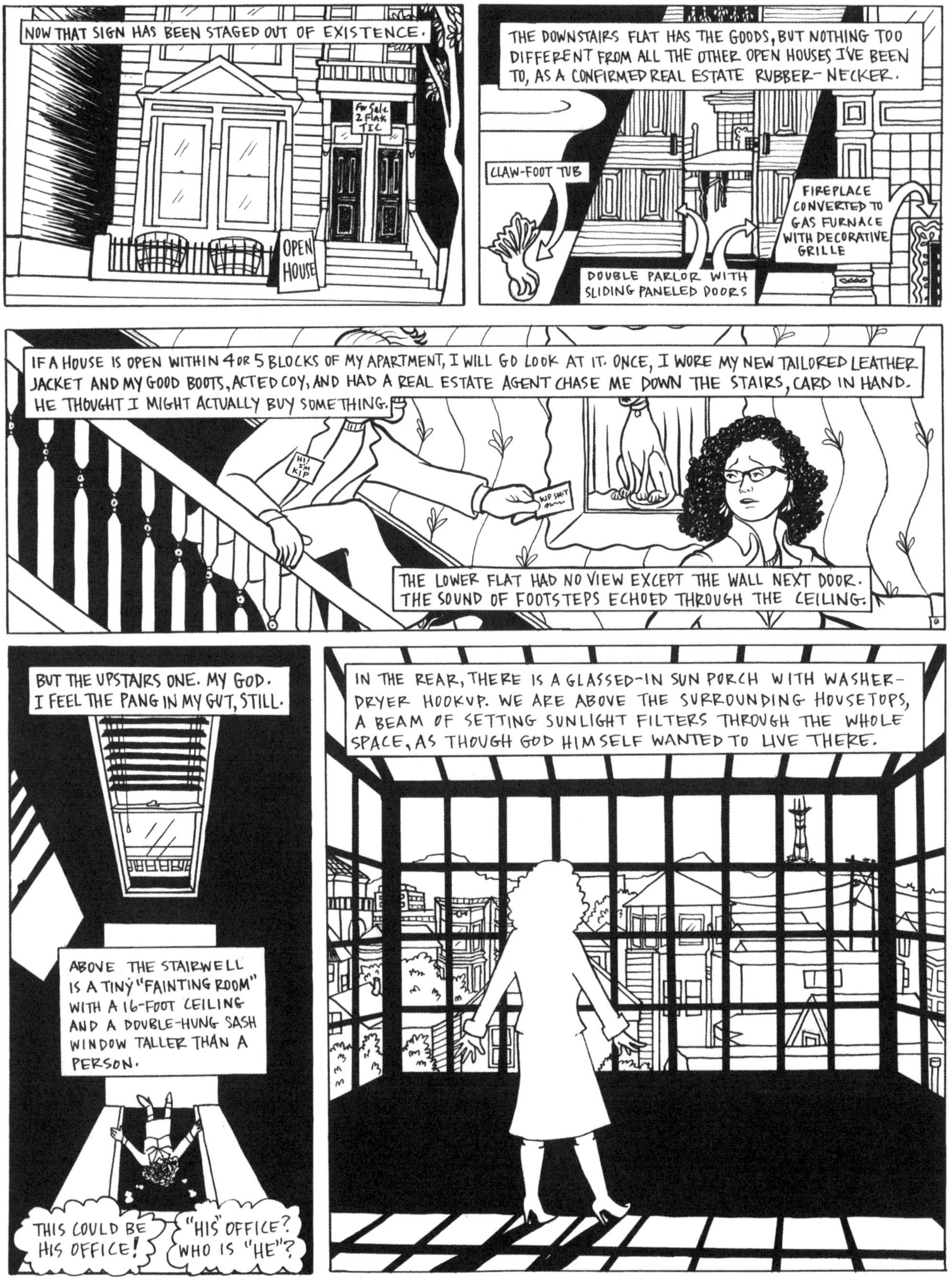
NOW THAT SIGN HAS BEEN STAGED OUT OF EXISTENCE.
For Sale 2 Flats TIC
OPEN HOUSE
THE DOWNSTAIRS FLAT HAS THE GOODS, BUT NOTHING TOO DIFFERENT FROM ALL THE OTHER OPEN HOUSES I'VE BEEN TO, AS A CONFIRMED REAL ESTATE RUBBER-NECKER.
CLAW-FOOT TUB
DOUBLE PARLOR WITH SLIDING PANELED DOORS
FIREPLACE CONVERTED TO GAS FURNACE WITH DECORATIVE GRILLE
IF A HOUSE IS OPEN WITHIN 4 OR 5 BLOCKS OF MY APARTMENT, I WILL GO LOOK AT IT. ONCE, I WORE MY NEW TAILORED LEATHER JACKET AND MY GOOD BOOTS, ACTED COY, AND HAD A REAL ESTATE AGENT CHASE ME DOWN THE STAIRS, CARD IN HAND. HE THOUGHT I MIGHT ACTUALLY BUY SOMETHING.
HI! I'M KIP
THE LOWER FLAT HAD NO VIEW EXCEPT THE WALL NEXT DOOR. THE SOUND OF FOOTSTEPS ECHOED THROUGH THE CEILING.
BUT THE UPSTAIRS ONE. MY GOD. I FEEL THE PANG IN MY GUT, STILL.
ABOVE THE STAIRWELL IS A TINY "FAINTING ROOM" WITH A 16-FOOT CEILING AND A DOUBLE-HUNG SASH WINDOW TALLER THAN A PERSON.
THIS COULD BE HIS OFFICE!
"HIS" OFFICE? WHO IS "HE"?
IN THE REAR, THERE IS A GLASSED-IN SUN PORCH WITH WASHER-DRYER HOOKUP. WE ARE ABOVE THE SURROUNDING HOUSETOPS, A BEAM OF SETTING SUNLIGHT FILTERS THROUGH THE WHOLE SPACE, AS THOUGH GOD HIMSELF WANTED TO LIVE THERE.

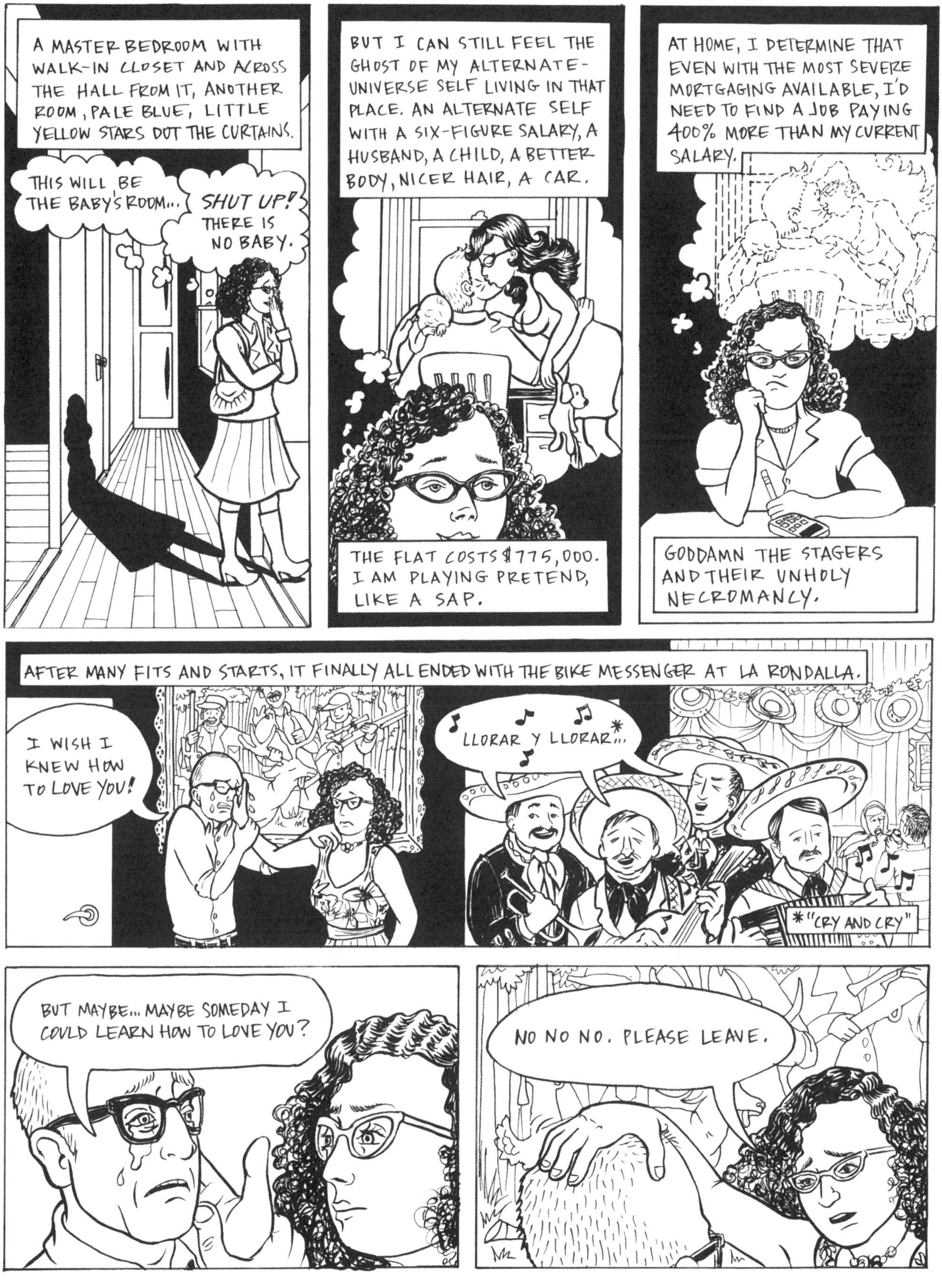

A MASTER BEDROOM WITH WALK-IN CLOSET AND ACROSS THE HALL FROM IT, ANOTHER ROOM, PALE BLUE, LITTLE YELLOW STARS DOT THE CURTAINS.
THIS WILL BE THE BABY'S ROOM...
SHUT UP! THERE IS NO BABY.
BUT I CAN STILL FEEL THE GHOST OF MY ALTERNATE-UNIVERSE SELF LIVING IN THAT PLACE. AN ALTERNATE SELF WITH A SIX-FIGURE SALARY, A HUSBAND, A CHILD, A BETTER BODY, NICER HAIR, A CAR.
THE FLAT COSTS $775,000. I AM PLAYING PRETEND, LIKE A SAP.
AT HOME, I DETERMINE THAT EVEN WITH THE MOST SEVERE MORTGAGING AVAILABLE, I'D NEED TO FIND A JOB PAYING 400% MORE THAN MY CURRENT SALARY.
GODDAMN THE STAGERS AND THEIR UNHOLY NECROMANCY.
AFTER MANY FITS AND STARTS, IT FINALLY ALL ENDED WITH THE BIKE MESSENGER AT LA RONDALLA.
I WISH I KNEW HOW TO LOVE YOU!
LLORAR Y LLORAR*...
*"CRY AND CRY"
BUT MAYBE... MAYBE SOMEDAY I COULD LEARN HOW TO LOVE YOU?
NO NO NO. PLEASE LEAVE.

"ACTUALLY, I'M NOT SURE WHY EITHER O<u>NE</u> OF US HAS NIPPLES."

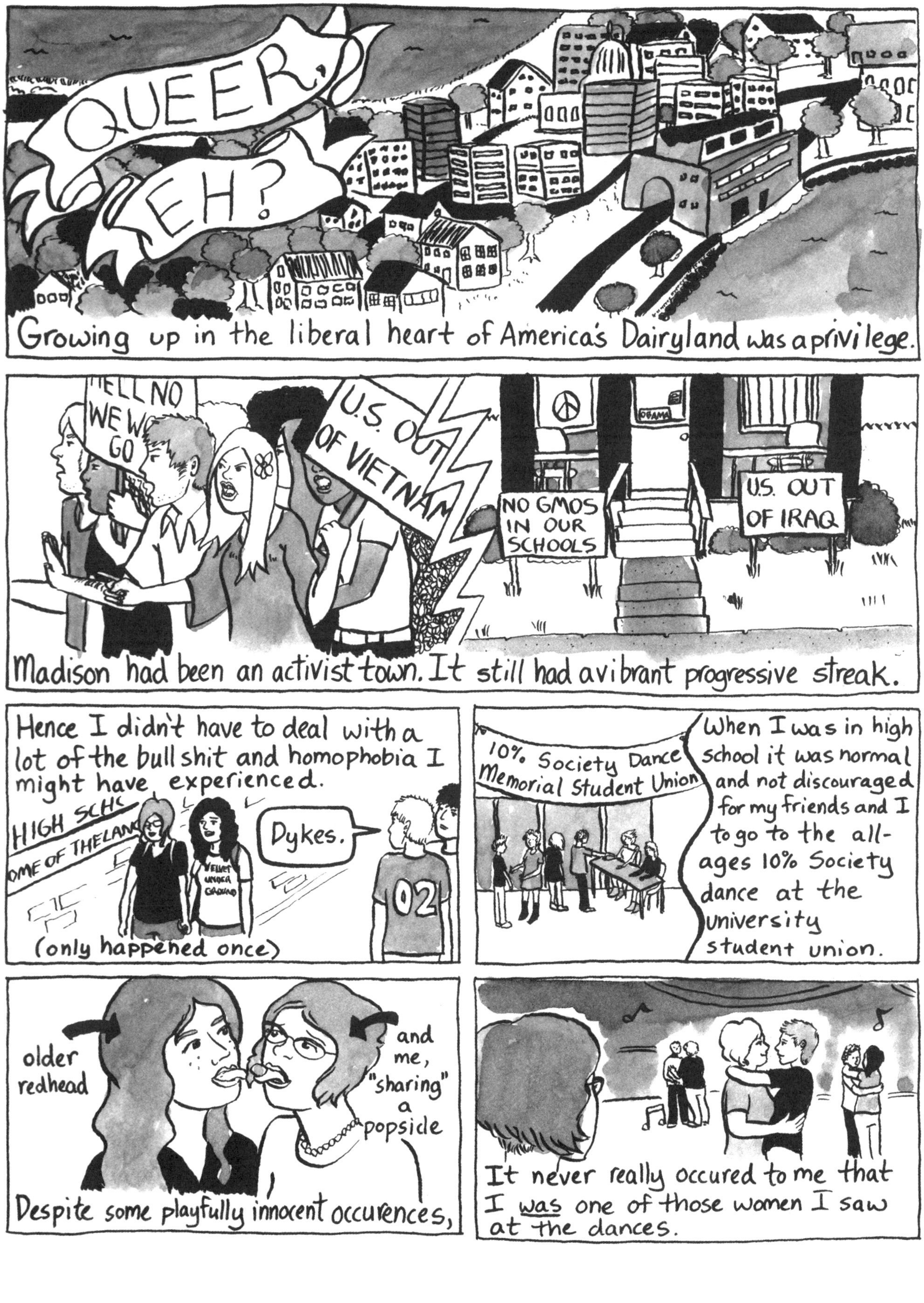
QUEER, EH?
Growing up in the liberal heart of America's Dairyland was a privilege.
U.S. OUT OF VIETNAM
NO GMOS IN OUR SCHOOLS
U.S. OUT OF IRAQ
Madison had been an activist town. It still had a vibrant progressive streak.
Hence I didn't have to deal with a lot of the bullshit and homophobia I might have experienced.
Dykes.
(only happened once)
10% Society Dance
Memorial Student Union
When I was in high school it was normal and not discouraged for my friends and I to go to the all-ages 10% Society dance at the university student union.
older redhead
and me, "sharing" a popsicle
Despite some playfully innocent occurences,
It never really occured to me that I was one of those women I saw at the dances.

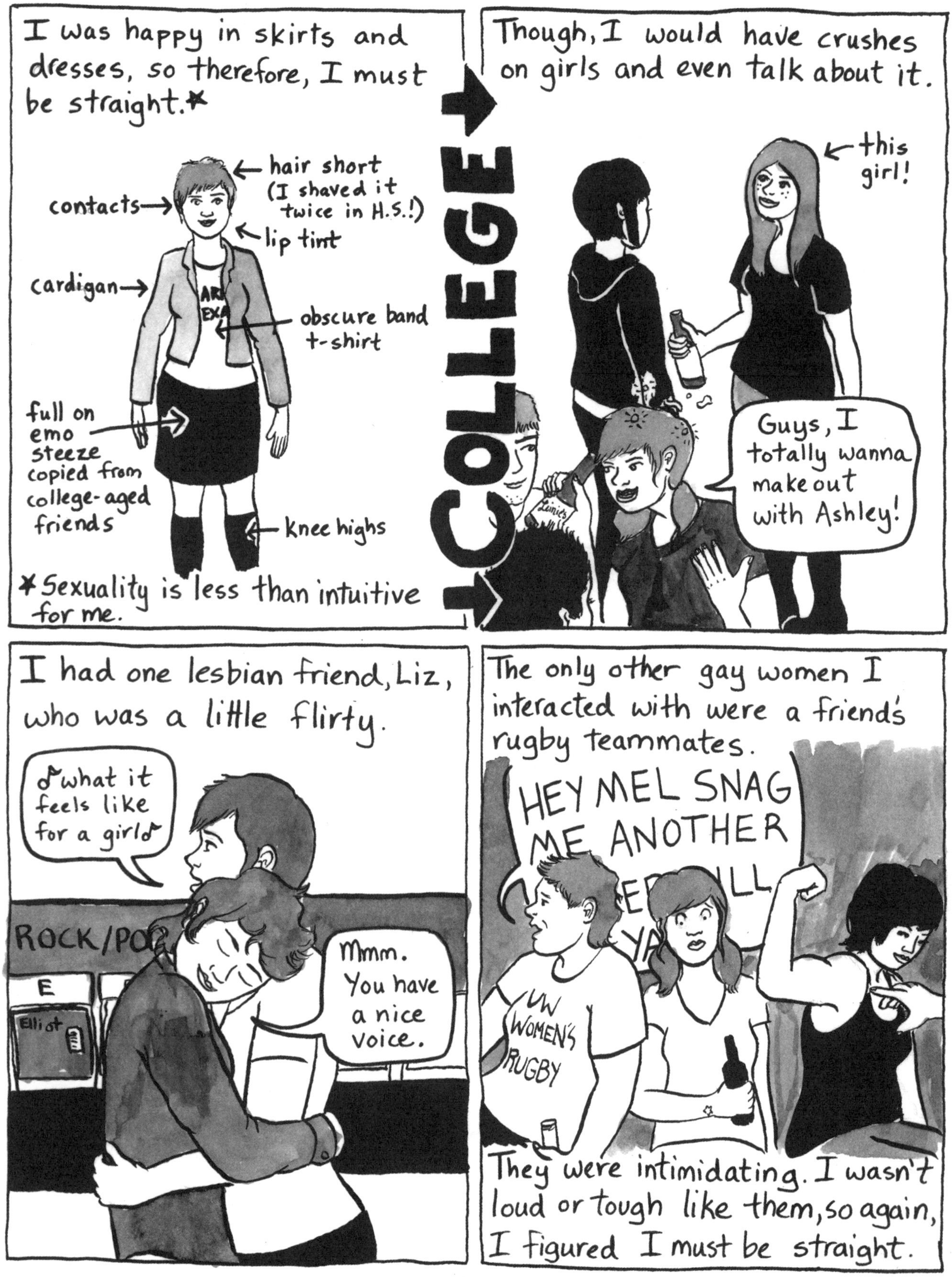
I was happy in skirts and dresses, so therefore, I must be straight.*
hair short (I shaved it twice in H.S.!)
contacts
lip tint
cardigan
obscure band t-shirt
full on emo steeze copied from college-aged friends
knee highs
*Sexuality is less than intuitive for me.
COLLEGE
Though, I would have crushes on girls and even talk about it.
this girl!
Guys, I totally wanna make out with Ashley!
I had one lesbian friend, Liz, who was a little flirty.
♪what it feels like for a girl♪
ROCK/POP
E
Mmm. You have a nice voice.
The only other gay women I interacted with were a friend's rugby teammates.
HEY MEL SNAG ME ANOTHER
UW WOMEN'S RUGBY
They were intimidating. I wasn't loud or tough like them, so again, I figured I must be straight.

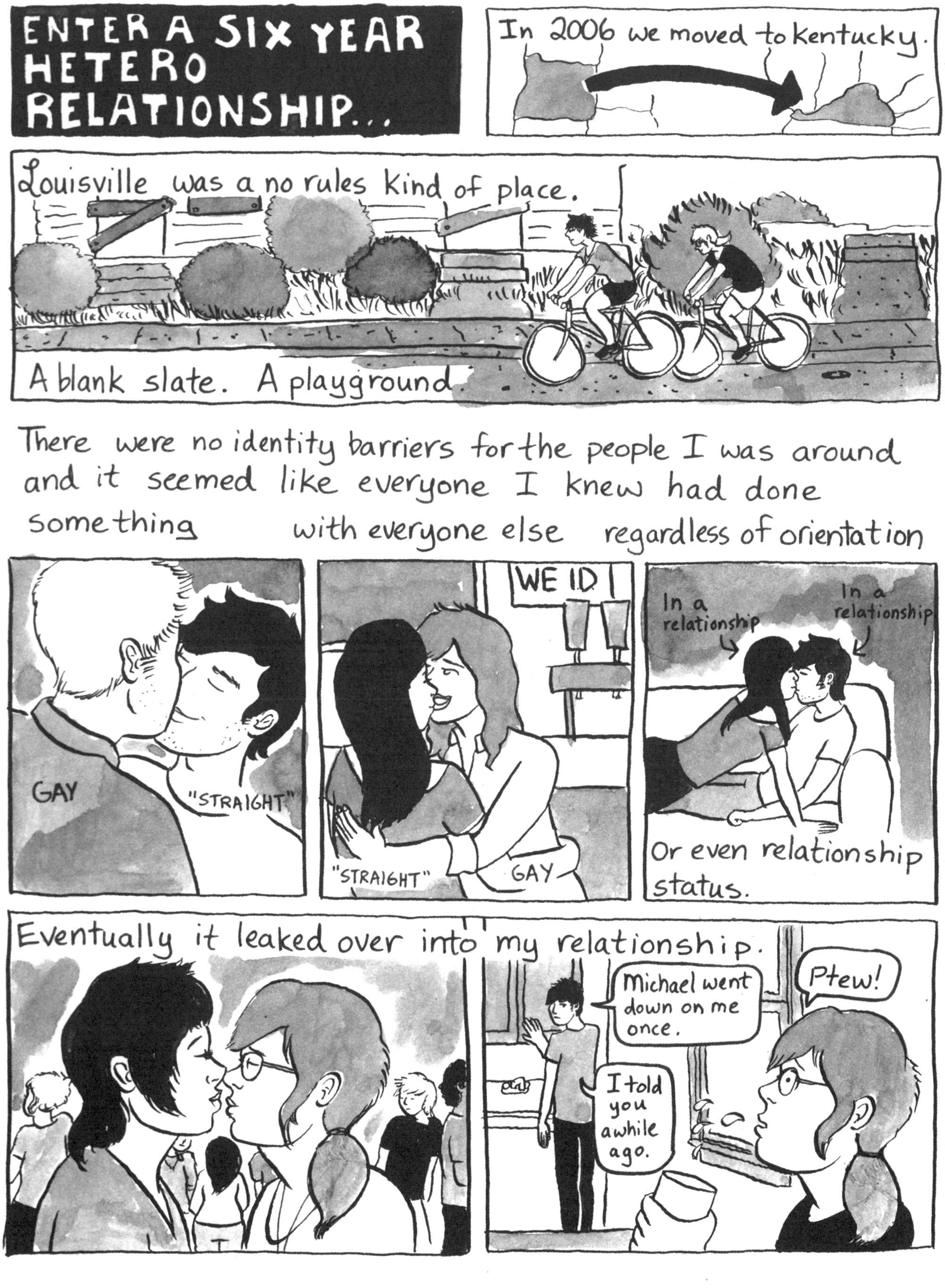
ENTER A SIX YEAR HETERO RELATIONSHIP...
In 2006 we moved to kentucky.
Louisville was a no rules kind of place.
A blank slate. A playground.
There were no identity barriers for the people I was around and it seemed like everyone I knew had done something with everyone else regardless of orientation
GAY
"STRAIGHT"
WE I.D.
"STRAIGHT"
GAY
In a relationship
In a relationship
Or even relationship status.
Eventually it leaked over into my relationship.
Michael went down on me once.
Ptew!
I told you awhile ago.

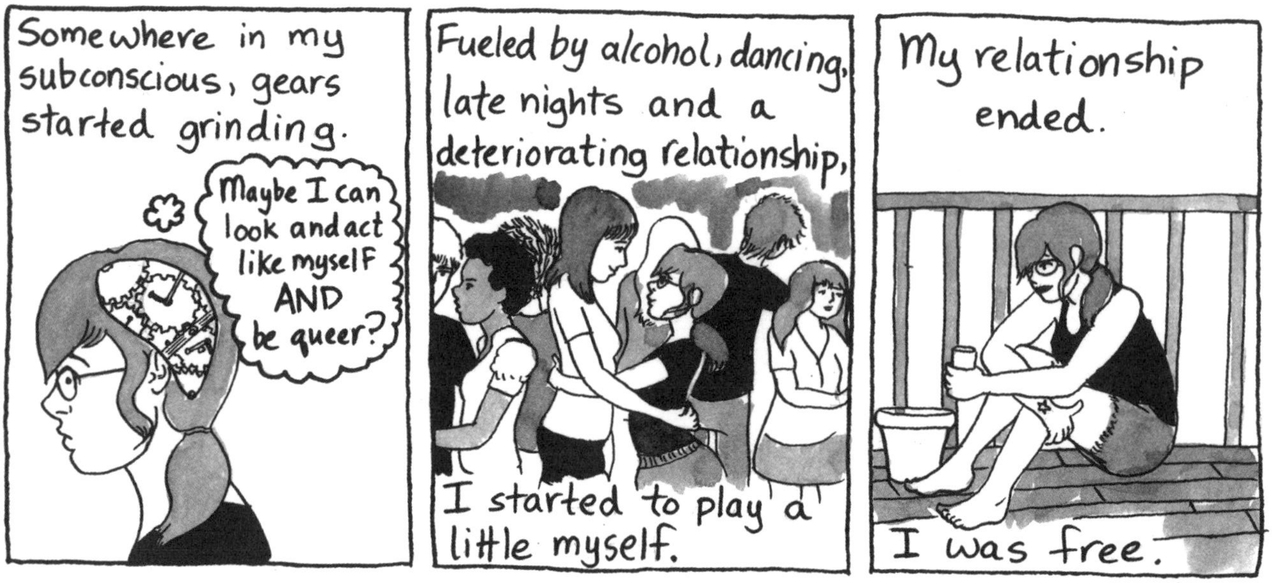
Somewhere in my subconscious, gears started grinding.
Maybe I can look and act like myself AND be queer?
Fueled by alcohol, dancing, late nights and a deteriorating relationship,
I started to play a little myself.
My relationship ended.
I was free.

Even though I was single, the carefree atmosphere was a little too much for me sometimes.

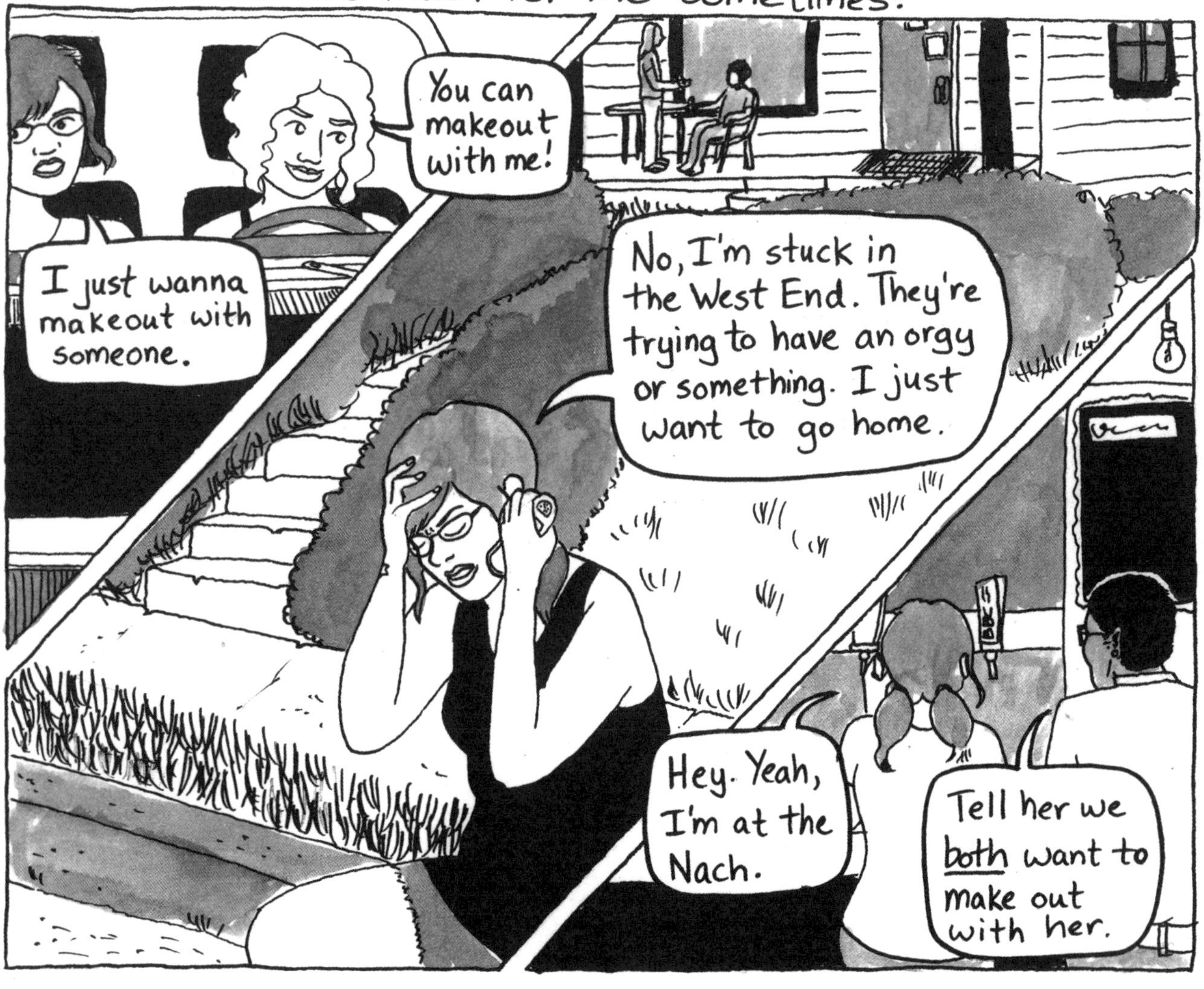
You can makeout with me!
I just wanna makeout with someone.
No, I'm stuck in the West End. They're trying to have an orgy or something. I just want to go home.
Hey. Yeah, I'm at the Nach.
Tell her we both want to make out with her.

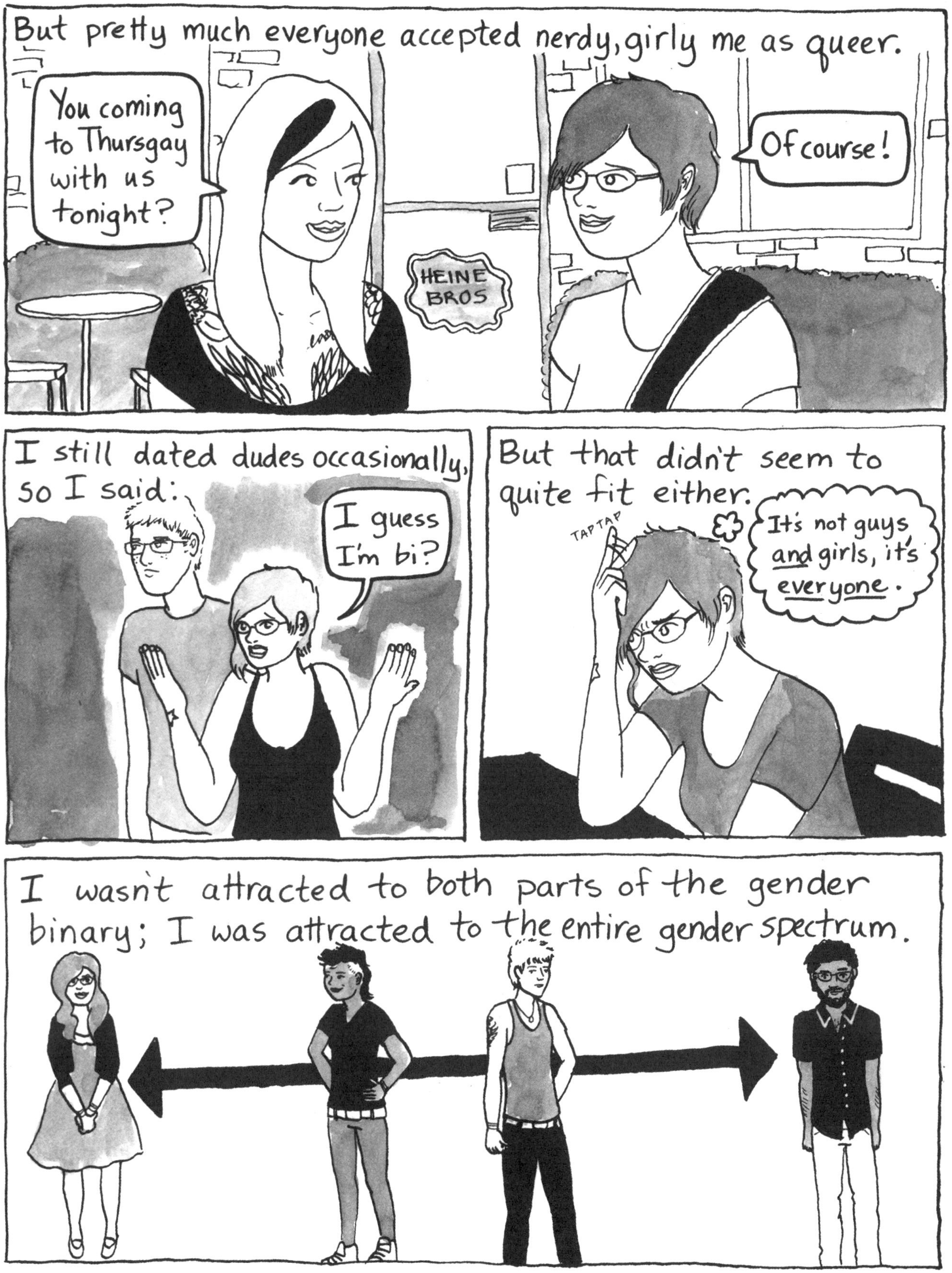
But pretty much everyone accepted nerdy, girly me as queer.
You coming to Thursgay with us tonight?
HEINE BROS
Of course!
I still dated dudes occasionally, so I said:
I guess I'm bi?
But that didn't seem to quite fit either.
TAPTAP
It's not guys and girls, it's everyone.
I wasn't attracted to both parts of the gender binary; I was attracted to the entire gender spectrum.

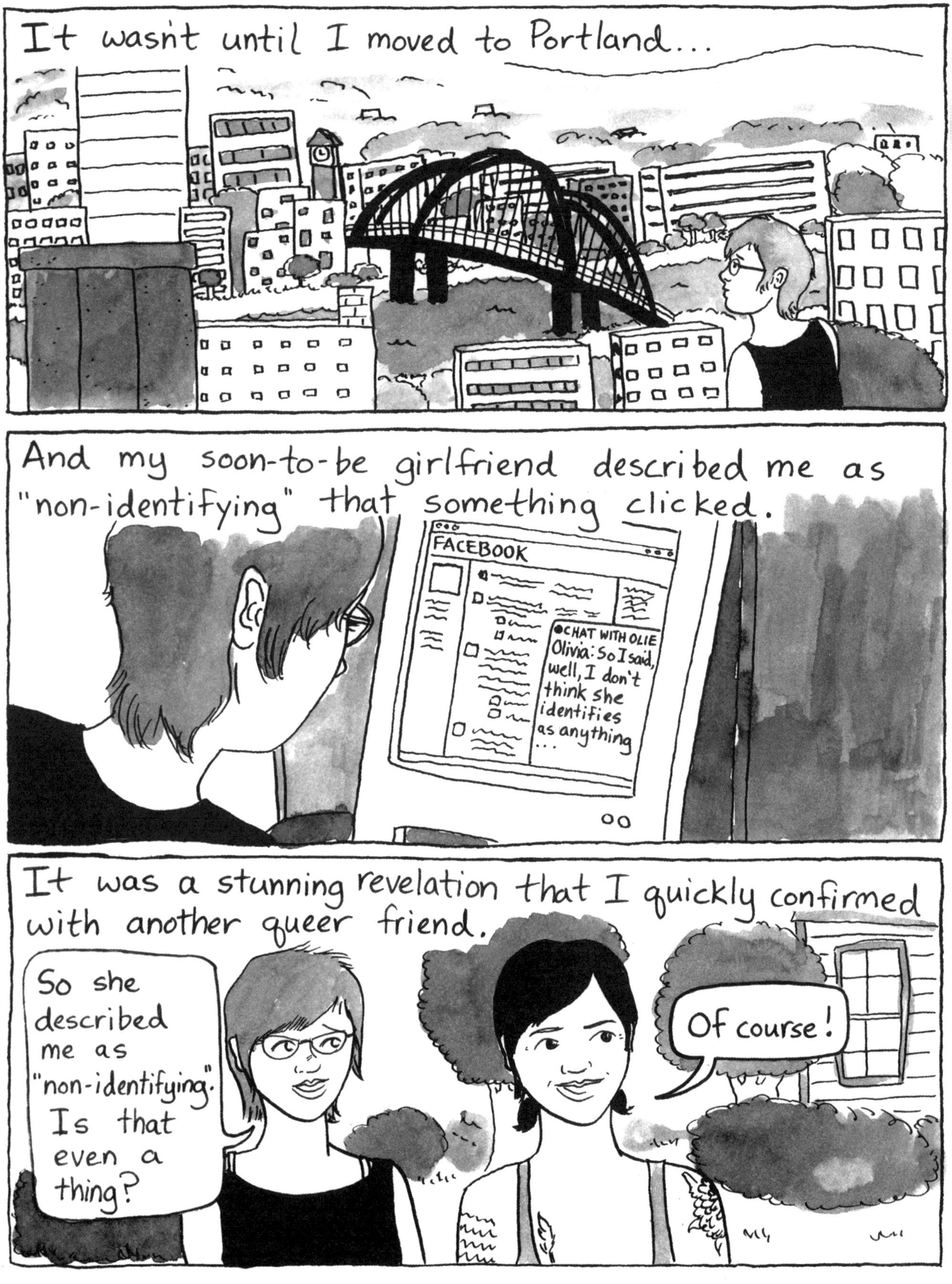
It wasn't until I moved to Portland...
And my soon-to-be girlfriend described me as "non-identifying" that something clicked.
FACEBOOK
CHAT WITH OLIE
Olivia: So I said, well, I don't think she identifies as anything ...
It was a stunning revelation that I quickly confirmed with another queer friend.
So she described me as "non-identifying." Is that even a thing?
Of course!

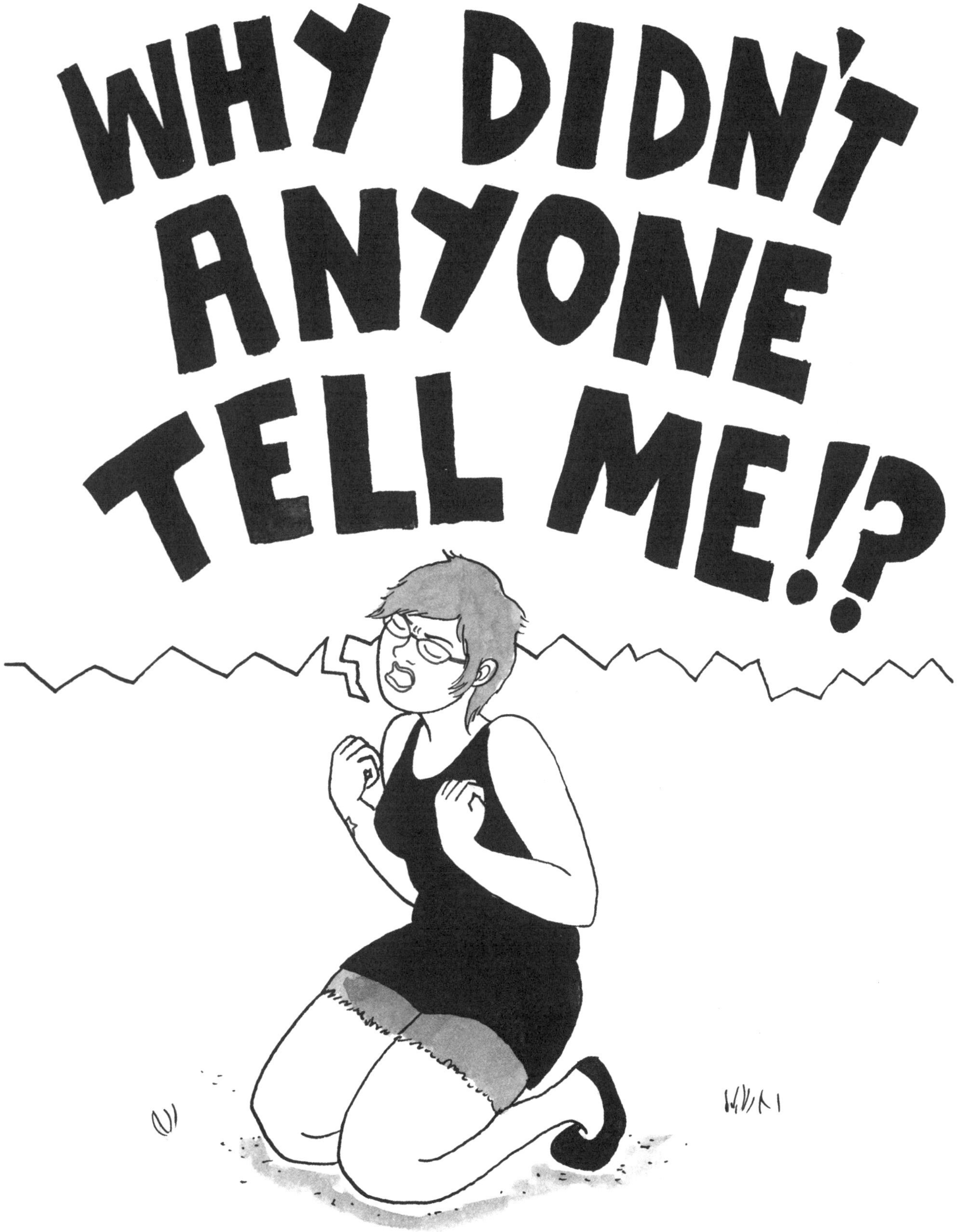
WHY DIDN'T ANYONE TELL ME!?

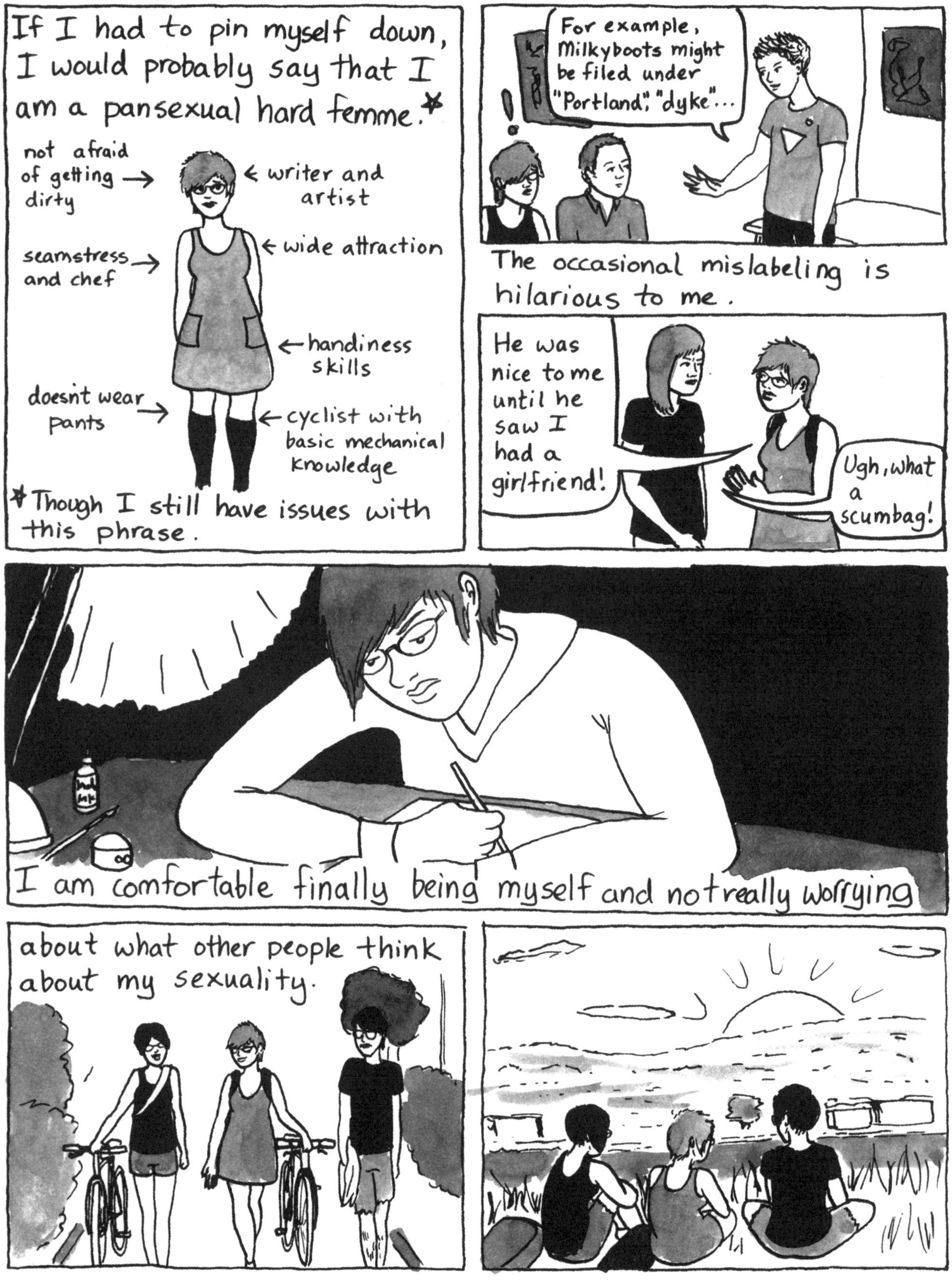
If I had to pin myself down, I would probably say that I am a pansexual hard femme.*
not afraid of getting dirty →
← writer and artist
seamstress and chef →
← wide attraction
← handiness skills
doesn't wear pants →
← cyclist with basic mechanical knowledge
*Though I still have issues with this phrase.
For example, Milkyboots might be filed under "Portland", "dyke"...
!
The occasional mislabeling is hilarious to me.
He was nice to me until he saw I had a girlfriend!
Ugh, what a scumbag!
I am comfortable finally being myself and not really worrying
about what other people think about my sexuality.

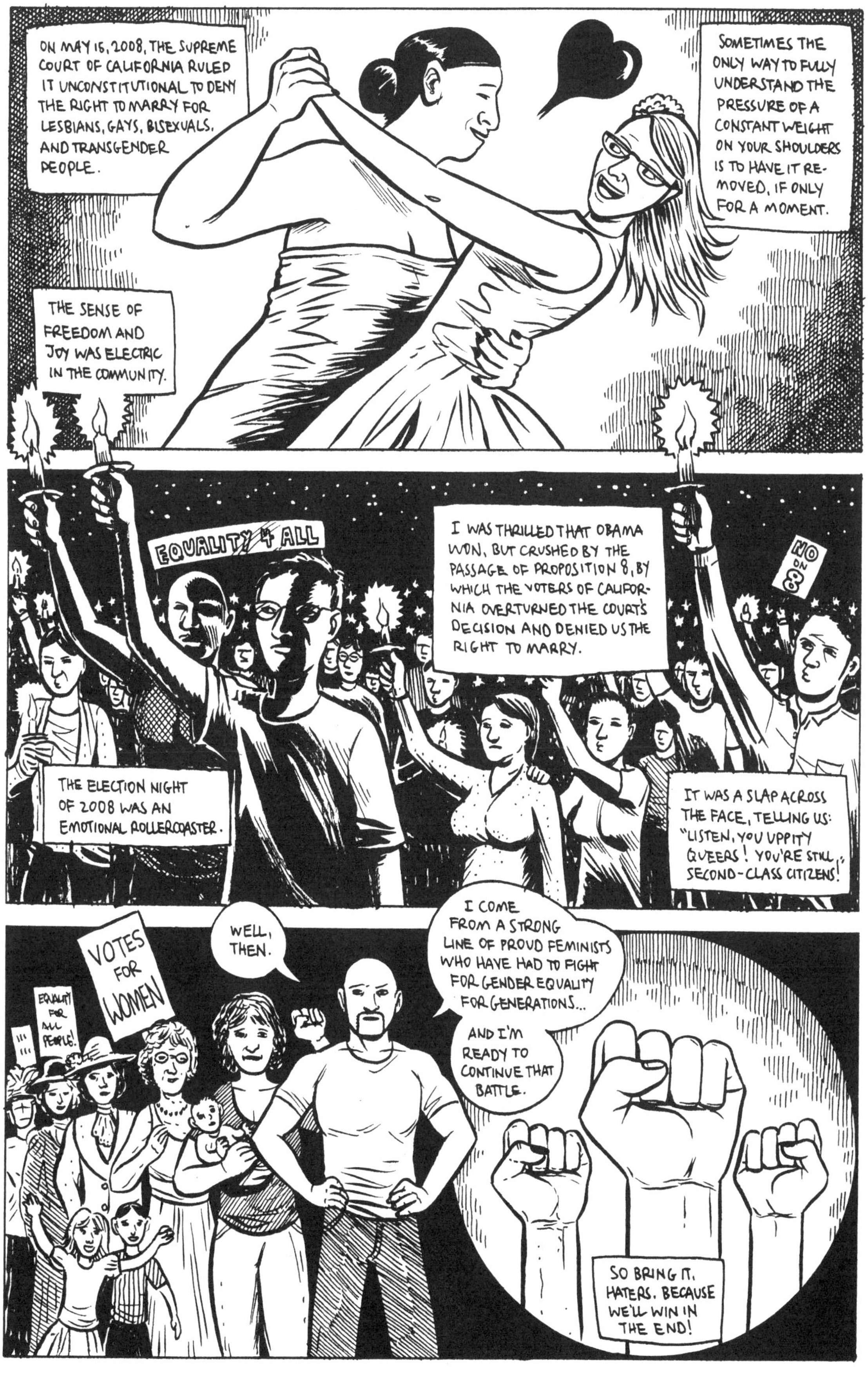

ON MAY 15, 2008, THE SUPREME COURT OF CALIFORNIA RULED IT UNCONSTITUTIONAL TO DENY THE RIGHT TO MARRY FOR LESBIANS, GAYS, BISEXUALS, AND TRANSGENDER PEOPLE.
SOMETIMES THE ONLY WAY TO FULLY UNDERSTAND THE PRESSURE OF A CONSTANT WEIGHT ON YOUR SHOULDERS IS TO HAVE IT REMOVED, IF ONLY FOR A MOMENT.
THE SENSE OF FREEDOM AND JOY WAS ELECTRIC IN THE COMMUNITY.
EQUALITY 4 ALL
I WAS THRILLED THAT OBAMA WON, BUT CRUSHED BY THE PASSAGE OF PROPOSITION 8, BY WHICH THE VOTERS OF CALIFORNIA OVERTURNED THE COURT'S DECISION AND DENIED US THE RIGHT TO MARRY.
NO ON 8
THE ELECTION NIGHT OF 2008 WAS AN EMOTIONAL ROLLERCOASTER.
IT WAS A SLAP ACROSS THE FACE, TELLING US: "LISTEN, YOU UPPITY QUEERS! YOU'RE STILL SECOND-CLASS CITIZENS!"
VOTES FOR WOMEN
EQUALITY FOR ALL PEOPLE!
WELL, THEN.
I COME FROM A STRONG LINE OF PROUD FEMINISTS WHO HAVE HAD TO FIGHT FOR GENDER EQUALITY FOR GENERATIONS...
AND I'M READY TO CONTINUE THAT BATTLE.
SO BRING IT, HATERS. BECAUSE WE'LL WIN IN THE END!

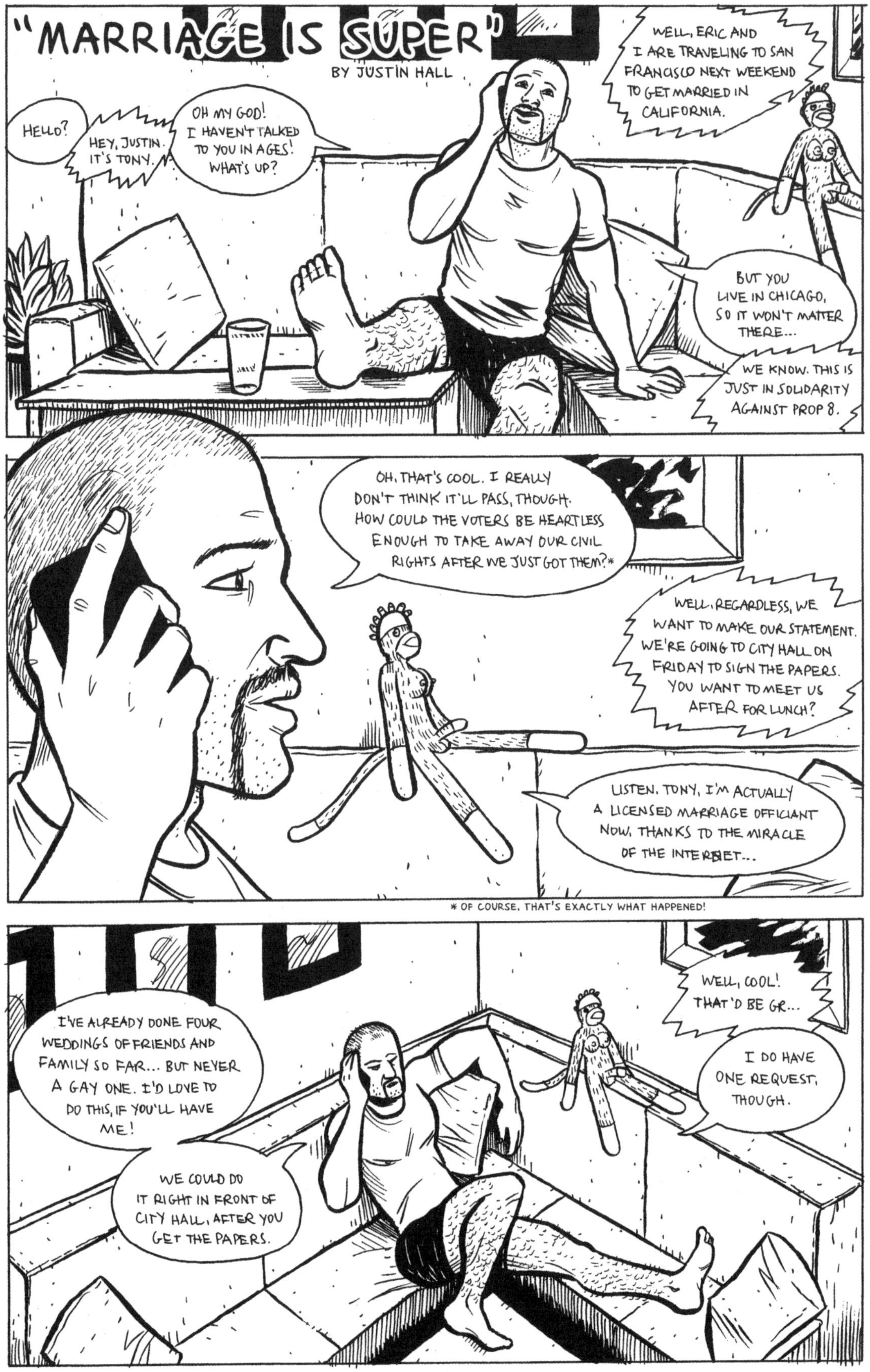
"MARRIAGE IS SUPER"
BY JUSTIN HALL
HELLO?
HEY, JUSTIN. IT'S TONY.
OH MY GOD! I HAVEN'T TALKED TO YOU IN AGES! WHAT'S UP?
WELL, ERIC AND I ARE TRAVELING TO SAN FRANCISCO NEXT WEEKEND TO GET MARRIED IN CALIFORNIA.
BUT YOU LIVE IN CHICAGO, SO IT WON'T MATTER THERE...
WE KNOW. THIS IS JUST IN SOLIDARITY AGAINST PROP 8.
OH, THAT'S COOL. I REALLY DON'T THINK IT'LL PASS, THOUGH. HOW COULD THE VOTERS BE HEARTLESS ENOUGH TO TAKE AWAY OUR CIVIL RIGHTS AFTER WE JUST GOT THEM?*
WELL, REGARDLESS, WE WANT TO MAKE OUR STATEMENT. WE'RE GOING TO CITY HALL ON FRIDAY TO SIGN THE PAPERS. YOU WANT TO MEET US AFTER FOR LUNCH?
LISTEN, TONY, I'M ACTUALLY A LICENSED MARRIAGE OFFICIANT NOW, THANKS TO THE MIRACLE OF THE INTERNET...
* OF COURSE, THAT'S EXACTLY WHAT HAPPENED!
WELL, COOL! THAT'D BE GR...
I'VE ALREADY DONE FOUR WEDDINGS OF FRIENDS AND FAMILY SO FAR... BUT NEVER A GAY ONE. I'D LOVE TO DO THIS, IF YOU'LL HAVE ME!
I DO HAVE ONE REQUEST, THOUGH.
WE COULD DO IT RIGHT IN FRONT OF CITY HALL, AFTER YOU GET THE PAPERS.

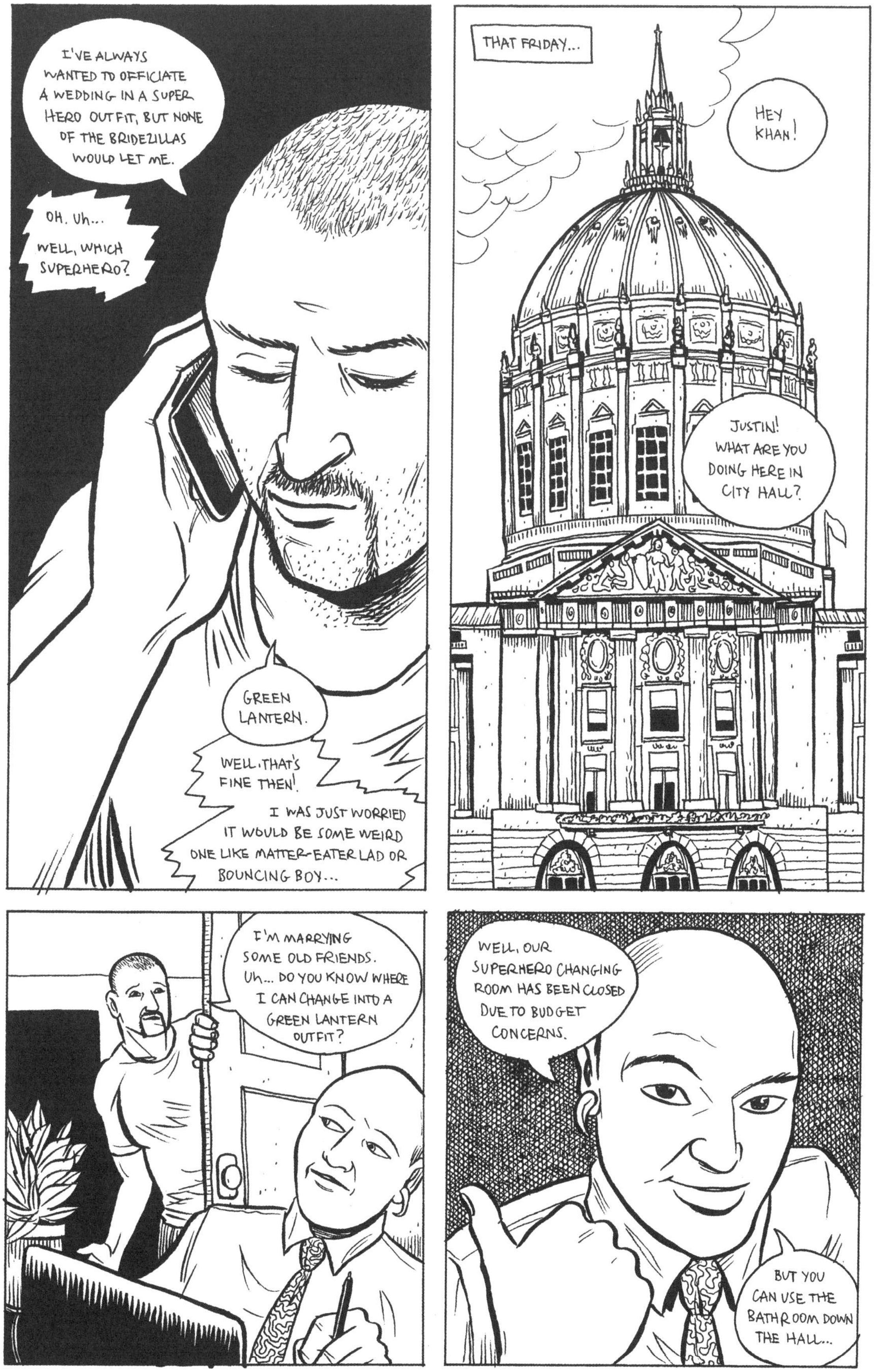

I'VE ALWAYS WANTED TO OFFICIATE A WEDDING IN A SUPER HERO OUTFIT, BUT NONE OF THE BRIDEZILLAS WOULD LET ME.
OH. Uh... WELL, WHICH SUPERHERO?
GREEN LANTERN.
WELL, THAT'S FINE THEN!
I WAS JUST WORRIED IT WOULD BE SOME WEIRD ONE LIKE MATTER-EATER LAD OR BOUNCING BOY...
THAT FRIDAY...
HEY KHAN!
JUSTIN! WHAT ARE YOU DOING HERE IN CITY HALL?
I'M MARRYING SOME OLD FRIENDS. Uh... DO YOU KNOW WHERE I CAN CHANGE INTO A GREEN LANTERN OUTFIT?
WELL, OUR SUPERHERO CHANGING ROOM HAS BEEN CLOSED DUE TO BUDGET CONCERNS.
BUT YOU CAN USE THE BATHROOM DOWN THE HALL...

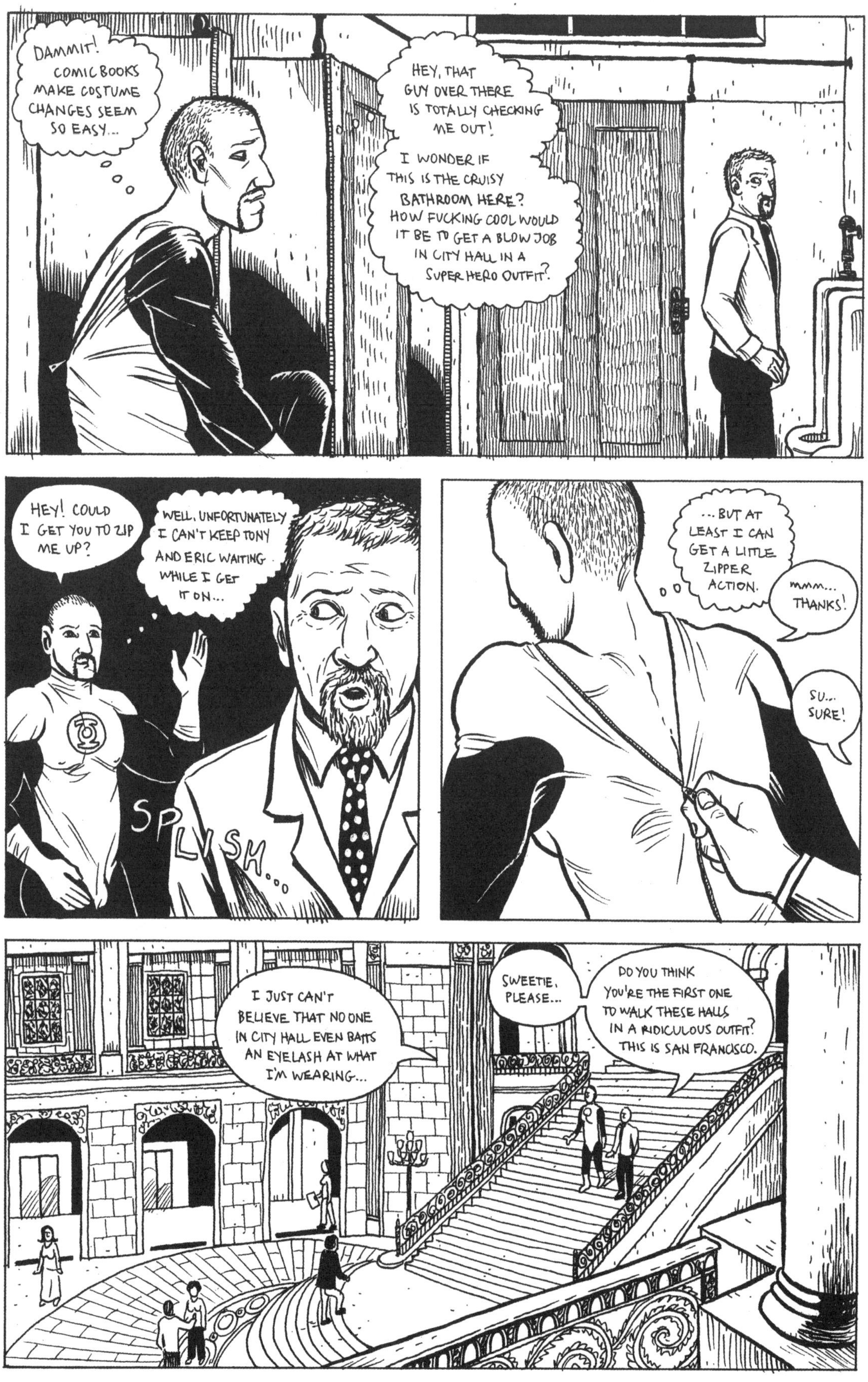
DAMMIT! COMIC BOOKS MAKE COSTUME CHANGES SEEM SO EASY...
HEY, THAT GUY OVER THERE IS TOTALLY CHECKING ME OUT!
I WONDER IF THIS IS THE CRUISY BATHROOM HERE? HOW FUCKING COOL WOULD IT BE TO GET A BLOW JOB IN CITY HALL IN A SUPER HERO OUTFIT?
HEY! COULD I GET YOU TO ZIP ME UP?
WELL, UNFORTUNATELY I CAN'T KEEP TONY AND ERIC WAITING WHILE I GET IT ON...
SPLISH...
...BUT AT LEAST I CAN GET A LITTLE ZIPPER ACTION.
mmm... THANKS!
SU... SURE!
I JUST CAN'T BELIEVE THAT NO ONE IN CITY HALL EVEN BATTS AN EYELASH AT WHAT I'M WEARING...
SWEETIE, PLEASE...
DO YOU THINK YOU'RE THE FIRST ONE TO WALK THESE HALLS IN A RIDICULOUS OUTFIT? THIS IS SAN FRANCISCO.

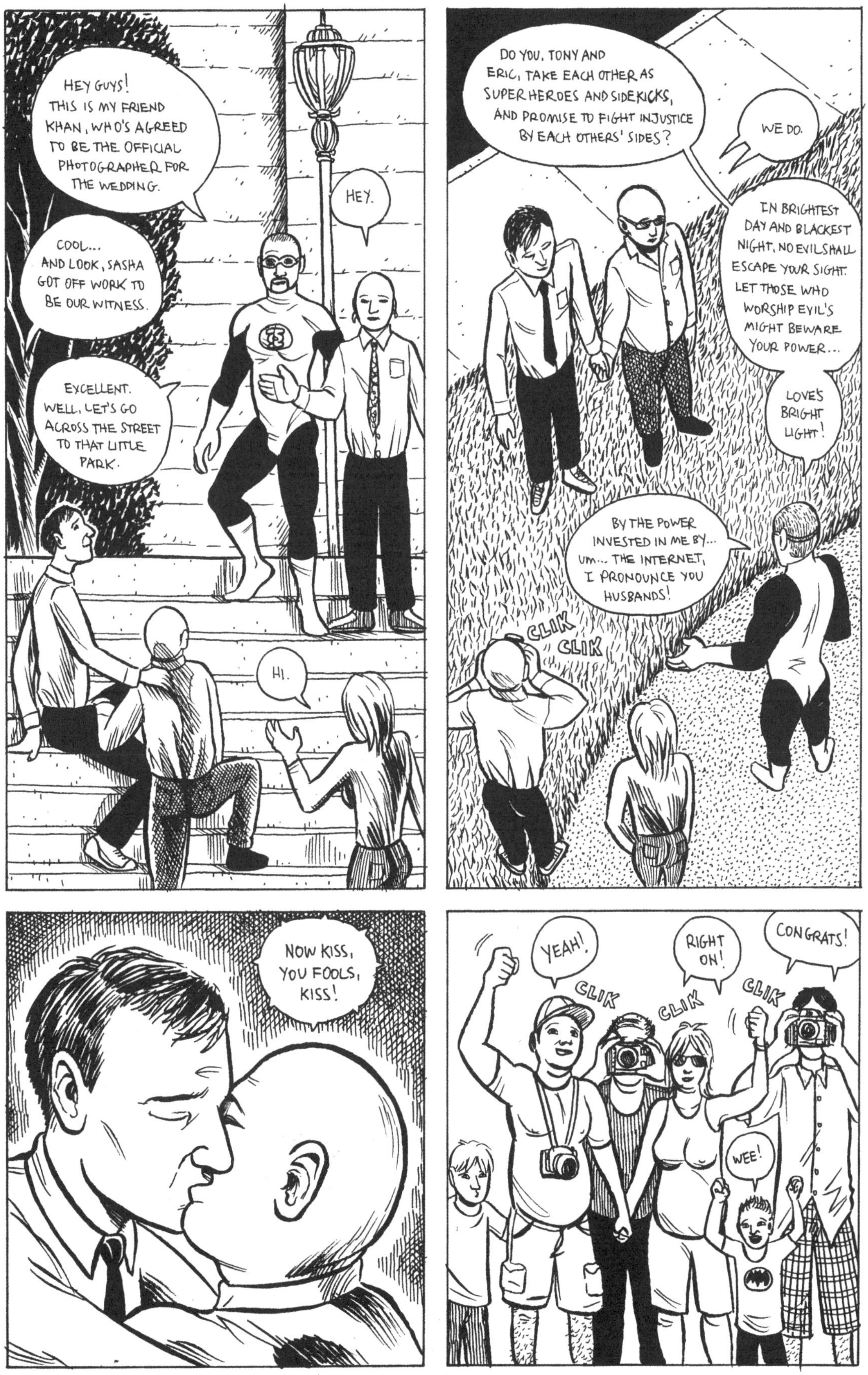
HEY GUYS! THIS IS MY FRIEND KHAN, WHO'S AGREED TO BE THE OFFICIAL PHOTOGRAPHER FOR THE WEDDING.
HEY.
COOL... AND LOOK, SASHA GOT OFF WORK TO BE OUR WITNESS.
EXCELLENT. WELL, LET'S GO ACROSS THE STREET TO THAT LITTLE PARK.
HI.
DO YOU, TONY AND ERIC, TAKE EACH OTHER AS SUPERHEROES AND SIDEKICKS, AND PROMISE TO FIGHT INJUSTICE BY EACH OTHERS' SIDES?
WE DO.
IN BRIGHTEST DAY AND BLACKEST NIGHT, NO EVIL SHALL ESCAPE YOUR SIGHT. LET THOSE WHO WORSHIP EVIL'S MIGHT BEWARE YOUR POWER...
LOVE'S BRIGHT LIGHT!
BY THE POWER INVESTED IN ME BY... UM... THE INTERNET, I PRONOUNCE YOU HUSBANDS!
CLIK
CLIK
NOW KISS, YOU FOOLS, KISS!
YEAH!
RIGHT ON!
CONGRATS!
CLIK
CLIK
CLIK
WEE!

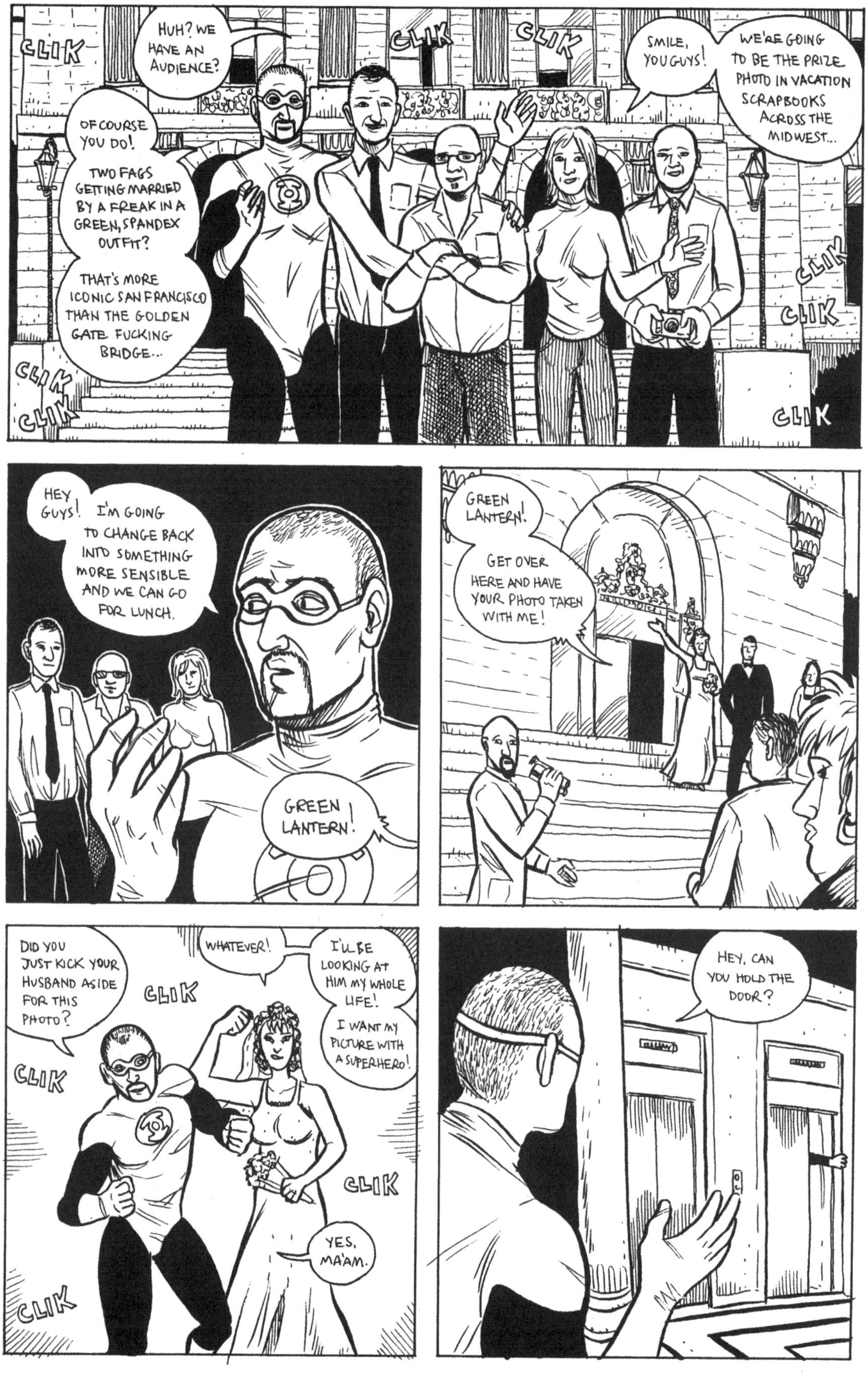

CLIK
HUH? WE HAVE AN AUDIENCE?
CLIK
CLIK
SMILE, YOU GUYS!
WE'RE GOING TO BE THE PRIZE PHOTO IN VACATION SCRAPBOOKS ACROSS THE MIDWEST...
OF COURSE YOU DO!
TWO FAGS GETTING MARRIED BY A FREAK IN A GREEN, SPANDEX OUTFIT?
THAT'S MORE ICONIC SAN FRANCISCO THAN THE GOLDEN GATE FUCKING BRIDGE...
CLIK
CLIK
CLIK
CLIK
CLIK
HEY GUYS! I'M GOING TO CHANGE BACK INTO SOMETHING MORE SENSIBLE AND WE CAN GO FOR LUNCH.
GREEN LANTERN!
GREEN LANTERN!
GET OVER HERE AND HAVE YOUR PHOTO TAKEN WITH ME!
DID YOU JUST KICK YOUR HUSBAND ASIDE FOR THIS PHOTO?
WHATEVER!
I'LL BE LOOKING AT HIM MY WHOLE LIFE!
I WANT MY PICTURE WITH A SUPERHERO!
CLIK
CLIK
CLIK
YES, MA'AM.
CLIK
HEY, CAN YOU HOLD THE DOOR?

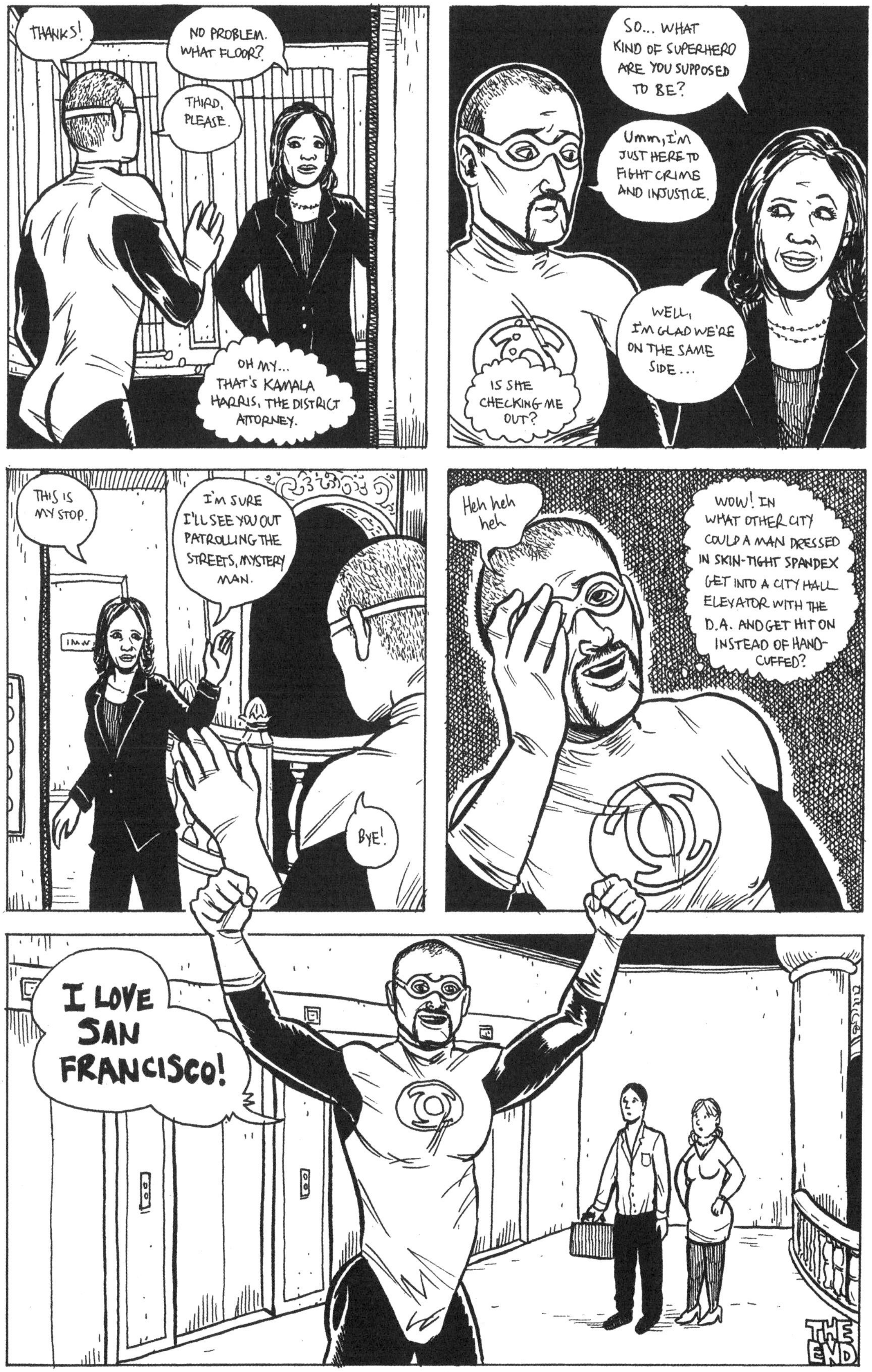
THANKS!
NO PROBLEM. WHAT FLOOR?
THIRD, PLEASE.
OH MY... THAT'S KAMALA HARRIS, THE DISTRICT ATTORNEY.
SO... WHAT KIND OF SUPERHERO ARE YOU SUPPOSED TO BE?
Umm, I'M JUST HERE TO FIGHT CRIME AND INJUSTICE.
WELL, I'M GLAD WE'RE ON THE SAME SIDE...
IS SHE CHECKING ME OUT?
THIS IS MY STOP.
I'M SURE I'LL SEE YOU OUT PATROLLING THE STREETS, MYSTERY MAN.
BYE!
Heh heh heh
WOW! IN WHAT OTHER CITY COULD A MAN DRESSED IN SKIN-TIGHT SPANDEX GET INTO A CITY HALL ELEVATOR WITH THE D.A. AND GET HIT ON INSTEAD OF HAND-CUFFED?
I LOVE SAN FRANCISCO!
THE END

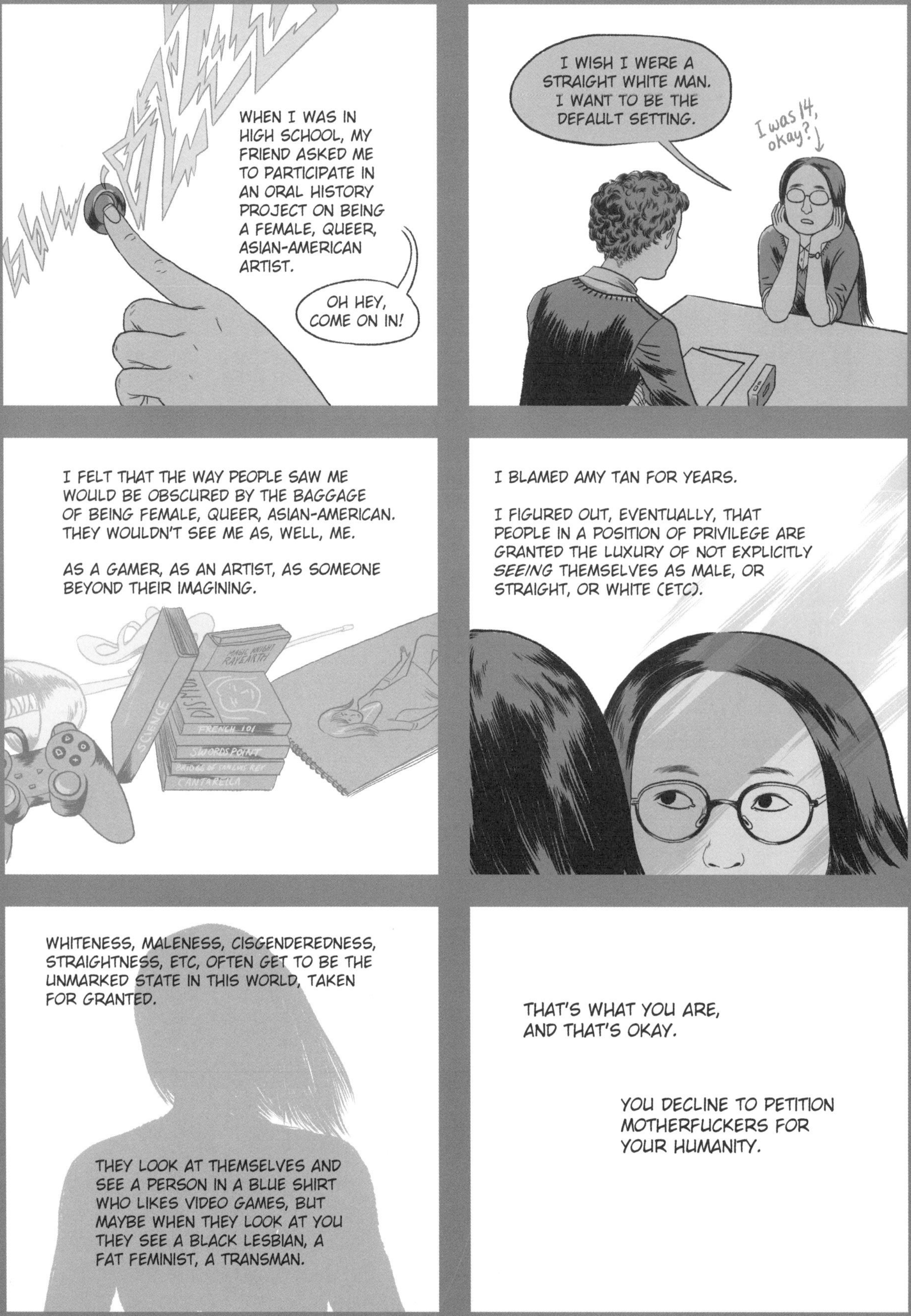
WHEN I WAS IN HIGH SCHOOL, MY FRIEND ASKED ME TO PARTICIPATE IN AN ORAL HISTORY PROJECT ON BEING A FEMALE, QUEER, ASIAN-AMERICAN ARTIST.
OH HEY, COME ON IN!
I WISH I WERE A STRAIGHT WHITE MAN. I WANT TO BE THE DEFAULT SETTING.
I was 14, okay?
I FELT THAT THE WAY PEOPLE SAW ME WOULD BE OBSCURED BY THE BAGGAGE OF BEING FEMALE, QUEER, ASIAN-AMERICAN. THEY WOULDN'T SEE ME AS, WELL, ME.
AS A GAMER, AS AN ARTIST, AS SOMEONE BEYOND THEIR IMAGINING.
SCIENCE
FRENCH 101
SWORDSPOINT
CANTARELLA
I BLAMED AMY TAN FOR YEARS.
I FIGURED OUT, EVENTUALLY, THAT PEOPLE IN A POSITION OF PRIVILEGE ARE GRANTED THE LUXURY OF NOT EXPLICITLY *SEEING* THEMSELVES AS MALE, OR STRAIGHT, OR WHITE (ETC).
WHITENESS, MALENESS, CISGENDEREDNESS, STRAIGHTNESS, ETC, OFTEN GET TO BE THE UNMARKED STATE IN THIS WORLD, TAKEN FOR GRANTED.
THEY LOOK AT THEMSELVES AND SEE A PERSON IN A BLUE SHIRT WHO LIKES VIDEO GAMES, BUT MAYBE WHEN THEY LOOK AT YOU THEY SEE A BLACK LESBIAN, A FAT FEMINIST, A TRANSMAN.
THAT'S WHAT YOU ARE, AND THAT'S OKAY.
YOU DECLINE TO PETITION MOTHERFUCKERS FOR YOUR HUMANITY.

BUT HAVING EXPERIENCED THIS DEHUMANIZATION DOESN'T AUTOMATICALLY MAKE PEOPLE MORE SYMPATHETIC TO SOMEONE ELSE'S PAIN.

SEXISM IS MORE IMPORTANT!

RACISM IS MORE IMPORTANT!

UH...

OPPRESSION IS NOT, IN AND OF ITSELF, ENNOBLING. GAY MEN ARE NOT FEMINIST BY DEFAULT; WHITE FEMINISTS ARE NOT NECESSARILY AWARE OF RACIAL PRIVILEGE. MY CHINESE-AMERICAN RELATIVES ARE BLATANTLY RACIST, AND I HAD TO BE EDUCATED ON TRANS ISSUES.

AND THE WORK OF LISTENING IS HARD AND OFTEN HUMILIATING.

ONLINE, THE FEMINIST MOVEMENT IS ONE PART OF AN INTERSECTIONAL APPROACH TAKING INTO ACCOUNT RACE, GENDER IDENTITY, ORIENTATION, ABILITY, CLASS, BODY SHAPE, ETC,

YOU MIGHT FIND PLENTY TO DISAGREE WITH, BUT YOU'LL ALSO FIND IDEAS THAT RESONATE WITH YOU.

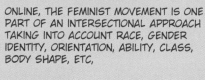

I READ A LOT OF TA-NEHISI COATES, EVEN THOUGH HE STUMBLES SOMETIMES ON FEMINIST ISSUES (AND APOLOGIZES AND DOESN'T GET DEFENSIVE). I BORROWED "DECLINE ALL OFFERS TO PETITION MOTHERFUCKERS FOR MY HUMANITY" AND "OPPRESSION IS NOT ENNOBLING" FROM HIS BLOG, FYI.

THERE ARE PLENTY OF BLOGS FOCUSED ON THE SUBJECT OF SOCIAL JUSTICE. CHECK AROUND, DIG IN.

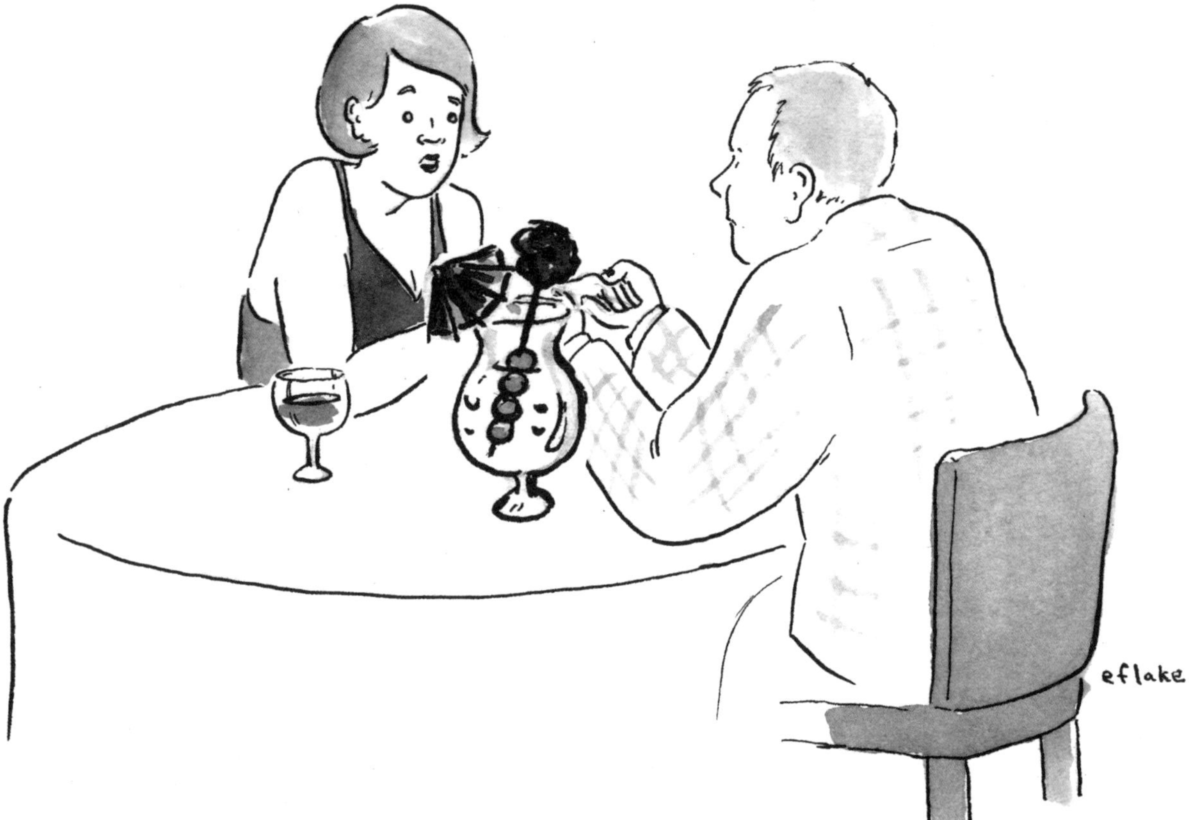
eflake

"IT'S NOT SO MUCH THAT YOU DRINK, IT'S WHAT YOU DRINK."

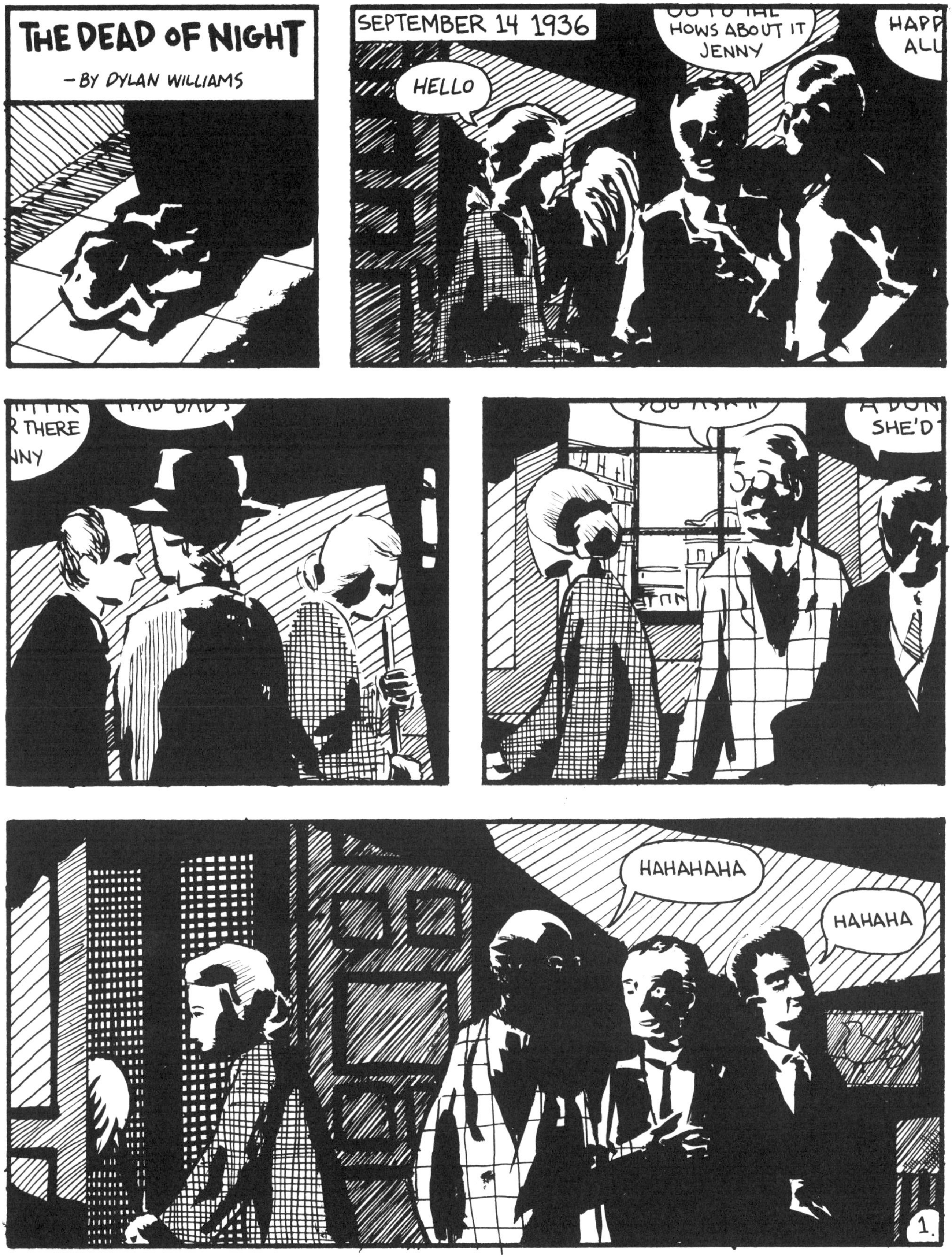
THE DEAD OF NIGHT
- BY DYLAN WILLIAMS
SEPTEMBER 14 1936
HELLO
HOWS ABOUT IT
JENNY
SHE'D
HAHAHAHA
HAHAHA
1.

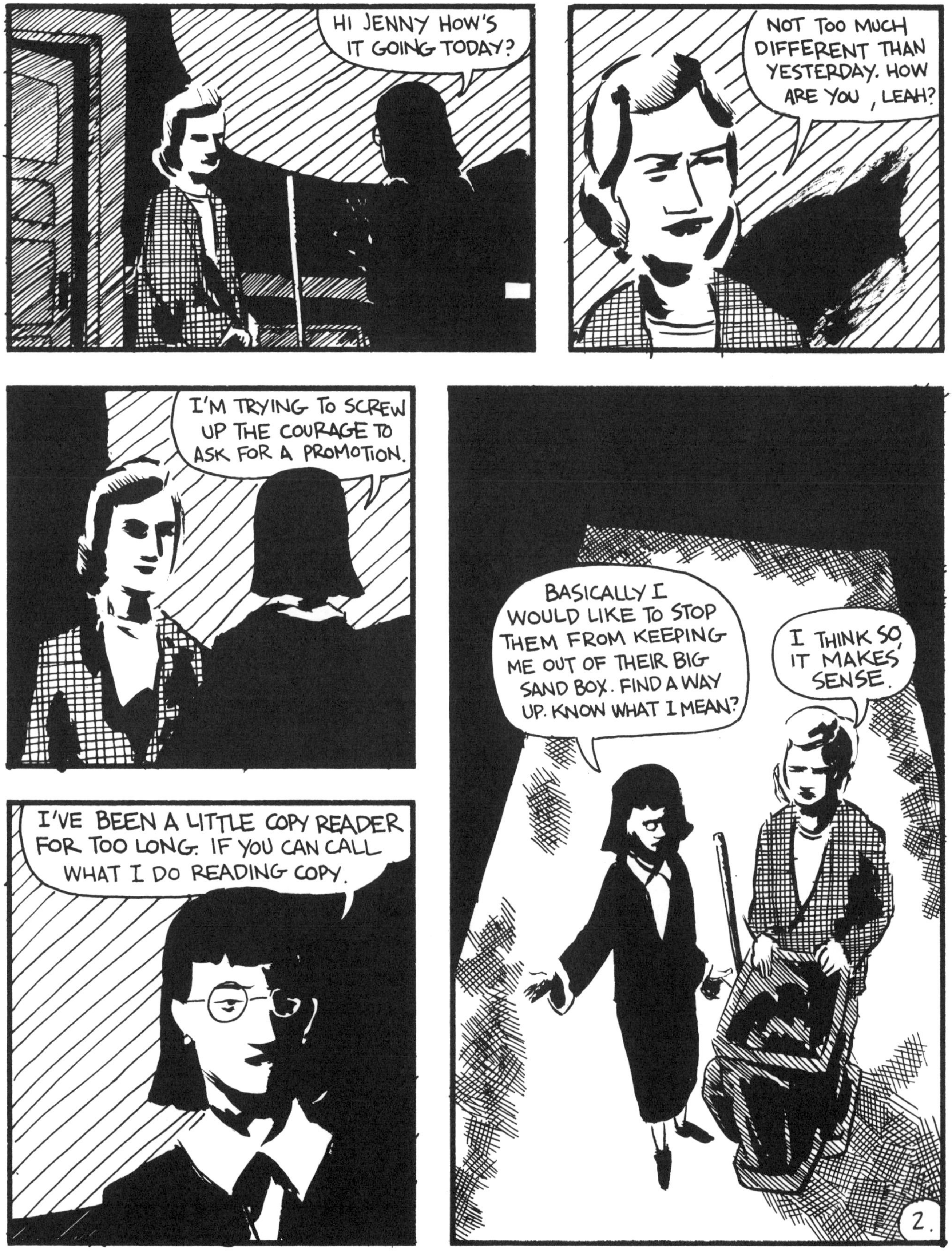
HI JENNY HOW'S IT GOING TODAY?
NOT TOO MUCH DIFFERENT THAN YESTERDAY. HOW ARE YOU, LEAH?
I'M TRYING TO SCREW UP THE COURAGE TO ASK FOR A PROMOTION.
I'VE BEEN A LITTLE COPY READER FOR TOO LONG. IF YOU CAN CALL WHAT I DO READING COPY.
BASICALLY I WOULD LIKE TO STOP THEM FROM KEEPING ME OUT OF THEIR BIG SAND BOX. FIND A WAY UP. KNOW WHAT I MEAN?
I THINK SO, IT MAKES SENSE.
2.

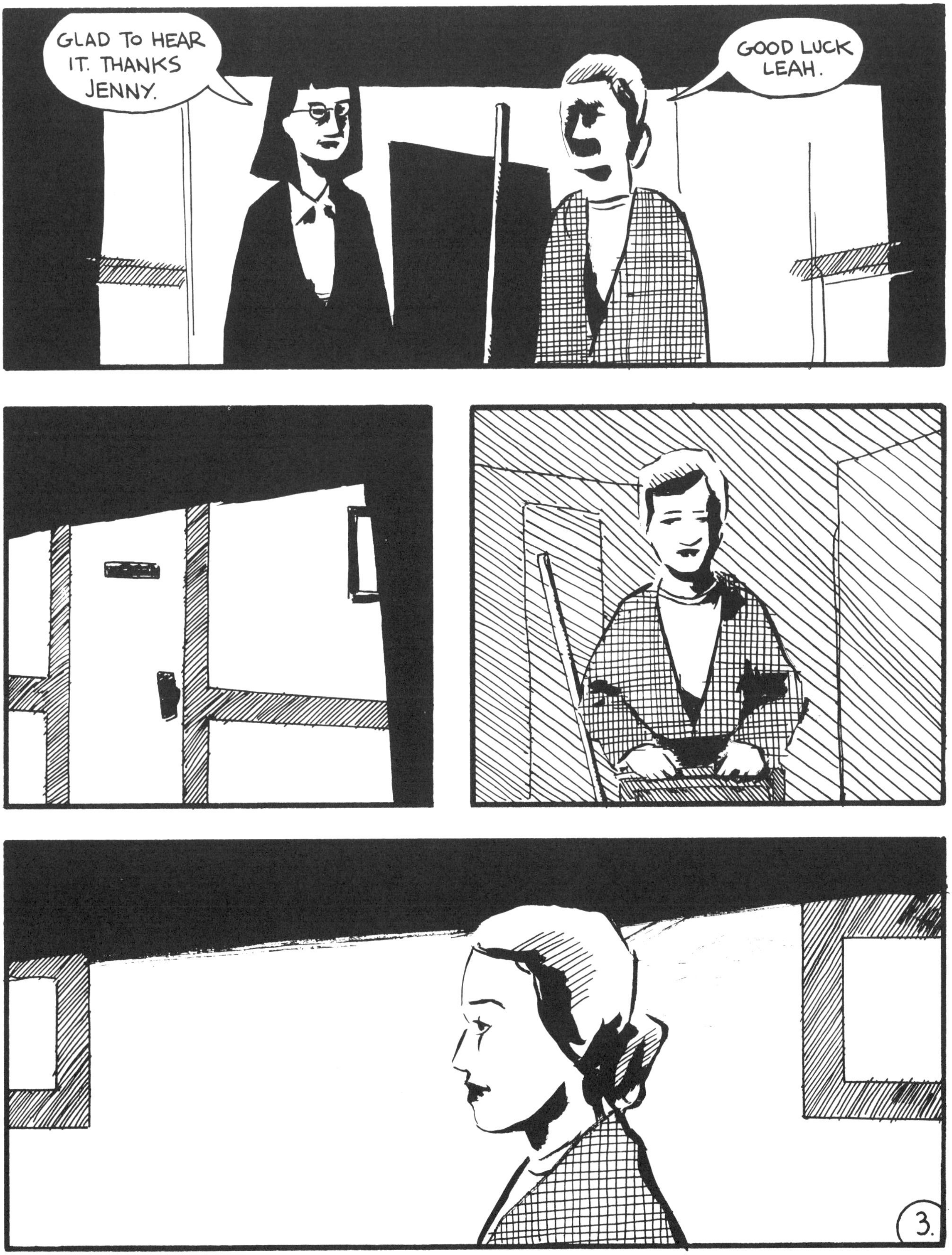
GLAD TO HEAR IT. THANKS JENNY.
GOOD LUCK LEAH.
3.

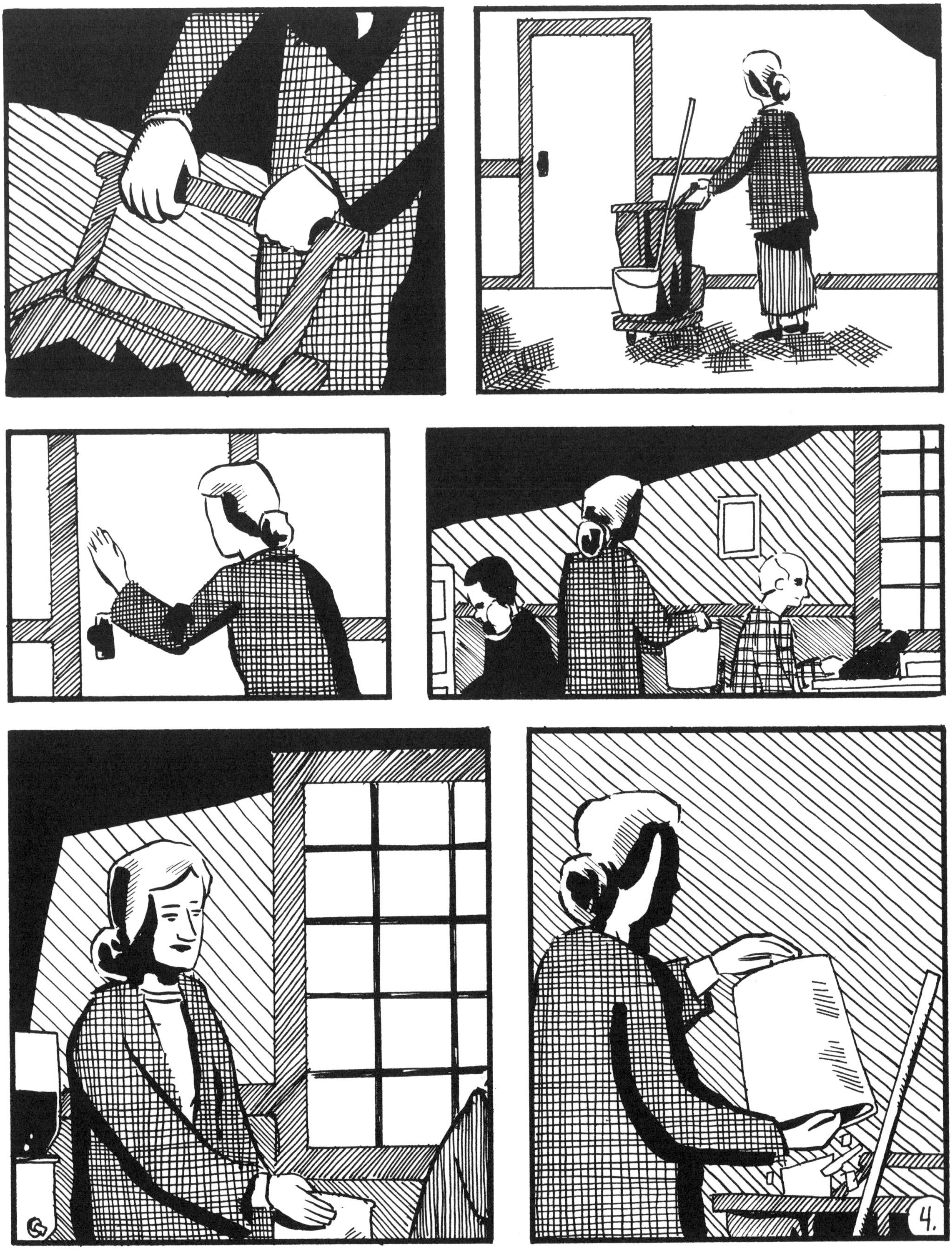
4.

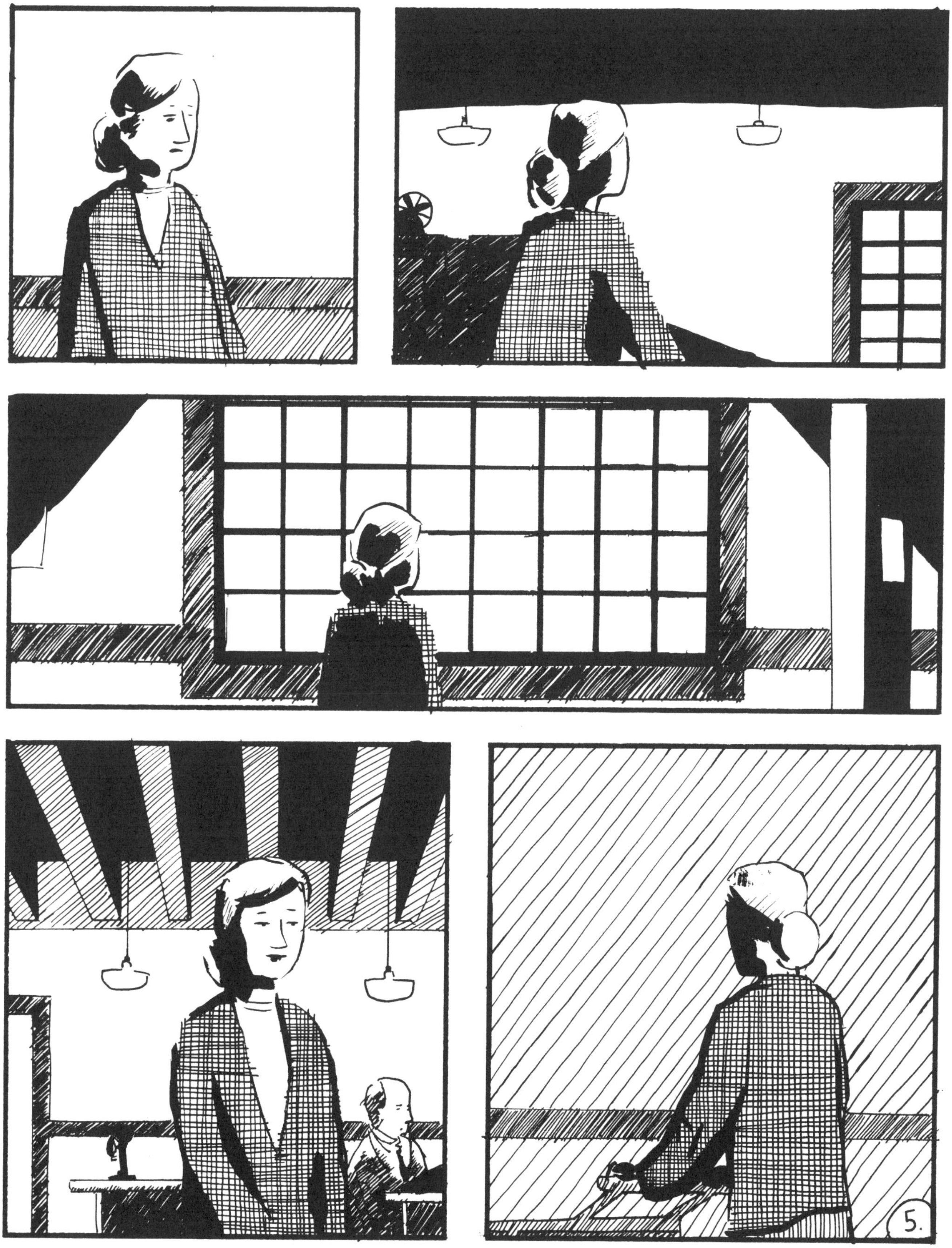
5.

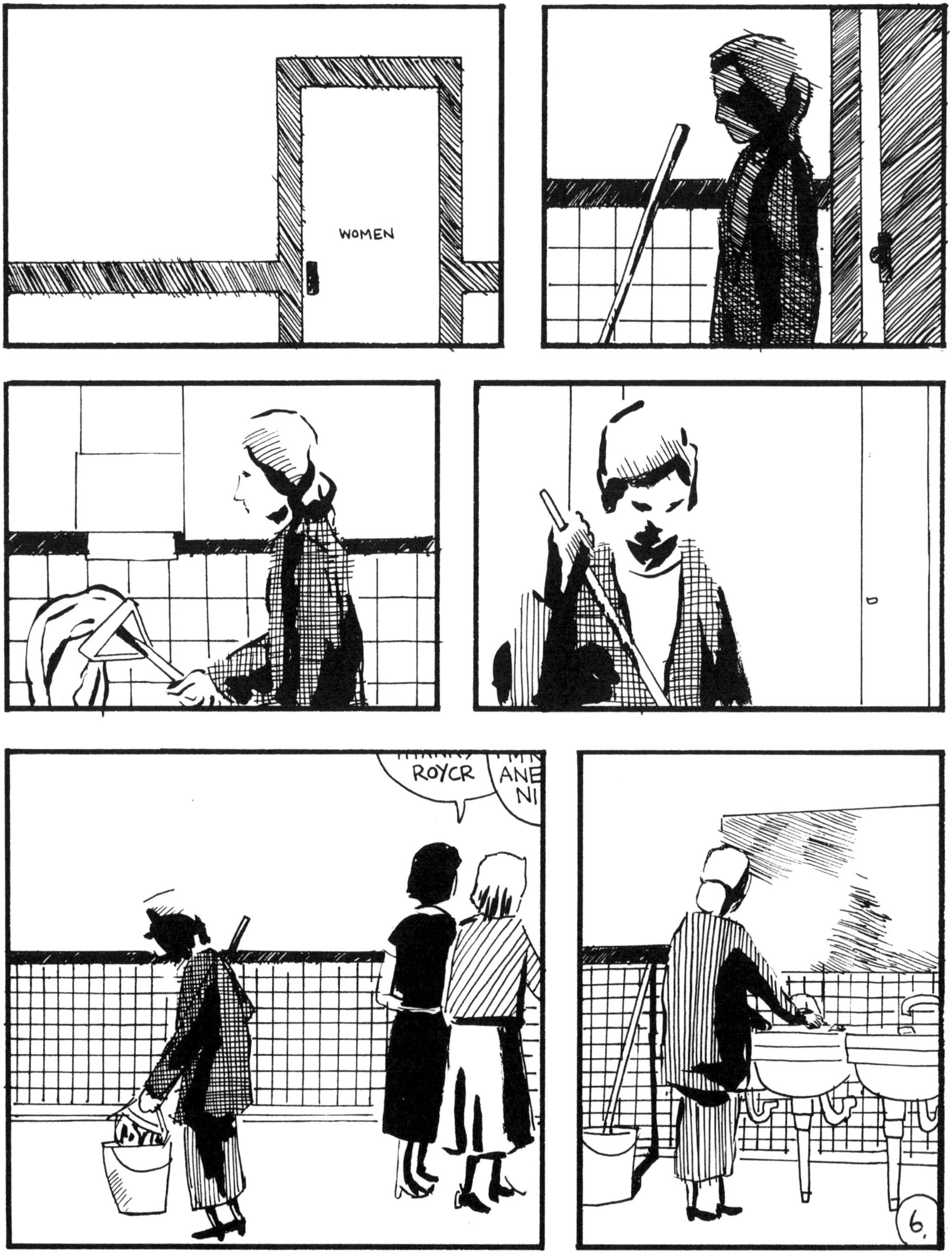
WOMEN
ROYCR

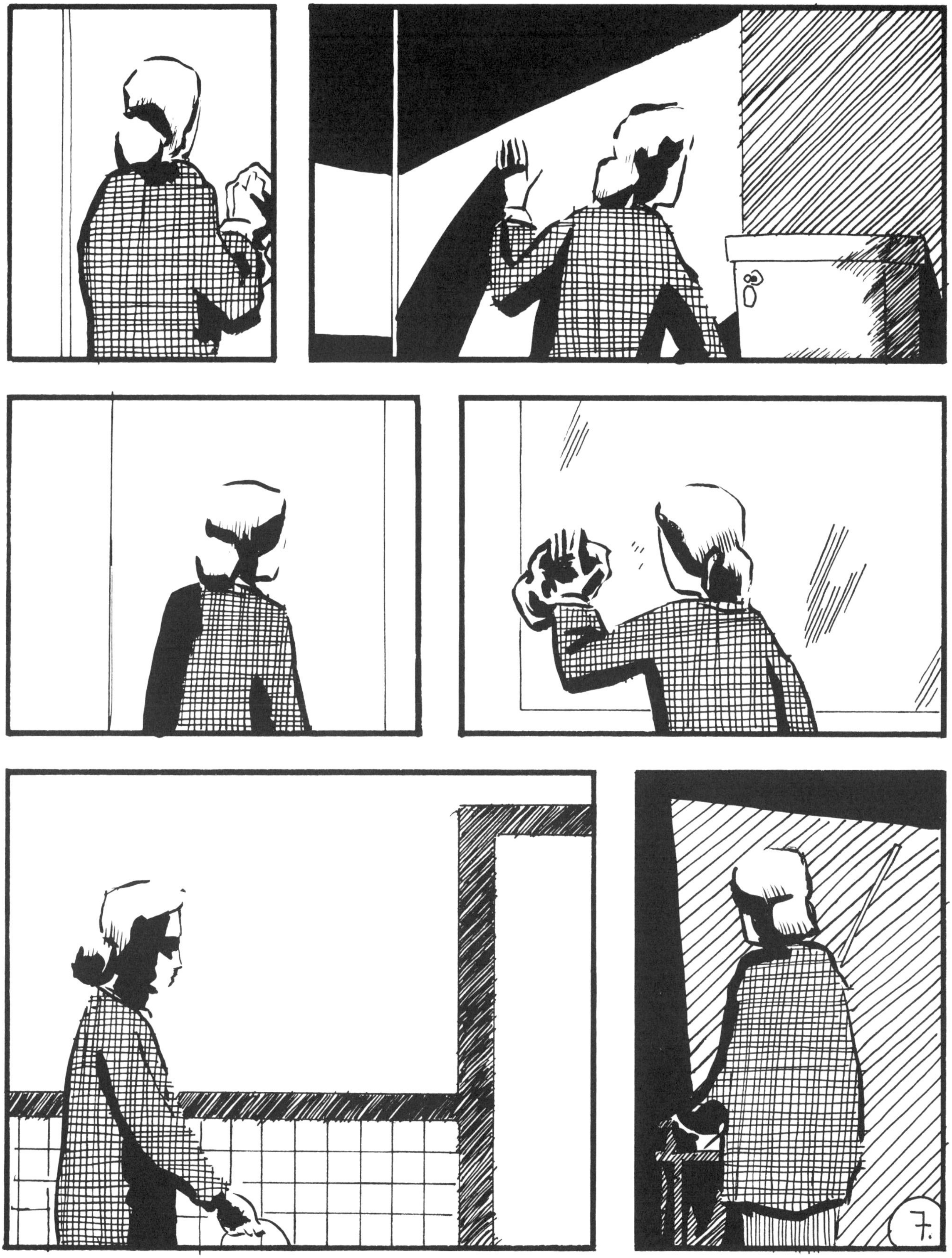
7.

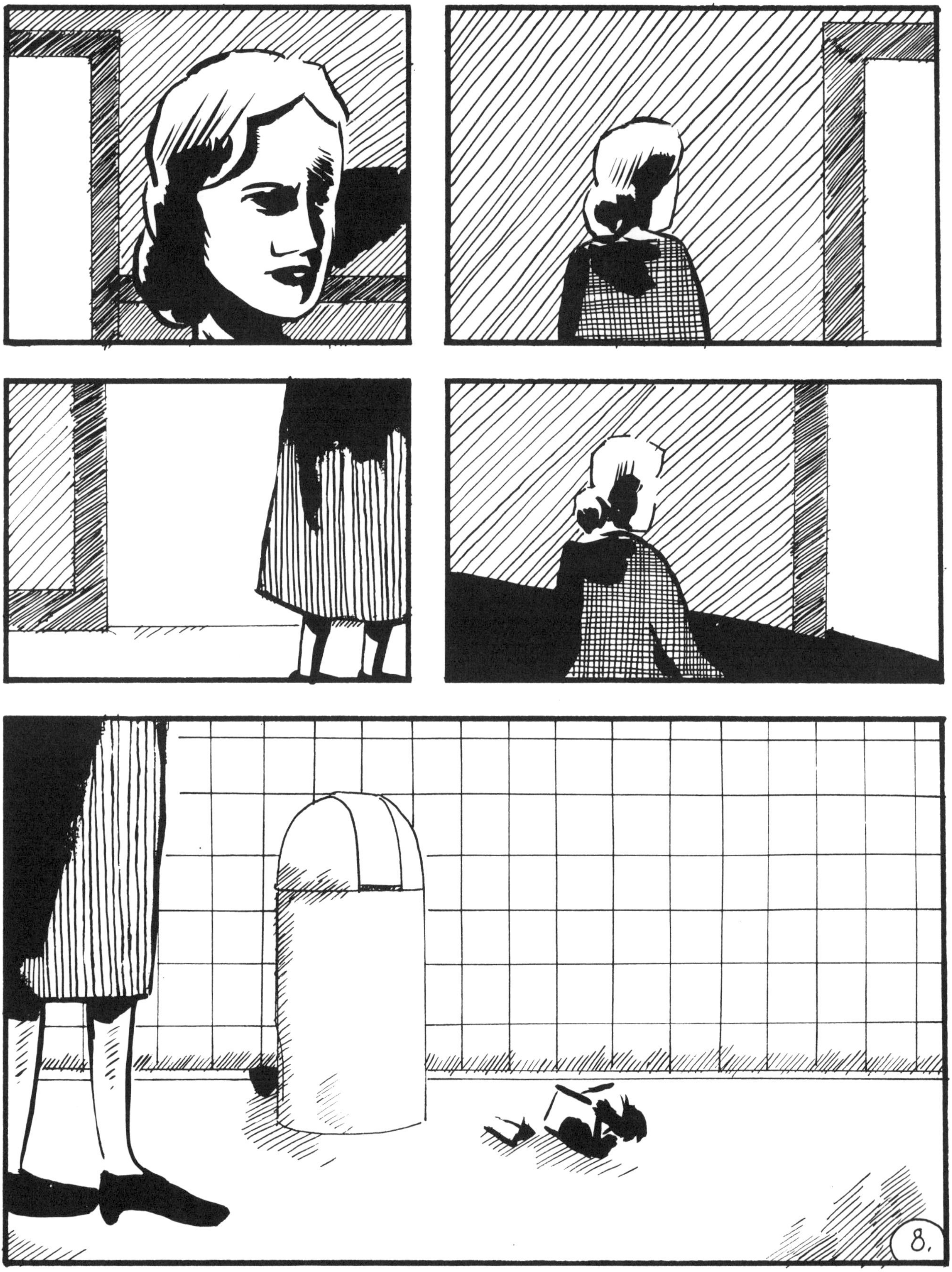
8.

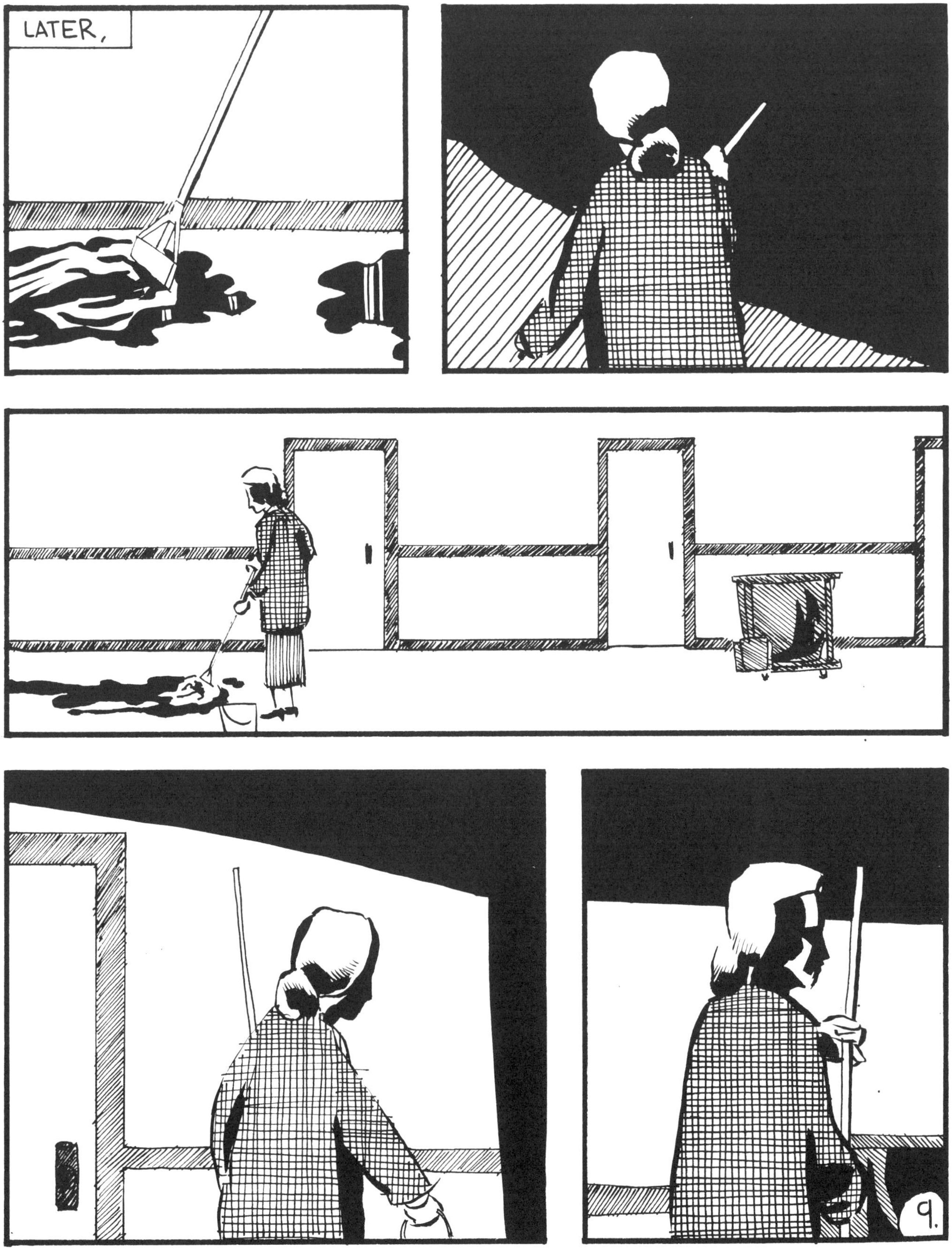
LATER,
9.

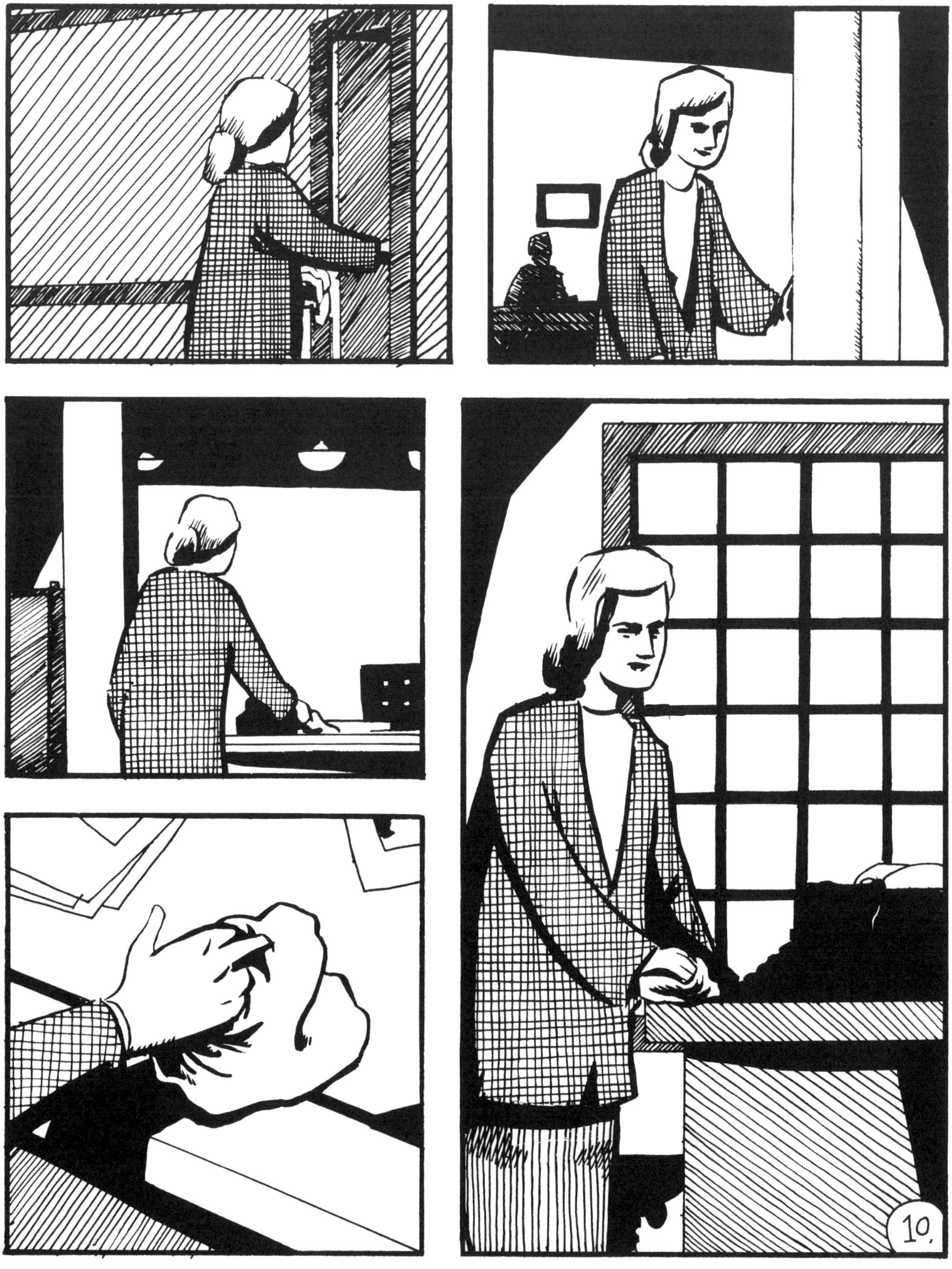
10.

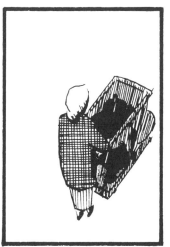

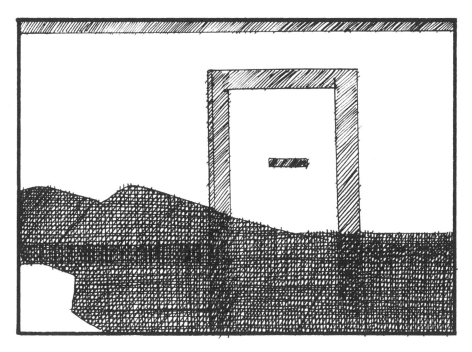

11.

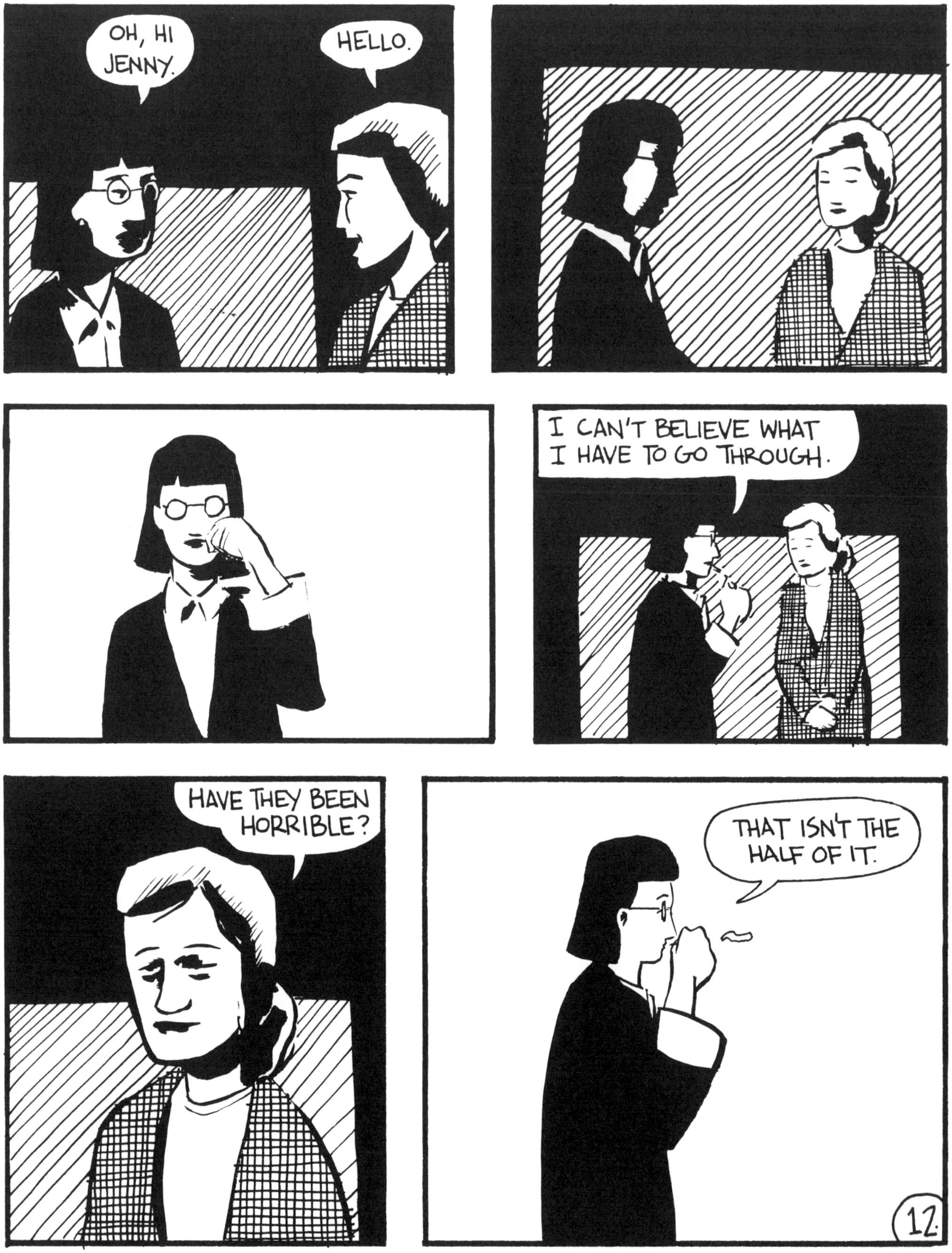
OH, HI JENNY.
HELLO.
I CAN'T BELIEVE WHAT I HAVE TO GO THROUGH.
HAVE THEY BEEN HORRIBLE?
THAT ISN'T THE HALF OF IT.
12.

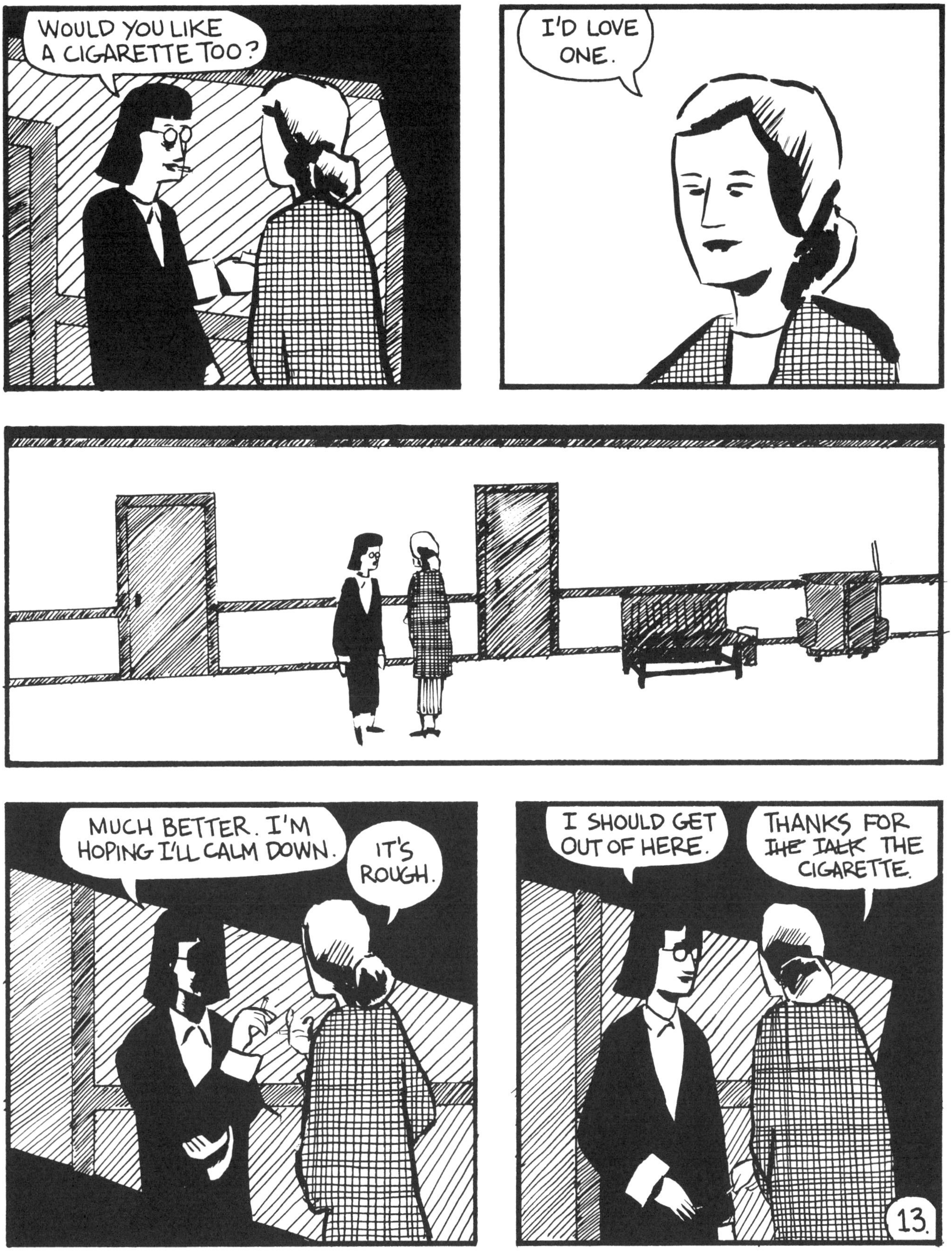
WOULD YOU LIKE A CIGARETTE TOO?
I'D LOVE ONE.
MUCH BETTER. I'M HOPING I'LL CALM DOWN.
IT'S ROUGH.
I SHOULD GET OUT OF HERE.
THANKS FOR ~~THE TALK~~ THE CIGARETTE.
13.

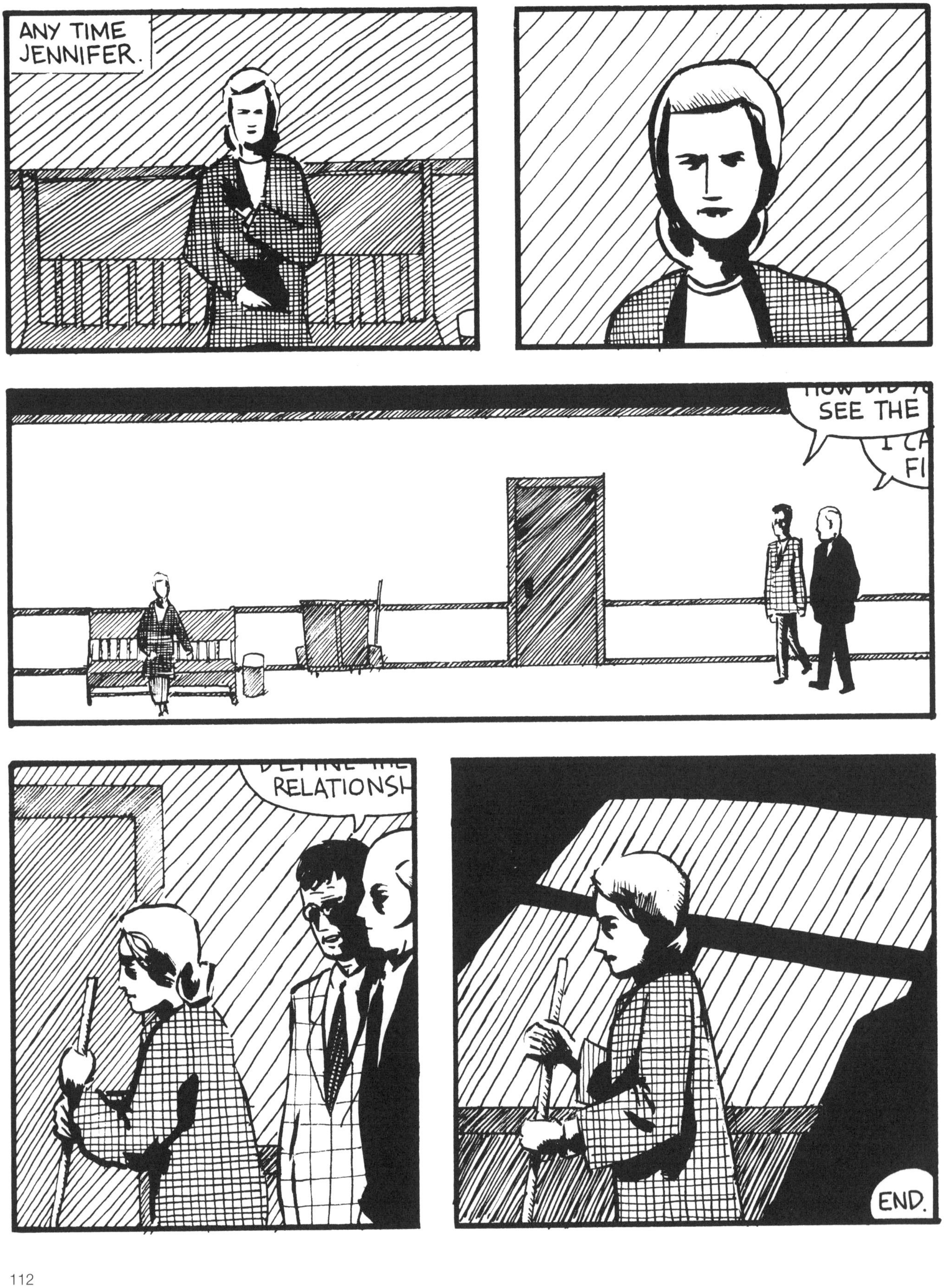
ANY TIME JENNIFER.
SEE THE
RELATIONSH
END.

# SKADI'S WOLVES

BY SARAH OLEKSYK

BEING A CARTOONIST, I'M A VISUAL THINKER. I USE SYMBOLS AND IMAGES AS MNEMONIC DEVICES, ESPECIALLY WHEN I'M TRYING TO MAKE CHANGES IN MY LIFE.

HEY LADY!

HEY!

OOH, SHE AIN'T LISTENING!

HEY!

TAP TAP TAP TAP TAP

I'VE USED THIS TECHNIQUE FOR ALL SORTS OF SITUATIONS: TO REMEMBER THINGS, TO CHEER MYSELF UP, TO CALM MYSELF DOWN. BUT IT'S NOT CALMNESS I NEED MOST THESE DAYS— IT'S STRENGTH. FEMALE STRENGTH.

I BEGAN TO SEEK A WAY TO VISUALIZE MY OWN POWER WITH A SYMBOL THAT SPOKE TO ME.

AND THEN I FOUND IT.

MY PERFECT FEMINIST ICON OF POWER IS A WARRIOR.
A POWERFUL FEMALE, ABLE TO FIGHT, COMMAND,
TRAVEL ALONE AND MEET ANY CHALLENGE.
THERE ARE SO FEW WOMEN IN OUR CULTURE
WHO HAVE BECOME SYMBOLIC OF POWER,
EVEN FEWER WHO HAVE DONE IT INDEPEN-
DENTLY OF THEIR ASSOCIATIONS WITH
POWERFUL MEN. FOR THE ANSWER TO
MY SEARCH, I TURNED TO A MYTHOLOGY
I'D LONG BEEN FASCINATED BY—
ONE THAT SPOKE POWERFULLY TO ME—
THAT OF THE NORSE. AND IN ITS
LEGENDS I DISCOVERED:

# SKÅDI

## NORSE GODDESS OF WINTER

A JÖTUNN, OR FROST GIANT, SHE ROAMS
THE NORTHERNMOST MOUNTAIN SIDES
OF THE SCANDINAVIAN PENINSULA,
ARMED WITH BOW AND ARROWS AND
FLANKED BY HER LOYAL WOLVES.
TO AVENGE HER MURDERED FATHER,
SHE DEMANDED A HUSBAND FROM
THE GODS — BUT LEFT HIM AND HIS
SEASIDE HOME TO ONCE AGAIN
LIVE ALONE IN THE MOUNTAINS.

NORSE LEGENDS CONTAINED AN EQUAL MIX OF
POWER THROUGH MALE AND FEMALE DIVINITIES,
AND THOSE SURROUNDING SKÅDI ESPECIALLY HAD
ELEMENTS OF GENDER ROLE REVERSAL, WHICH
CHARMED AND INTRIGUED ME. THE MORE I
LEARNED ABOUT HER, THE MORE I LIKED HER.

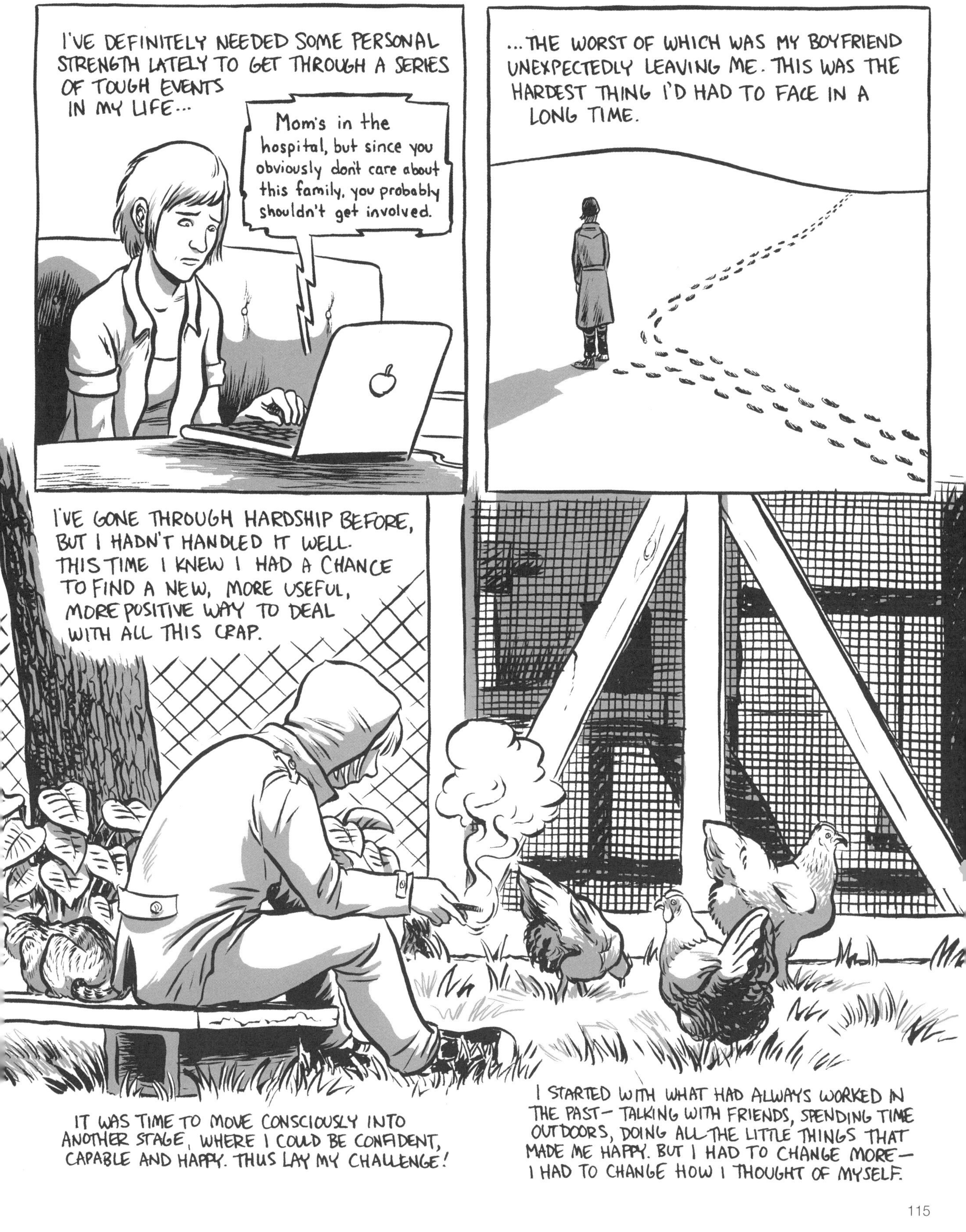
I'VE DEFINITELY NEEDED SOME PERSONAL STRENGTH LATELY TO GET THROUGH A SERIES OF TOUGH EVENTS IN MY LIFE...
Mom's in the hospital, but since you obviously don't care about this family, you probably shouldn't get involved.
...THE WORST OF WHICH WAS MY BOYFRIEND UNEXPECTEDLY LEAVING ME. THIS WAS THE HARDEST THING I'D HAD TO FACE IN A LONG TIME.
I'VE GONE THROUGH HARDSHIP BEFORE, BUT I HADN'T HANDLED IT WELL. THIS TIME I KNEW I HAD A CHANCE TO FIND A NEW, MORE USEFUL, MORE POSITIVE WAY TO DEAL WITH ALL THIS CRAP.
IT WAS TIME TO MOVE CONSCIOUSLY INTO ANOTHER STAGE, WHERE I COULD BE CONFIDENT, CAPABLE AND HAPPY. THUS LAY MY CHALLENGE!
I STARTED WITH WHAT HAD ALWAYS WORKED IN THE PAST- TALKING WITH FRIENDS, SPENDING TIME OUTDOORS, DOING ALL THE LITTLE THINGS THAT MADE ME HAPPY. BUT I HAD TO CHANGE MORE- I HAD TO CHANGE HOW I THOUGHT OF MYSELF.

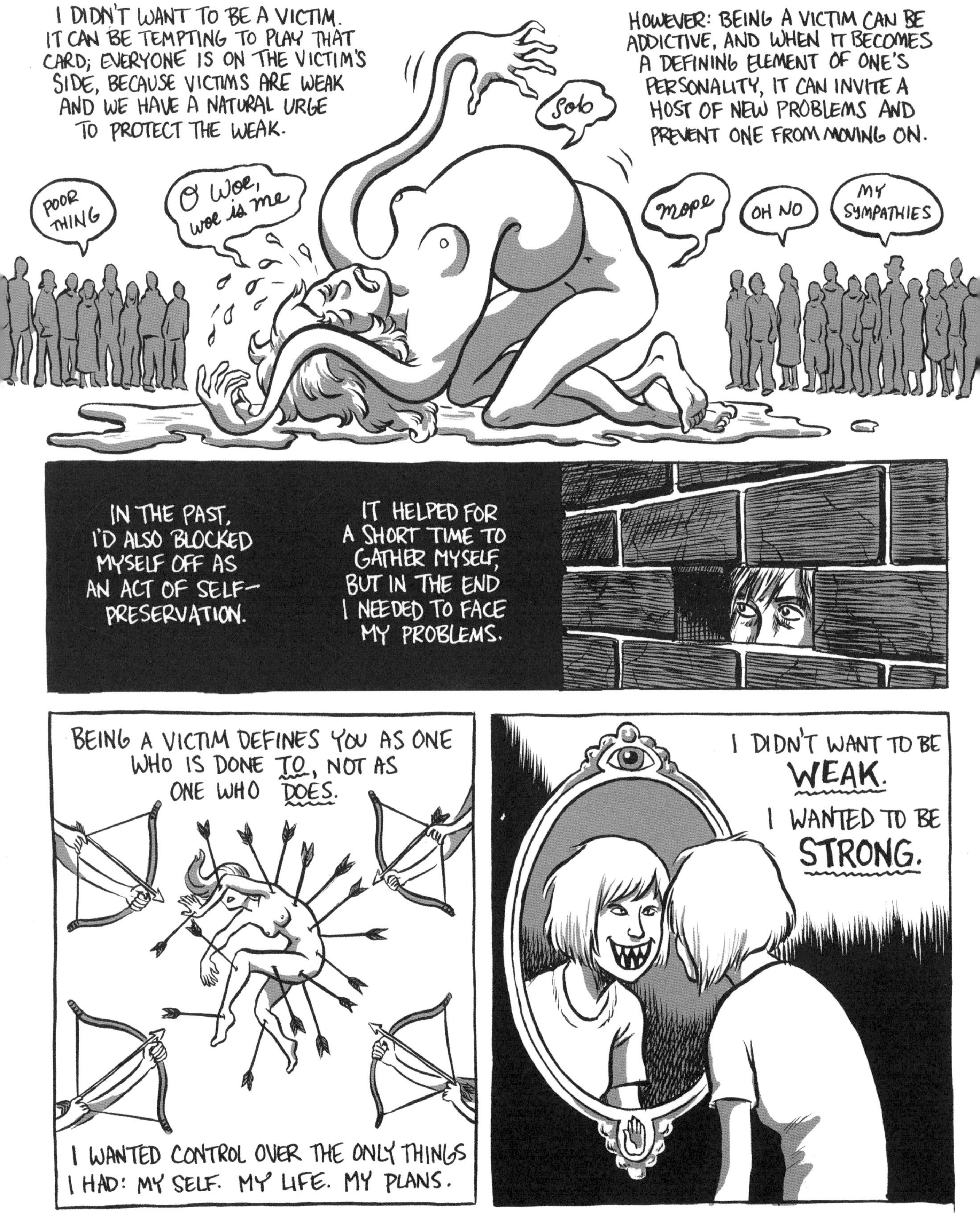
I DIDN'T WANT TO BE A VICTIM. IT CAN BE TEMPTING TO PLAY THAT CARD; EVERYONE IS ON THE VICTIM'S SIDE, BECAUSE VICTIMS ARE WEAK AND WE HAVE A NATURAL URGE TO PROTECT THE WEAK.
Sob
HOWEVER: BEING A VICTIM CAN BE ADDICTIVE, AND WHEN IT BECOMES A DEFINING ELEMENT OF ONE'S PERSONALITY, IT CAN INVITE A HOST OF NEW PROBLEMS AND PREVENT ONE FROM MOVING ON.
POOR THING
O Woe, woe is me
mope
OH NO
MY SYMPATHIES
IN THE PAST, I'D ALSO BLOCKED MYSELF OFF AS AN ACT OF SELF-PRESERVATION.
IT HELPED FOR A SHORT TIME TO GATHER MYSELF, BUT IN THE END I NEEDED TO FACE MY PROBLEMS.
BEING A VICTIM DEFINES YOU AS ONE WHO IS DONE TO, NOT AS ONE WHO DOES.
I WANTED CONTROL OVER THE ONLY THINGS I HAD: MY SELF. MY LIFE. MY PLANS.
I DIDN'T WANT TO BE WEAK.
I WANTED TO BE STRONG.

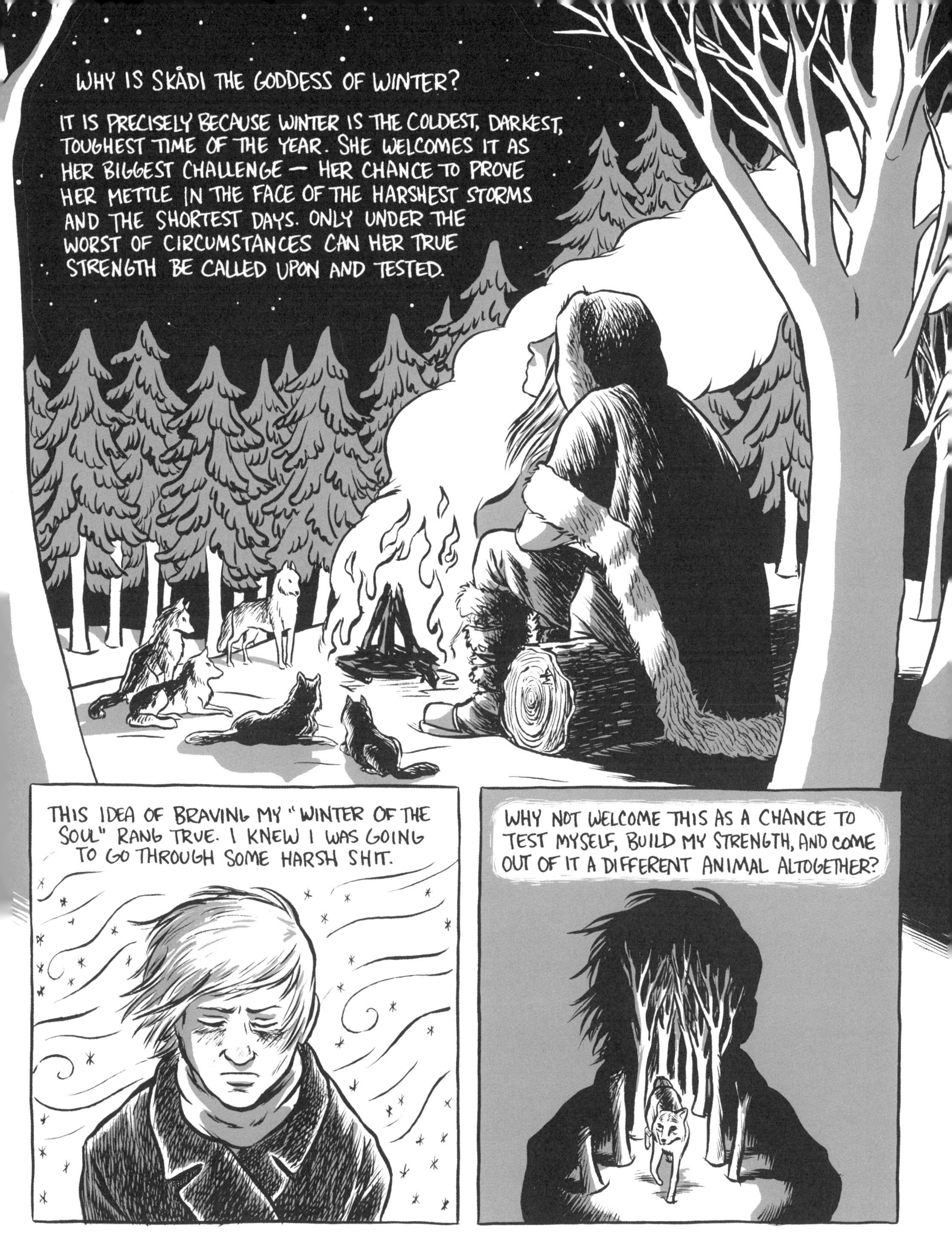
WHY IS SKÅDI THE GODDESS OF WINTER?
IT IS PRECISELY BECAUSE WINTER IS THE COLDEST, DARKEST, TOUGHEST TIME OF THE YEAR. SHE WELCOMES IT AS HER BIGGEST CHALLENGE — HER CHANCE TO PROVE HER METTLE IN THE FACE OF THE HARSHEST STORMS AND THE SHORTEST DAYS. ONLY UNDER THE WORST OF CIRCUMSTANCES CAN HER TRUE STRENGTH BE CALLED UPON AND TESTED.
THIS IDEA OF BRAVING MY "WINTER OF THE SOUL" RANG TRUE. I KNEW I WAS GOING TO GO THROUGH SOME HARSH SHIT.
WHY NOT WELCOME THIS AS A CHANCE TO TEST MYSELF, BUILD MY STRENGTH, AND COME OUT OF IT A DIFFERENT ANIMAL ALTOGETHER?

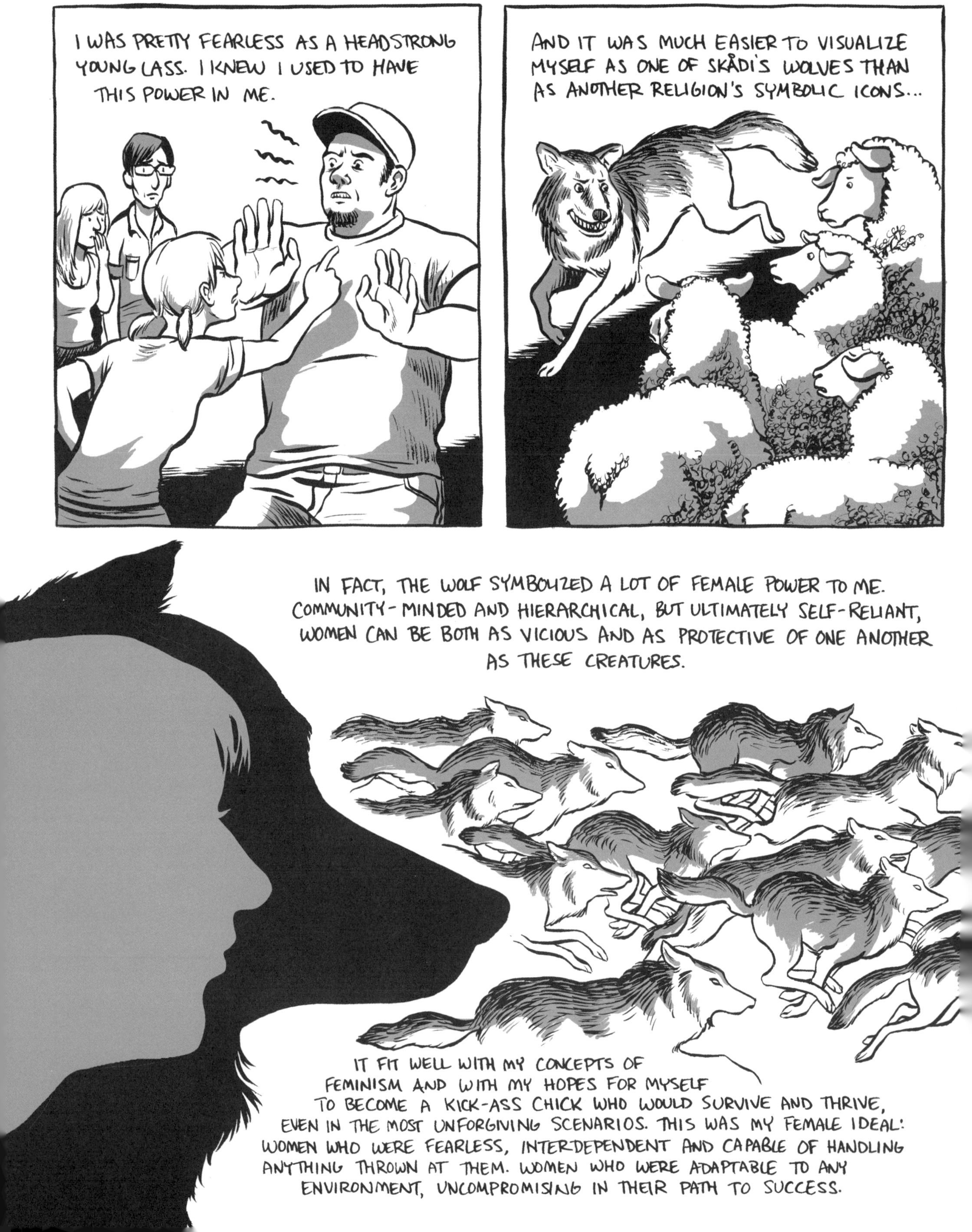
I WAS PRETTY FEARLESS AS A HEADSTRONG YOUNG LASS. I KNEW I USED TO HAVE THIS POWER IN ME.
AND IT WAS MUCH EASIER TO VISUALIZE MYSELF AS ONE OF SKÅDI'S WOLVES THAN AS ANOTHER RELIGION'S SYMBOLIC ICONS...
IN FACT, THE WOLF SYMBOLIZED A LOT OF FEMALE POWER TO ME. COMMUNITY-MINDED AND HIERARCHICAL, BUT ULTIMATELY SELF-RELIANT, WOMEN CAN BE BOTH AS VICIOUS AND AS PROTECTIVE OF ONE ANOTHER AS THESE CREATURES.
IT FIT WELL WITH MY CONCEPTS OF FEMINISM AND WITH MY HOPES FOR MYSELF TO BECOME A KICK-ASS CHICK WHO WOULD SURVIVE AND THRIVE, EVEN IN THE MOST UNFORGIVING SCENARIOS. THIS WAS MY FEMALE IDEAL: WOMEN WHO WERE FEARLESS, INTERDEPENDENT AND CAPABLE OF HANDLING ANYTHING THROWN AT THEM. WOMEN WHO WERE ADAPTABLE TO ANY ENVIRONMENT, UNCOMPROMISING IN THEIR PATH TO SUCCESS.

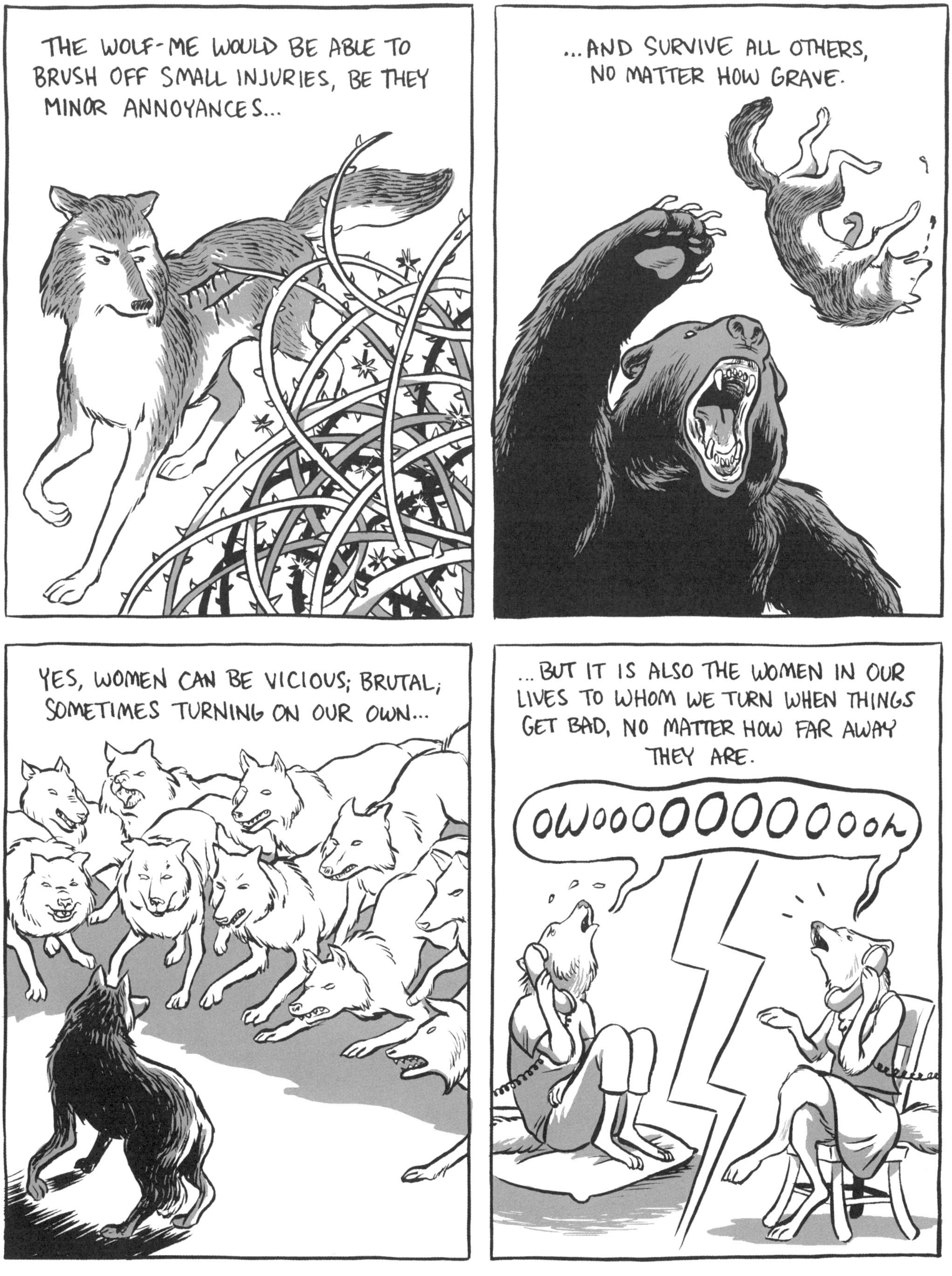
THE WOLF-ME WOULD BE ABLE TO BRUSH OFF SMALL INJURIES, BE THEY MINOR ANNOYANCES...
...AND SURVIVE ALL OTHERS, NO MATTER HOW GRAVE.
YES, WOMEN CAN BE VICIOUS; BRUTAL; SOMETIMES TURNING ON OUR OWN...
...BUT IT IS ALSO THE WOMEN IN OUR LIVES TO WHOM WE TURN WHEN THINGS GET BAD, NO MATTER HOW FAR AWAY THEY ARE.
OWoooOOOOOOooh

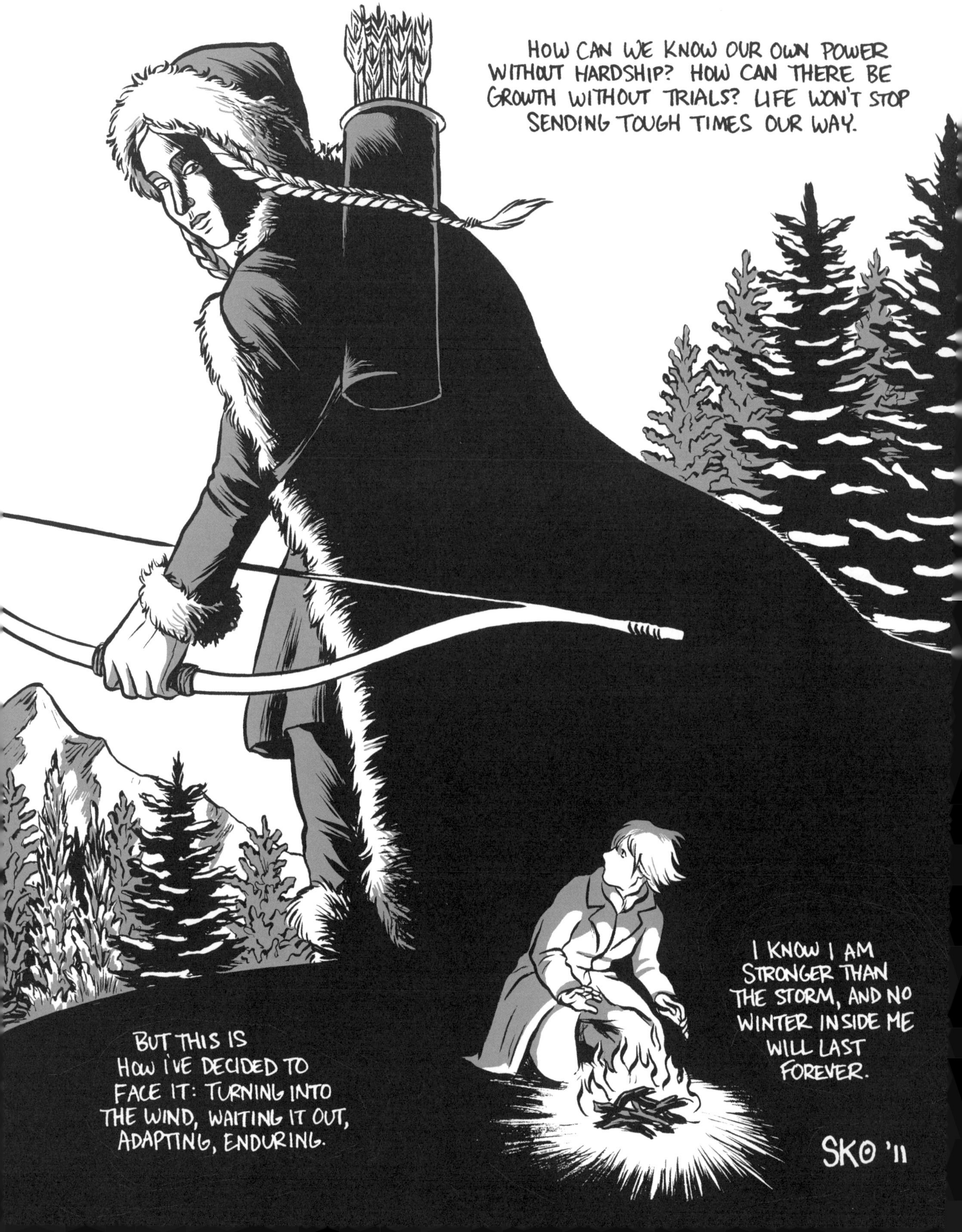
HOW CAN WE KNOW OUR OWN POWER WITHOUT HARDSHIP? HOW CAN THERE BE GROWTH WITHOUT TRIALS? LIFE WON'T STOP SENDING TOUGH TIMES OUR WAY.
BUT THIS IS HOW I'VE DECIDED TO FACE IT: TURNING INTO THE WIND, WAITING IT OUT, ADAPTING, ENDURING.
I KNOW I AM STRONGER THAN THE STORM, AND NO WINTER INSIDE ME WILL LAST FOREVER.
SKO '11

# PROSTITUTES: FOR TEENS

BY JEN WANG

I never thought I'd care so much about what other people think.

A teenage girl becomes madam to a bunch of other teen girl prostitutes, and they join forces with other societal victims to take over the establishment that wronged them.

I thought it was pretty much the best idea, ever. Anyone who thought otherwise was a hater of justice and fun.

Then I started getting the blank stares,

and the polite nods.

I didn't even mention the part where I wanted to write it for a teenage audience.

Prostitution. Not just the world's oldest profession, but one of the most divisive ones. Ask 10 different feminists whether they think it should be legal and you'll get 10 different answers and a bunch of "I don't know"s.

The problem is the subject is so expansive.

The upper-middle class collegiates with their wealthy sugar daddies are very different from...

the internet dominatrix entrepreneurs

the homeless teen drug addicts,

from Cambodian trafficked sex slaves.

One could argue all prostitution supports the exploitation of women, but does that would leave out gay and female clients?

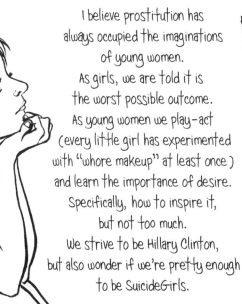

I believe prostitution has always occupied the imaginations of young women.
As girls, we are told it is the worst possible outcome.
As young women we play-act (every little girl has experimented with "whore makeup" at least once) and learn the importance of desire.
Specifically, how to inspire it, but not too much.
We strive to be Hillary Clinton, but also wonder if we're pretty enough to be SuicideGirls.

Being close friends with a self-sufficient prostitute meant a neverending stream of questioning. There always exists a level of mystery, and fantasy.

How much did he pay you?

Was he married?

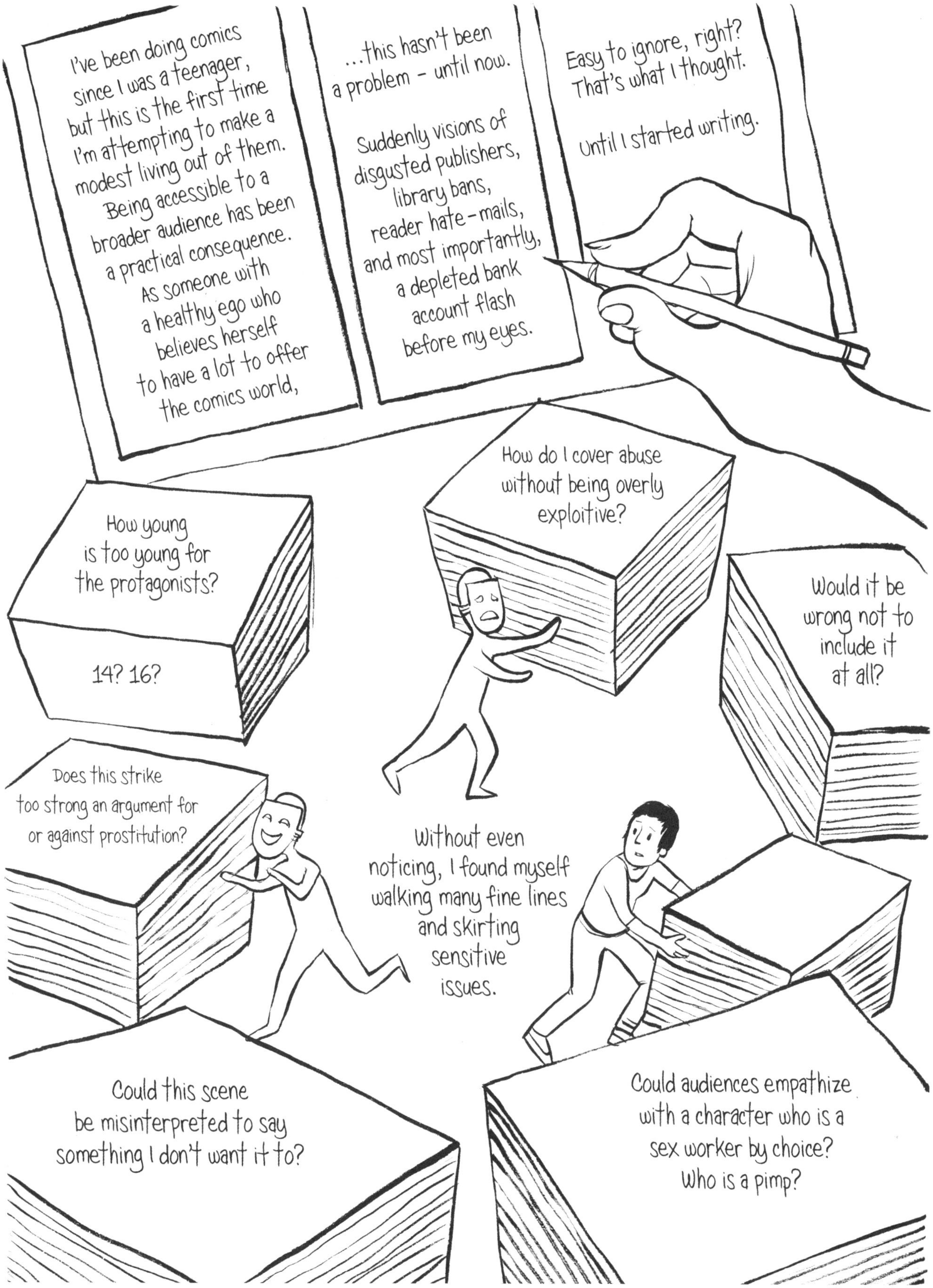
I've been doing comics since I was a teenager, but this is the first time I'm attempting to make a modest living out of them. Being accessible to a broader audience has been a practical consequence. As someone with a healthy ego who believes herself to have a lot to offer the comics world,
...this hasn't been a problem – until now.
Suddenly visions of disgusted publishers, library bans, reader hate-mails, and most importantly, a depleted bank account flash before my eyes.
Easy to ignore, right? That's what I thought.
Until I started writing.
How do I cover abuse without being overly exploitive?
How young is too young for the protagonists?
14? 16?
Would it be wrong not to include it at all?
Does this strike too strong an argument for or against prostitution?
Without even noticing, I found myself walking many fine lines and skirting sensitive issues.
Could this scene be misinterpreted to say something I don't want it to?
Could audiences empathize with a character who is a sex worker by choice? Who is a pimp?

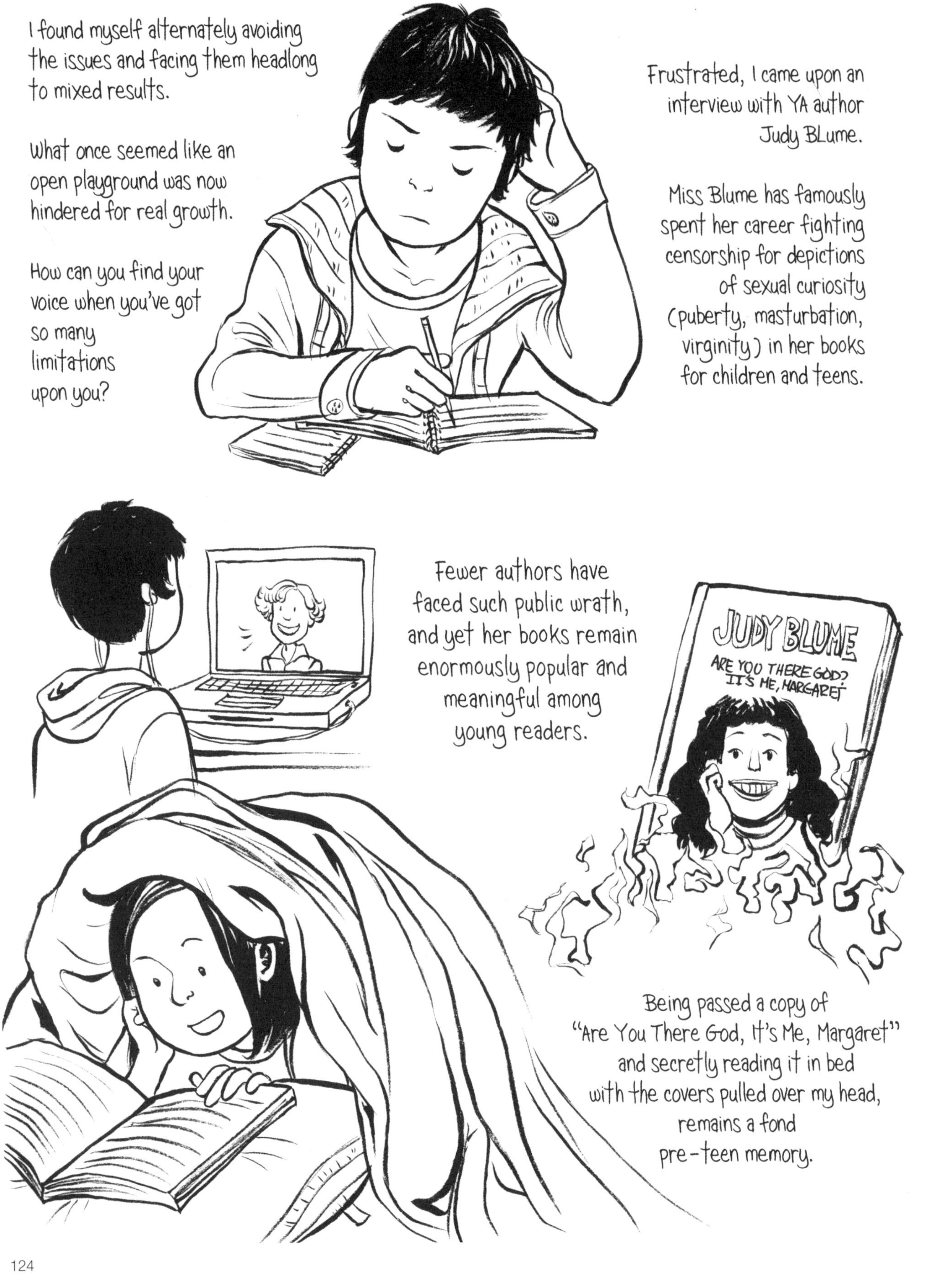
I found myself alternately avoiding the issues and facing them headlong to mixed results.
What once seemed like an open playground was now hindered for real growth.
How can you find your voice when you've got so many limitations upon you?
Frustrated, I came upon an interview with YA author Judy BLume.
Miss Blume has famously spent her career fighting censorship for depictions of sexual curiosity (puberty, masturbation, virginity) in her books for children and teens.
Fewer authors have faced such public wrath, and yet her books remain enormously popular and meaningful among young readers.
JUDY BLUME
ARE YOU THERE GOD? IT'S ME, MARGARET
Being passed a copy of "Are You There God, It's Me, Margaret" and secretly reading it in bed with the covers pulled over my head, remains a fond pre-teen memory.

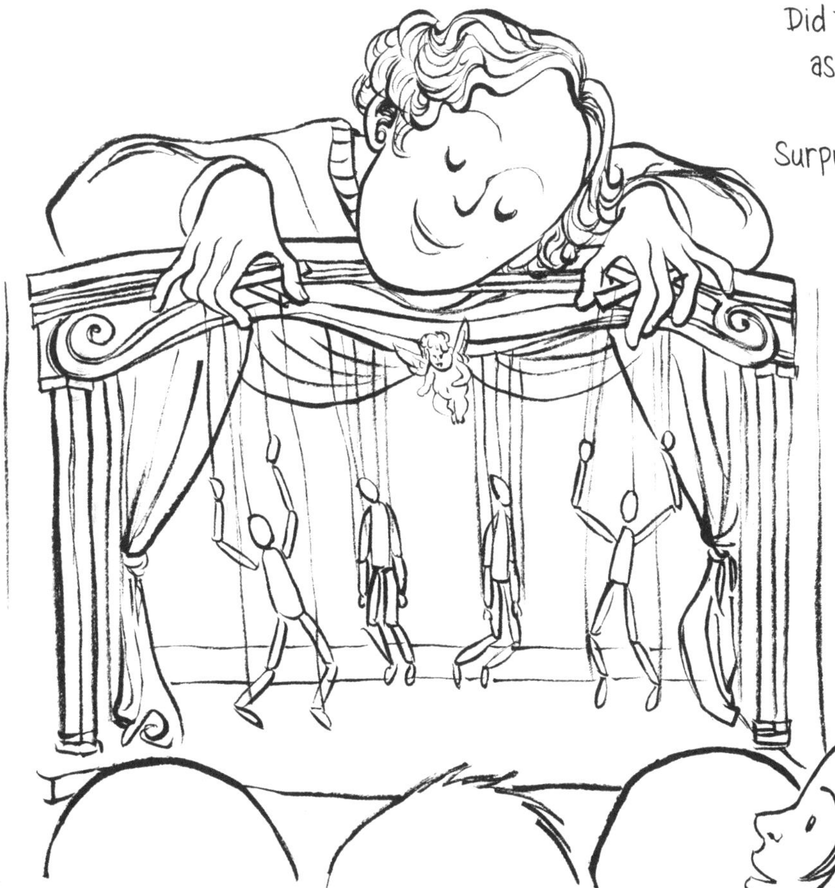

Did the author, the interviewer asked, set out with an agenda when she wrote her books? Surprisingly, the answer was no. The one time she did, the writing felt forced and stilted.

The key, she said, was to focus on drafting empathetic characters and telling an engaging story. The audience isn't interested in reading a lecture.

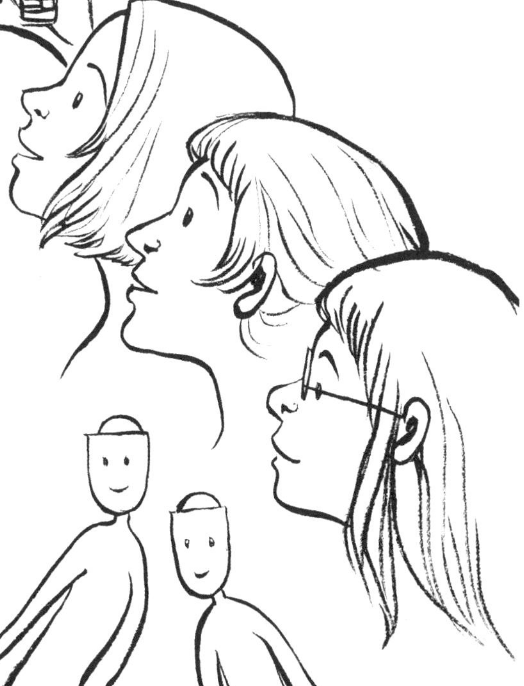

Clouded by pressure over subject matter, I'd completely ignored the most neutralizing feature in fiction, the ability to live in a character's head. If people could come to love Hannibal Lector, Patrick Bateman, and Humbert Humbert, did I really have that much to worry about?

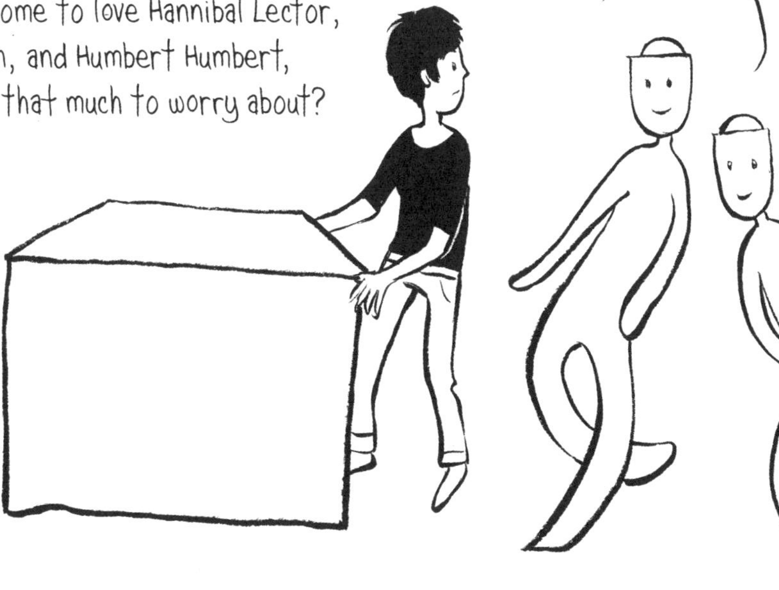

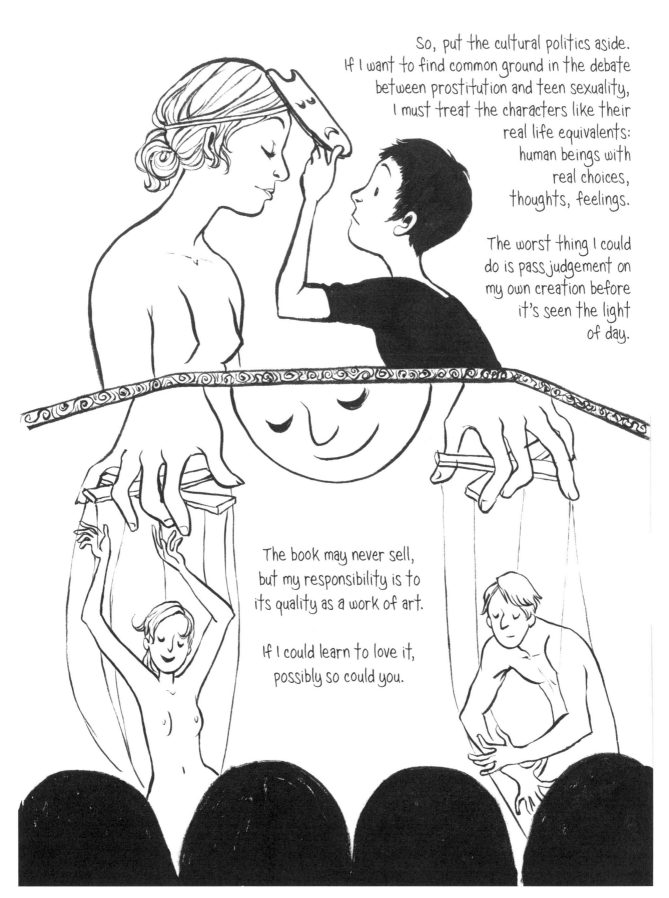

So, put the cultural politics aside. If I want to find common ground in the debate between prostitution and teen sexuality, I must treat the characters like their real life equivalents: human beings with real choices, thoughts, feelings.

The worst thing I could do is pass judgement on my own creation before it's seen the light of day.

The book may never sell, but my responsibility is to its quality as a work of art.

If I could learn to love it, possibly so could you.

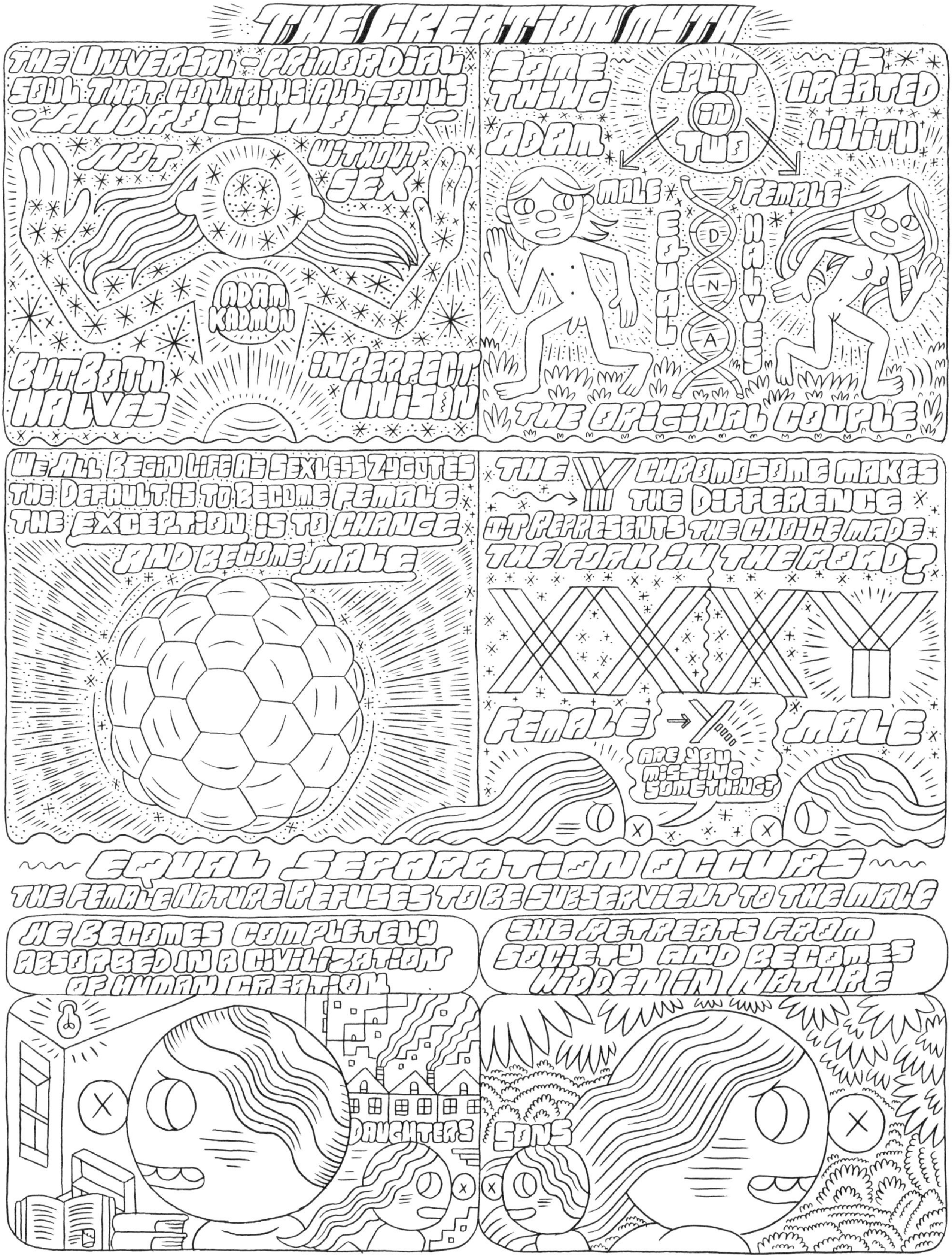
THE CREATION MYTH
THE UNIVERSAL - PRIMORDIAL SOUL THAT CONTAINS ALL SOULS - ANDROGYNOUS -
NOT WITHOUT SEX
ADAM KADMON
BUT BOTH HALVES
IN PERFECT UNISON
SAME THING
SPLIT IN TWO
IS CREATED
ADAM
LILITH
MALE
FEMALE
EQUAL
HALVES
D N A
THE ORIGINAL COUPLE
WE ALL BEGIN LIFE AS SEXLESS ZYGOTES THE DEFAULT IS TO BECOME FEMALE THE EXCEPTION IS TO CHANGE AND BECOME MALE
THE Y CHROMOSOME MAKES THE DIFFERENCE IT REPRESENTS THE CHOICE MADE THE FORK IN THE ROAD?
XX XY
FEMALE
MALE
ARE YOU MISSING SOMETHING?
EQUAL SEPARATION OCCURS
THE FEMALE NATURE REFUSES TO BE SUBSERVIENT TO THE MALE
HE BECOMES COMPLETELY ABSORBED IN A CIVILIZATION OF HUMAN CREATION
SHE RETREATS FROM SOCIETY AND BECOMES HIDDEN IN NATURE
DAUGHTERS
SONS

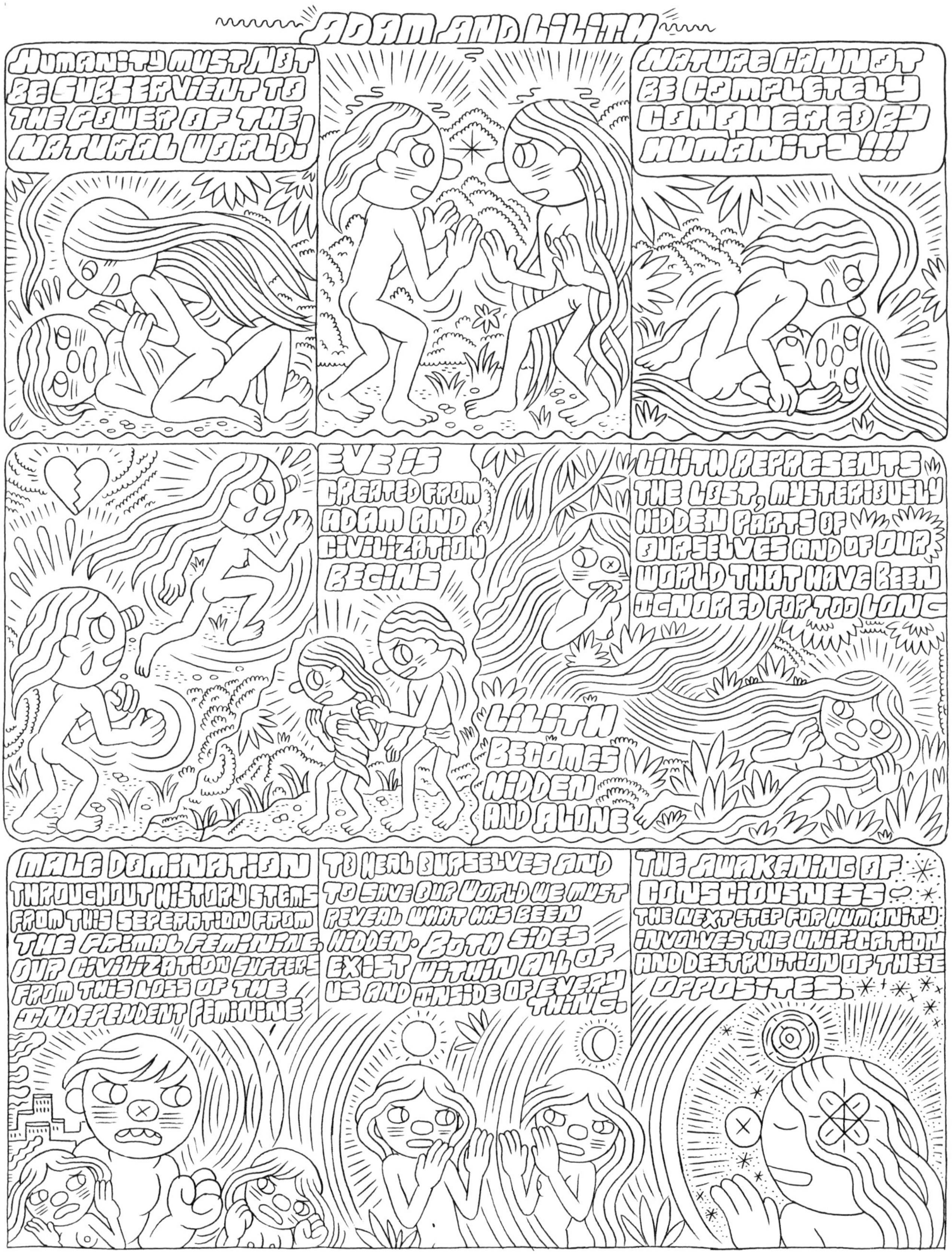
ADAM AND LILITH
HUMANITY MUST NOT BE SUBSERVIENT TO THE POWER OF THE NATURAL WORLD!
NATURE CANNOT BE COMPLETELY CONQUERED BY HUMANITY!!!
EVE IS CREATED FROM ADAM AND CIVILIZATION BEGINS
LILITH REPRESENTS THE LOST, MYSTERIOUSLY HIDDEN PARTS OF OURSELVES AND OF OUR WORLD THAT HAVE BEEN IGNORED FOR TOO LONG
LILITH BECOMES HIDDEN AND ALONE
MALE DOMINATION THROUGHOUT HISTORY STEMS FROM THIS SEPERATION FROM THE PRIMAL FEMININE. OUR CIVILIZATION SUFFERS FROM THIS LOSS OF THE INDEPENDENT FEMININE
TO HEAL OURSELVES AND TO SAVE OUR WORLD WE MUST REVEAL WHAT HAS BEEN HIDDEN. BOTH SIDES EXIST WITHIN ALL OF US AND INSIDE OF EVERY THING.
THE AWAKENING OF CONSCIOUSNESS - THE NEXT STEP FOR HUMANITY INVOLVES THE UNIFICATION AND DESTRUCTION OF THESE OPPOSITES.

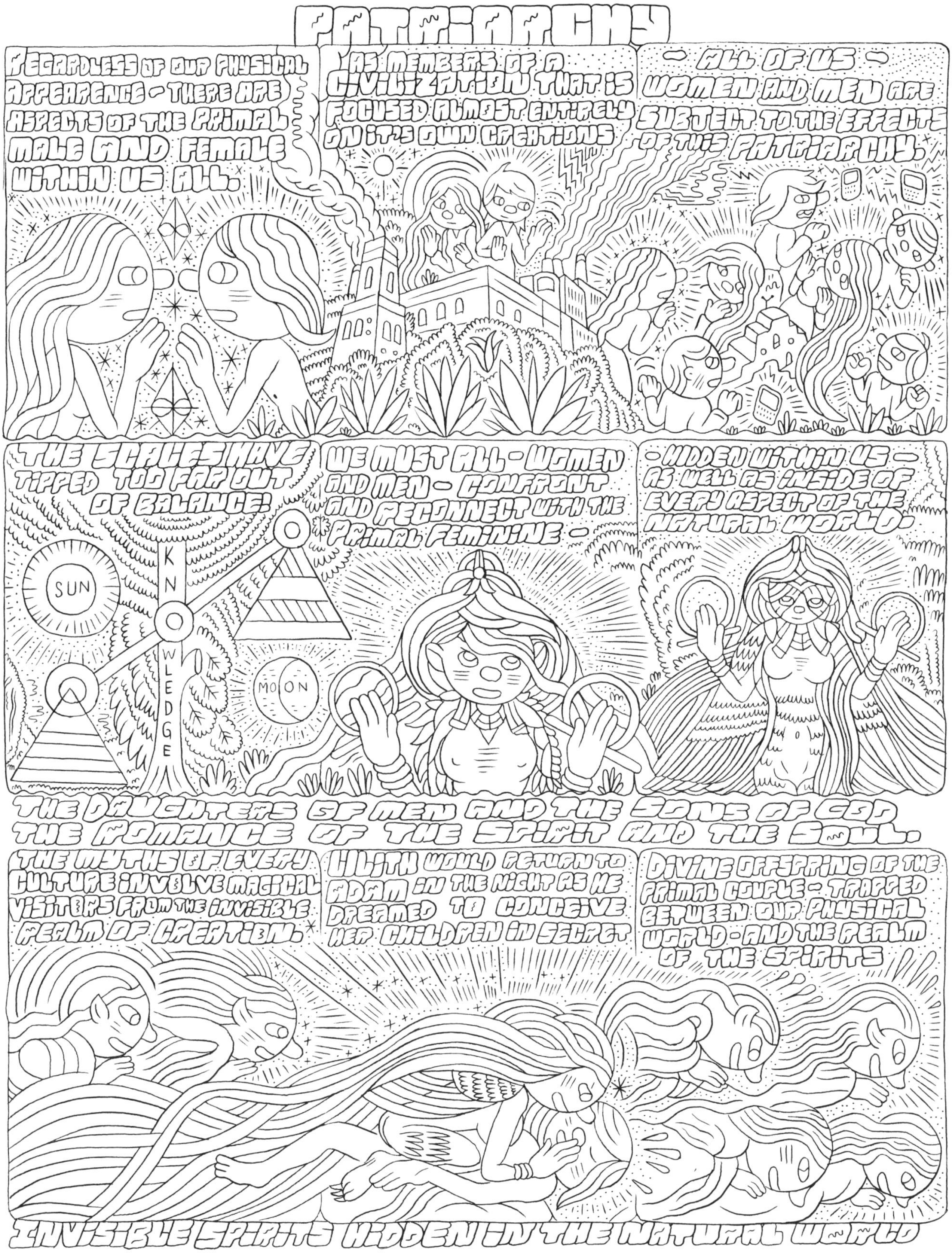
PATRIARCHY
REGARDLESS OF OUR PHYSICAL APPEARENCE - THERE ARE ASPECTS OF THE PRIMAL MALE AND FEMALE WITHIN US ALL.
AS MEMBERS OF A CIVILIZATION THAT IS FOCUSED ALMOST ENTIRELY ON IT'S OWN CREATIONS
- ALL OF US - WOMEN AND MEN ARE SUBJECT TO THE EFFECTS OF THIS PATRIARCHY.
THE SCALES HAVE TIPPED TOO FAR OUT OF BALANCE!
SUN
KNOWLEDGE
MOON
WE MUST ALL - WOMEN AND MEN - CONFRONT AND RECONNECT WITH THE PRIMAL FEMININE -
- HIDDEN WITHIN US - AS WELL AS INSIDE OF EVERY ASPECT OF THE NATURAL WORLD.
THE DAUGHTERS OF MEN AND THE SONS OF GOD
THE ROMANCE OF THE SPIRIT AND THE SOUL.
THE MYTHS OF EVERY CULTURE INVOLVE MAGICAL VISITORS FROM THE INVISIBLE REALM OF CREATION.
LILITH WOULD RETURN TO ADAM IN THE NIGHT AS HE DREAMED TO CONCEIVE HER CHILDREN IN SECRET
DIVINE OFFSPRING OF THE PRIMAL COUPLE - TRAPPED BETWEEN OUR PHYSICAL WORLD - AND THE REALM OF THE SPIRITS
INVISIBLE SPIRITS HIDDEN IN THE NATURAL WORLD

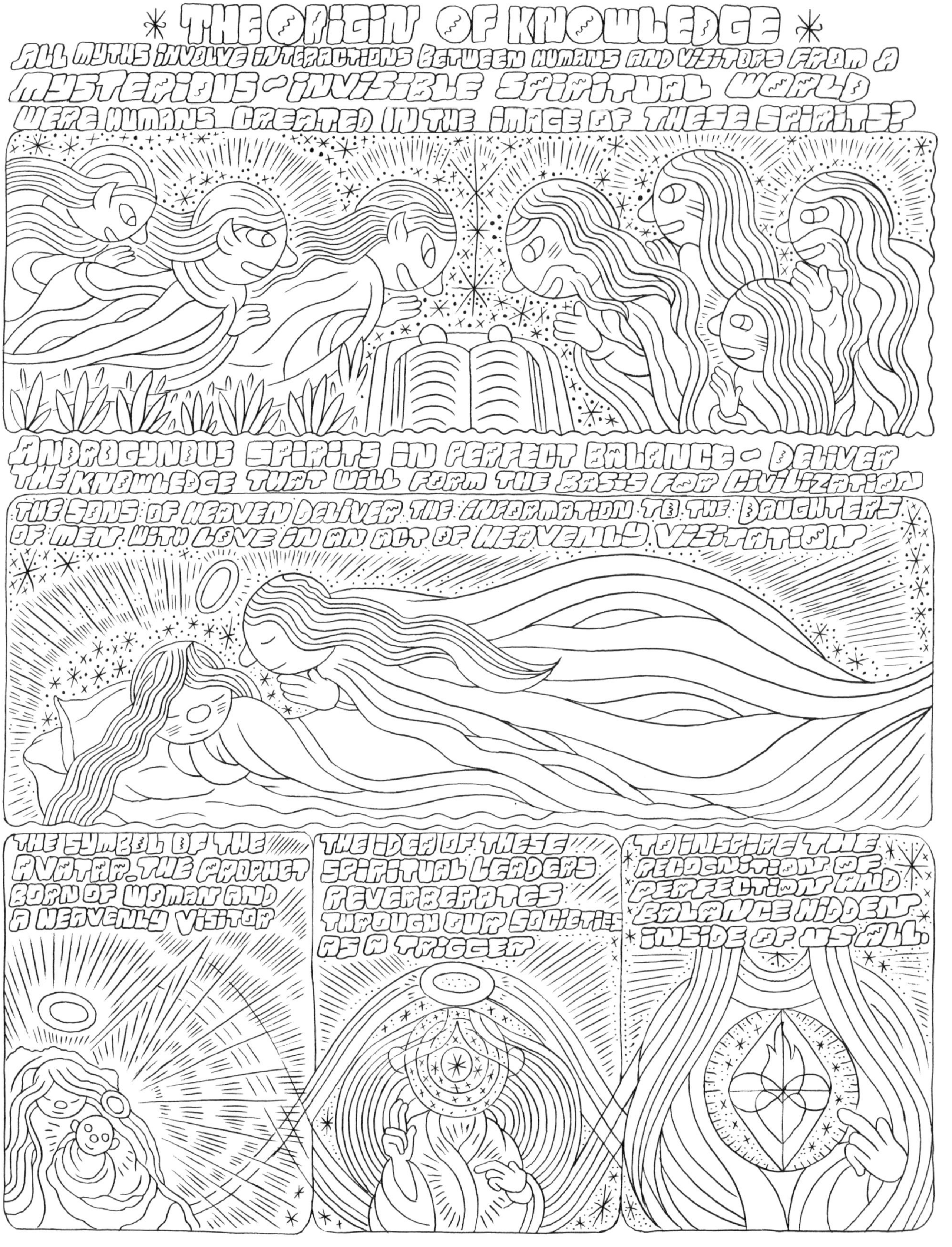
THE ORIGIN OF KNOWLEDGE
ALL MYTHS INVOLVE INTERACTIONS BETWEEN HUMANS AND VISITORS FROM A MYSTERIOUS ~ INVISIBLE SPIRITUAL WORLD
WERE HUMANS CREATED IN THE IMAGE OF THESE SPIRITS?
ANDROGYNOUS SPIRITS IN PERFECT BALANCE - DELIVER THE KNOWLEDGE THAT WILL FORM THE BASIS FOR CIVILIZATION
THE SONS OF HEAVEN DELIVER THE INFORMATION TO THE DAUGHTERS OF MEN WITH LOVE IN AN ACT OF HEAVENLY VISITATION
THE SYMBOL OF THE AVATAR_THE PROPHET BORN OF WOMAN AND A HEAVENLY VISITOR
THE IDEA OF THESE SPIRITUAL LEADERS REVERBERATES THROUGH OUR SOCIETIES AS A TRIGGER
TO INSPIRE THE RECOGNITION OF PERFECTION AND BALANCE HIDDEN INSIDE OF US ALL.

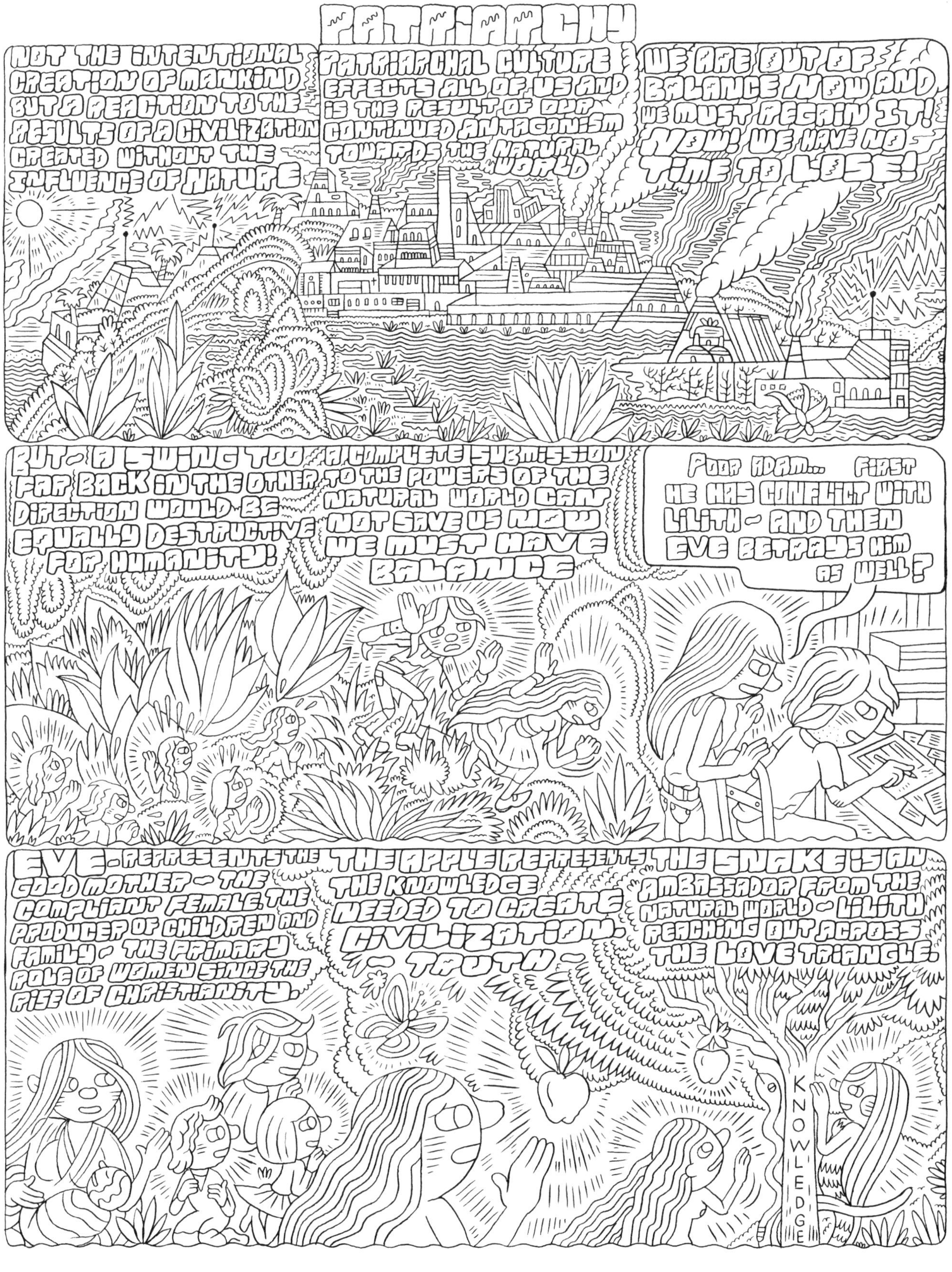
PATRIARCHY
NOT THE INTENTIONAL CREATION OF MANKIND BUT A REACTION TO THE RESULTS OF A CIVILIZATION CREATED WITHOUT THE INFLUENCE OF NATURE
PATRIARCHAL CULTURE EFFECTS ALL OF US AND IS THE RESULT OF OUR CONTINUED ANTAGONISM TOWARDS THE NATURAL WORLD
WE ARE OUT OF BALANCE NOW AND WE MUST REGAIN IT! NOW! WE HAVE NO TIME TO LOSE!
BUT - A SWING TOO FAR BACK IN THE OTHER DIRECTION WOULD BE EQUALLY DESTRUCTIVE FOR HUMANITY!
A COMPLETE SUBMISSION TO THE POWERS OF THE NATURAL WORLD CAN NOT SAVE US NOW WE MUST HAVE BALANCE
POOR ADAM... FIRST HE HAS CONFLICT WITH LILITH - AND THEN EVE BETRAYS HIM AS WELL?
EVE - REPRESENTS THE GOOD MOTHER - THE COMPLIANT FEMALE. THE PRODUCER OF CHILDREN AND FAMILY - THE PRIMARY ROLE OF WOMEN SINCE THE RISE OF CHRISTIANITY.
THE APPLE REPRESENTS THE KNOWLEDGE NEEDED TO CREATE CIVILIZATION. - TRUTH -
THE SNAKE IS AN AMBASSADOR FROM THE NATURAL WORLD - LILITH REACHING OUT ACROSS THE LOVE TRIANGLE.
KNOWLEDGE

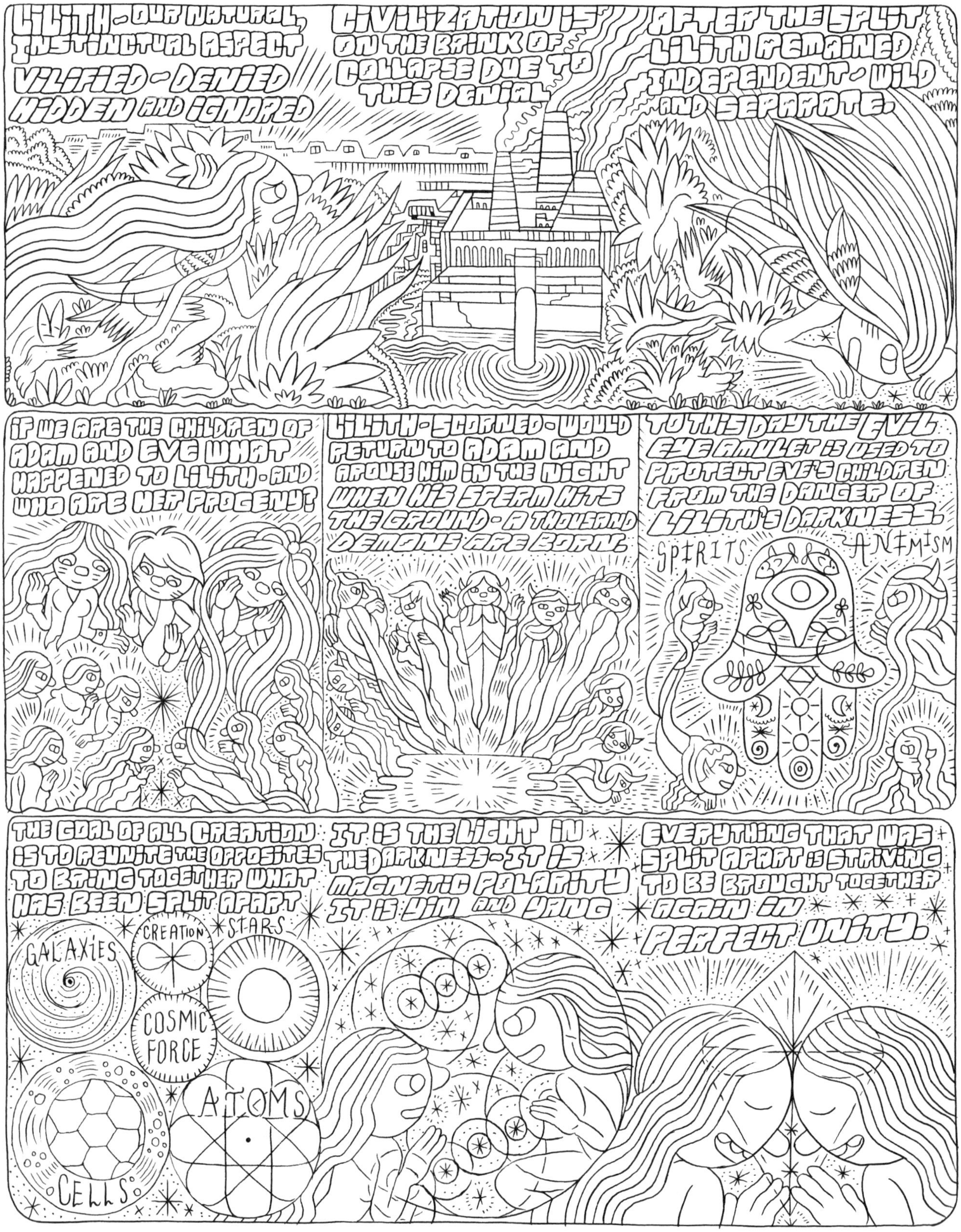
LILITH - OUR NATURAL, INSTINCTUAL ASPECT
VILIFIED - DENIED HIDDEN AND IGNORED
CIVILIZATION IS ON THE BRINK OF COLLAPSE DUE TO THIS DENIAL
AFTER THE SPLIT LILITH REMAINED INDEPENDENT - WILD AND SEPARATE.
IF WE ARE THE CHILDREN OF ADAM AND EVE WHAT HAPPENED TO LILITH - AND WHO ARE HER PROGENY?
LILITH - SCORNED - WOULD RETURN TO ADAM AND AROUSE HIM IN THE NIGHT WHEN HIS SPERM HITS THE GROUND - A THOUSAND DEMONS ARE BORN.
TO THIS DAY THE EVIL EYE AMULET IS USED TO PROTECT EVE'S CHILDREN FROM THE DANGER OF LILITH'S DARKNESS.
SPIRITS
ANIMISM
THE GOAL OF ALL CREATION IS TO REUNITE THE OPPOSITES TO BRING TOGETHER WHAT HAS BEEN SPLIT APART
GALAXIES
CREATION
STARS
COSMIC FORCE
ATOMS
CELLS
IT IS THE LIGHT IN THE DARKNESS - IT IS MAGNETIC POLARITY IT IS YIN AND YANG
EVERYTHING THAT WAS SPLIT APART IS STRIVING TO BE BROUGHT TOGETHER AGAIN IN PERFECT UNITY.

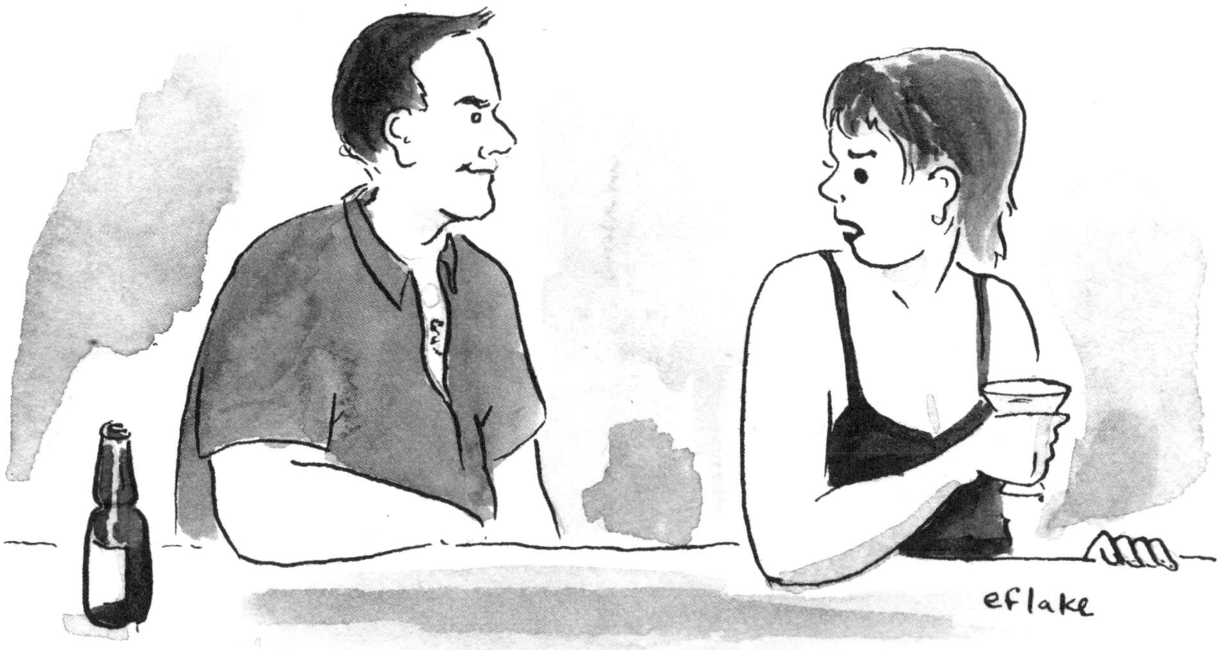
eflake

"NO THANKS, PAL- I CAN BUY MY OWN ROOFIES."

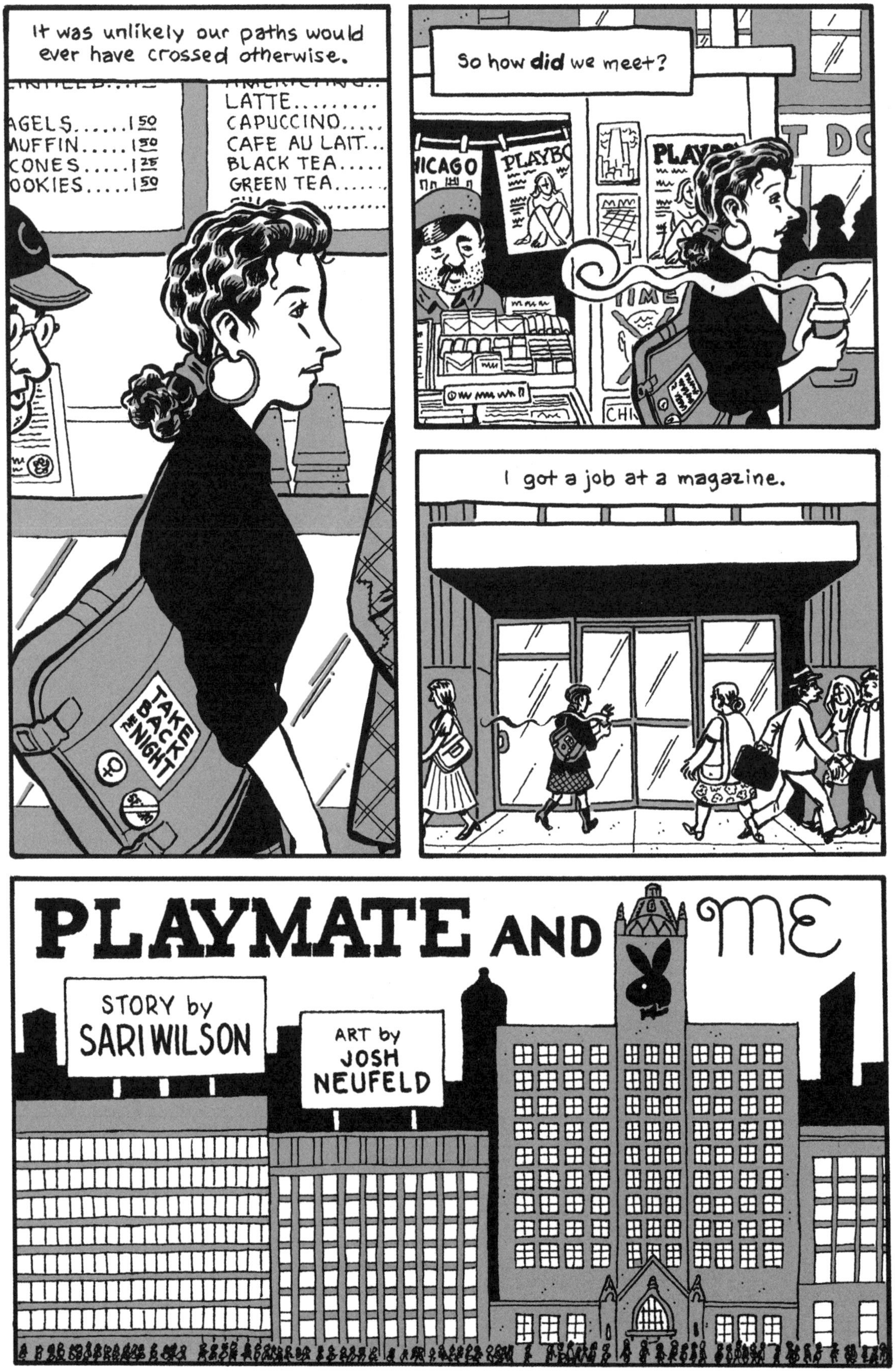
It was unlikely our paths would ever have crossed otherwise.
LATTE
CAPUCCINO
CAFE AU LAIT
BLACK TEA
GREEN TEA
TAKE BACK THE NIGHT
So how did we meet?
PLAYBO
ICAGO
I got a job at a magazine.
PLAYMATE AND ME
STORY by SARI WILSON
ART by JOSH NEUFELD

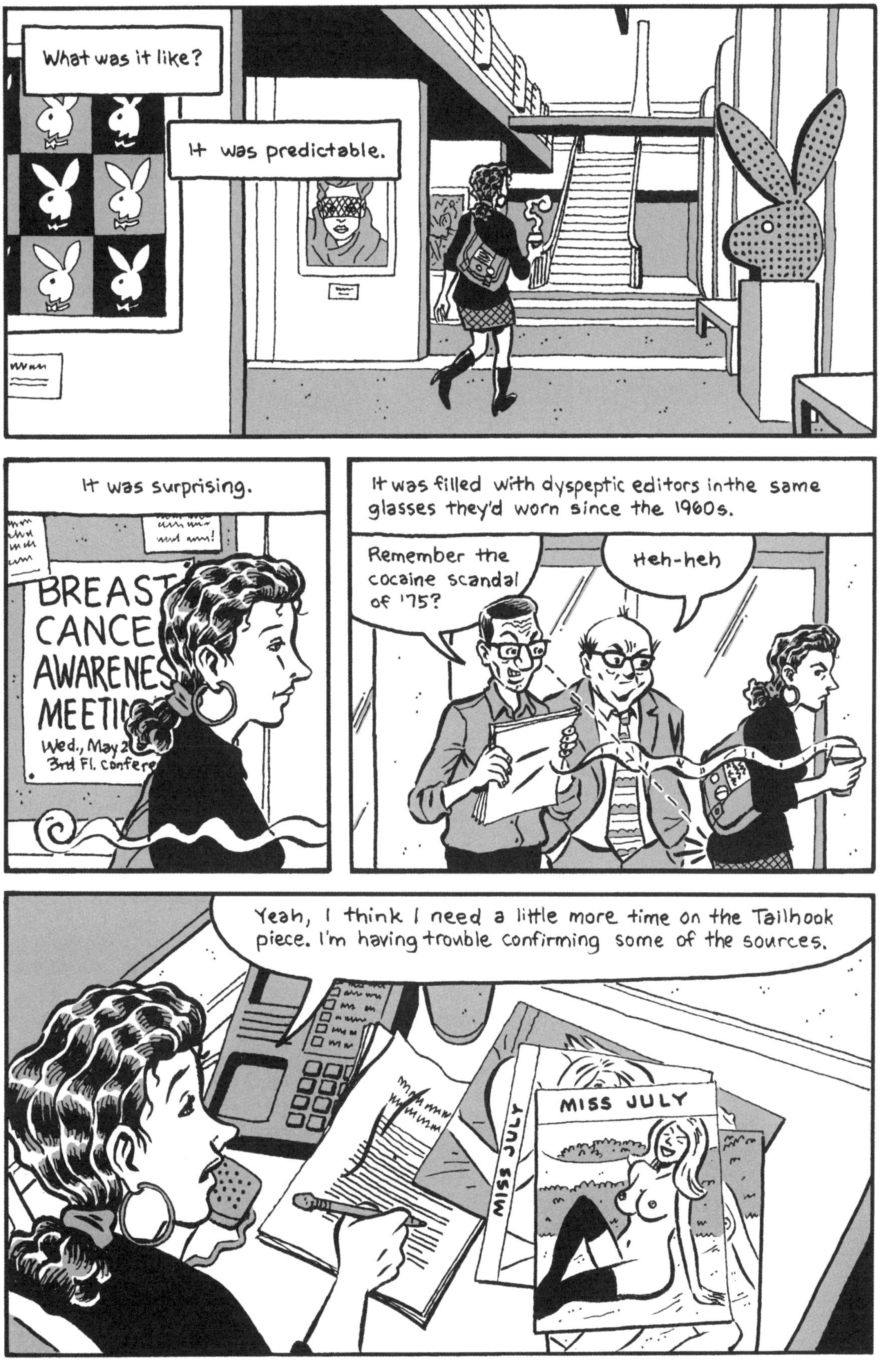
What was it like?
It was predictable.
It was surprising.
BREAST CANCE AWARENES MEETI
Wed., May 2
3rd Fl. confere
It was filled with dyspeptic editors in the same glasses they'd worn since the 1960s.
Remember the cocaine scandal of '75?
Heh-heh
Yeah, I think I need a little more time on the Tailhook piece. I'm having trouble confirming some of the sources.
MISS JULY
MISS JULY

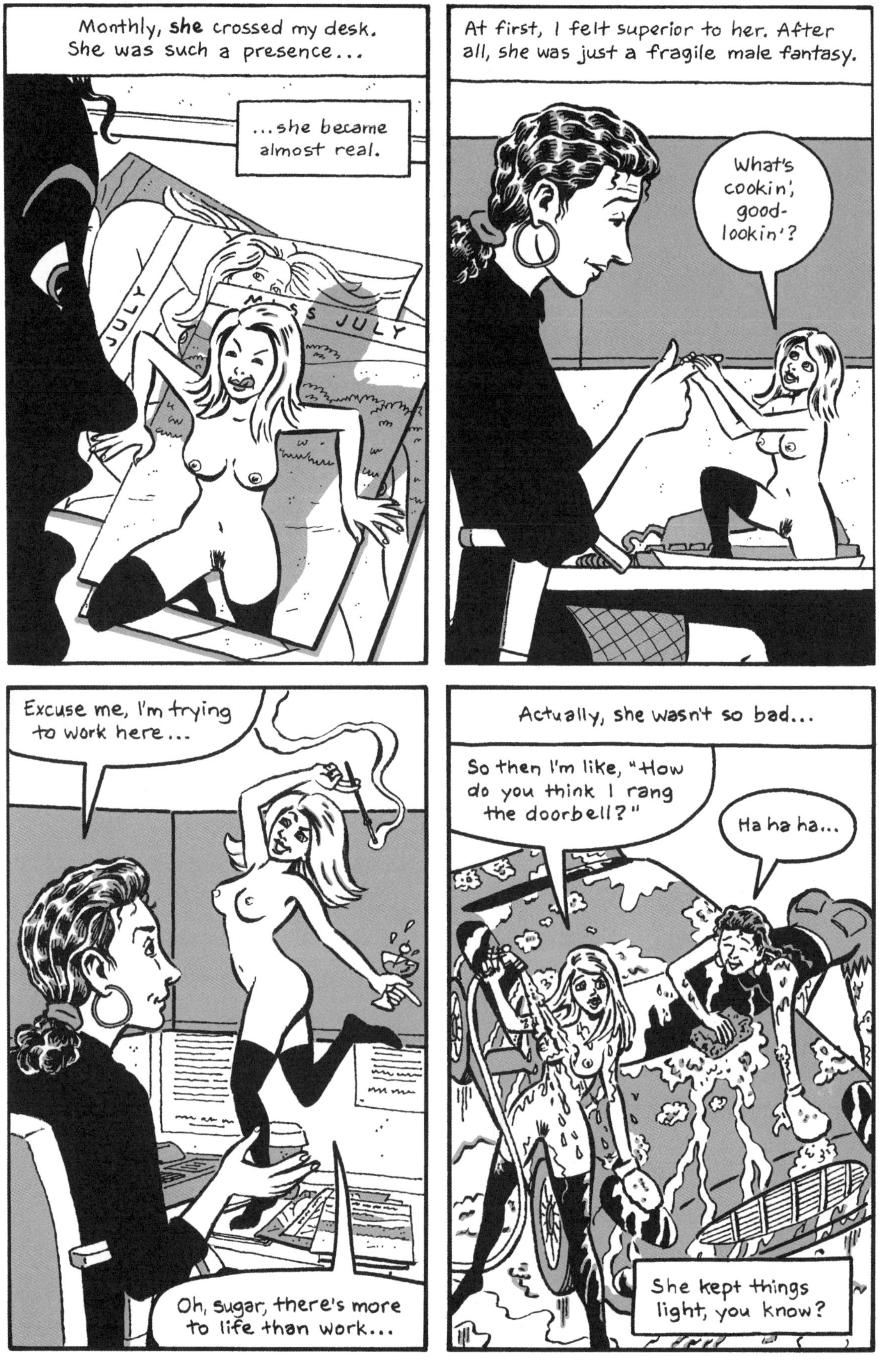
Monthly, she crossed my desk. She was such a presence...
...she became almost real.
JULY
JULY
At first, I felt superior to her. After all, she was just a fragile male fantasy.
What's cookin', good-lookin'?
Excuse me, I'm trying to work here...
Oh, sugar, there's more to life than work...
Actually, she wasn't so bad...
So then I'm like, "How do you think I rang the doorbell?"
Ha ha ha...
She kept things light, you know?

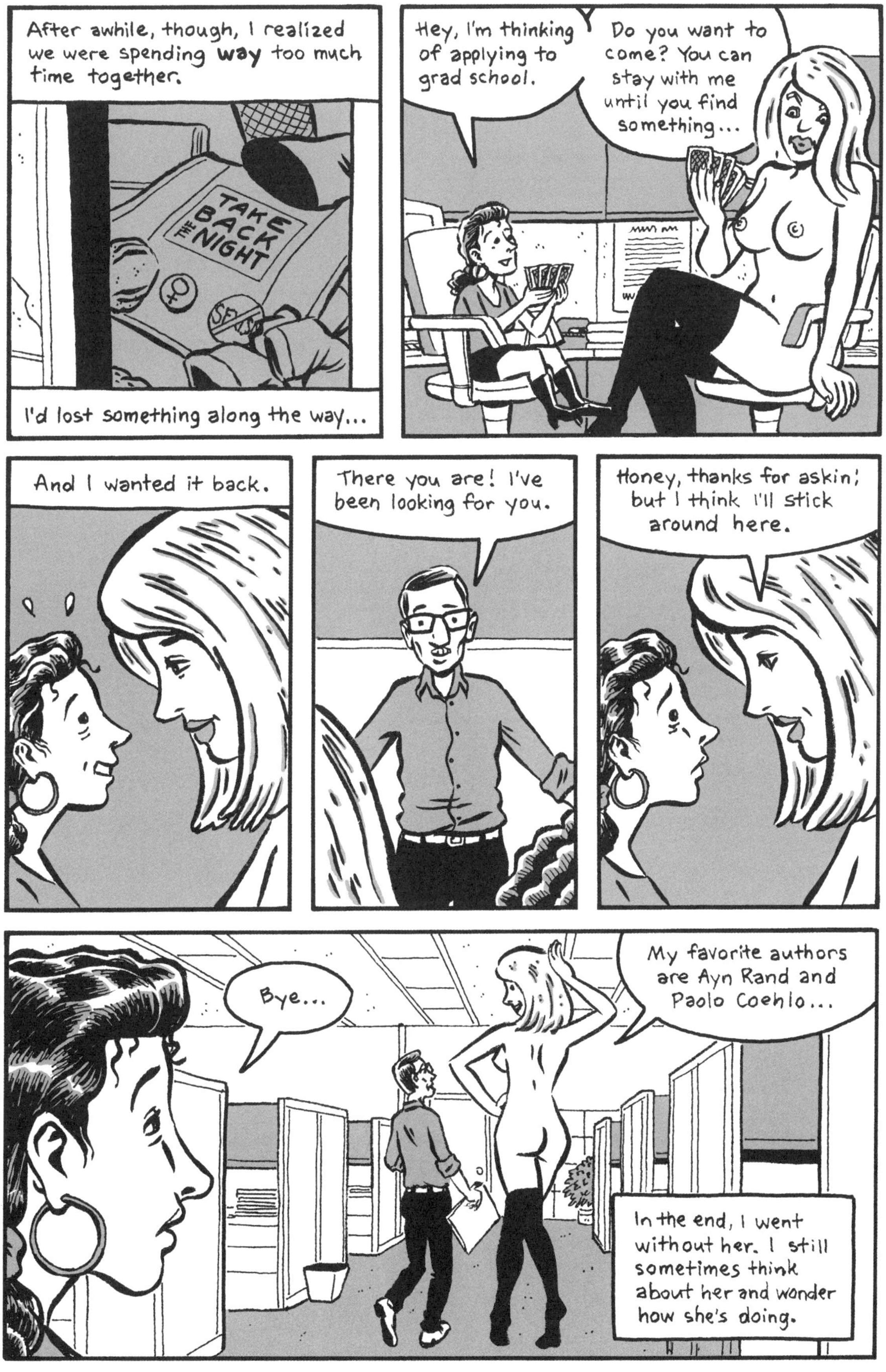
After awhile, though, I realized we were spending **way** too much time together.
TAKE BACK THE NIGHT
I'd lost something along the way...
Hey, I'm thinking of applying to grad school.
Do you want to come? You can stay with me until you find something...
And I wanted it back.
There you are! I've been looking for you.
Honey, thanks for askin', but I think I'll stick around here.
Bye...
My favorite authors are Ayn Rand and Paolo Coehlo...
In the end, I went without her. I still sometimes think about her and wonder how she's doing.

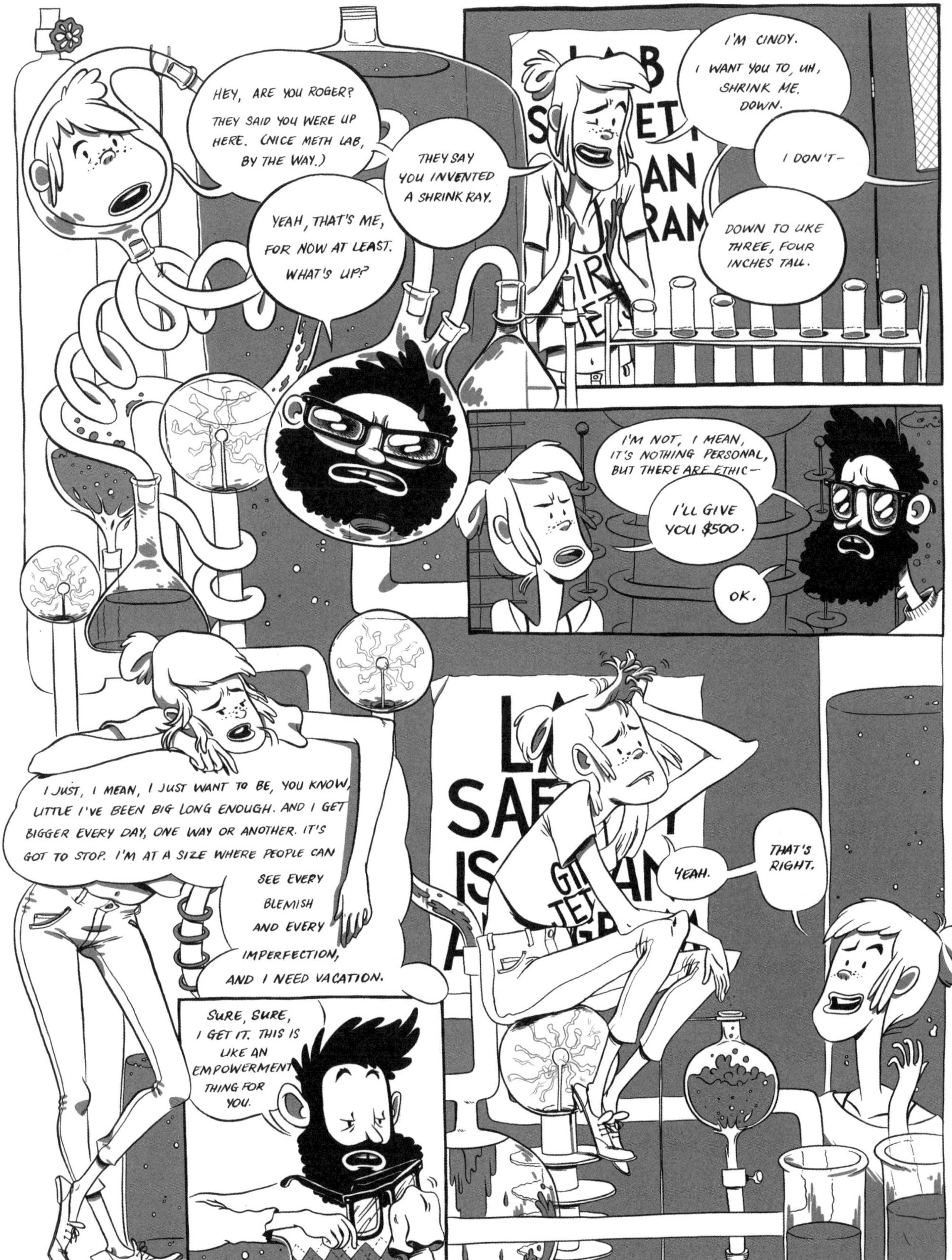
HEY, ARE YOU ROGER? THEY SAID YOU WERE UP HERE. (NICE METH LAB, BY THE WAY.)
THEY SAY YOU INVENTED A SHRINK RAY.
YEAH, THAT'S ME, FOR NOW AT LEAST. WHAT'S UP?
I'M CINDY.
I WANT YOU TO, UH, SHRINK ME. DOWN.
I DON'T-
DOWN TO LIKE THREE, FOUR INCHES TALL.
LAB SAFETY IS AN ...RAM
I'M NOT, I MEAN, IT'S NOTHING PERSONAL, BUT THERE ARE ETHIC—
I'LL GIVE YOU $500.
OK.
I JUST, I MEAN, I JUST WANT TO BE, YOU KNOW, LITTLE I'VE BEEN BIG LONG ENOUGH. AND I GET BIGGER EVERY DAY, ONE WAY OR ANOTHER. IT'S GOT TO STOP. I'M AT A SIZE WHERE PEOPLE CAN SEE EVERY BLEMISH AND EVERY IMPERFECTION, AND I NEED VACATION.
SURE, SURE, I GET IT. THIS IS LIKE AN EMPOWERMENT THING FOR YOU.
YEAH.
THAT'S RIGHT.

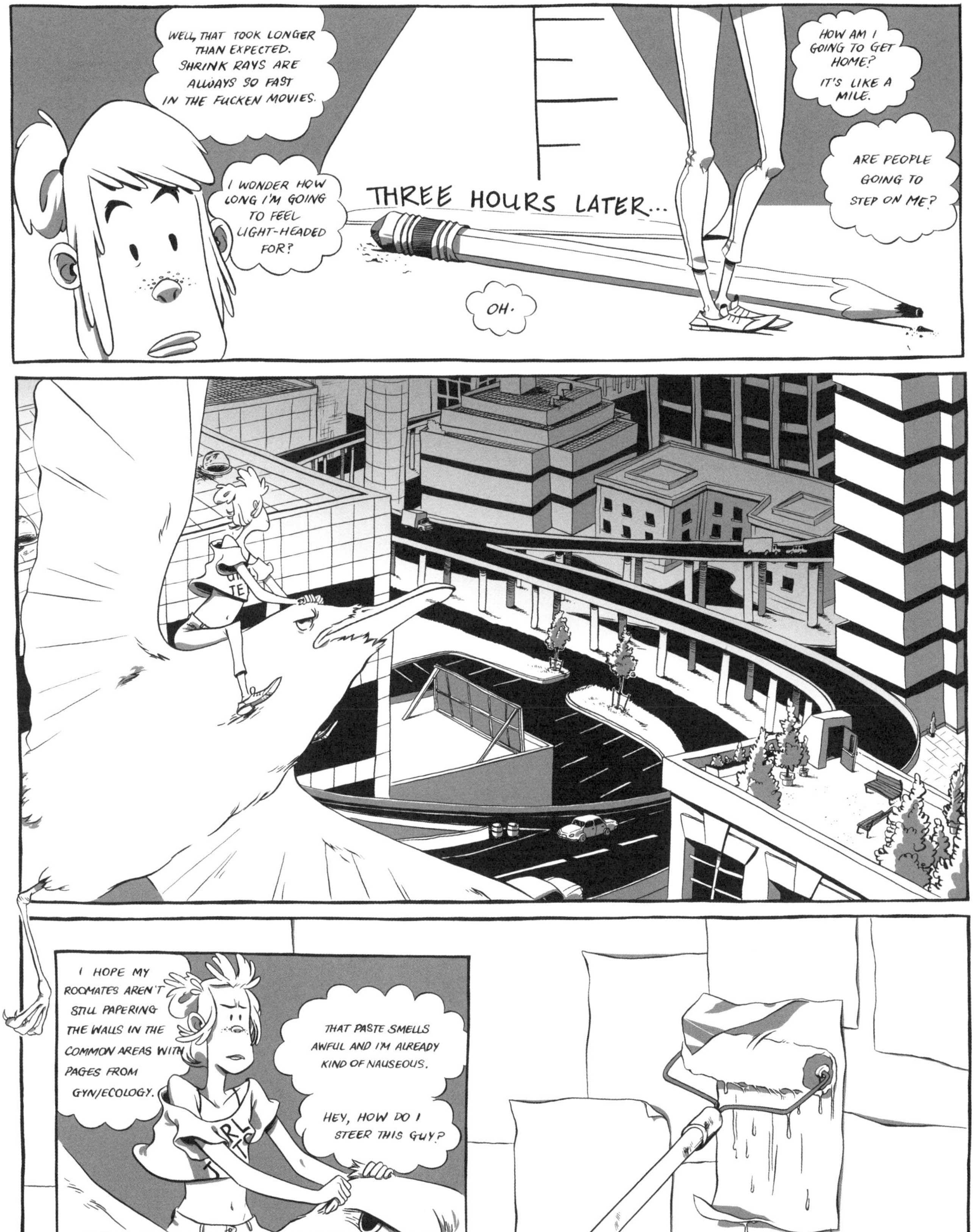
WELL, THAT TOOK LONGER THAN EXPECTED. SHRINK RAYS ARE ALWAYS SO FAST IN THE FUCKEN MOVIES.
I WONDER HOW LONG I'M GOING TO FEEL LIGHT-HEADED FOR?
THREE HOURS LATER...
OH.
HOW AM I GOING TO GET HOME?
IT'S LIKE A MILE.
ARE PEOPLE GOING TO STEP ON ME?
I HOPE MY ROOMATES AREN'T STILL PAPERING THE WALLS IN THE COMMON AREAS WITH PAGES FROM GYN/ECOLOGY.
THAT PASTE SMELLS AWFUL AND I'M ALREADY KIND OF NAUSEOUS.
HEY, HOW DO I STEER THIS GUY?

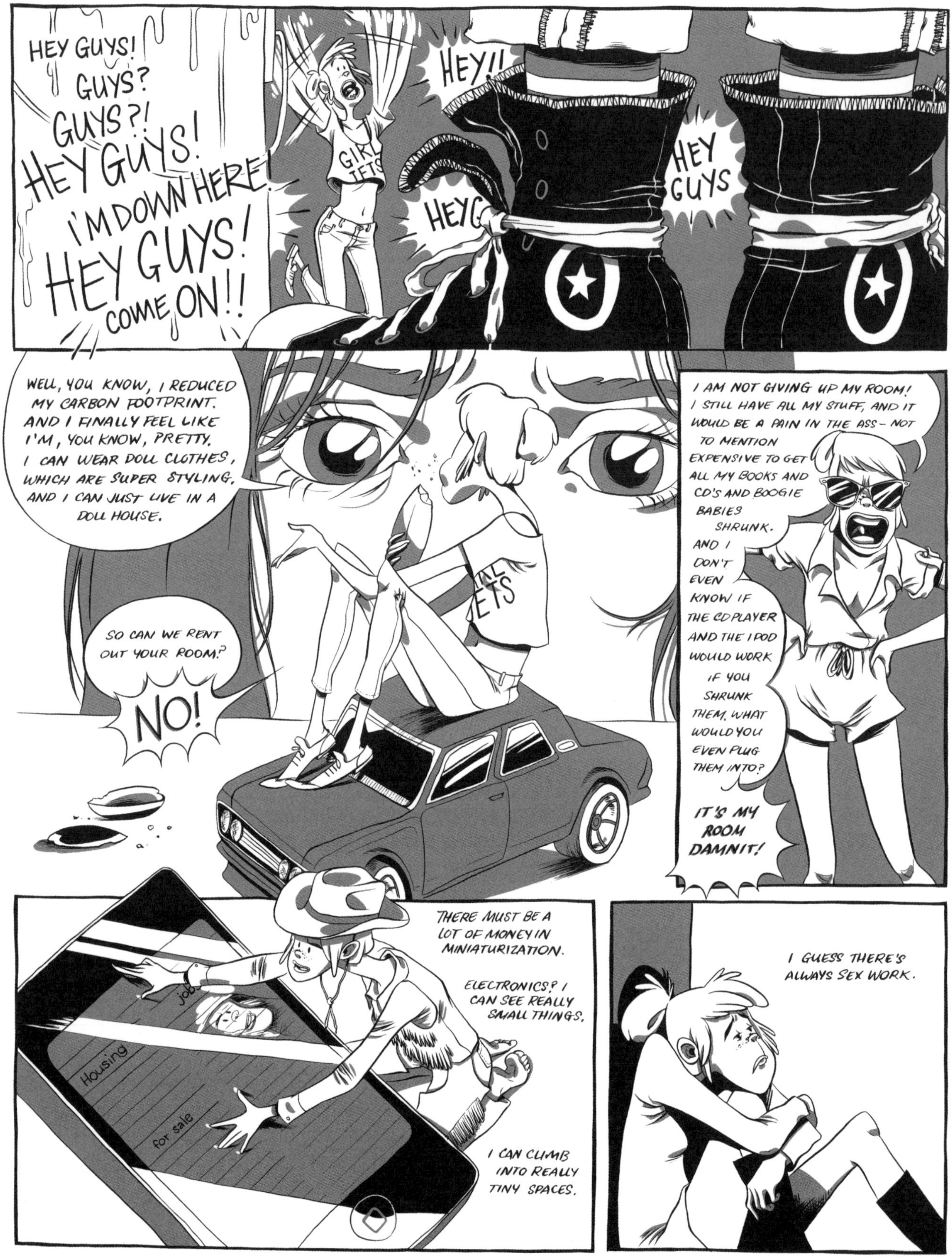
HEY GUYS!
GUYS?
GUYS?!
HEY GUYS!
I'M DOWN HERE!
HEY GUYS!
COME ON!!
HEY!!
HEY G
HEY GUYS
WELL, YOU KNOW, I REDUCED MY CARBON FOOTPRINT. AND I FINALLY FEEL LIKE I'M, YOU KNOW, PRETTY. I CAN WEAR DOLL CLOTHES, WHICH ARE SUPER STYLING. AND I CAN JUST LIVE IN A DOLL HOUSE.
SO CAN WE RENT OUT YOUR ROOM?
NO!
I AM NOT GIVING UP MY ROOM! I STILL HAVE ALL MY STUFF, AND IT WOULD BE A PAIN IN THE ASS - NOT TO MENTION EXPENSIVE TO GET ALL MY BOOKS AND CD'S AND BOOGIE BABIES SHRUNK. AND I DON'T EVEN KNOW IF THE CD PLAYER AND THE IPOD WOULD WORK IF YOU SHRUNK THEM. WHAT WOULD YOU EVEN PLUG THEM INTO?
IT'S MY ROOM DAMNIT!
jobs
Housing
for sale
THERE MUST BE A LOT OF MONEY IN MINIATURIZATION.
ELECTRONICS? I CAN SEE REALLY SMALL THINGS.
I CAN CLIMB INTO REALLY TINY SPACES.
I GUESS THERE'S ALWAYS SEX WORK.

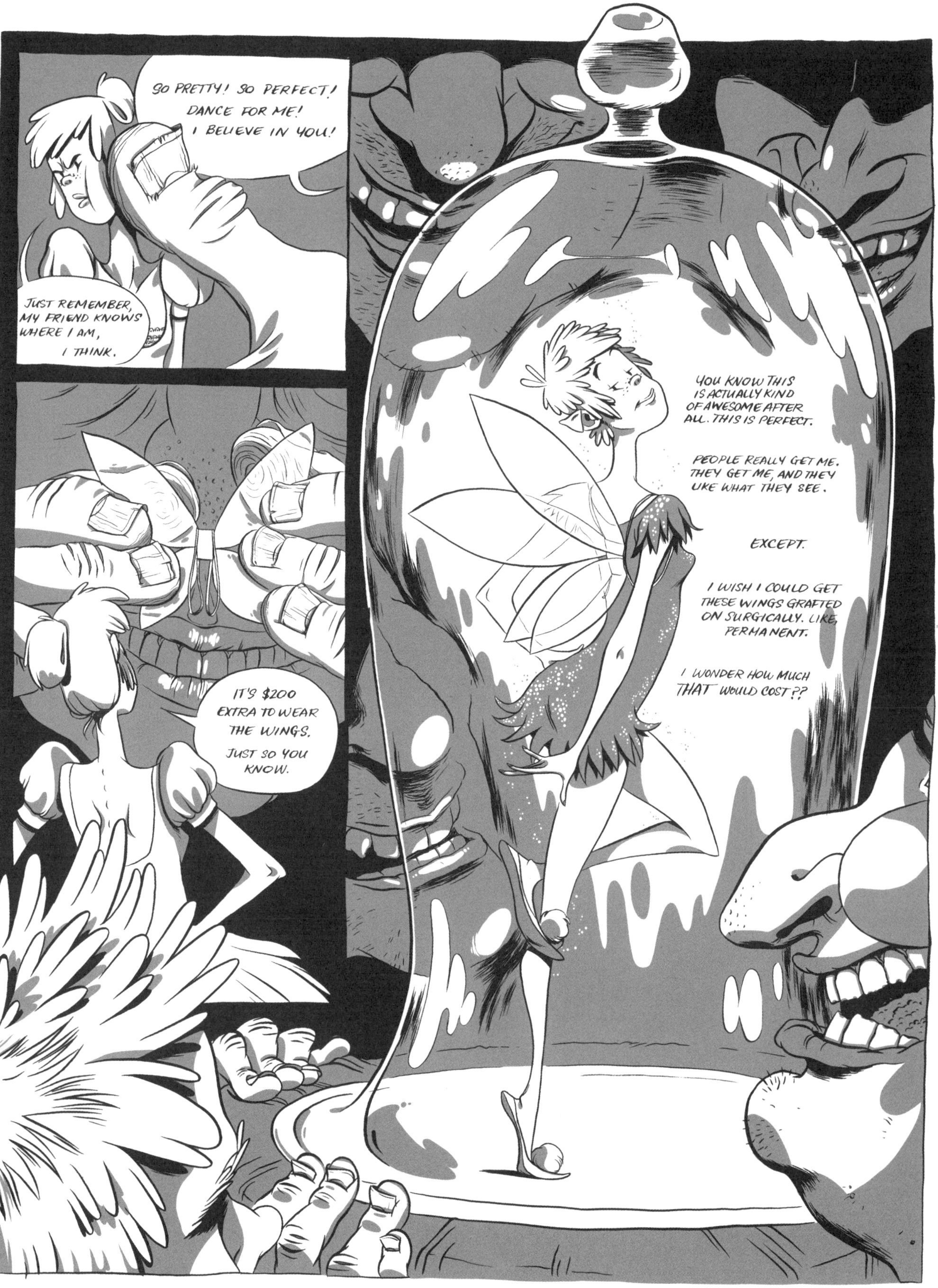
SO PRETTY! SO PERFECT! DANCE FOR ME! I BELIEVE IN YOU!
JUST REMEMBER, MY FRIEND KNOWS WHERE I AM, I THINK.
IT'S $200 EXTRA TO WEAR THE WINGS.
JUST SO YOU KNOW.
YOU KNOW THIS IS ACTUALLY KIND OF AWESOME AFTER ALL. THIS IS PERFECT.
PEOPLE REALLY GET ME. THEY GET ME, AND THEY LIKE WHAT THEY SEE.
EXCEPT.
I WISH I COULD GET THESE WINGS GRAFTED ON SURGICALLY. LIKE, PERMANENT.
I WONDER HOW MUCH THAT WOULD COST??

# HER FAT FEMINIST ASS ulli lust & kai pfeiffer 2011

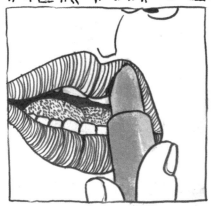

I never put on suspenders just to go for a walk and feel the wind between my legs.

Suspenders, I'll only be wearing them if they are really appreciated.

I'll go now.

Ok, bye.

SMAK

What is this drawing? What's that supposed to represent?

A nipple.

That doesn't look like a nipple.

I'm sorry, but I need to concentrate...

Look! That's what a tit looks like!

Stop that, I'm in the middle of chatting

>SORRY DARLING<

sorry, darling. your tits are always worthy of my highest attention.

it's just, i have to concentrate, chatting with that impatient sweet little Miss B.

pff

ok, i'm really going now

bye, sweetie. have fun.

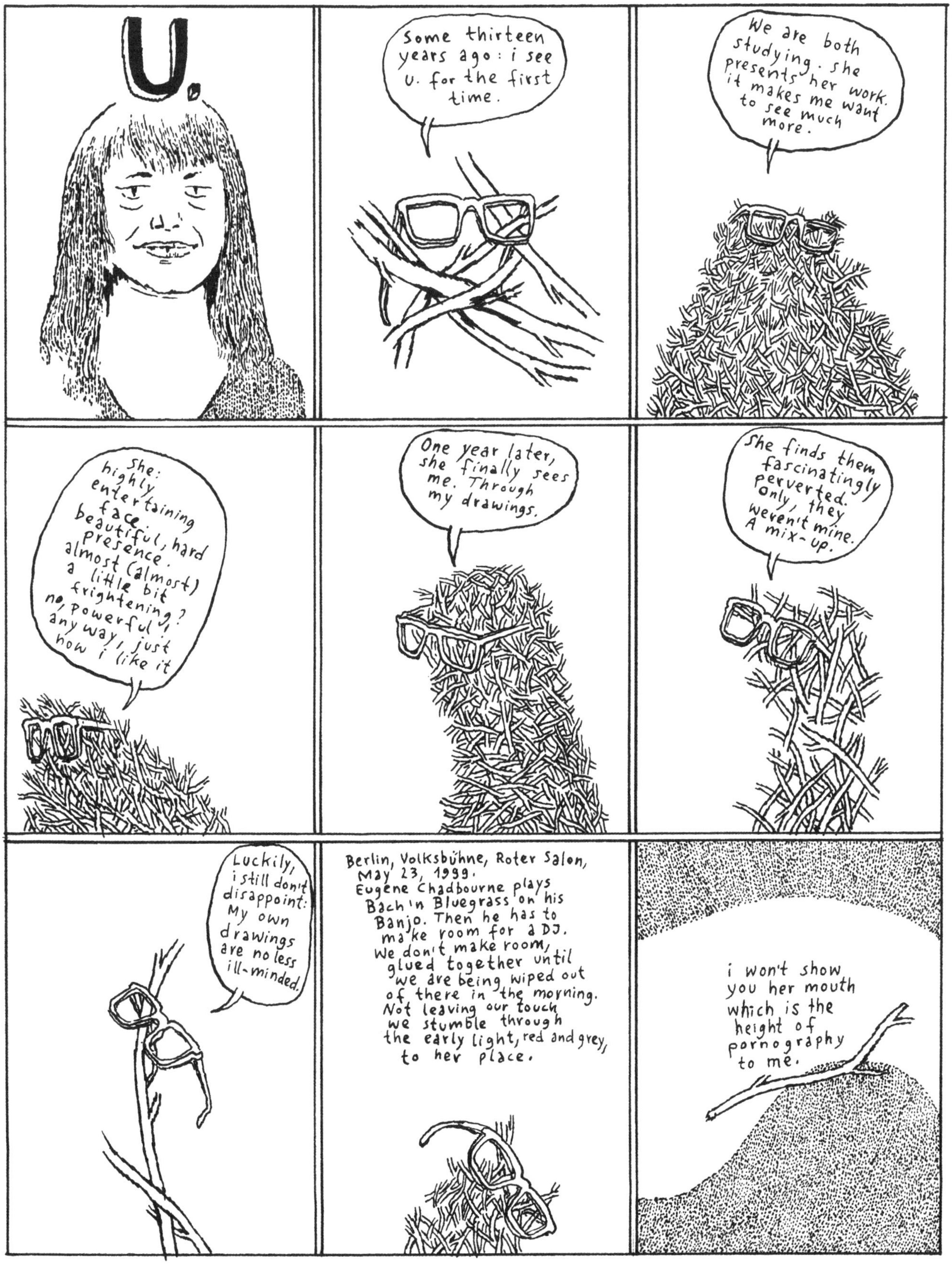
U.
Some thirteen years ago: i see U. for the first time.
We are both studying. she presents her work. it makes me want to see much more.
She: highly entertaining face. beautiful, hard presence. almost (almost) a little bit frightening? no, powerful, anyway, just how i like it
One year later, she finally sees me. Through my drawings.
She finds them fascinatingly perverted. Only, they weren't mine. A mix-up.
Luckily, i still don't disappoint: My own drawings are no less ill-minded.
Berlin, Volksbühne, Roter Salon, May 23, 1999. Eugene Chadbourne plays Bach in Bluegrass on his Banjo. Then he has to make room for a DJ. We don't make room, glued together until we are being wiped out of there in the morning. Not leaving our touch we stumble through the early light, red and grey, to her place.
i won't show you her mouth which is the height of pornography to me.

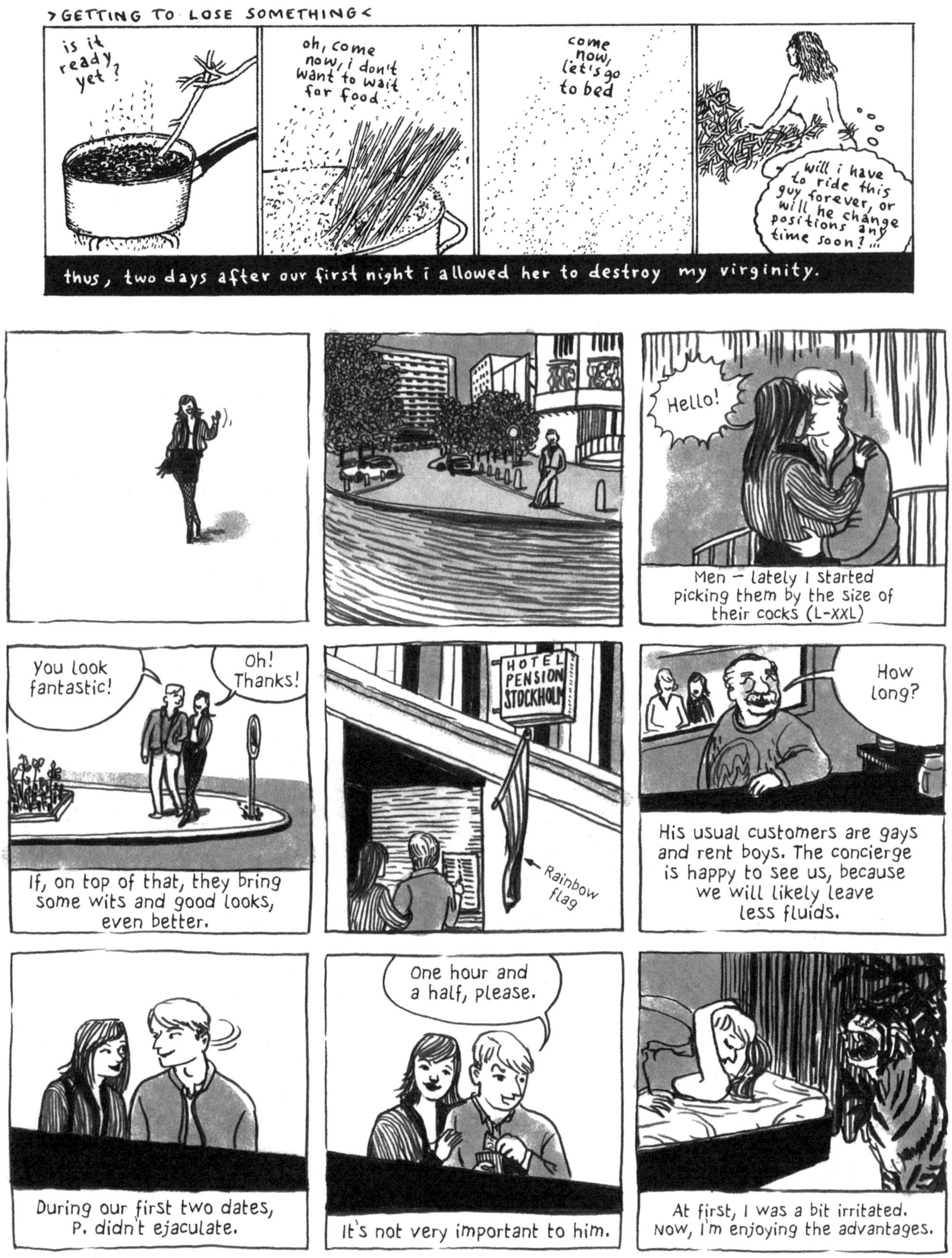
>GETTING TO LOSE SOMETHING<
is it ready yet?
oh, come now, i don't want to wait for food
come now, let's go to bed
will i have to ride this guy forever, or will he change positions any time soon?...
thus, two days after our first night i allowed her to destroy my virginity.
Hello!
Men – lately I started picking them by the size of their cocks (L-XXL)
You look fantastic!
Oh! Thanks!
If, on top of that, they bring some wits and good looks, even better.
HOTEL PENSION STOCKHOLM
Rainbow flag
How long?
His usual customers are gays and rent boys. The concierge is happy to see us, because we will likely leave less fluids.
During our first two dates, P. didn't ejaculate.
One hour and a half, please.
It's not very important to him.
At first, I was a bit irritated. Now, I'm enjoying the advantages.

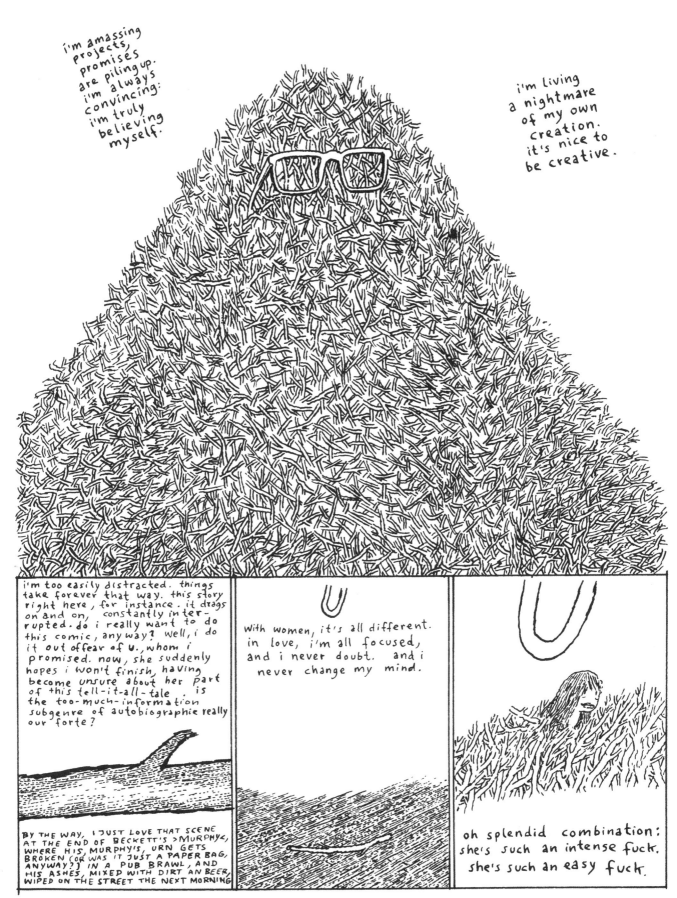

i'm amassing projects, promises are piling up. i'm always convincing: i'm truly believing myself.

i'm living a nightmare of my own creation. it's nice to be creative.

i'm too easily distracted. things take forever that way. this story right here, for instance. it drags on and on, constantly interrupted. do i really want to do this comic, anyway? well, i do it out of fear of U., whom i promised. now, she suddenly hopes i won't finish, having become unsure about her part of this tell-it-all-tale. is the too-much-information subgenre of autobiographie really our forte?

BY THE WAY, I JUST LOVE THAT SCENE AT THE END OF BECKETT'S >MURPHY<, WHERE HIS, MURPHY'S, URN GETS BROKEN (OR WAS IT JUST A PAPER BAG, ANYWAY?) IN A PUB BRAWL, AND HIS ASHES, MIXED WITH DIRT AN BEER, WIPED ON THE STREET THE NEXT MORNING

With women, it's all different. in love, i'm all focused, and i never doubt. and i never change my mind.

oh splendid combination: she's such an intense fuck. she's such an easy fuck.

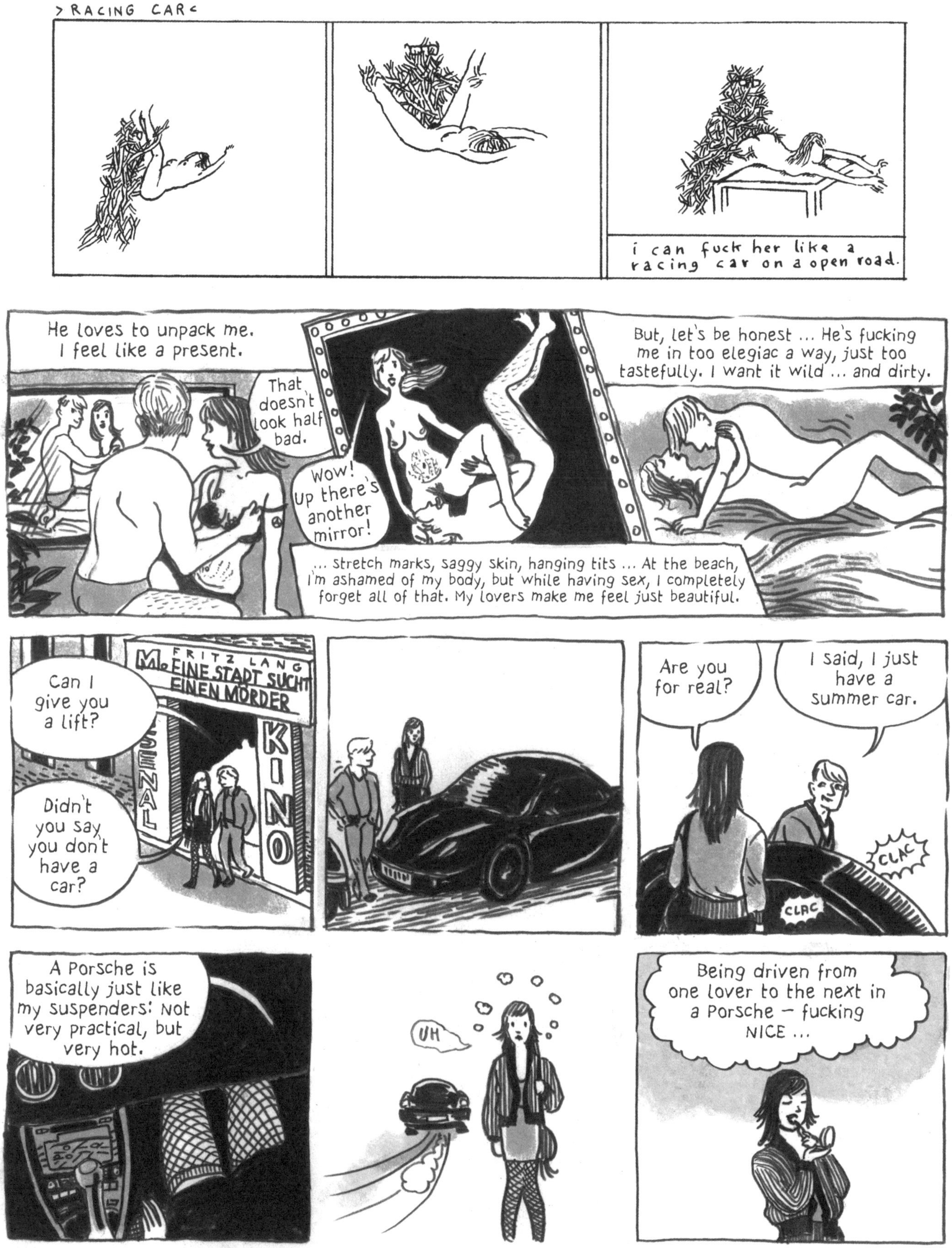

> RACING CAR <
i can fuck her like a racing car on a open road.
He loves to unpack me. I feel like a present.
That doesn't look half bad.
Wow! Up there's another mirror!
But, let's be honest ... He's fucking me in too elegiac a way, just too tastefully. I want it wild ... and dirty.
... stretch marks, saggy skin, hanging tits ... At the beach, I'm ashamed of my body, but while having sex, I completely forget all of that. My lovers make me feel just beautiful.
FRITZ LANG
M. EINE STADT SUCHT EINEN MÖRDER
ARSENAL
KINO
Can I give you a lift?
Didn't you say you don't have a car?
Are you for real?
I said, I just have a summer car.
CLAC
CLAC
A Porsche is basically just like my suspenders: Not very practical, but very hot.
UH
Being driven from one lover to the next in a Porsche – fucking NICE ...

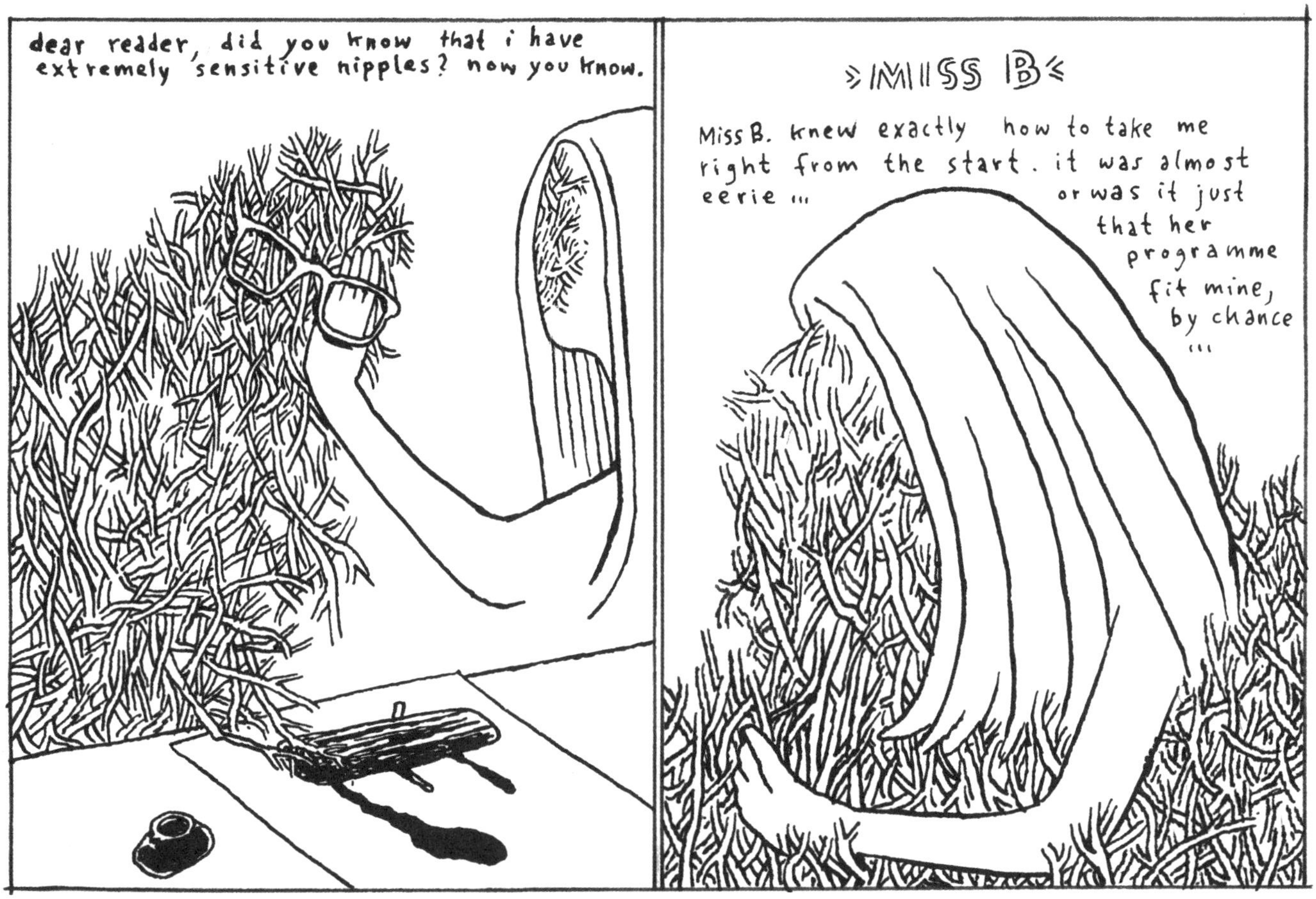
dear reader, did you know that i have extremely sensitive nipples? now you know.
>MISS B<
Miss B. knew exactly how to take me right from the start. it was almost eerie ...
or was it just that her programme fit mine, by chance ...

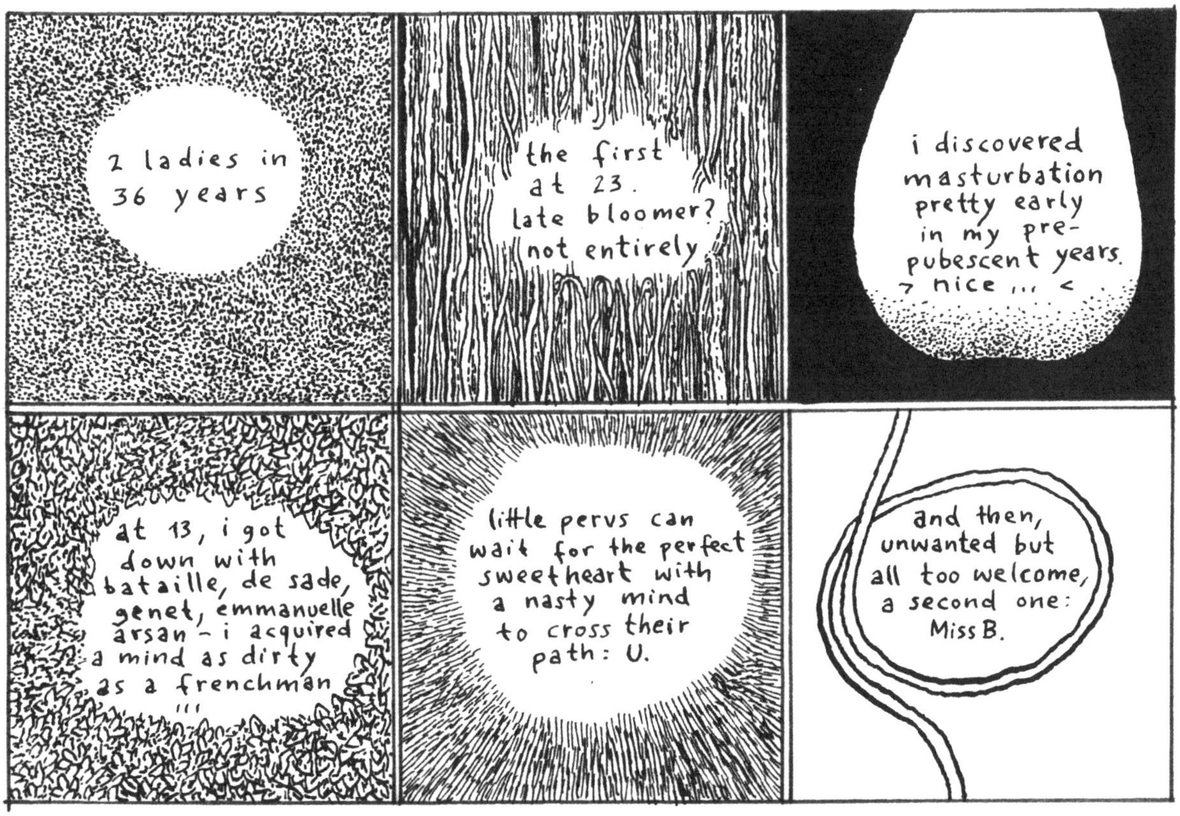
2 ladies in 36 years
the first at 23. late bloomer? not entirely
i discovered masturbation pretty early in my pre-pubescent years.
> nice ... <
at 13, i got down with bataille, de sade, genet, emmanuelle arsan - i acquired a mind as dirty as a frenchman ...
little pervs can wait for the perfect sweetheart with a nasty mind to cross their path: U.
and then, unwanted but all too welcome, a second one: Miss B.

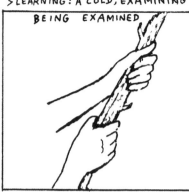

>LEARNING: A COLD, EXAMINING LOOK, SEAMINGLY PASSIONLESS, ALMOST BORED = SEXUAL TRANCE<
BEING EXAMINED
BY MISS B.
IS, FOR A FEW MARVELOUS MOMENTS OF ODDITY, TO
BECOME A NUMINOUS OBJECT. TAKEN. OWNED. LOST TO HER.
Since I began to turn my erotic fantasies into reality three months ago, I have lost six pounds without starving at all ...
DRINNN
I've lost my appetite for sweets – before, I used to eat half a bar of chocolate each day.
Look at that ...
CLAC
OOH How wet you are.
mmmmm
I am a 44 years old woman, emancipated and self-confident.
Come.
... and I like to feel that he is stronger than me.
There, stay like this.

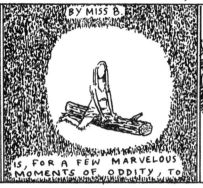

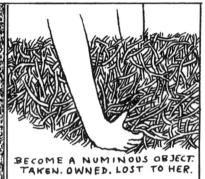

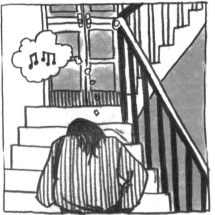

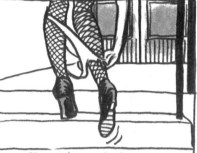

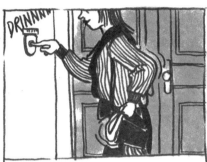

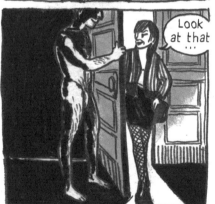

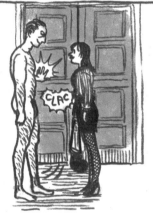

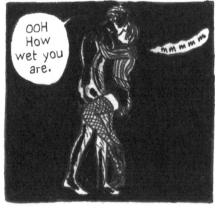

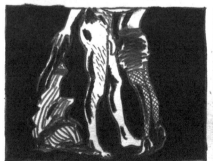

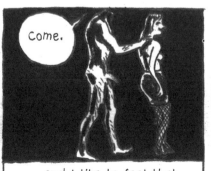

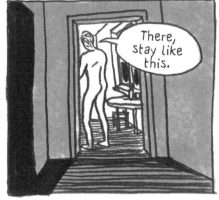

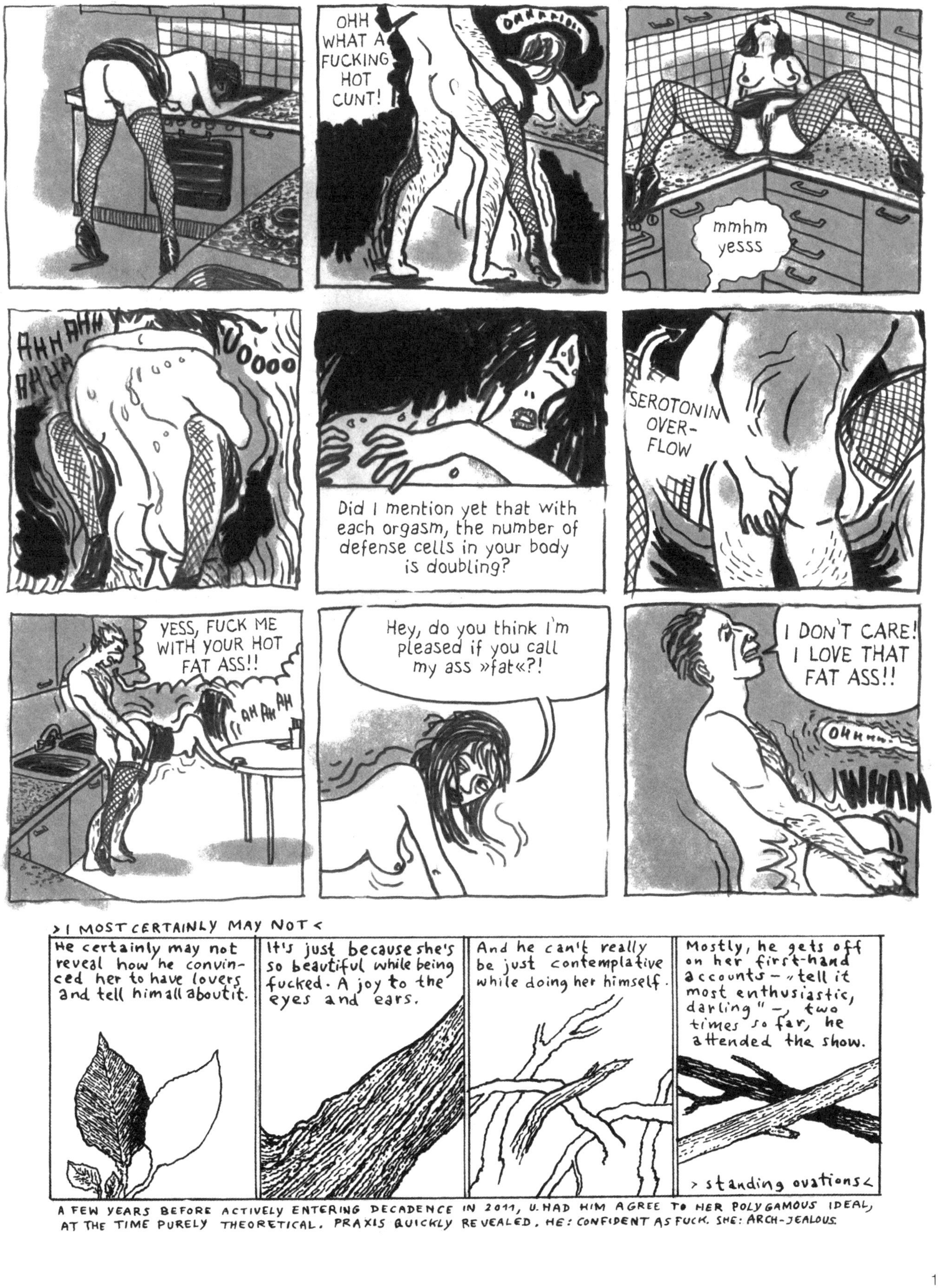
OHH WHAT A FUCKING HOT CUNT!
mmhm yesss
SEROTONIN OVER-FLOW
Did I mention yet that with each orgasm, the number of defense cells in your body is doubling?
YESS, FUCK ME WITH YOUR HOT FAT ASS!!
AH AH AH
Hey, do you think I'm pleased if you call my ass »fat«?!
I DON'T CARE! I LOVE THAT FAT ASS!!
WHAM
>I MOST CERTAINLY MAY NOT<
He certainly may not reveal how he convinced her to have lovers and tell him all about it.
It's just because she's so beautiful while being fucked. A joy to the eyes and ears.
And he can't really be just contemplative while doing her himself.
Mostly, he gets off on her first-hand accounts – „tell it most enthusiastic, darling" –, two times so far, he attended the show.
>standing ovations<
A FEW YEARS BEFORE ACTIVELY ENTERING DECADENCE IN 2011, U. HAD HIM AGREE TO HER POLYGAMOUS IDEAL, AT THE TIME PURELY THEORETICAL. PRAXIS QUICKLY REVEALED. HE: CONFIDENT AS FUCK. SHE: ARCH-JEALOUS.

MISS B. IN A BATHTUB

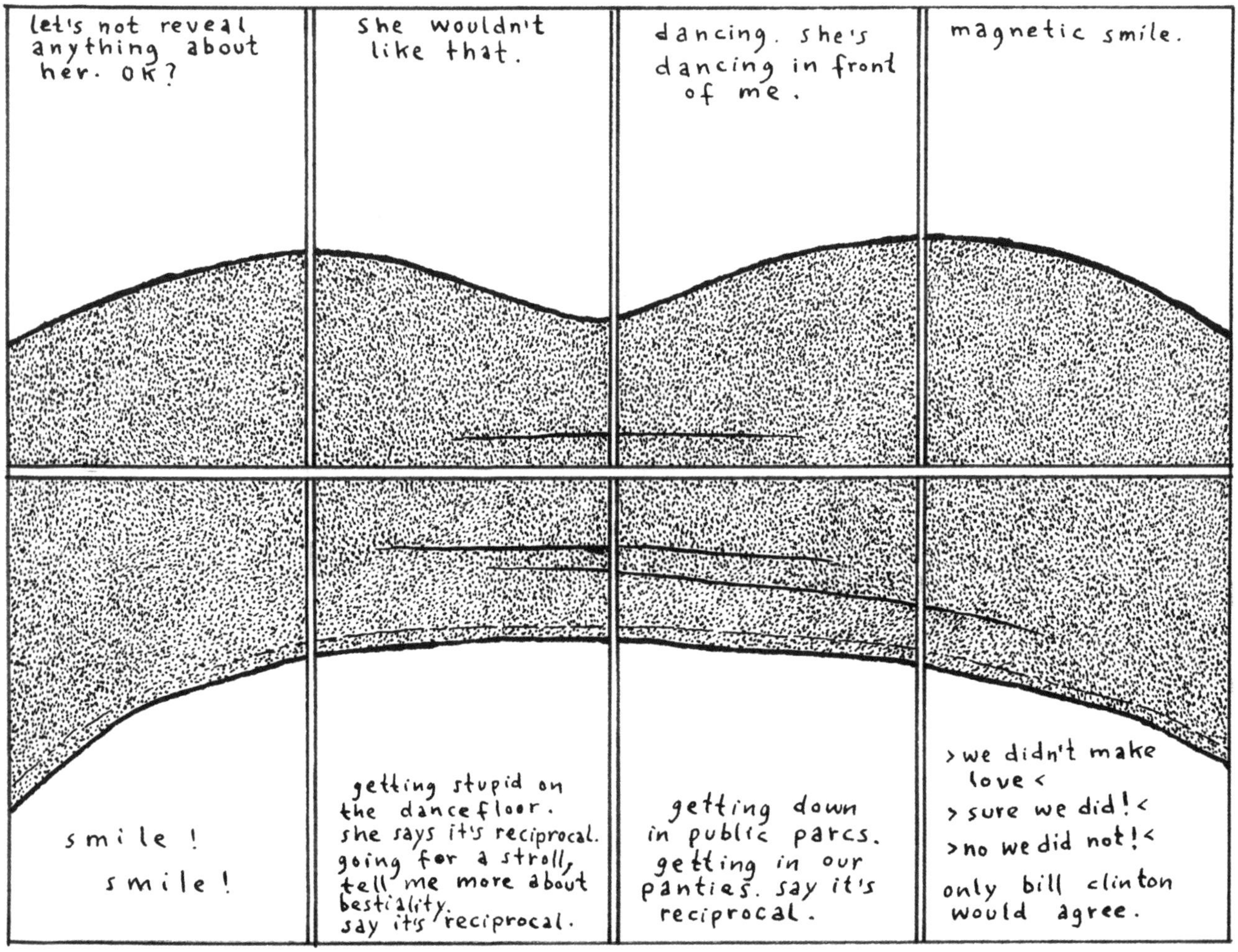

| let's not reveal anything about her. ok? | she wouldn't like that. | dancing. she's dancing in front of me. | magnetic smile. |
|---|---|---|---|
| smile ! smile ! | getting stupid on the dancefloor. she says it's reciprocal. going for a stroll, tell me more about bestiality. say it's reciprocal. | getting down in public parcs. getting in our panties. say it's reciprocal. | >we didn't make love < > sure we did ! < >no we did not ! < only bill clinton would agree. |

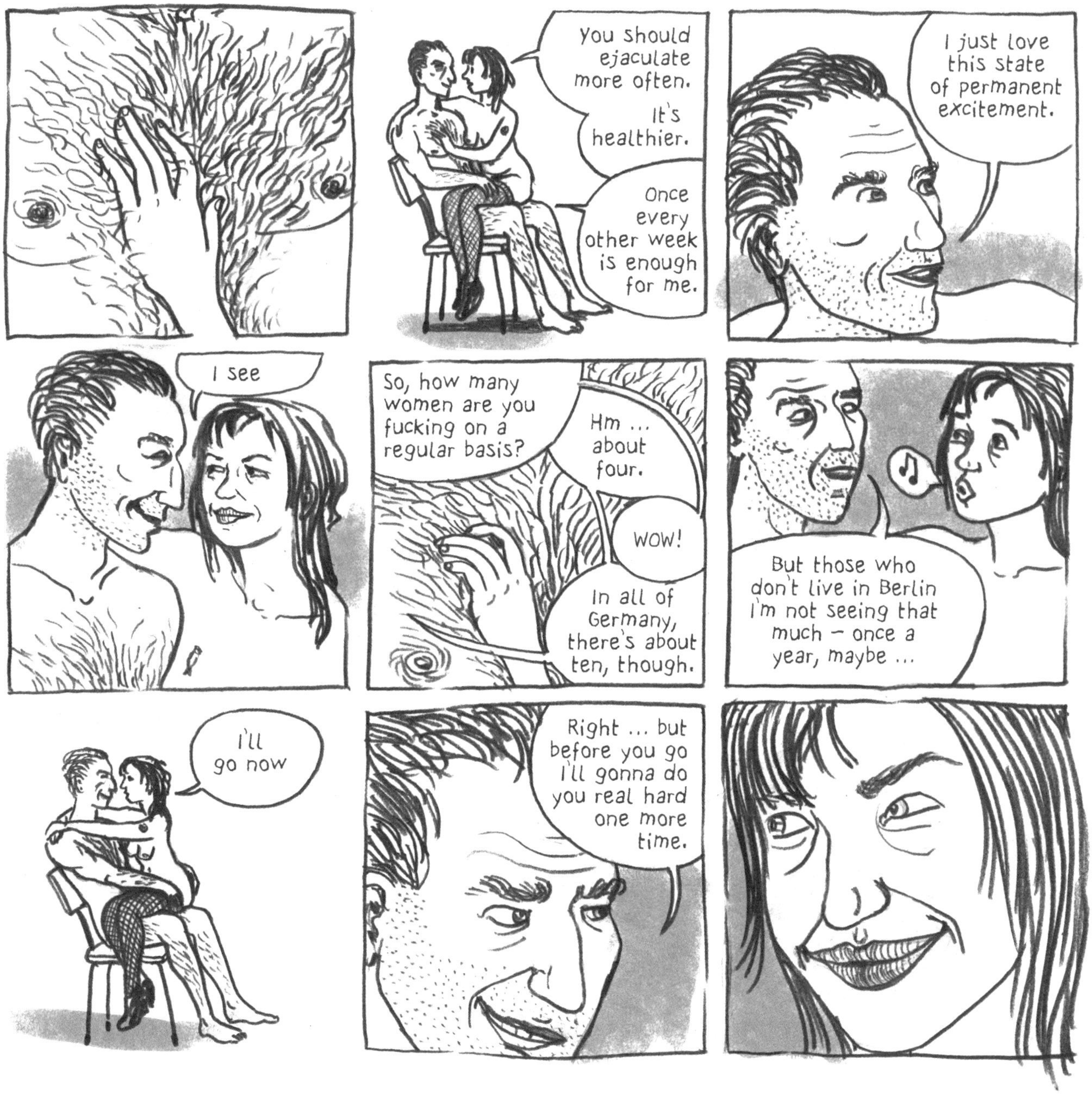
You should ejaculate more often.
It's healthier.
Once every other week is enough for me.
I just love this state of permanent excitement.
I see
So, how many women are you fucking on a regular basis?
Hm ... about four.
WOW!
In all of Germany, there's about ten, though.
♪
But those who don't live in Berlin I'm not seeing that much – once a year, maybe ...
I'll go now
Right ... but before you go I'll gonna do you real hard one more time.

>JUST ETHICS. HOT DAMN...<

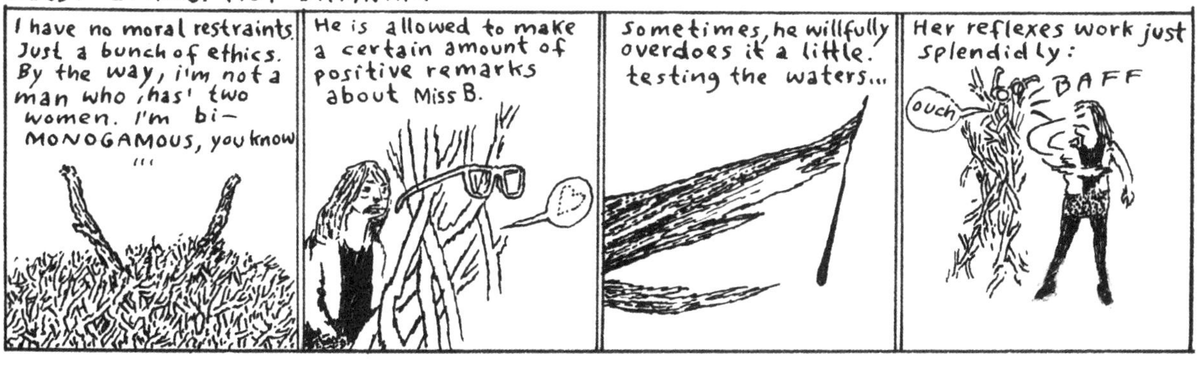
I have no moral restraints. Just a bunch of ethics. By the way, i'm not a man who 'has' two women. I'm bi-MONOGAMOUS, you know ...
He is allowed to make a certain amount of positive remarks about Miss B.
Sometimes, he willfully overdoes it a little. testing the waters...
Her reflexes work just splendidly:
ouch
BAFF

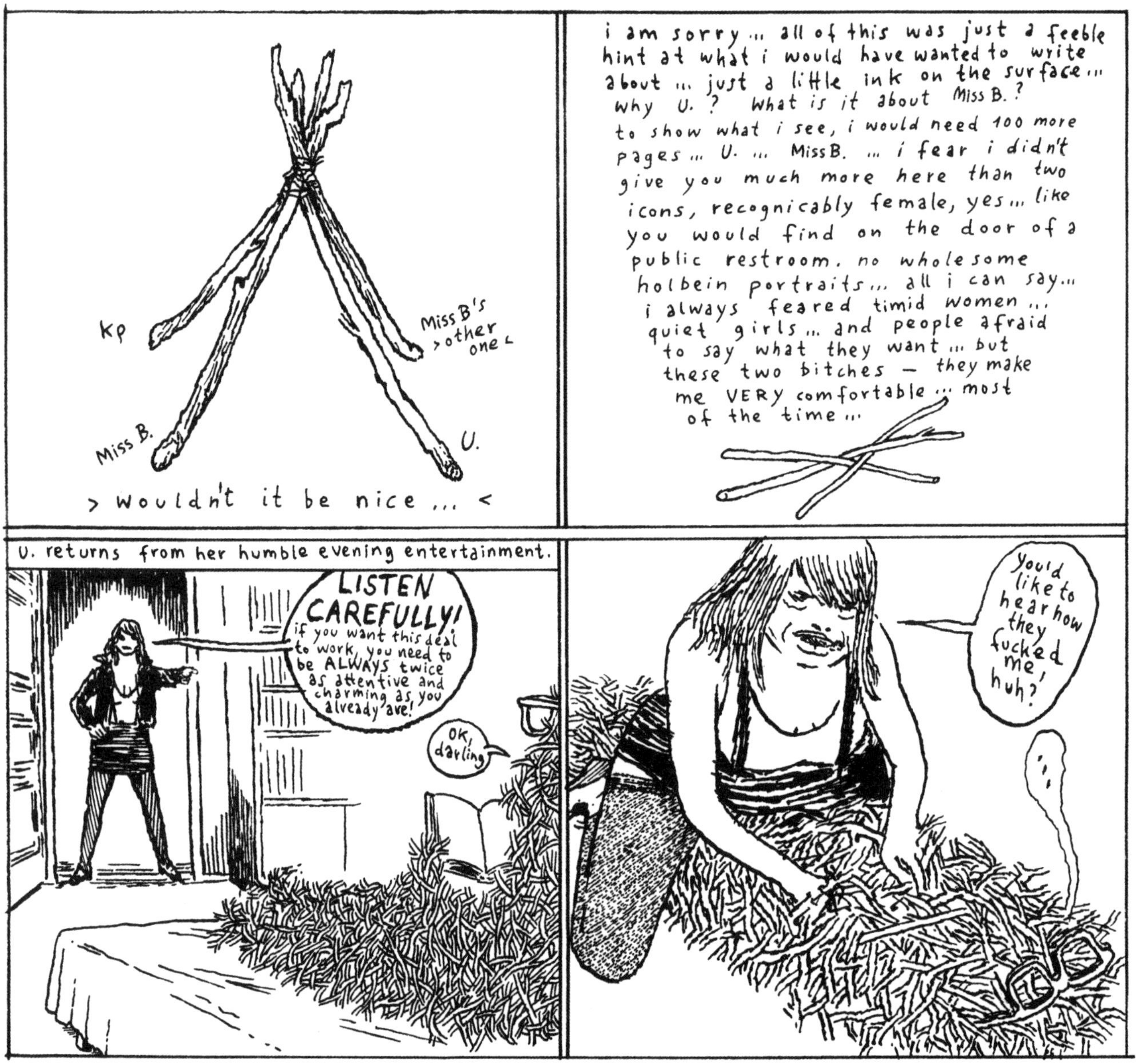
Kp
Miss B's >other one<
Miss B.
U.
> wouldn't it be nice ... <
i am sorry ... all of this was just a feeble hint at what i would have wanted to write about ... just a little ink on the surface ... why U. ? What is it about Miss B. ? to show what i see, i would need 100 more pages ... U. ... Miss B. ... i fear i didn't give you much more here than two icons, recognicably female, yes ... like you would find on the door of a public restroom. no wholesome holbein portraits ... all i can say ... i always feared timid women ... quiet girls ... and people afraid to say what they want ... but these two bitches – they make me VERY comfortable ... most of the time ...
U. returns from her humble evening entertainment.
LISTEN CAREFULLY! if you want this deal to work, you need to be ALWAYS twice as attentive and charming as you already are!
OK, darling
You'd like to hear how they fucked me, huh?

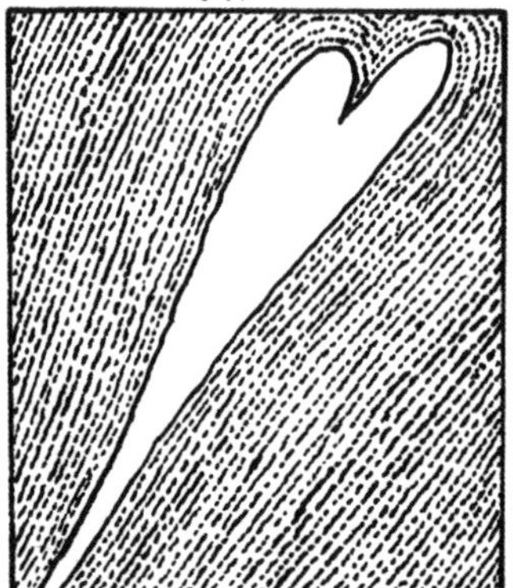
uh –

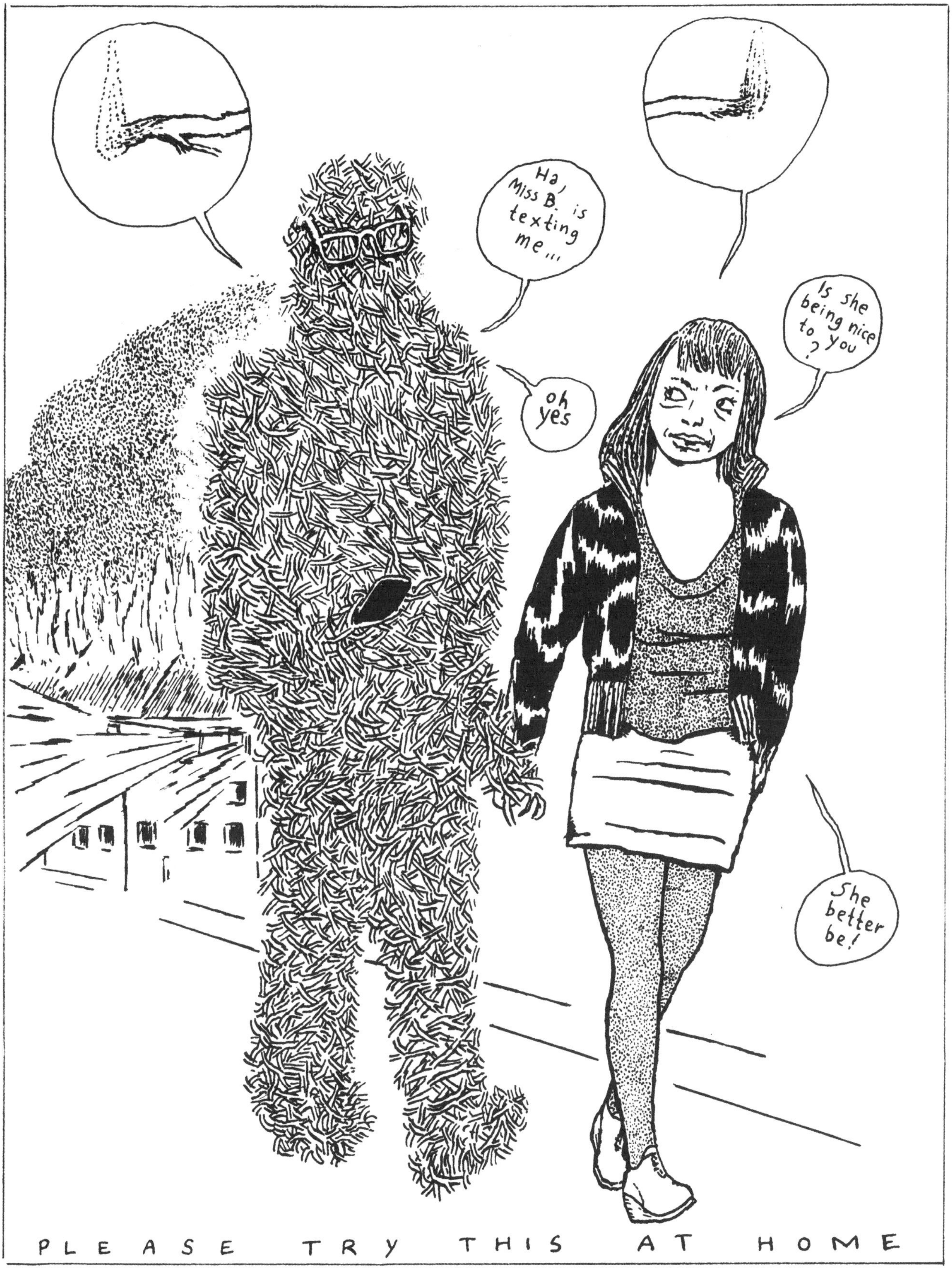
Ha, Miss B. is texting me...
oh yes
Is she being nice to you?
She better be!
PLEASE TRY THIS AT HOME

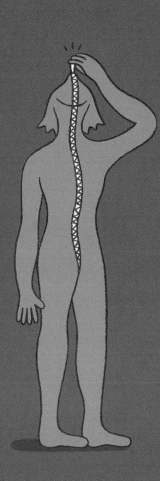

My body is a vessel
for gathering and keeping,
a pitcher on wheels
being filled with impression
as it travels.

Going off-road,
splashing over,
leaving a trail.

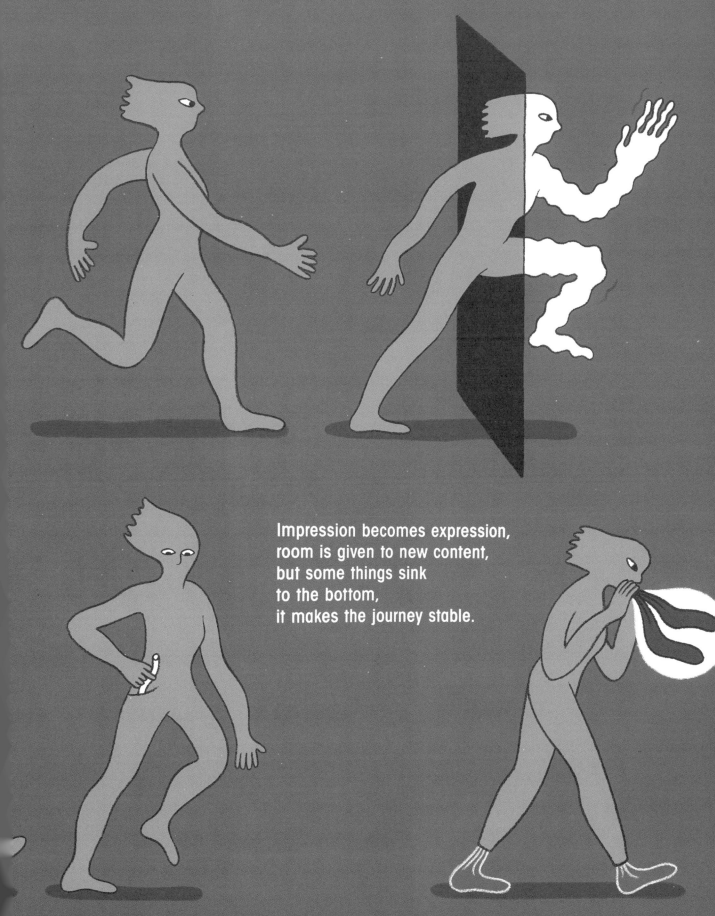

Impression becomes expression,
room is given to new content,
but some things sink
to the bottom,
it makes the journey stable.

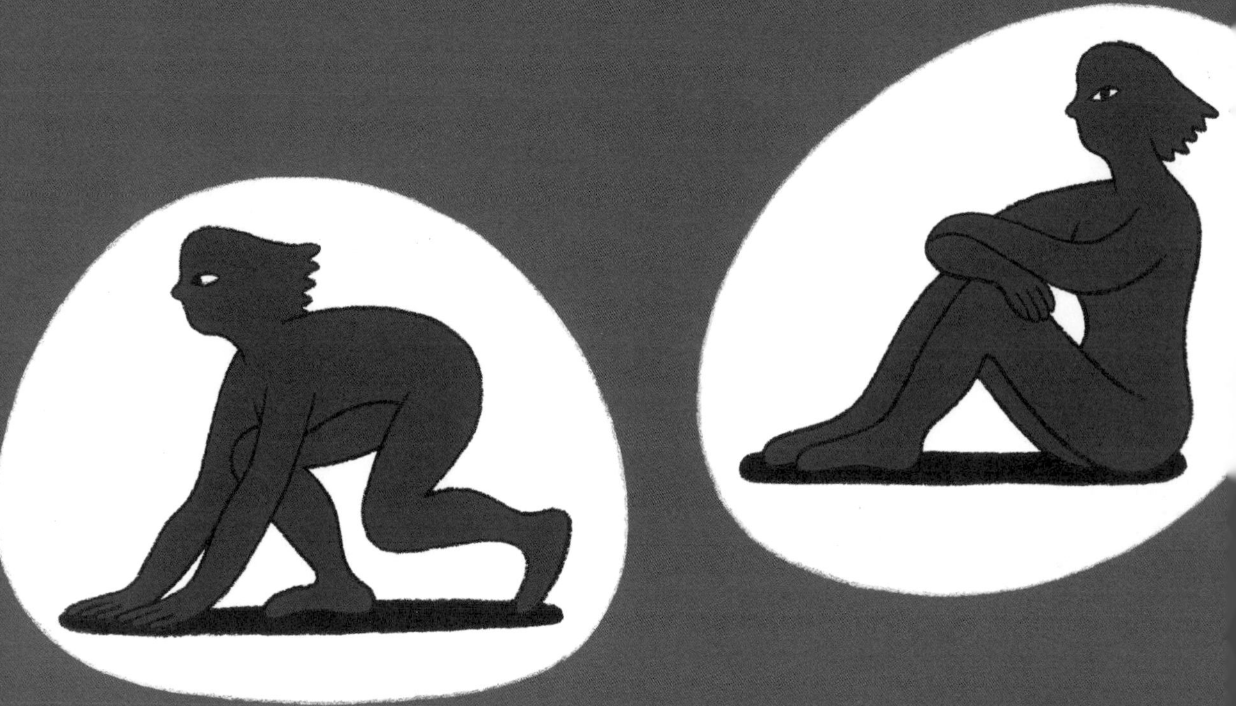

Learning to steer
between pits and fires,
has a focus:
quench, fill, nourish, destroy.

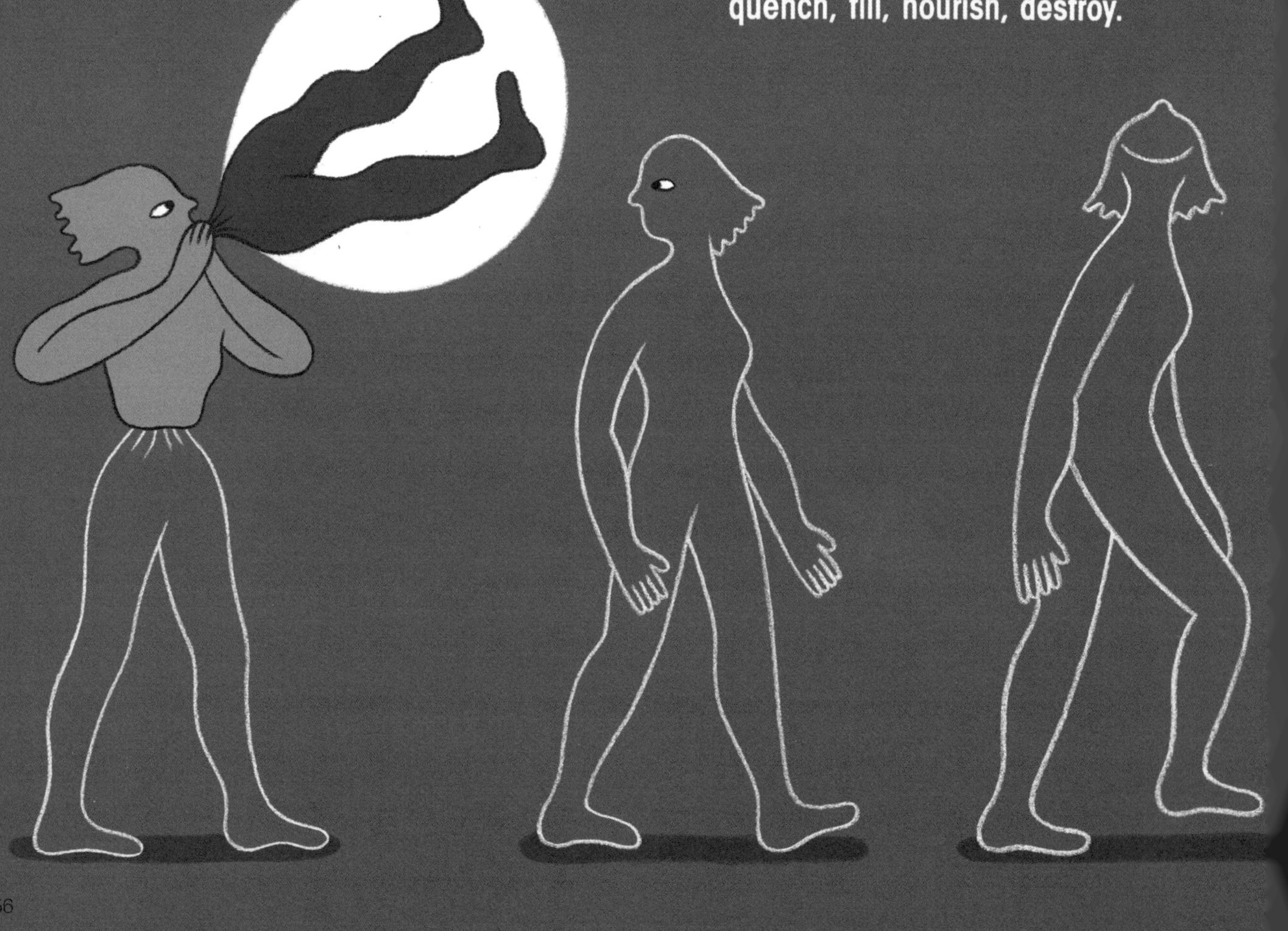

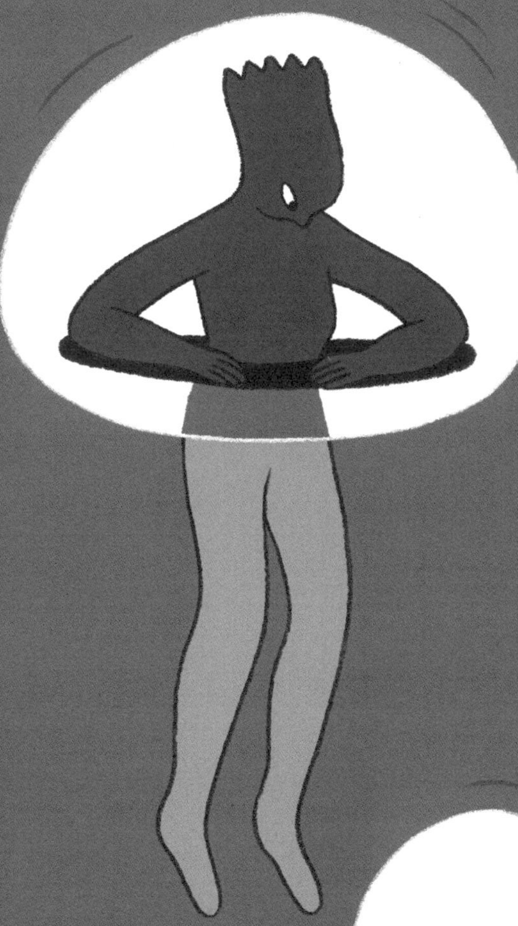

I´am water, petrol and acid
my body is a vessel.

Come on body,
cruise for me!

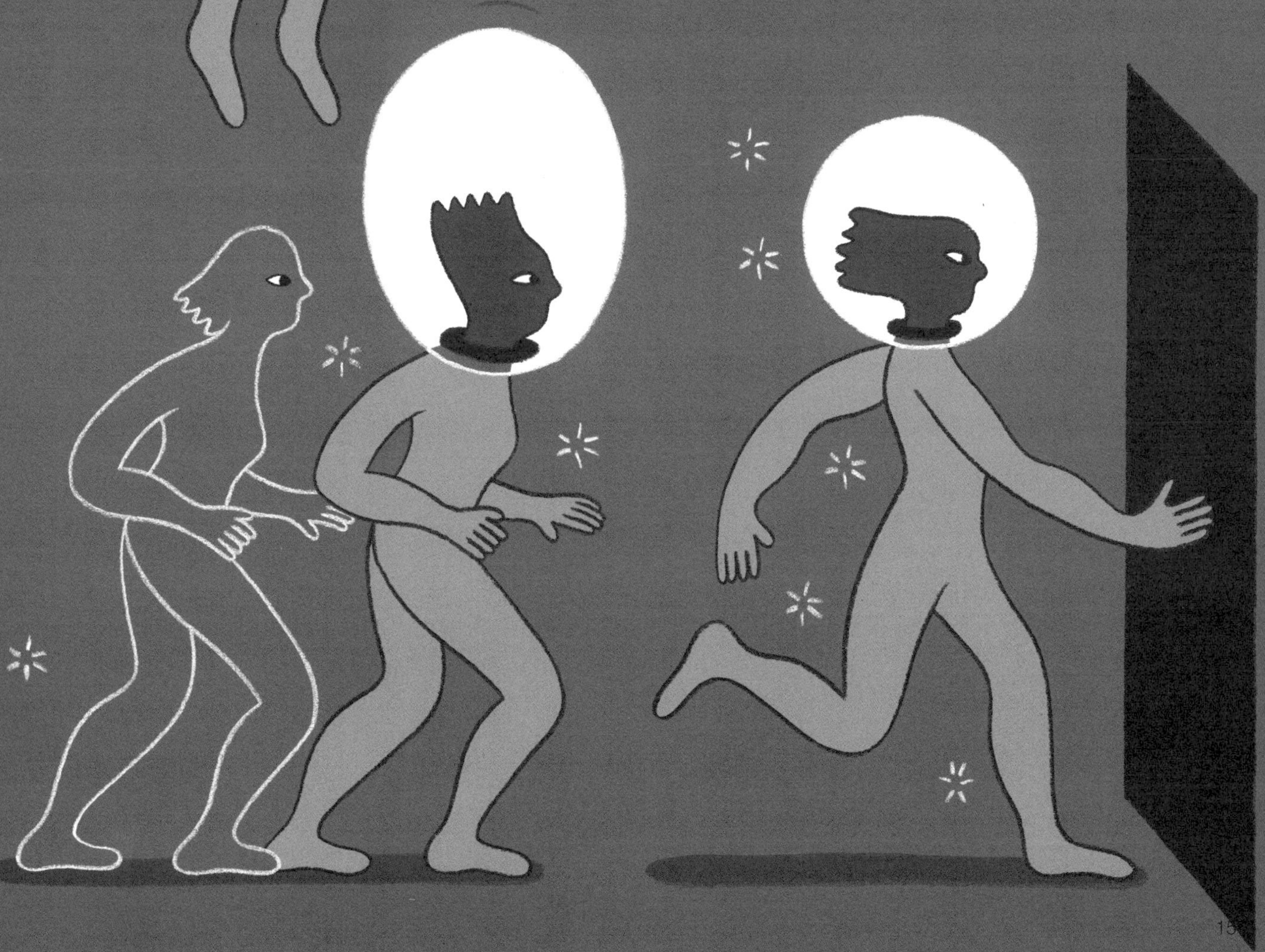

STINA LÖFGREN

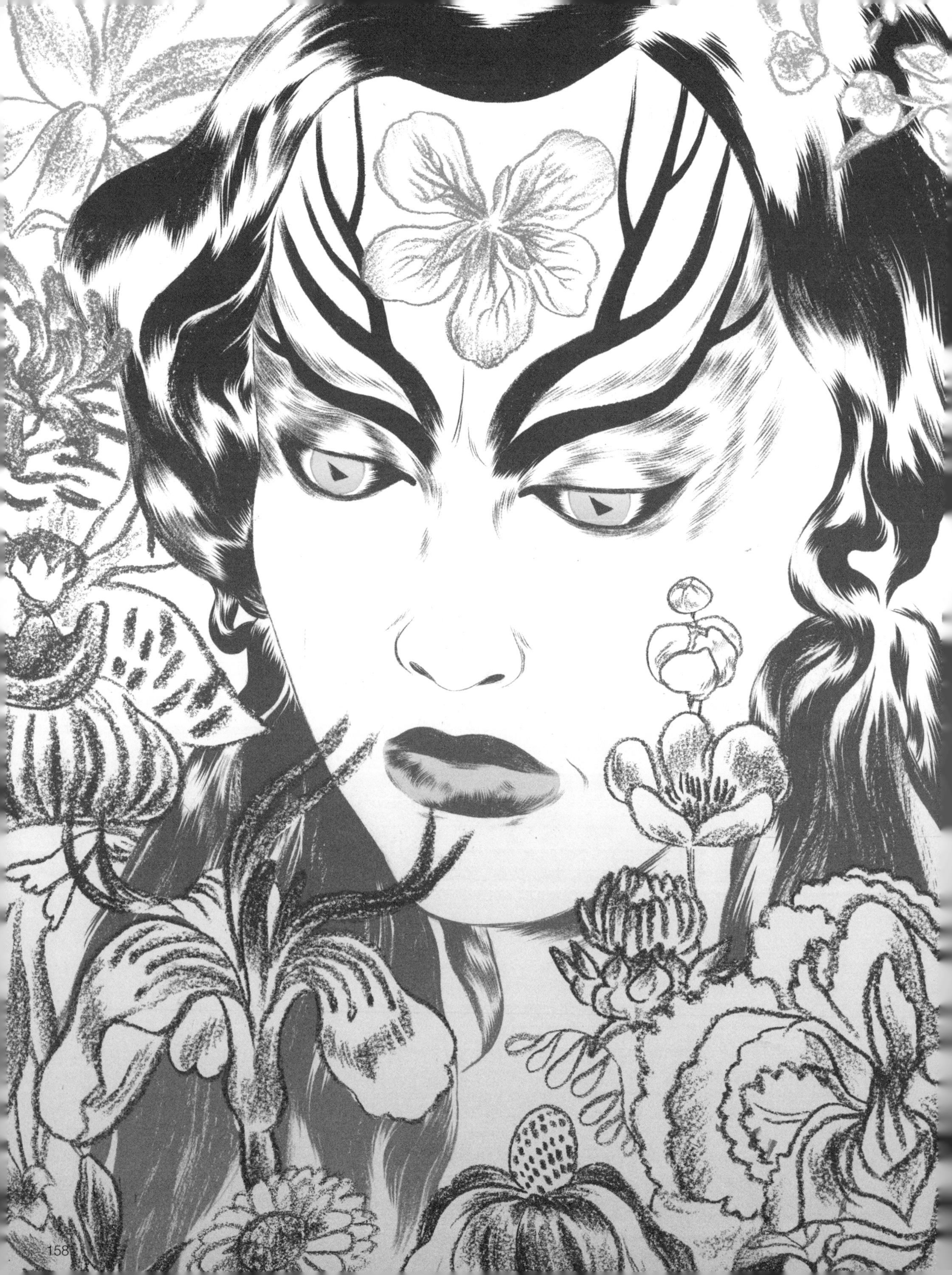

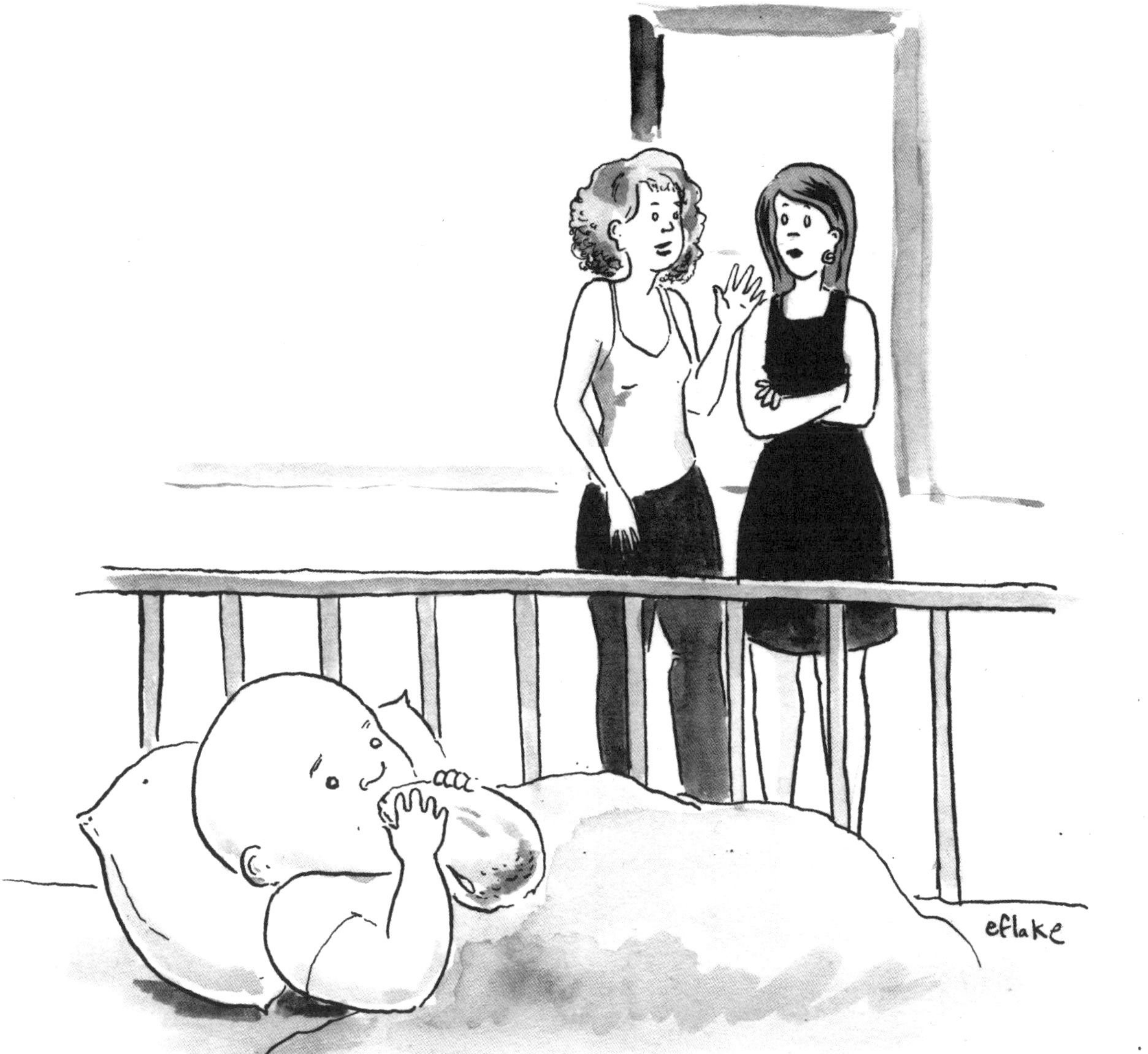
eflake

"TURNS OUT MY OLD IMPLANTS MAKE PERFECT WOOBIES."

# Untethered

### A STORY BY LISA ULLMANN
### ART BY KAT ROBERTS
### LAYOUTS BY JOAN REILLY

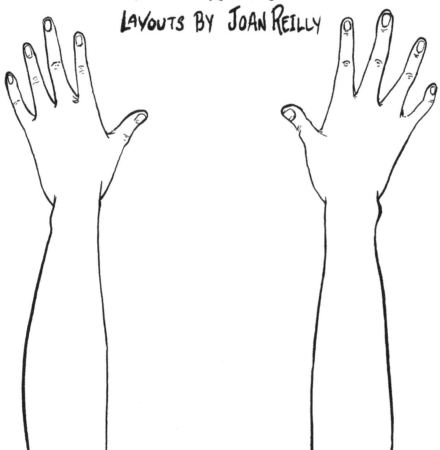

IT ALL STARTED IN MY GYNECOLOGIST'S OFFICE, A FEW WEEKS AFTER MY 39TH BIRTHDAY.

I'D BEEN SEEING DR. WERTZ FOR YEARS.

ALRIGHT I'M GOING TO GIVE YOU A BREAST EXAM.

AT ALMOST EVERY APPOINTMENT IN MY 30'S HE URGED ME TO TAKE PREGNANCY VERY SERIOUSLY.

YOU GIVE YOURSELF BREAST EXAMS RIGHT?

NO, NOT REALLY.

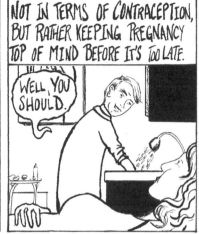

NOT IN TERMS OF CONTRACEPTION, BUT RATHER KEEPING PREGNANCY TOP OF MIND BEFORE IT'S TOO LATE.

WELL, YOU SHOULD.

AS ALARMING AS THESE WARNINGS HAVE BEEN, I'M NEVER OFFENDED BY HIS CANDOR.

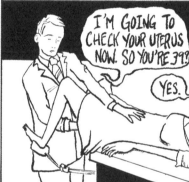

I'M GOING TO CHECK YOUR UTERUS NOW. SO YOU'RE 39?

YES.

AS A GYNECOLOGIST, HALF OF HIS JOB IS LIKELY TELLING WOMEN THEY CAN'T GET PREGNANT.

YOU'LL NEED TO START GETTING MAMMOGRAMS NEXT YEAR KEEP IN MIND.

GIVEN THAT SCENARIO I'D LIKE TO DISCUSS MY FERTILITY OPTIONS.

SIGH, OKAY.

I'M JUST TRYING TO FIGURE OUT WHAT, IF ANYTHING I SHOULD DO.

YOU'RE NOT SEEING ANYONE RIGHT NOW I TAKE IT.

NO.

YOU HAVE TO BE RUTHLESSLY HONEST WITH YOURSELF. WILL YOUR LIFE BE TRULY UNFULFILLED IF YOU DON'T HAVE CHILDREN?

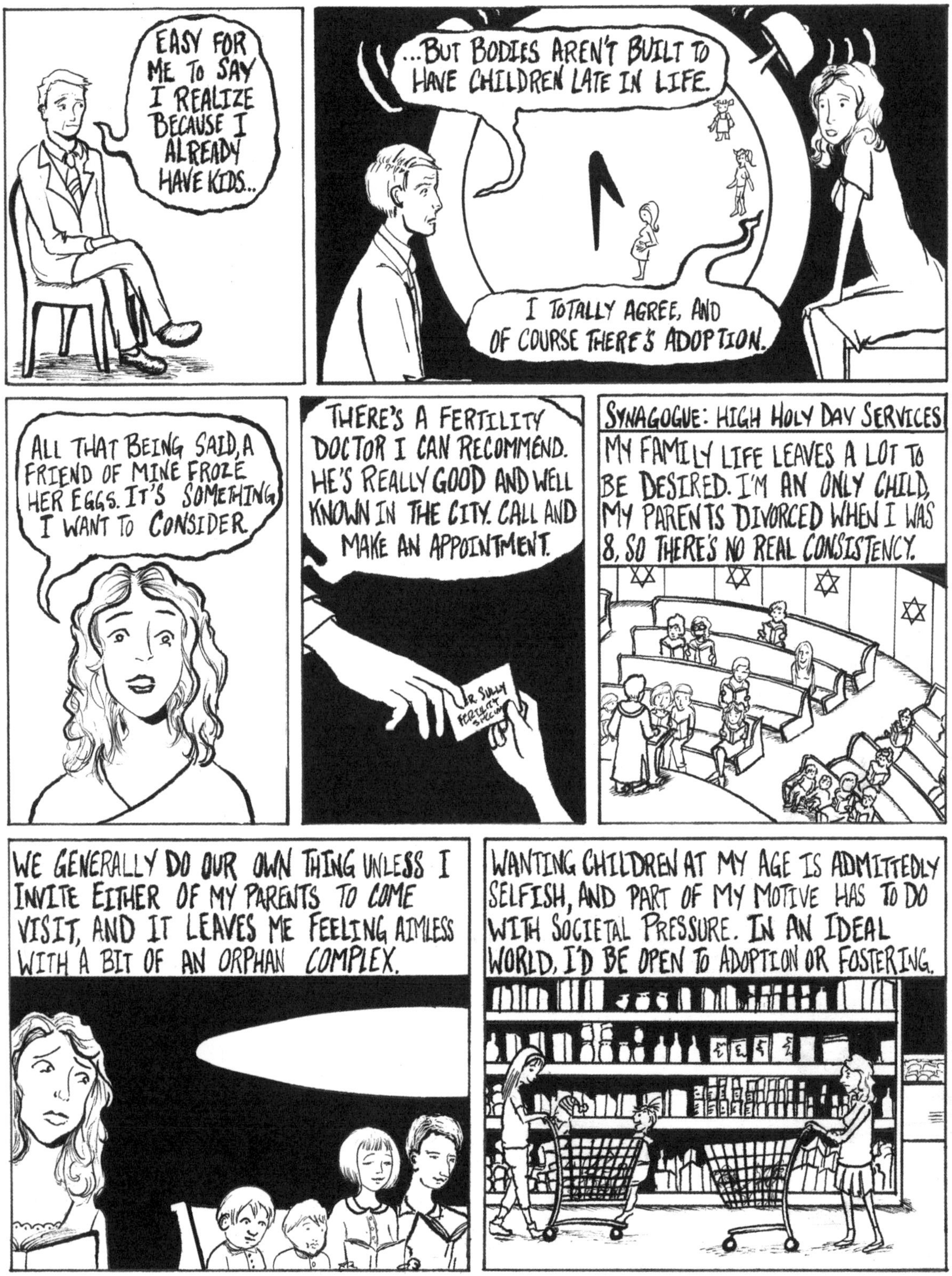
EASY FOR ME TO SAY I REALIZE BECAUSE I ALREADY HAVE KIDS...
...BUT BODIES AREN'T BUILT TO HAVE CHILDREN LATE IN LIFE.
I TOTALLY AGREE, AND OF COURSE THERE'S ADOPTION.
ALL THAT BEING SAID, A FRIEND OF MINE FROZE HER EGGS. IT'S SOMETHING I WANT TO CONSIDER.
THERE'S A FERTILITY DOCTOR I CAN RECOMMEND. HE'S REALLY GOOD AND WELL KNOWN IN THE CITY. CALL AND MAKE AN APPOINTMENT.
SYNAGOGUE: HIGH HOLY DAY SERVICES
MY FAMILY LIFE LEAVES A LOT TO BE DESIRED. I'M AN ONLY CHILD, MY PARENTS DIVORCED WHEN I WAS 8, SO THERE'S NO REAL CONSISTENCY.
WE GENERALLY DO OUR OWN THING UNLESS I INVITE EITHER OF MY PARENTS TO COME VISIT, AND IT LEAVES ME FEELING AIMLESS WITH A BIT OF AN ORPHAN COMPLEX.
WANTING CHILDREN AT MY AGE IS ADMITTEDLY SELFISH, AND PART OF MY MOTIVE HAS TO DO WITH SOCIETAL PRESSURE. IN AN IDEAL WORLD, I'D BE OPEN TO ADOPTION OR FOSTERING.

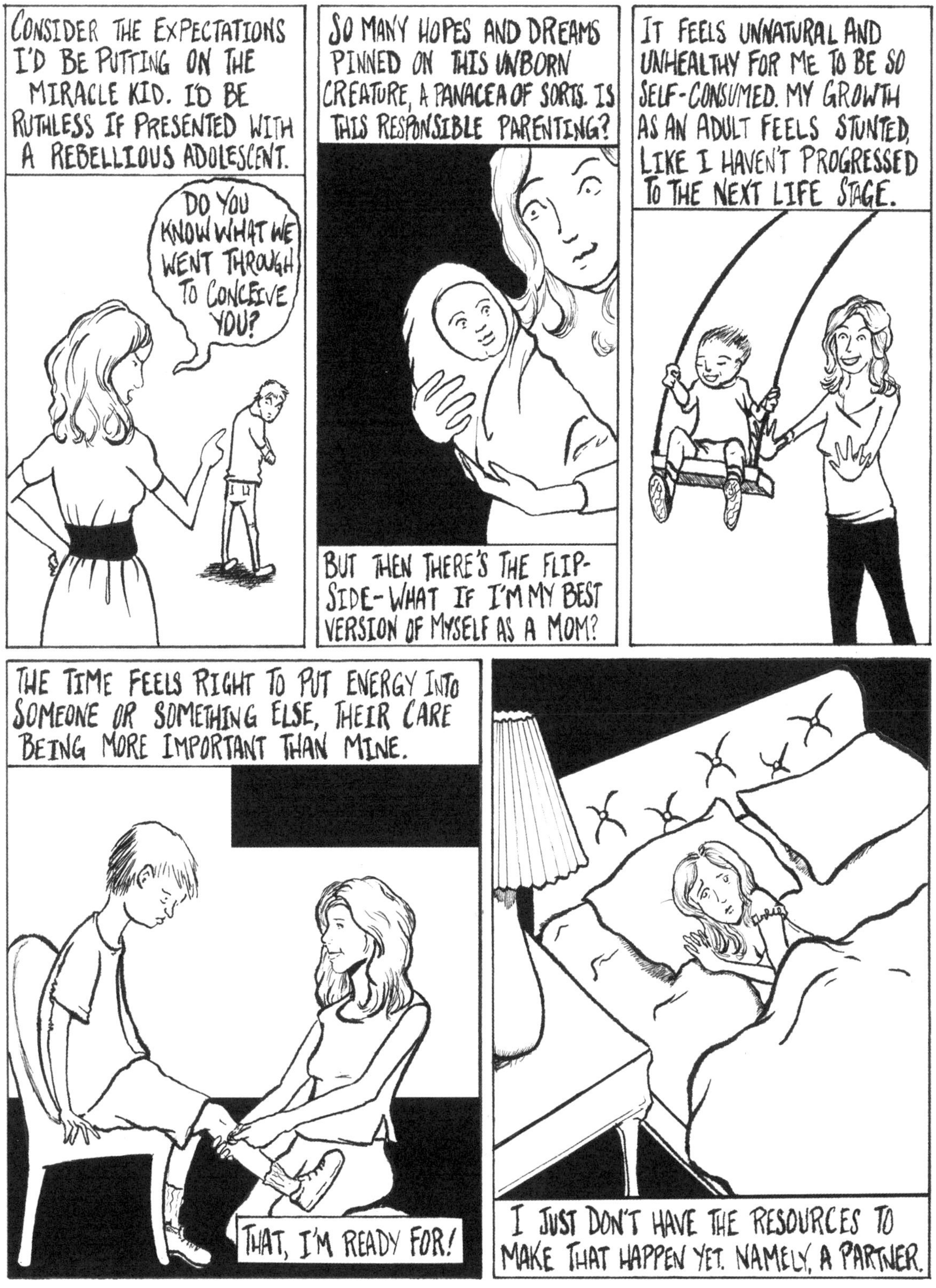
CONSIDER THE EXPECTATIONS I'D BE PUTTING ON THE MIRACLE KID. I'D BE RUTHLESS IF PRESENTED WITH A REBELLIOUS ADOLESCENT.
DO YOU KNOW WHAT WE WENT THROUGH TO CONCEIVE YOU?
SO MANY HOPES AND DREAMS PINNED ON THIS UNBORN CREATURE, A PANACEA OF SORTS. IS THIS RESPONSIBLE PARENTING?
BUT THEN THERE'S THE FLIP-SIDE- WHAT IF I'M MY BEST VERSION OF MYSELF AS A MOM?
IT FEELS UNNATURAL AND UNHEALTHY FOR ME TO BE SO SELF-CONSUMED. MY GROWTH AS AN ADULT FEELS STUNTED, LIKE I HAVEN'T PROGRESSED TO THE NEXT LIFE STAGE.
THE TIME FEELS RIGHT TO PUT ENERGY INTO SOMEONE OR SOMETHING ELSE, THEIR CARE BEING MORE IMPORTANT THAN MINE.
THAT, I'M READY FOR!
I JUST DON'T HAVE THE RESOURCES TO MAKE THAT HAPPEN YET. NAMELY, A PARTNER.

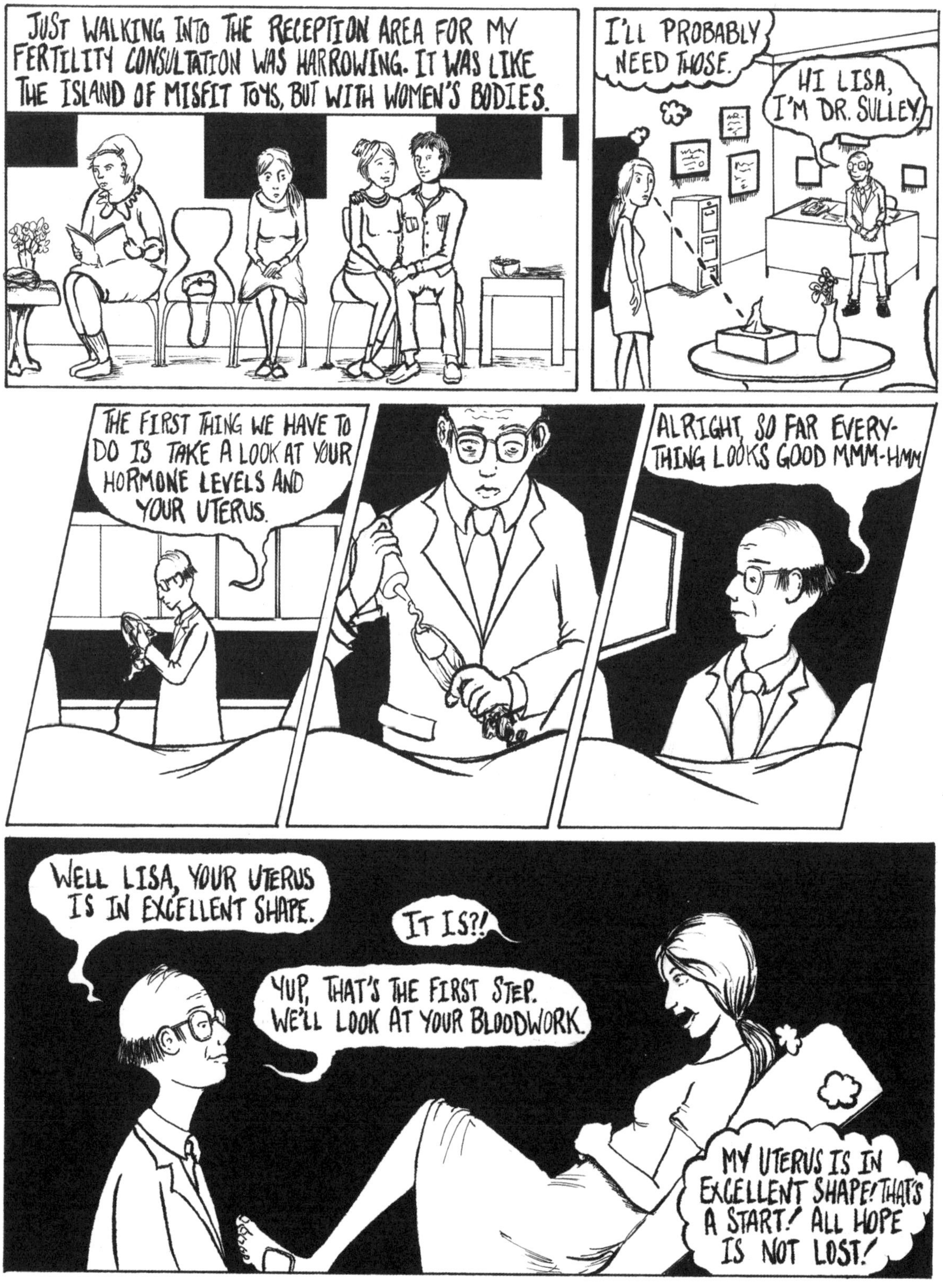

JUST WALKING INTO THE RECEPTION AREA FOR MY FERTILITY CONSULTATION WAS HARROWING. IT WAS LIKE THE ISLAND OF MISFIT TOYS, BUT WITH WOMEN'S BODIES.
I'LL PROBABLY NEED THOSE.
HI LISA, I'M DR. SULLEY.
THE FIRST THING WE HAVE TO DO IS TAKE A LOOK AT YOUR HORMONE LEVELS AND YOUR UTERUS.
ALRIGHT, SO FAR EVERY-THING LOOKS GOOD MMM-HMM
WELL LISA, YOUR UTERUS IS IN EXCELLENT SHAPE.
IT IS?!
YUP, THAT'S THE FIRST STEP. WE'LL LOOK AT YOUR BLOODWORK.
MY UTERUS IS IN EXCELLENT SHAPE! THAT'S A START! ALL HOPE IS NOT LOST!

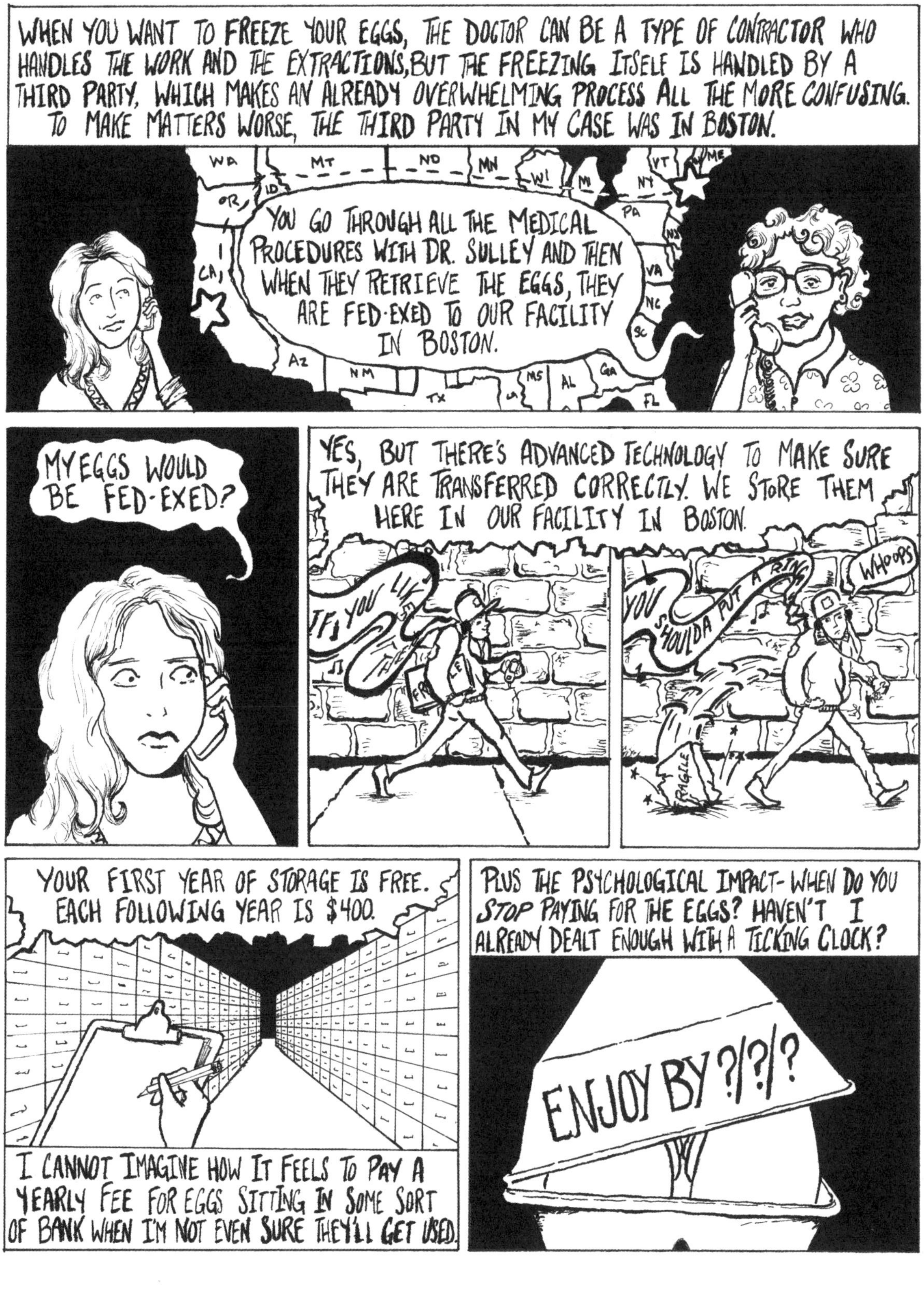
WHEN YOU WANT TO FREEZE YOUR EGGS, THE DOCTOR CAN BE A TYPE OF CONTRACTOR WHO HANDLES THE WORK AND THE EXTRACTIONS, BUT THE FREEZING ITSELF IS HANDLED BY A THIRD PARTY, WHICH MAKES AN ALREADY OVERWHELMING PROCESS ALL THE MORE CONFUSING. TO MAKE MATTERS WORSE, THE THIRD PARTY IN MY CASE WAS IN BOSTON.
WA
MT
ND
MN
WI
MI
VT
ME
NY
ID
OR
PA
CA
VA
NC
SC
AZ
NM
TX
MS
AL
GA
FL
YOU GO THROUGH ALL THE MEDICAL PROCEDURES WITH DR. SULLEY AND THEN WHEN THEY RETRIEVE THE EGGS, THEY ARE FED-EXED TO OUR FACILITY IN BOSTON.
MY EGGS WOULD BE FED-EXED?
YES, BUT THERE'S ADVANCED TECHNOLOGY TO MAKE SURE THEY ARE TRANSFERRED CORRECTLY. WE STORE THEM HERE IN OUR FACILITY IN BOSTON.
IF YOU LIKED IT
YOU SHOULDA PUT A RING
WHOOPS
FRAGILE
YOUR FIRST YEAR OF STORAGE IS FREE. EACH FOLLOWING YEAR IS $400.
I CANNOT IMAGINE HOW IT FEELS TO PAY A YEARLY FEE FOR EGGS SITTING IN SOME SORT OF BANK WHEN I'M NOT EVEN SURE THEY'LL GET USED.
PLUS THE PSYCHOLOGICAL IMPACT- WHEN DO YOU STOP PAYING FOR THE EGGS? HAVEN'T I ALREADY DEALT ENOUGH WITH A TICKING CLOCK?
ENJOY BY ?/?/?

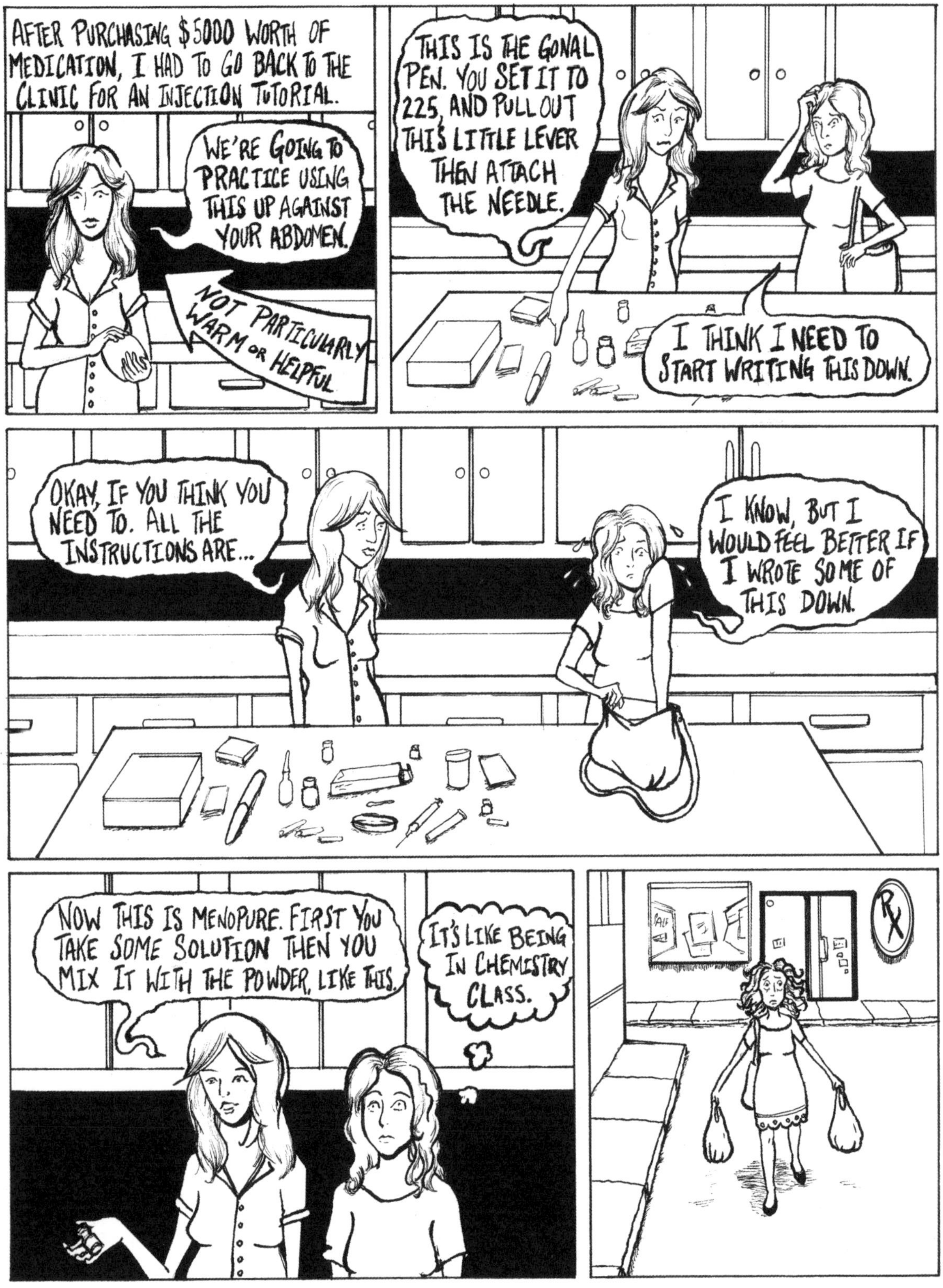
AFTER PURCHASING $5000 WORTH OF MEDICATION, I HAD TO GO BACK TO THE CLINIC FOR AN INJECTION TUTORIAL.
WE'RE GOING TO PRACTICE USING THIS UP AGAINST YOUR ABDOMEN.
NOT PARTICULARLY WARM OR HELPFUL
THIS IS THE GONAL PEN. YOU SET IT TO 225, AND PULL OUT THIS LITTLE LEVER THEN ATTACH THE NEEDLE.
I THINK I NEED TO START WRITING THIS DOWN.
OKAY, IF YOU THINK YOU NEED TO. ALL THE INSTRUCTIONS ARE...
I KNOW, BUT I WOULD FEEL BETTER IF I WROTE SOME OF THIS DOWN.
NOW THIS IS MENOPURE. FIRST YOU TAKE SOME SOLUTION THEN YOU MIX IT WITH THE POWDER, LIKE THIS.
IT'S LIKE BEING IN CHEMISTRY CLASS.
RX

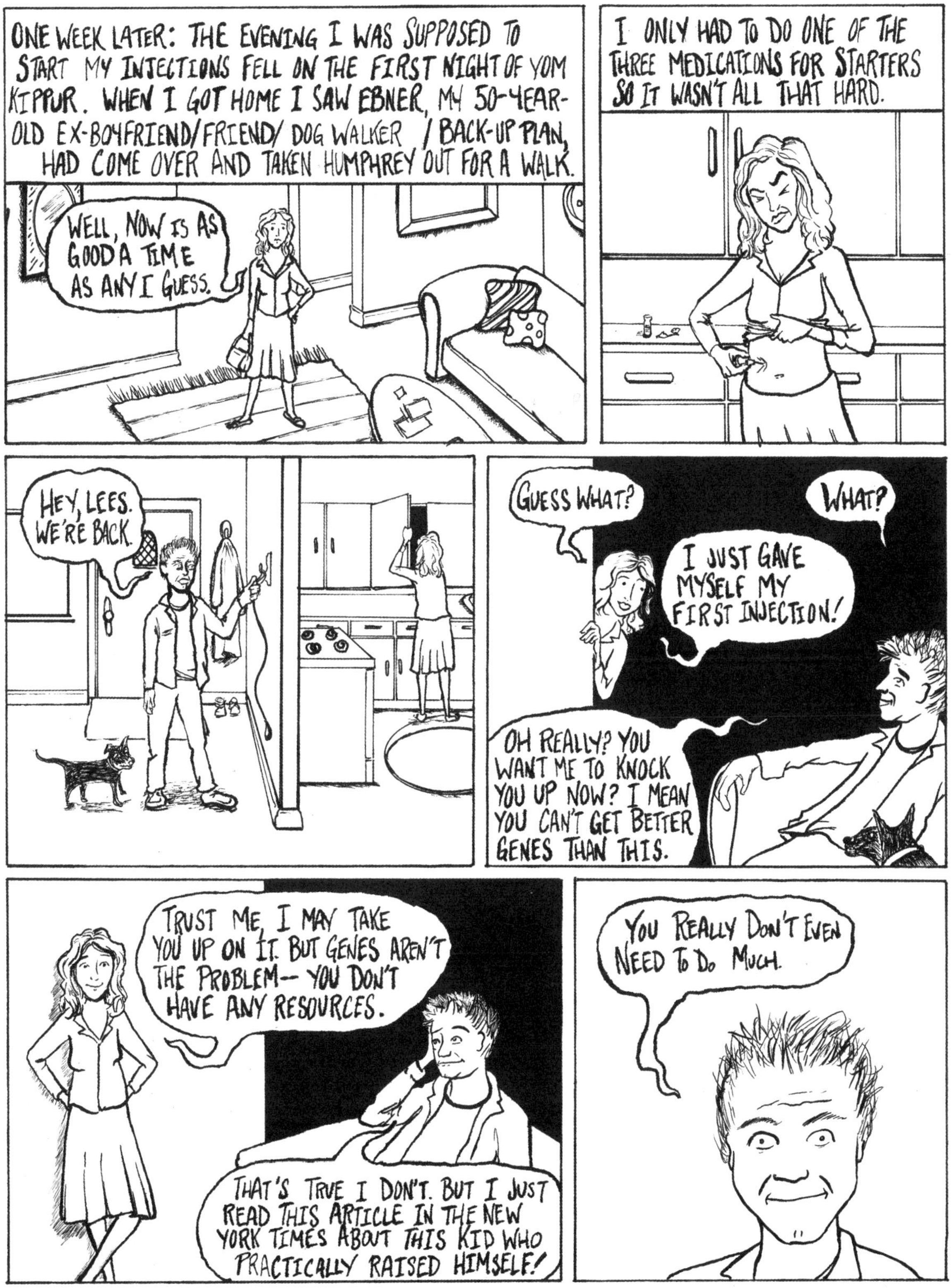
ONE WEEK LATER: THE EVENING I WAS SUPPOSED TO START MY INJECTIONS FELL ON THE FIRST NIGHT OF YOM KIPPUR. WHEN I GOT HOME I SAW EBNER, MY 50-YEAR-OLD EX-BOYFRIEND/FRIEND/ DOG WALKER / BACK-UP PLAN, HAD COME OVER AND TAKEN HUMPHREY OUT FOR A WALK.
WELL, NOW IS AS GOOD A TIME AS ANY I GUESS.
I ONLY HAD TO DO ONE OF THE THREE MEDICATIONS FOR STARTERS SO IT WASN'T ALL THAT HARD.
HEY, LEES. WE'RE BACK.
GUESS WHAT?
WHAT?
I JUST GAVE MYSELF MY FIRST INJECTION!
OH REALLY? YOU WANT ME TO KNOCK YOU UP NOW? I MEAN YOU CAN'T GET BETTER GENES THAN THIS.
TRUST ME, I MAY TAKE YOU UP ON IT. BUT GENES AREN'T THE PROBLEM-- YOU DON'T HAVE ANY RESOURCES.
THAT'S TRUE I DON'T. BUT I JUST READ THIS ARTICLE IN THE NEW YORK TIMES ABOUT THIS KID WHO PRACTICALLY RAISED HIMSELF!
YOU REALLY DON'T EVEN NEED TO DO MUCH.

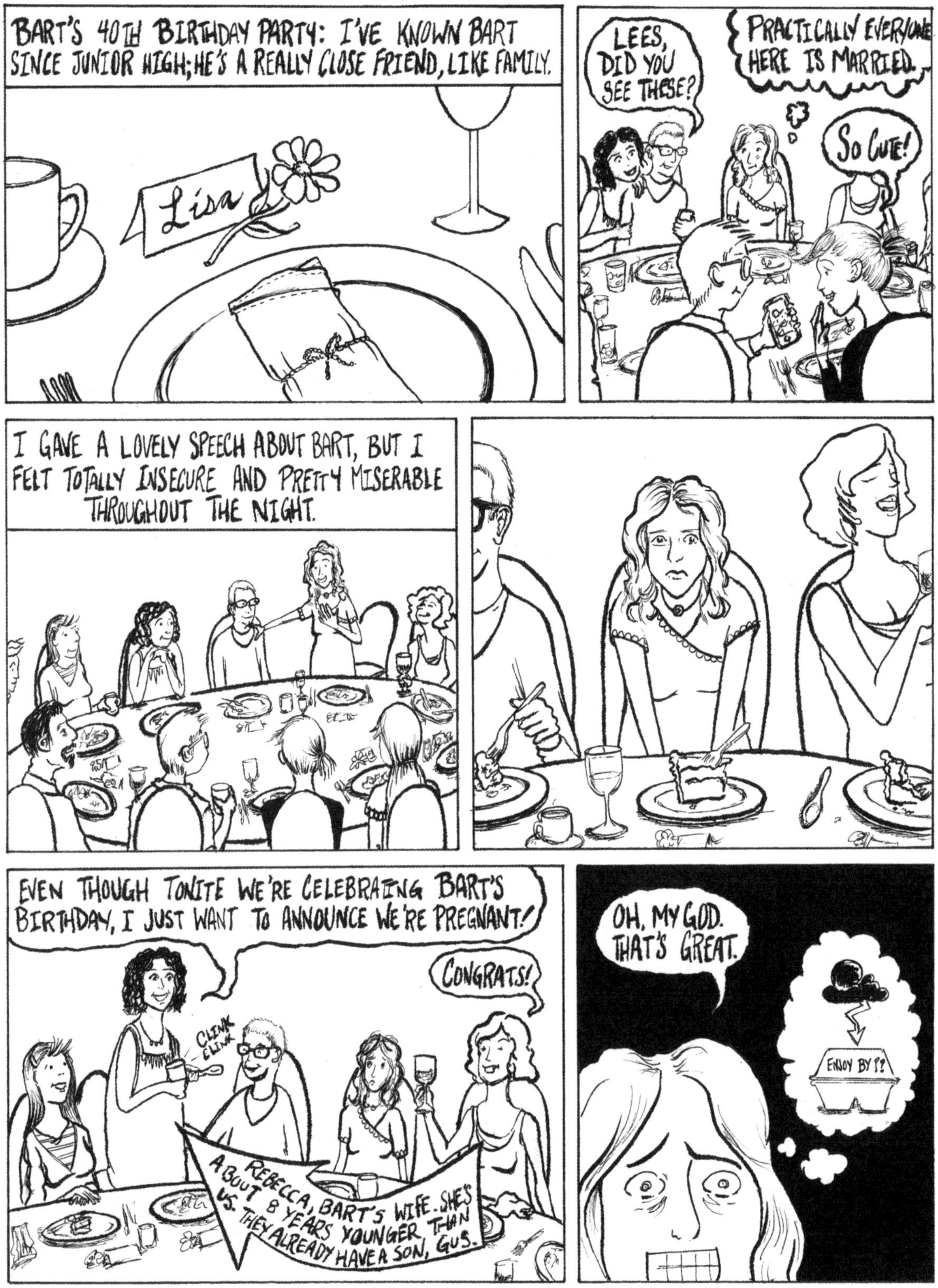
BART'S 40TH BIRTHDAY PARTY: I'VE KNOWN BART SINCE JUNIOR HIGH; HE'S A REALLY CLOSE FRIEND, LIKE FAMILY.
Lisa
LEES, DID YOU SEE THESE?
PRACTICALLY EVERYONE HERE IS MARRIED.
So CUTE!
I GAVE A LOVELY SPEECH ABOUT BART, BUT I FELT TOTALLY INSECURE AND PRETTY MISERABLE THROUGHOUT THE NIGHT.
EVEN THOUGH TONITE WE'RE CELEBRATING BART'S BIRTHDAY, I JUST WANT TO ANNOUNCE WE'RE PREGNANT!
CONGRATS!
CLINK CLINK
REBECCA, BART'S WIFE. SHE'S ABOUT 8 YEARS YOUNGER THAN US. THEY ALREADY HAVE A SON, GUS.
OH, MY GOD. THAT'S GREAT.
ENJOY BY ?!?

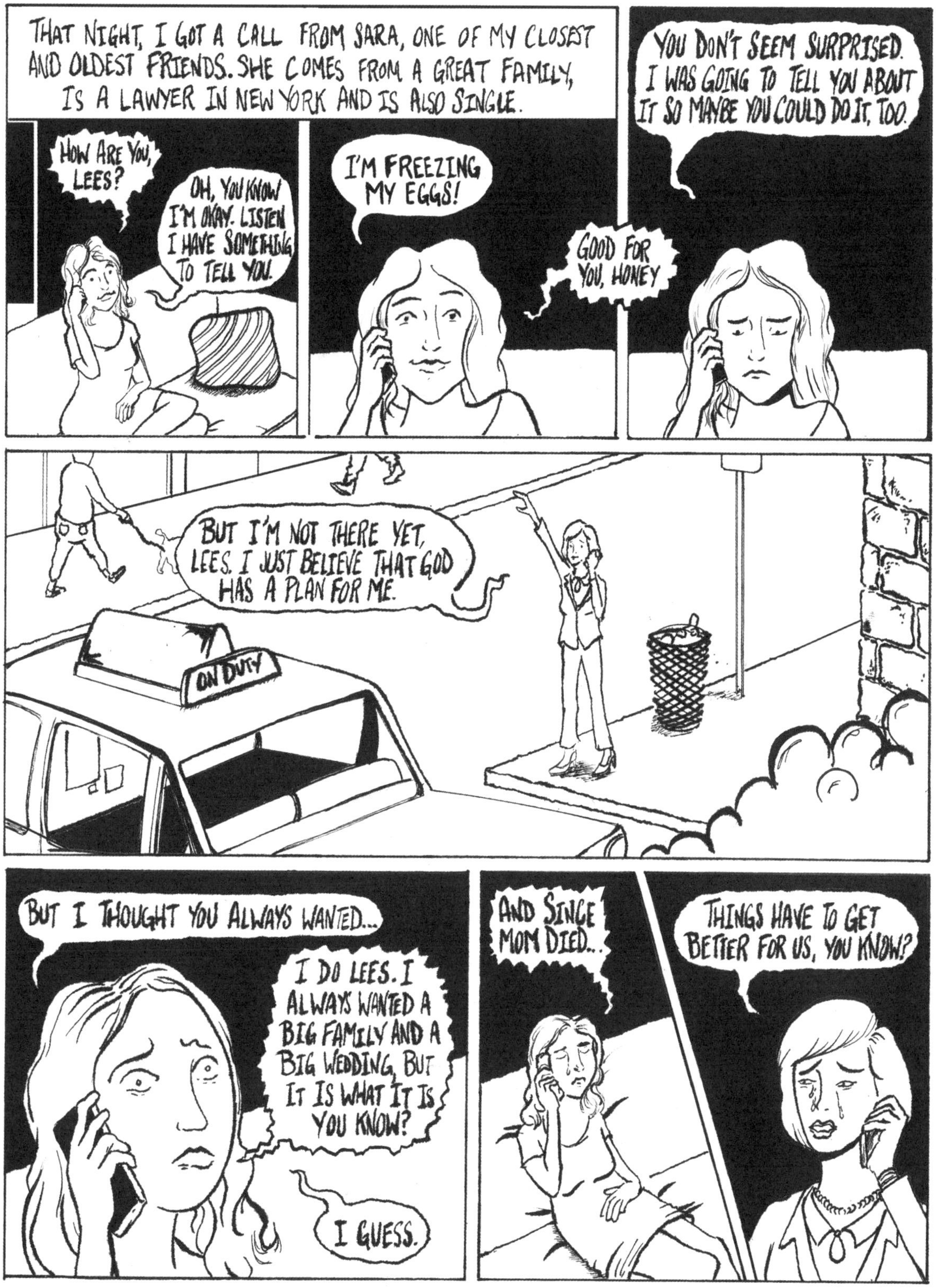
THAT NIGHT, I GOT A CALL FROM SARA, ONE OF MY CLOSEST AND OLDEST FRIENDS. SHE COMES FROM A GREAT FAMILY, IS A LAWYER IN NEW YORK AND IS ALSO SINGLE.
HOW ARE YOU, LEES?
OH, YOU KNOW I'M OKAY. LISTEN I HAVE SOMETHING TO TELL YOU.
I'M FREEZING MY EGGS!
GOOD FOR YOU, HONEY
YOU DON'T SEEM SURPRISED. I WAS GOING TO TELL YOU ABOUT IT SO MAYBE YOU COULD DO IT, TOO.
BUT I'M NOT THERE YET, LEES. I JUST BELIEVE THAT GOD HAS A PLAN FOR ME.
ON DUTY
BUT I THOUGHT YOU ALWAYS WANTED...
I DO LEES. I ALWAYS WANTED A BIG FAMILY AND A BIG WEDDING, BUT IT IS WHAT IT IS YOU KNOW?
I GUESS.
AND SINCE MOM DIED...
THINGS HAVE TO GET BETTER FOR US, YOU KNOW?

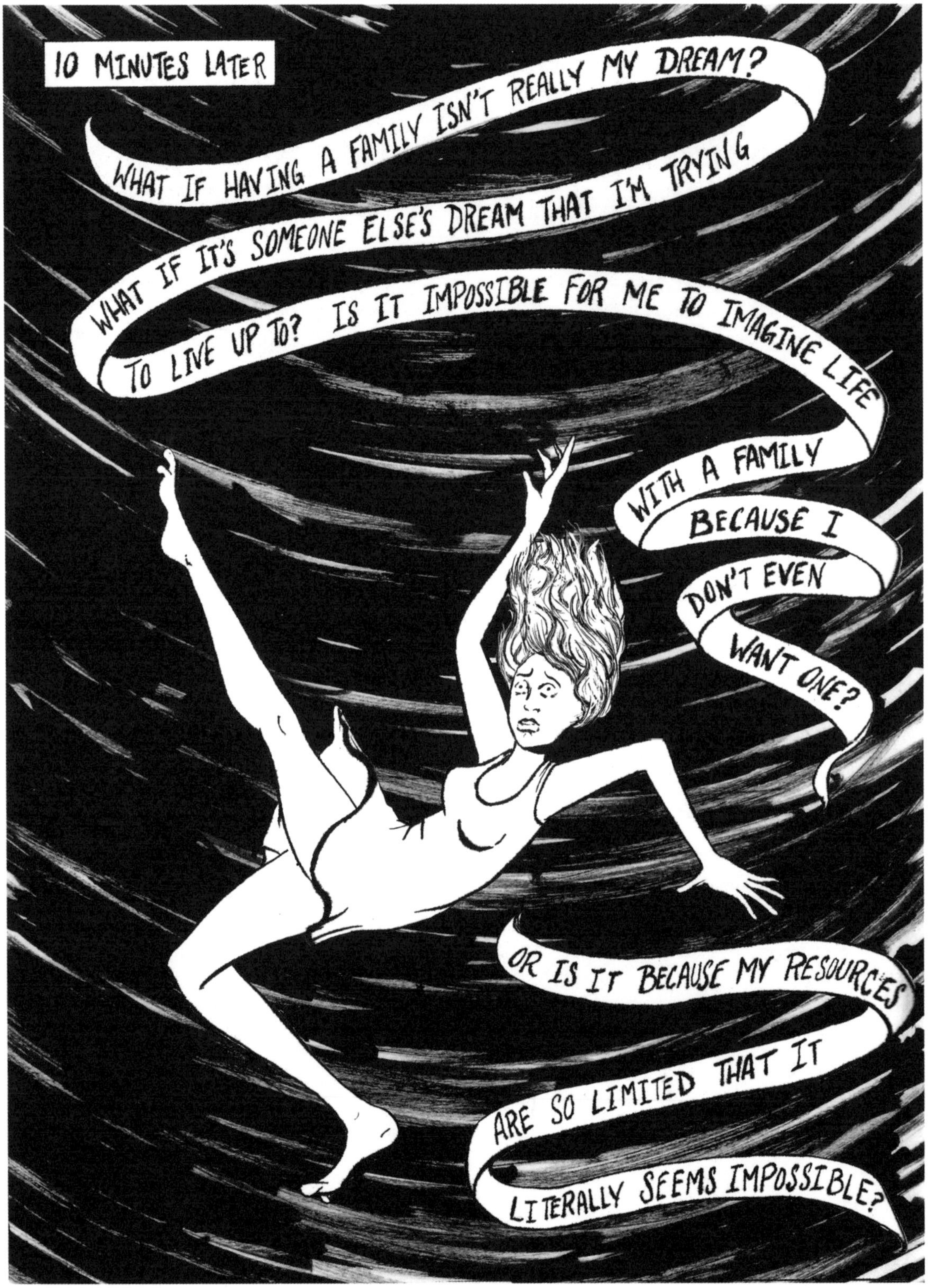
10 MINUTES LATER
WHAT IF HAVING A FAMILY ISN'T REALLY MY DREAM?
WHAT IF IT'S SOMEONE ELSE'S DREAM THAT I'M TRYING
TO LIVE UP TO? IS IT IMPOSSIBLE FOR ME TO IMAGINE LIFE
WITH A FAMILY
BECAUSE I
DON'T EVEN
WANT ONE?
OR IS IT BECAUSE MY RESOURCES
ARE SO LIMITED THAT IT
LITERALLY SEEMS IMPOSSIBLE?

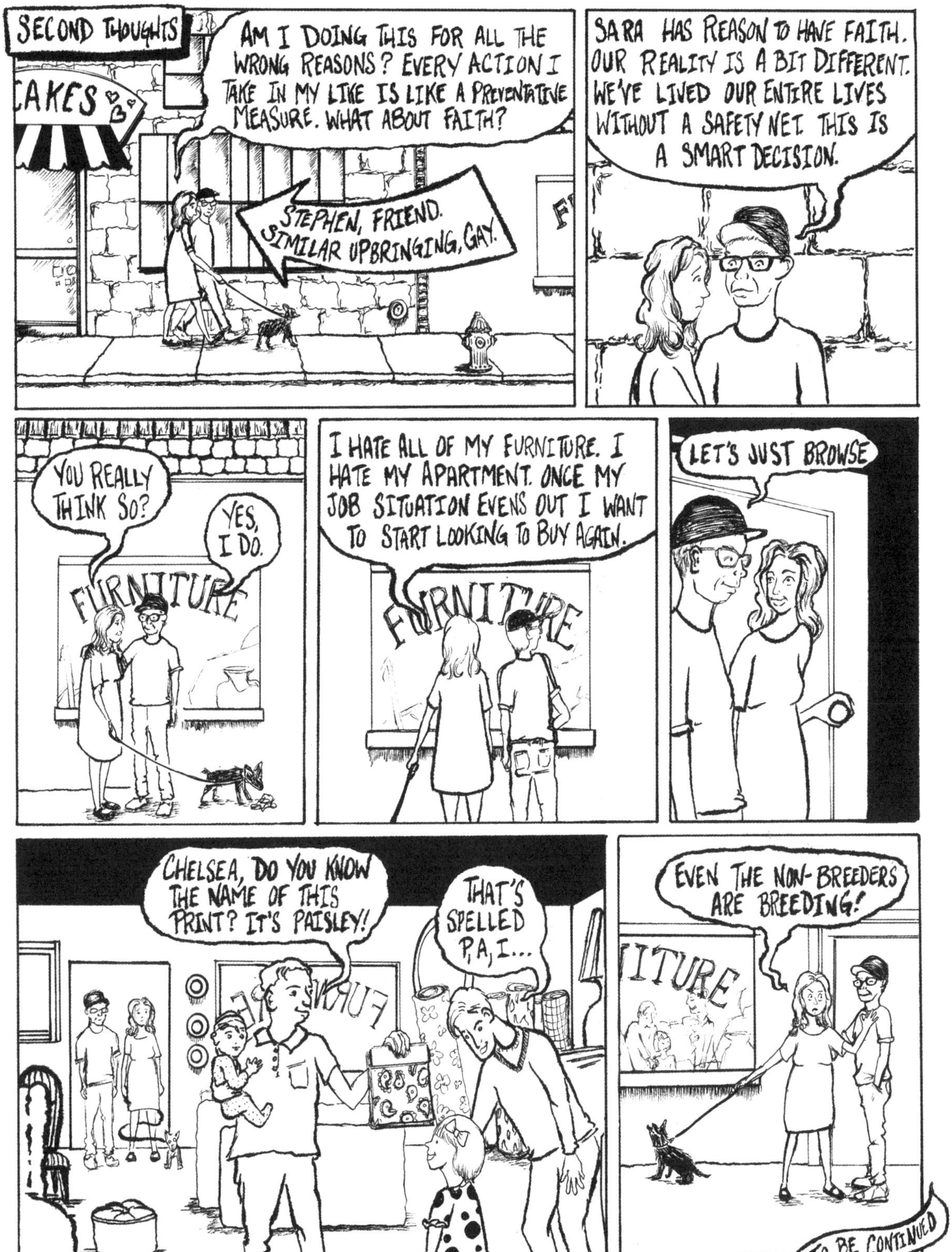
SECOND THOUGHTS
AM I DOING THIS FOR ALL THE WRONG REASONS? EVERY ACTION I TAKE IN MY LIKE IS LIKE A PREVENTATIVE MEASURE. WHAT ABOUT FAITH?
CAKES
STEPHEN, FRIEND. SIMILAR UPBRINGING, GAY.
SARA HAS REASON TO HAVE FAITH. OUR REALITY IS A BIT DIFFERENT. WE'VE LIVED OUR ENTIRE LIVES WITHOUT A SAFETY NET. THIS IS A SMART DECISION.
YOU REALLY THINK SO?
YES, I DO.
FURNITURE
I HATE ALL OF MY FURNITURE. I HATE MY APARTMENT. ONCE MY JOB SITUATION EVENS OUT I WANT TO START LOOKING TO BUY AGAIN.
FURNITURE
LET'S JUST BROWSE
CHELSEA, DO YOU KNOW THE NAME OF THIS PRINT? IT'S PAISLEY!
THAT'S SPELLED P, A, I...
EVEN THE NON-BREEDERS ARE BREEDING!
ITURE
TO BE CONTINUED

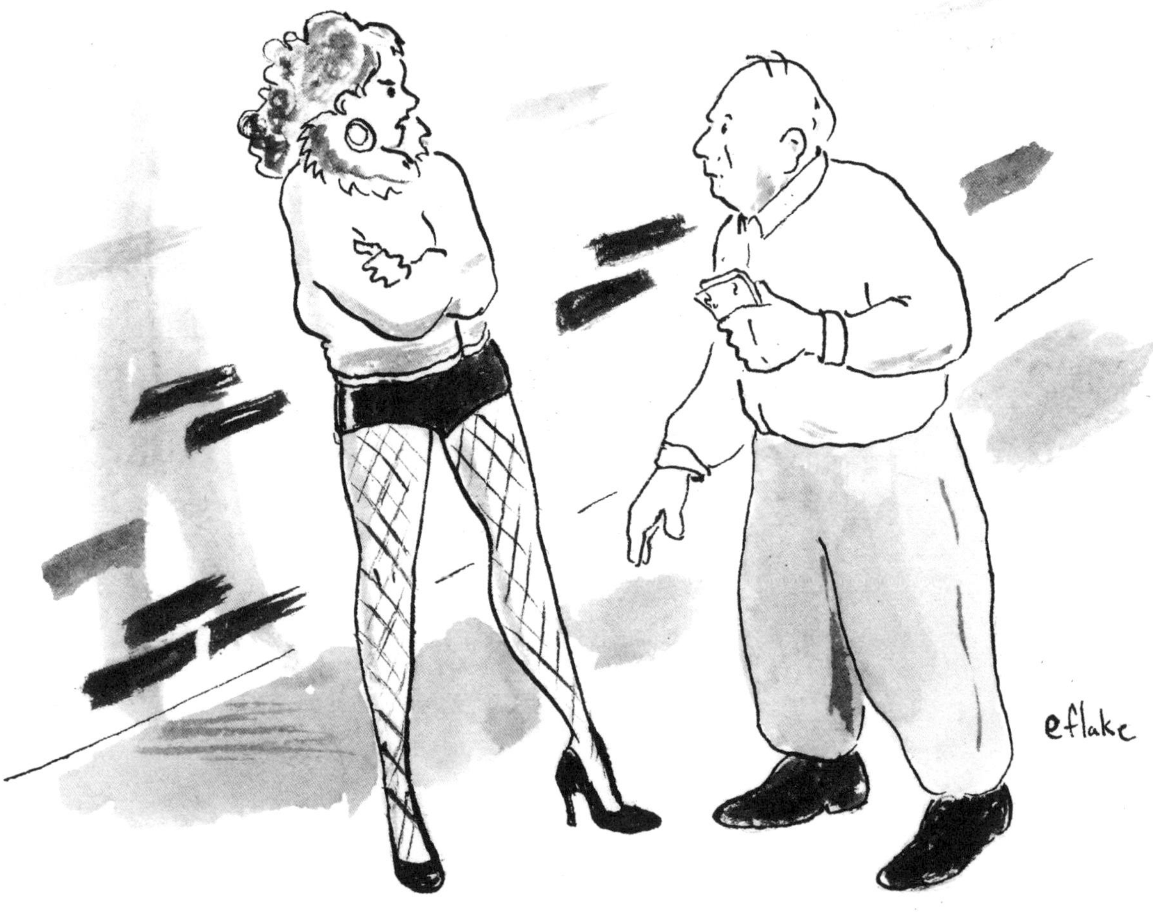
eflake

"AND AN EXTRA $10 IF YOU START TELLING ME ABOUT YOUR GRANDKIDS."

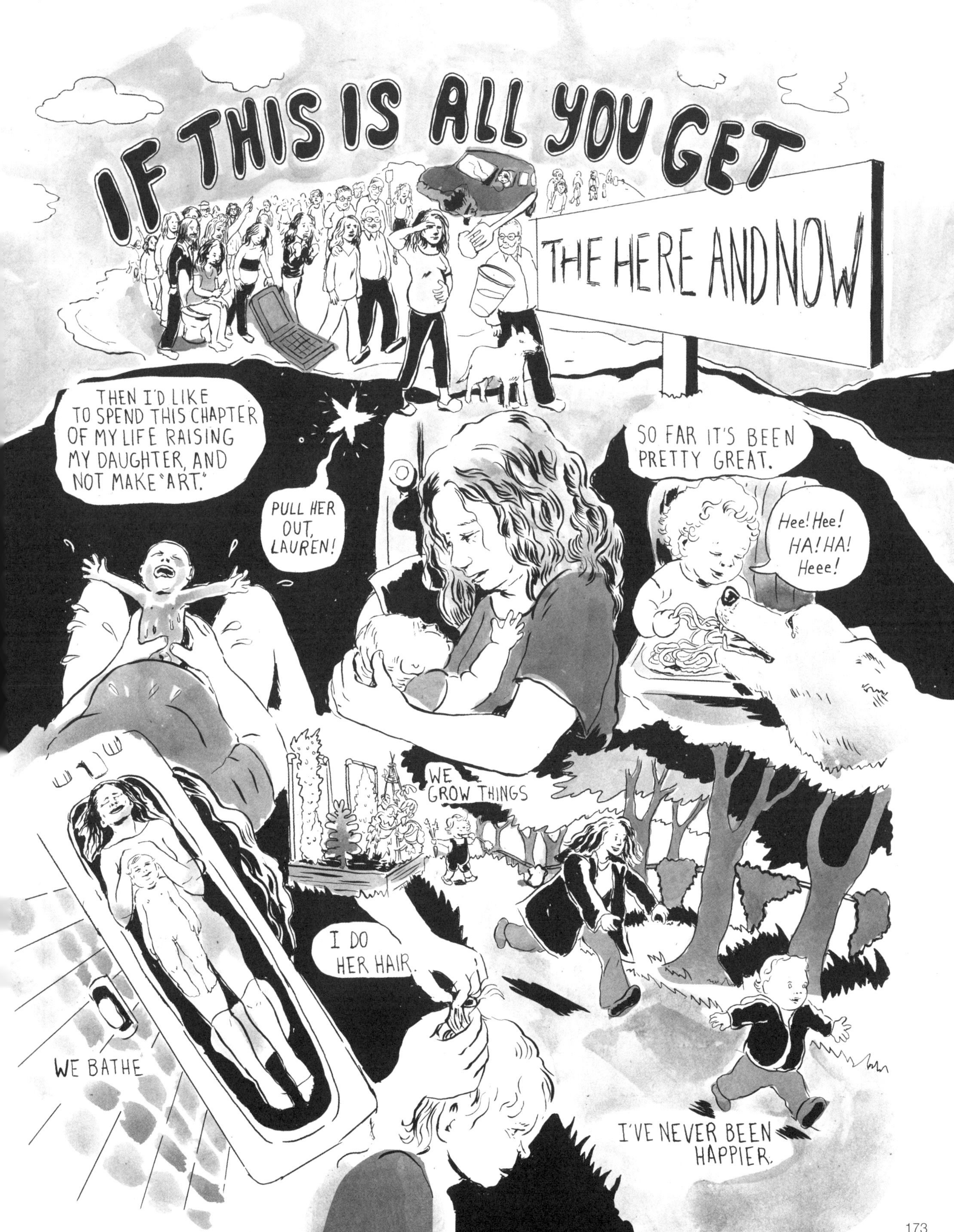
IF THIS IS ALL YOU GET
THE HERE AND NOW
THEN I'D LIKE TO SPEND THIS CHAPTER OF MY LIFE RAISING MY DAUGHTER, AND NOT MAKE "ART."
PULL HER OUT, LAUREN!
SO FAR IT'S BEEN PRETTY GREAT.
Hee! Hee! HA! HA! Heee!
WE GROW THINGS
I DO HER HAIR.
WE BATHE
I'VE NEVER BEEN HAPPIER.

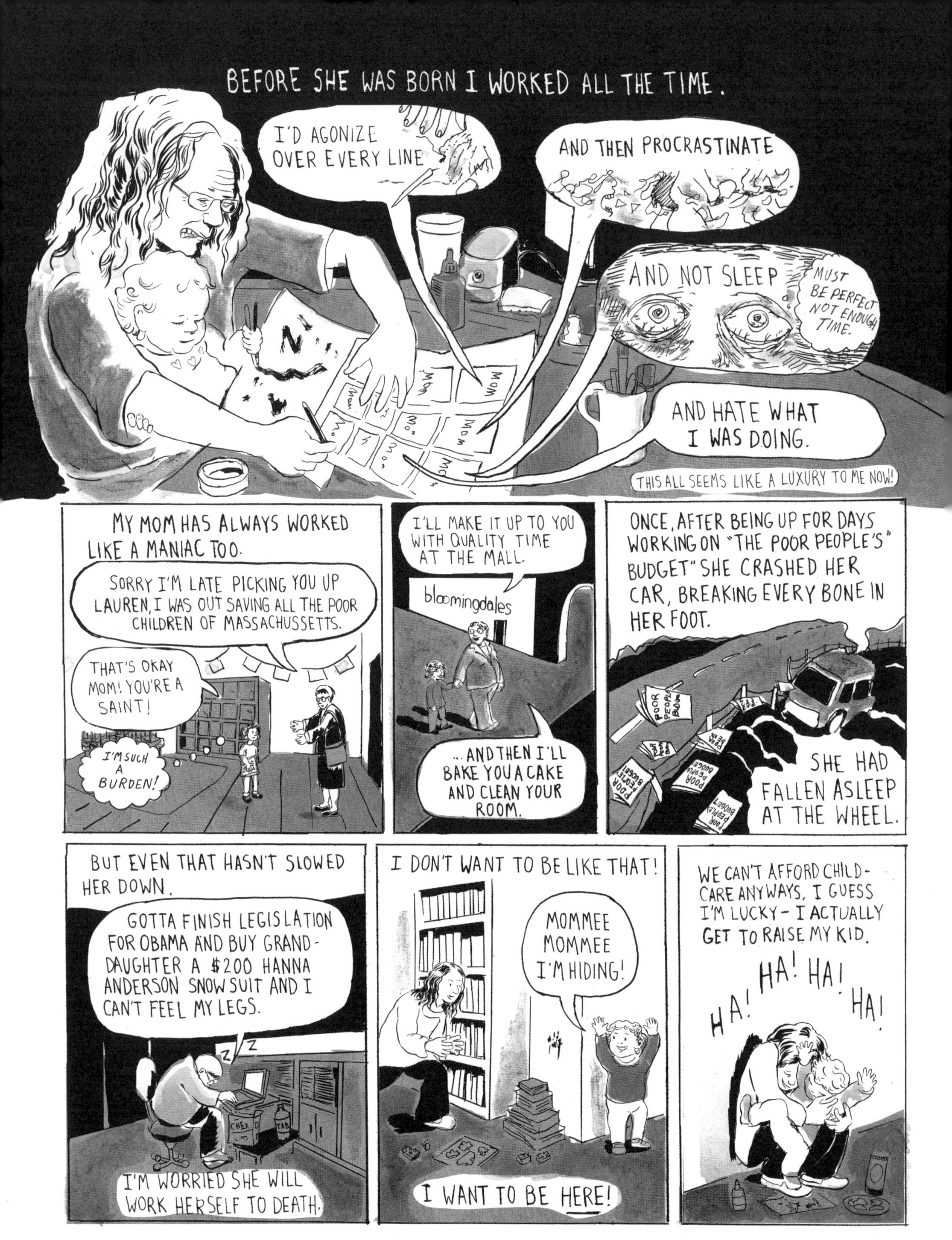
BEFORE SHE WAS BORN I WORKED ALL THE TIME.
I'D AGONIZE OVER EVERY LINE
AND THEN PROCRASTINATE
AND NOT SLEEP
MUST BE PERFECT NOT ENOUGH TIME.
AND HATE WHAT I WAS DOING.
THIS ALL SEEMS LIKE A LUXURY TO ME NOW!
MY MOM HAS ALWAYS WORKED LIKE A MANIAC TOO.
SORRY I'M LATE PICKING YOU UP LAUREN, I WAS OUT SAVING ALL THE POOR CHILDREN OF MASSACHUSSETTS.
THAT'S OKAY MOM! YOU'RE A SAINT!
I'M SUCH A BURDEN!
I'LL MAKE IT UP TO YOU WITH QUALITY TIME AT THE MALL.
bloomingdales
...AND THEN I'LL BAKE YOU A CAKE AND CLEAN YOUR ROOM.
ONCE, AFTER BEING UP FOR DAYS WORKING ON "THE POOR PEOPLE'S" BUDGET" SHE CRASHED HER CAR, BREAKING EVERY BONE IN HER FOOT.
SHE HAD FALLEN ASLEEP AT THE WHEEL.
BUT EVEN THAT HASN'T SLOWED HER DOWN.
GOTTA FINISH LEGISLATION FOR OBAMA AND BUY GRAND-DAUGHTER A $200 HANNA ANDERSON SNOW SUIT AND I CAN'T FEEL MY LEGS.
Z Z
I'M WORRIED SHE WILL WORK HERSELF TO DEATH.
I DON'T WANT TO BE LIKE THAT!
MOMMEE MOMMEE I'M HIDING!
I WANT TO BE HERE!
WE CAN'T AFFORD CHILD-CARE ANYWAYS. I GUESS I'M LUCKY - I ACTUALLY GET TO RAISE MY KID.
HA! HA! HA! HA!

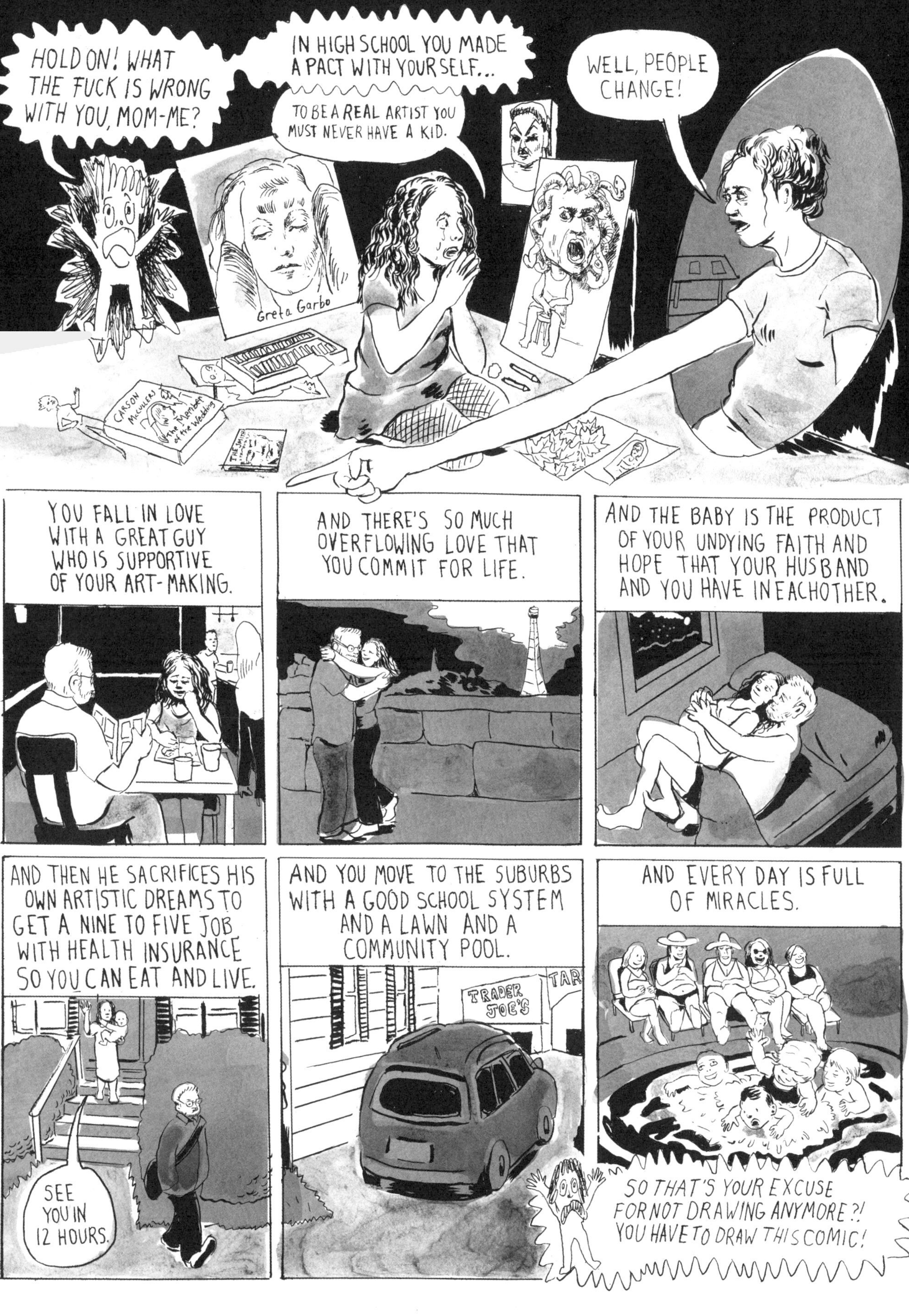
HOLD ON! WHAT THE FUCK IS WRONG WITH YOU, MOM-ME?
IN HIGH SCHOOL YOU MADE A PACT WITH YOURSELF...
TO BE A REAL ARTIST YOU MUST NEVER HAVE A KID.
WELL, PEOPLE CHANGE!
Greta Garbo
CARSON McCULLERS
The Member of the Wedding
YOU FALL IN LOVE WITH A GREAT GUY WHO IS SUPPORTIVE OF YOUR ART-MAKING.
AND THERE'S SO MUCH OVERFLOWING LOVE THAT YOU COMMIT FOR LIFE.
AND THE BABY IS THE PRODUCT OF YOUR UNDYING FAITH AND HOPE THAT YOUR HUSBAND AND YOU HAVE IN EACHOTHER.
AND THEN HE SACRIFICES HIS OWN ARTISTIC DREAMS TO GET A NINE TO FIVE JOB WITH HEALTH INSURANCE SO YOU CAN EAT AND LIVE.
SEE YOU IN 12 HOURS.
AND YOU MOVE TO THE SUBURBS WITH A GOOD SCHOOL SYSTEM AND A LAWN AND A COMMUNITY POOL.
TRADER JOE'S
TAR
AND EVERY DAY IS FULL OF MIRACLES.
SO THAT'S YOUR EXCUSE FOR NOT DRAWING ANYMORE?! YOU HAVE TO DRAW THIS COMIC!

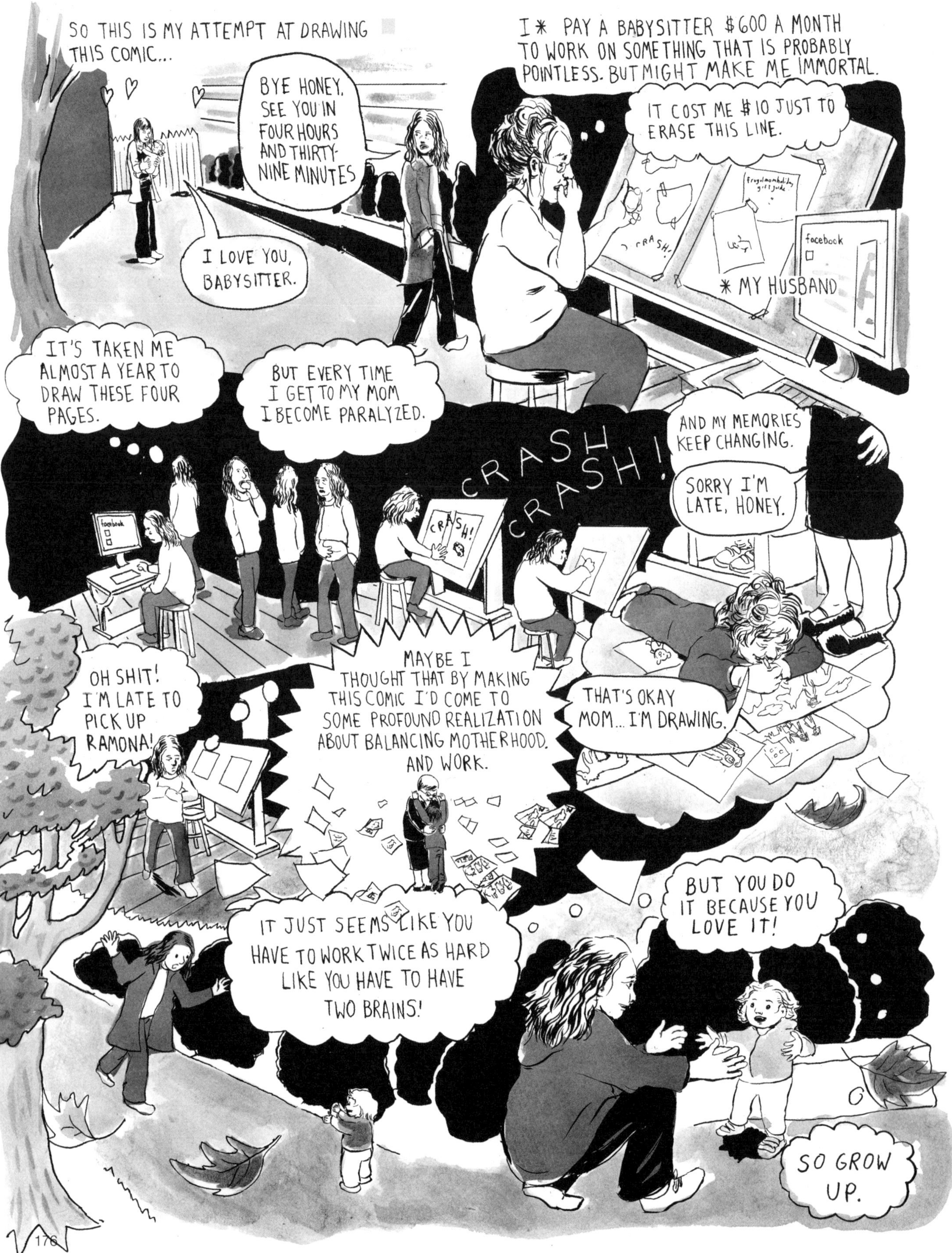

SO THIS IS MY ATTEMPT AT DRAWING THIS COMIC...
BYE HONEY. SEE YOU IN FOUR HOURS AND THIRTY-NINE MINUTES
I LOVE YOU, BABYSITTER.
I* PAY A BABYSITTER $600 A MONTH TO WORK ON SOMETHING THAT IS PROBABLY POINTLESS. BUT MIGHT MAKE ME IMMORTAL.
IT COST ME $10 JUST TO ERASE THIS LINE.
facebook
* MY HUSBAND
IT'S TAKEN ME ALMOST A YEAR TO DRAW THESE FOUR PAGES.
BUT EVERY TIME I GET TO MY MOM I BECOME PARALYZED.
facebook
CRASH!
CRASH CRASH!
AND MY MEMORIES KEEP CHANGING.
SORRY I'M LATE, HONEY.
OH SHIT! I'M LATE TO PICK UP RAMONA!
MAYBE I THOUGHT THAT BY MAKING THIS COMIC I'D COME TO SOME PROFOUND REALIZATION ABOUT BALANCING MOTHERHOOD. AND WORK.
THAT'S OKAY MOM... I'M DRAWING.
IT JUST SEEMS LIKE YOU HAVE TO WORK TWICE AS HARD LIKE YOU HAVE TO HAVE TWO BRAINS!
BUT YOU DO IT BECAUSE YOU LOVE IT!
SO GROW UP.

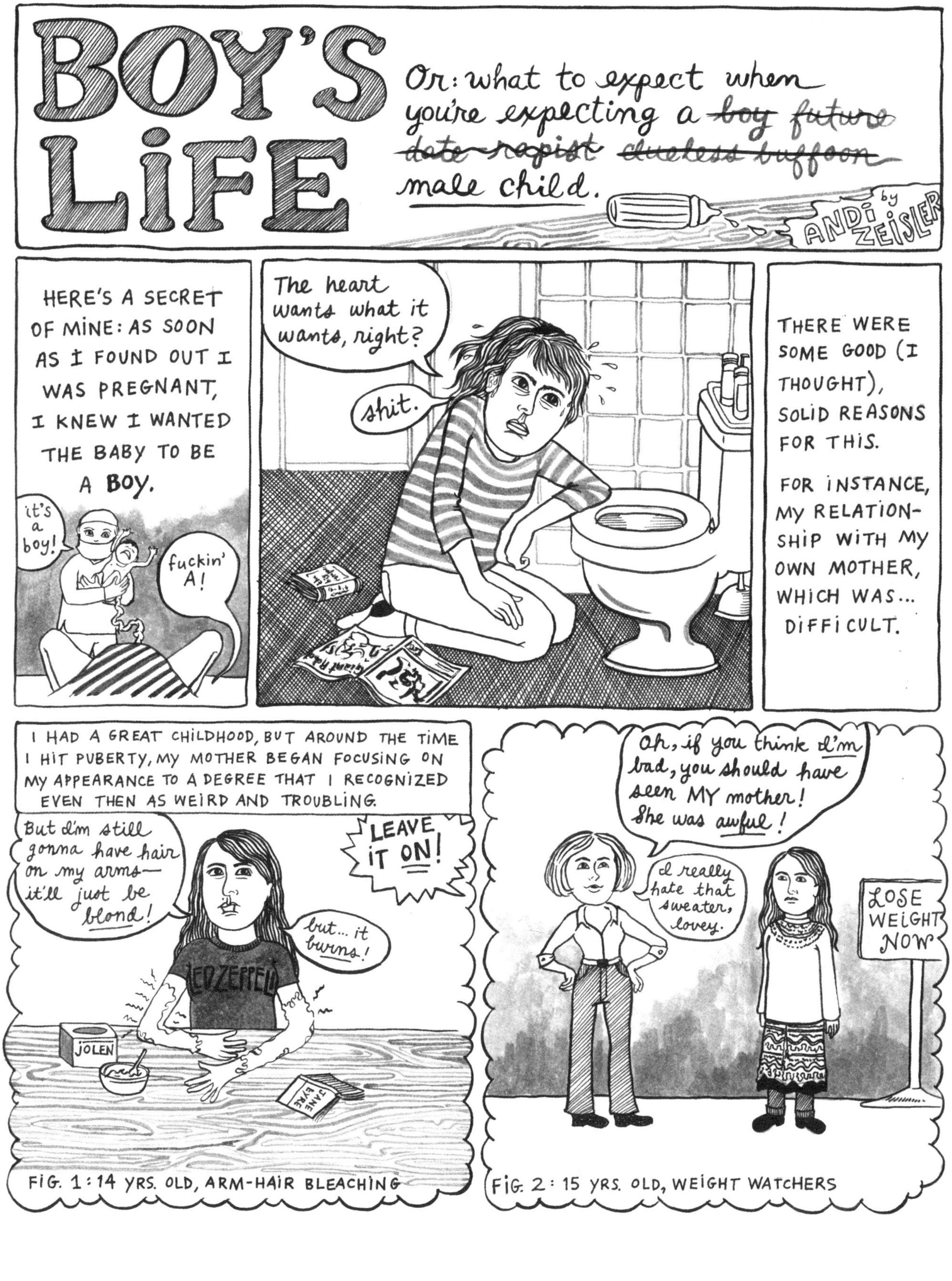
BOY'S LiFE
Or: what to expect when you're expecting a ~~boy future date rapist clueless buffoon~~ male child.
by ANDi ZEISLER
HERE'S A SECRET OF MiNE: AS SOON AS I FOUND OUT I WAS PREGNANT, I KNEW I WANTED THE BABY TO BE A BOY.
it's a boy!
fuckin' A!
The heart wants what it wants, right?
shit.
THERE WERE SOME GOOD (I THOUGHT), SOLID REASONS FOR THIS.
FOR INSTANCE, MY RELATIONSHIP WITH MY OWN MOTHER, WHICH WAS... DIFFICULT.
I HAD A GREAT CHILDHOOD, BUT AROUND THE TIME I HIT PUBERTY, MY MOTHER BEGAN FOCUSING ON MY APPEARANCE TO A DEGREE THAT I RECOGNIZED EVEN THEN AS WEIRD AND TROUBLING.
But I'm still gonna have hair on my arms— it'll just be blond!
LEAVE IT ON!
but... it burns!
JOLEN
JANE EYRE
FIG. 1: 14 YRS. OLD, ARM-HAIR BLEACHING
Oh, if you think I'm bad, you should have seen MY mother! She was awful!
I really hate that sweater, lovey.
LOSE WEIGHT NOW
FIG. 2: 15 YRS. OLD, WEIGHT WATCHERS

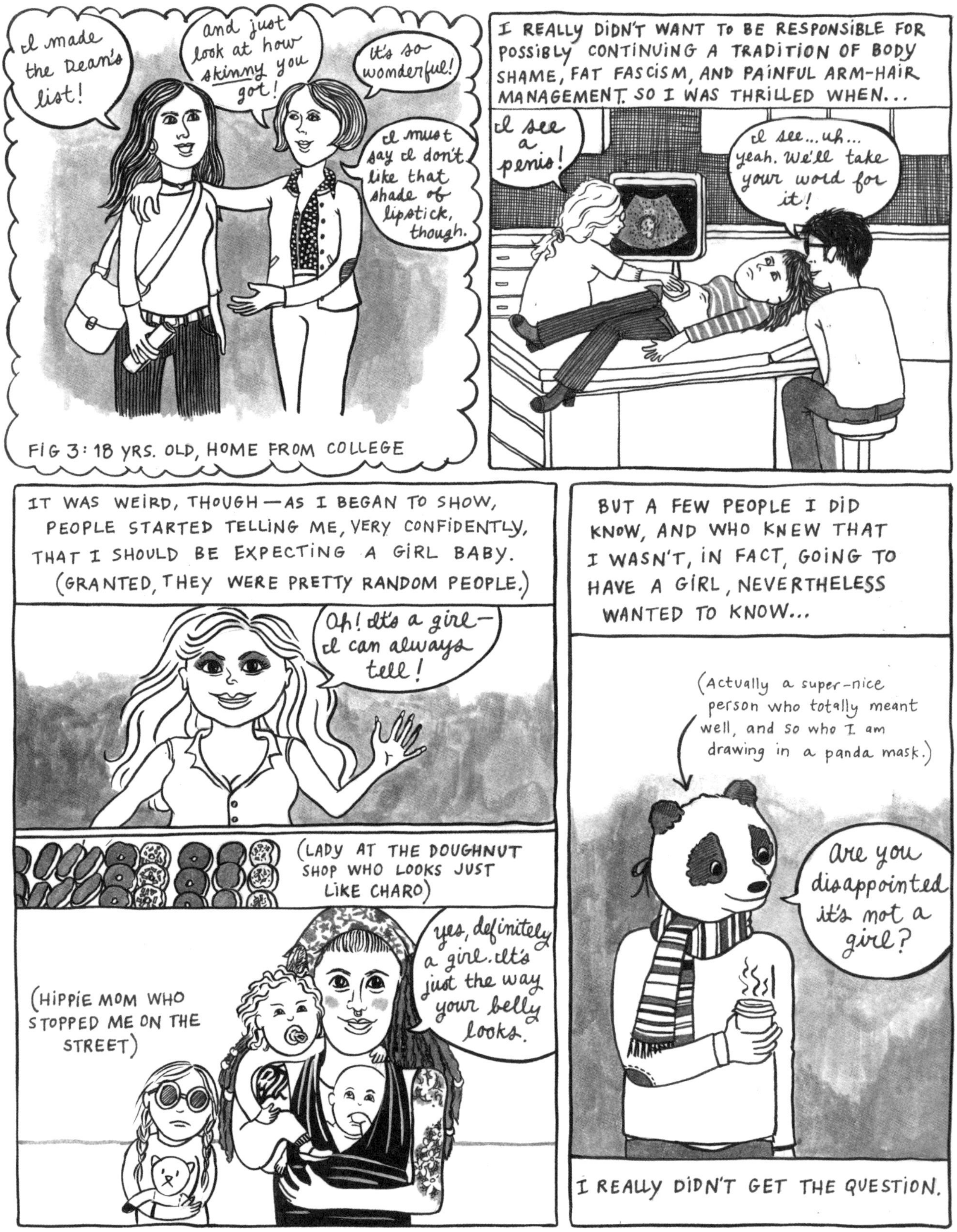
I made the Dean's list!
and just look at how skinny you got!
It's so wonderful!
I must say I don't like that shade of lipstick, though.
FIG 3: 18 YRS. OLD, HOME FROM COLLEGE
I REALLY DIDN'T WANT TO BE RESPONSIBLE FOR POSSIBLY CONTINUING A TRADITION OF BODY SHAME, FAT FASCISM, AND PAINFUL ARM-HAIR MANAGEMENT. SO I WAS THRILLED WHEN...
I see a penis!
I see... uh... yeah. We'll take your word for it!
IT WAS WEIRD, THOUGH — AS I BEGAN TO SHOW, PEOPLE STARTED TELLING ME, VERY CONFIDENTLY, THAT I SHOULD BE EXPECTING A GIRL BABY. (GRANTED, THEY WERE PRETTY RANDOM PEOPLE.)
Oh! It's a girl— I can always tell!
(LADY AT THE DOUGHNUT SHOP WHO LOOKS JUST LIKE CHARO)
yes, definitely a girl. It's just the way your belly looks.
(HIPPIE MOM WHO STOPPED ME ON THE STREET)
BUT A FEW PEOPLE I DID KNOW, AND WHO KNEW THAT I WASN'T, IN FACT, GOING TO HAVE A GIRL, NEVERTHELESS WANTED TO KNOW...
(Actually a super-nice person who totally meant well, and so who I am drawing in a panda mask.)
Are you disappointed it's not a girl?
I REALLY DIDN'T GET THE QUESTION.

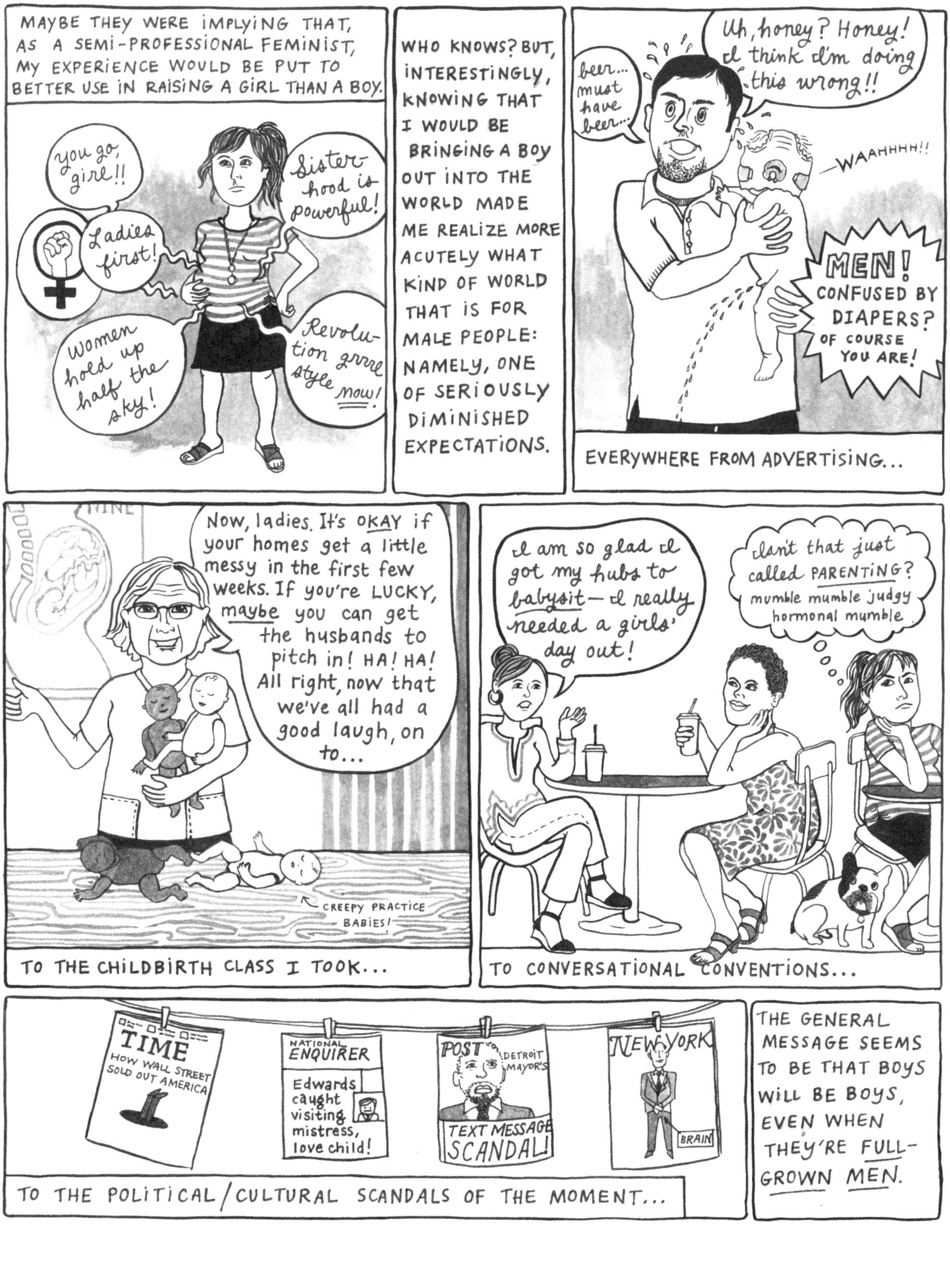
MAYBE THEY WERE IMPLYING THAT, AS A SEMI-PROFESSIONAL FEMINIST, MY EXPERIENCE WOULD BE PUT TO BETTER USE IN RAISING A GIRL THAN A BOY.
you go, girl!!
Sister-hood is powerful!
Ladies first!
Women hold up half the sky!
Revolution grrrl style now!
WHO KNOWS? BUT, INTERESTINGLY, KNOWING THAT I WOULD BE BRINGING A BOY OUT INTO THE WORLD MADE ME REALIZE MORE ACUTELY WHAT KIND OF WORLD THAT IS FOR MALE PEOPLE: NAMELY, ONE OF SERIOUSLY DIMINISHED EXPECTATIONS.
beer... must have beer...
Uh, honey? Honey! I think I'm doing this wrong!!
—WAAHHHH!!
MEN! CONFUSED BY DIAPERS? OF COURSE YOU ARE!
EVERYWHERE FROM ADVERTISING...
NINE
Now, ladies. It's OKAY if your homes get a little messy in the first few weeks. If you're LUCKY, maybe you can get the husbands to pitch in! HA! HA! All right, now that we've all had a good laugh, on to...
CREEPY PRACTICE BABIES!
TO THE CHILDBIRTH CLASS I TOOK...
I am so glad I got my hubs to babysit—I really needed a girls' day out!
Isn't that just called PARENTING? mumble mumble judgy hormonal mumble
TO CONVERSATIONAL CONVENTIONS...
TIME
HOW WALL STREET SOLD OUT AMERICA
NATIONAL ENQUIRER
Edwards caught visiting mistress, love child!
POST
DETROIT MAYOR'S
TEXT MESSAGE SCANDAL!
NEW YORK
BRAIN
TO THE POLITICAL/CULTURAL SCANDALS OF THE MOMENT...
THE GENERAL MESSAGE SEEMS TO BE THAT BOYS WILL BE BOYS, EVEN WHEN THEY'RE FULL-GROWN MEN.

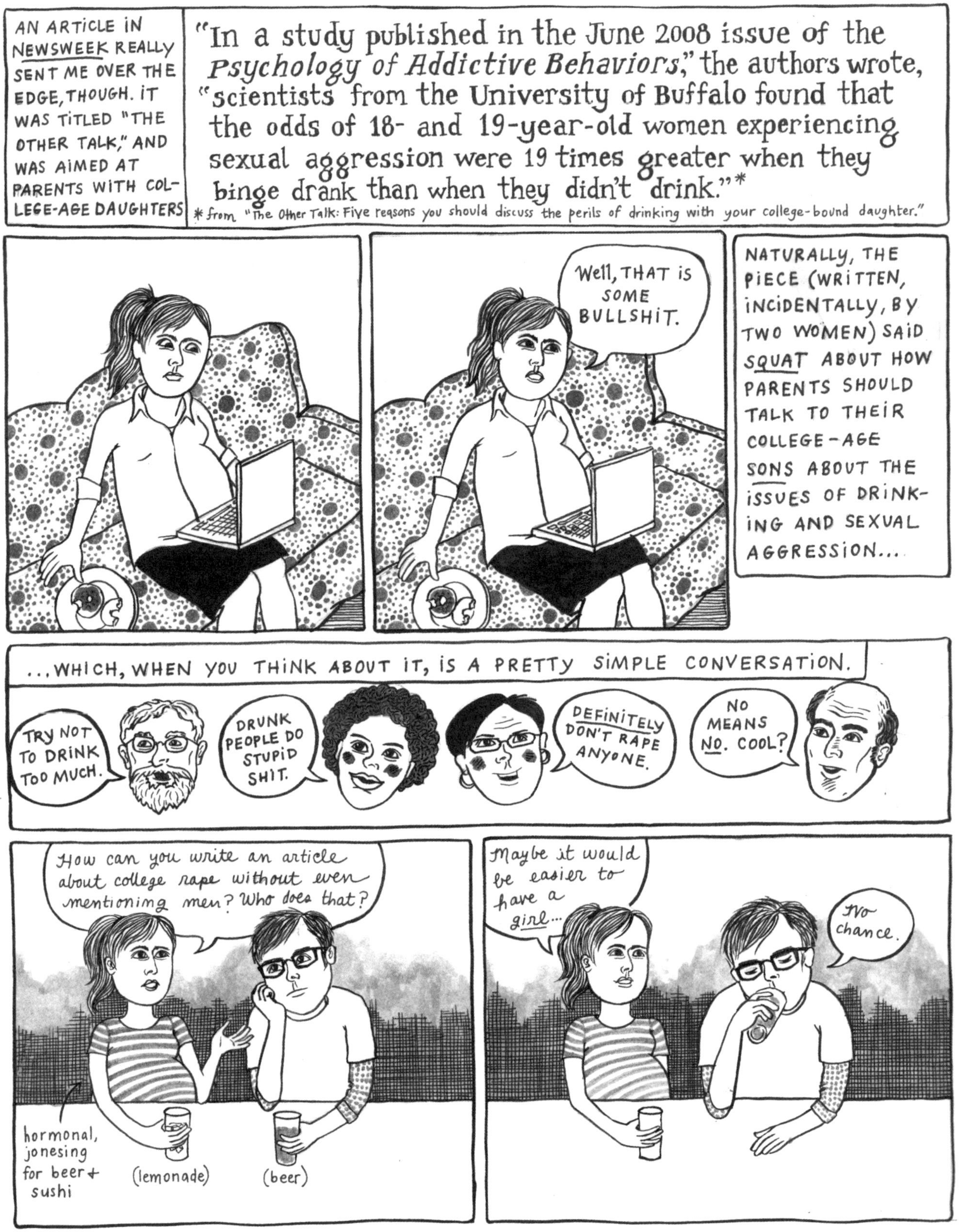
AN ARTICLE IN NEWSWEEK REALLY SENT ME OVER THE EDGE, THOUGH. IT WAS TITLED "THE OTHER TALK," AND WAS AIMED AT PARENTS WITH COLLEGE-AGE DAUGHTERS
"In a study published in the June 2008 issue of the Psychology of Addictive Behaviors," the authors wrote, "scientists from the University of Buffalo found that the odds of 18- and 19-year-old women experiencing sexual aggression were 19 times greater when they binge drank than when they didn't drink."*
* from "The Other Talk: Five reasons you should discuss the perils of drinking with your college-bound daughter."
Well, THAT is SOME BULLSHIT.
NATURALLY, THE PIECE (WRITTEN, INCIDENTALLY, BY TWO WOMEN) SAID SQUAT ABOUT HOW PARENTS SHOULD TALK TO THEIR COLLEGE-AGE SONS ABOUT THE ISSUES OF DRINKING AND SEXUAL AGGRESSION...
...WHICH, WHEN YOU THINK ABOUT IT, IS A PRETTY SIMPLE CONVERSATION.
TRY NOT TO DRINK TOO MUCH.
DRUNK PEOPLE DO STUPID SHIT.
DEFINITELY DON'T RAPE ANYONE.
NO MEANS NO. COOL?
How can you write an article about college rape without even mentioning men? Who does that?
hormonal, jonesing for beer + sushi
(lemonade)
(beer)
Maybe it would be easier to have a girl...
No chance.

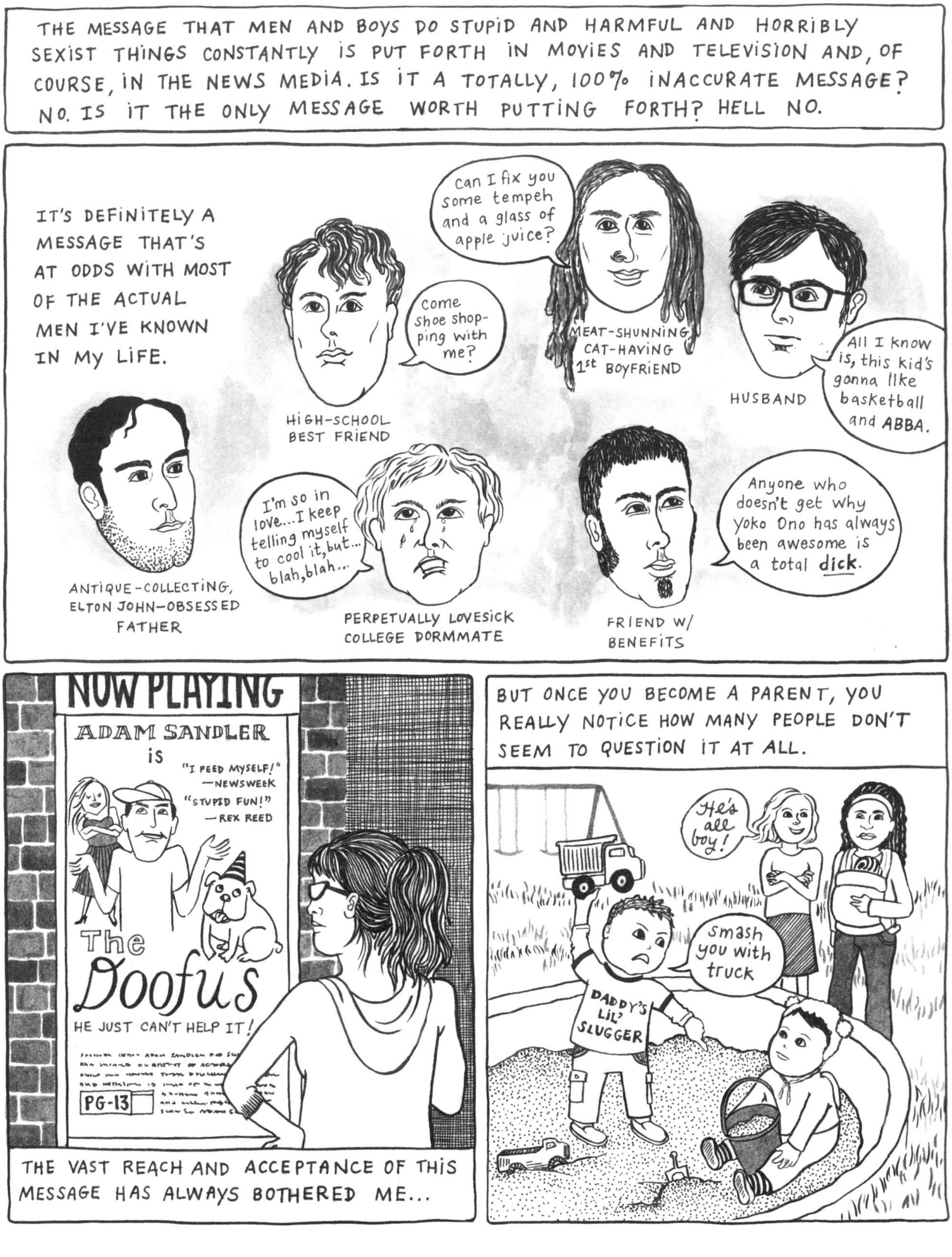
THE MESSAGE THAT MEN AND BOYS DO STUPID AND HARMFUL AND HORRIBLY SEXIST THINGS CONSTANTLY IS PUT FORTH IN MOVIES AND TELEVISION AND, OF COURSE, IN THE NEWS MEDIA. IS IT A TOTALLY, 100% INACCURATE MESSAGE? NO. IS IT THE ONLY MESSAGE WORTH PUTTING FORTH? HELL NO.
IT'S DEFINITELY A MESSAGE THAT'S AT ODDS WITH MOST OF THE ACTUAL MEN I'VE KNOWN IN MY LIFE.
Come shoe shopping with me?
HIGH-SCHOOL BEST FRIEND
Can I fix you some tempeh and a glass of apple juice?
MEAT-SHUNNING CAT-HAVING 1st BOYFRIEND
All I know is, this kid's gonna like basketball and ABBA.
HUSBAND
ANTIQUE-COLLECTING, ELTON JOHN-OBSESSED FATHER
I'm so in love...I keep telling myself to cool it, but... blah, blah...
PERPETUALLY LOVESICK COLLEGE DORMMATE
Anyone who doesn't get why Yoko Ono has always been awesome is a total dick.
FRIEND W/ BENEFITS
NOW PLAYING
ADAM SANDLER is
"I FEED MYSELF!" —NEWSWEEK
"STUPID FUN!" —REX REED
The Doofus
HE JUST CAN'T HELP IT!
PG-13
THE VAST REACH AND ACCEPTANCE OF THIS MESSAGE HAS ALWAYS BOTHERED ME...
BUT ONCE YOU BECOME A PARENT, YOU REALLY NOTICE HOW MANY PEOPLE DON'T SEEM TO QUESTION IT AT ALL.
He's all boy!
smash you with truck
DADDY'S LIL' SLUGGER

OBVIOUSLY, THE GENDERED MESSAGES ABOUT GIRLS ARE JUST AS STRONG, JUST AS PERNICIOUS, AND IN MANY INSTANCES JUST AS UNQUESTIONED.

(EXHIBIT A: THOSE DUMB-ASS PINK HEADBANDS PEOPLE PUT ON THEIR BALD NEWBORNS)

We hate when people think she's a boy!

COULD NOT GIVE A TINY RAT'S ASS.

AND THE FORCES OF BOTH POP CULTURE AND CAPITALISM WORK TO ENSURE THAT BOYS & GIRLS ARE CATEGORIES, NOT PEOPLE.

2011

UNISEX "BIG WHEEL" VS.

1976

PINK "PRINCESS COACH"
+
"TOUGH-TALKING JEEP"

I DEFINITELY DON'T HAVE ANY ILLUSIONS ABOUT RAISING THE PERFECT FEMINIST SON. I'M NOT SURE WHAT THAT WOULD EVEN LOOK LIKE.

Do you know what "cis-gender" is? I do!

Can I learn to bake?

I'm doing my book report on this!

the SECOND SEX

FAVORITE BAND: ABBA
SECOND FAVORITE: VAN HALEN*

OBSESSED WITH FRUIT

WILL TELL YOU WHEN ANYONE FARTED

PICKED OUT DISNEY PRINCESS KITE

LIKES TO HEAD-BUTT THE DOG

WANTS TO TALK ABOUT FLAG AT THE GAS STATION A FEW HUNDRED TIMES.

*David Lee Roth-era

ESPECIALLY SINCE RIGHT NOW, HE'S STILL A TODDLER, WITH ONLY THE FAINTEST CONCEPT OF "BOY" AND "GIRL."

STILL, I'M THINKING AHEAD. AS MUCH AS I WANT TO LIVE IN A WORLD WHERE LOW EXPECTATIONS FOR MEN ARE PUT UNDER THE SAME CRITICAL LENS AS LOW EXPECTATIONS OF WOMEN HAVE BEEN, I'M NOT SUPER OPTIMISTIC.

BUT RIGHT NOW, IT'S ENOUGH TO JUST BE MY SON'S MOTHER...

...Goodnight noises everywhere.

...USUALLY.

If I ever hear you use the phrase "Bros before hos," I will ground the shit out of you.

Okay won't say dat.

END 20 11

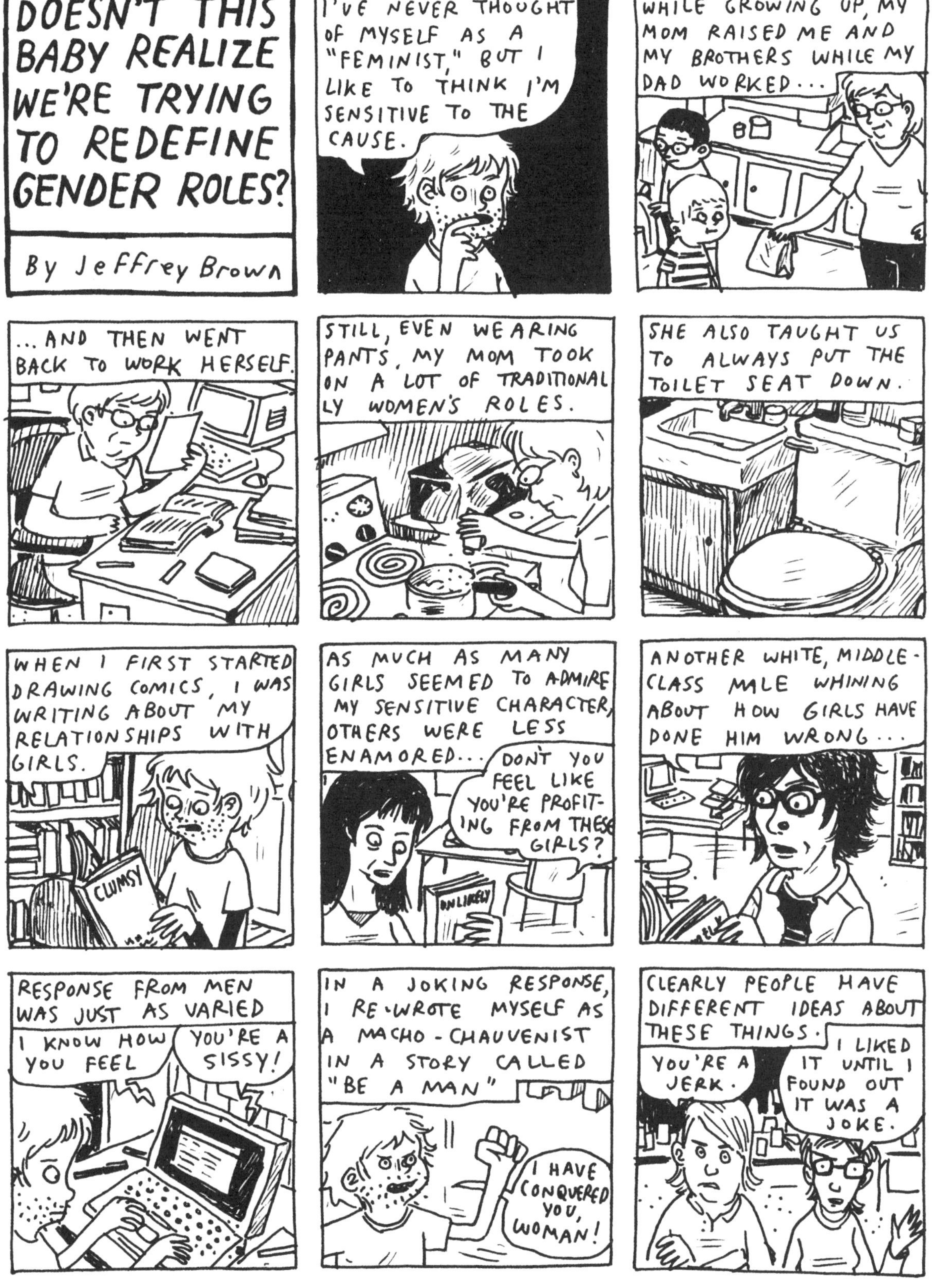
DOESN'T THIS BABY REALIZE WE'RE TRYING TO REDEFINE GENDER ROLES?
By Jeffrey Brown
I'VE NEVER THOUGHT OF MYSELF AS A "FEMINIST," BUT I LIKE TO THINK I'M SENSITIVE TO THE CAUSE.
WHILE GROWING UP, MY MOM RAISED ME AND MY BROTHERS WHILE MY DAD WORKED...
...AND THEN WENT BACK TO WORK HERSELF.
STILL, EVEN WEARING PANTS, MY MOM TOOK ON A LOT OF TRADITIONALLY WOMEN'S ROLES.
SHE ALSO TAUGHT US TO ALWAYS PUT THE TOILET SEAT DOWN.
WHEN I FIRST STARTED DRAWING COMICS, I WAS WRITING ABOUT MY RELATIONSHIPS WITH GIRLS.
CLUMSY
AS MUCH AS MANY GIRLS SEEMED TO ADMIRE MY SENSITIVE CHARACTER, OTHERS WERE LESS ENAMORED...
DON'T YOU FEEL LIKE YOU'RE PROFITING FROM THESE GIRLS?
UNLIKELY
ANOTHER WHITE, MIDDLE-CLASS MALE WHINING ABOUT HOW GIRLS HAVE DONE HIM WRONG...
RESPONSE FROM MEN WAS JUST AS VARIED
I KNOW HOW YOU FEEL
YOU'RE A SISSY!
IN A JOKING RESPONSE, I RE-WROTE MYSELF AS A MACHO-CHAUVENIST IN A STORY CALLED "BE A MAN"
I HAVE CONQUERED YOU, WOMAN!
CLEARLY PEOPLE HAVE DIFFERENT IDEAS ABOUT THESE THINGS.
YOU'RE A JERK.
I LIKED IT UNTIL I FOUND OUT IT WAS A JOKE.

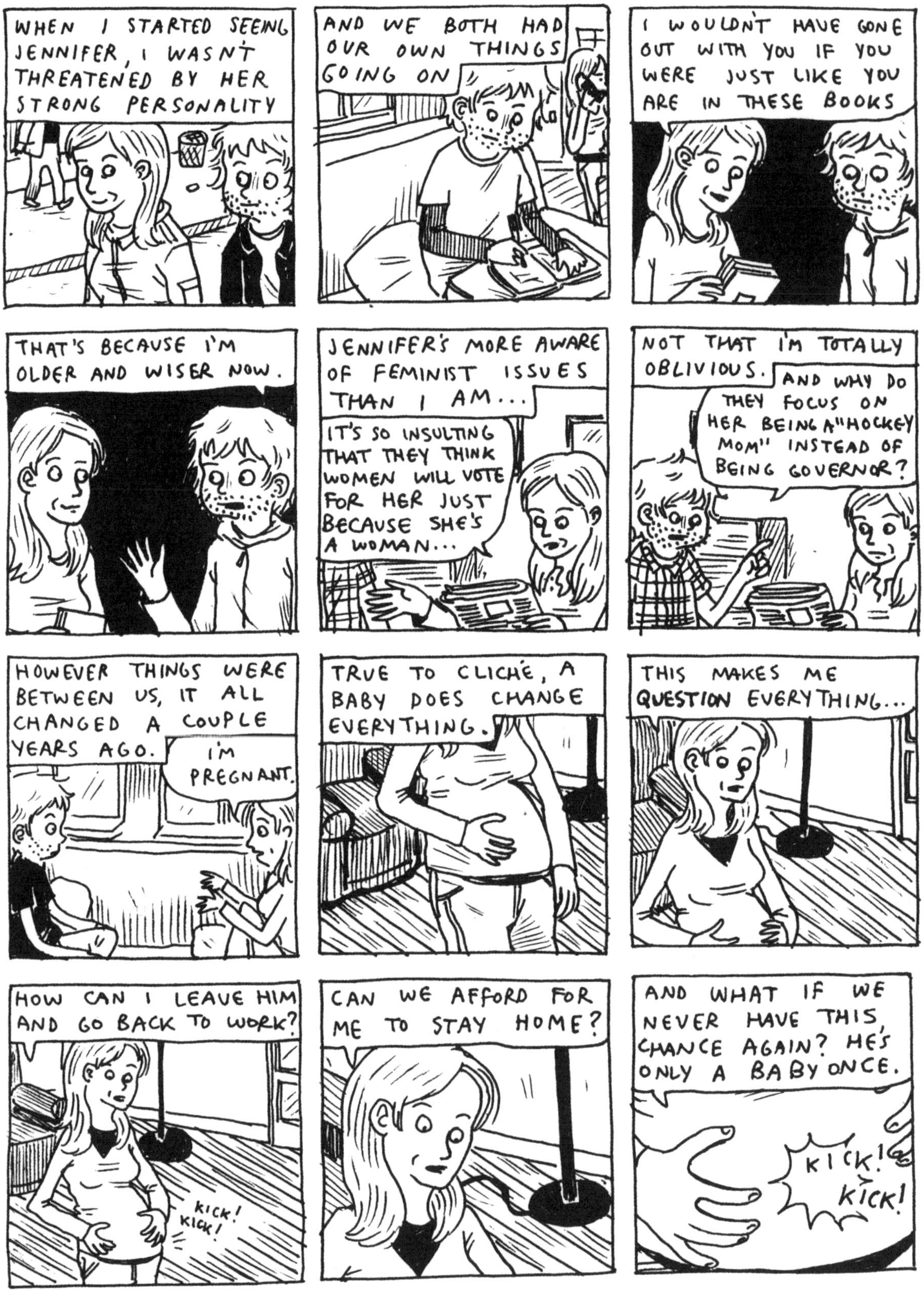
WHEN I STARTED SEEING JENNIFER, I WASN'T THREATENED BY HER STRONG PERSONALITY
AND WE BOTH HAD OUR OWN THINGS GOING ON
I WOULDN'T HAVE GONE OUT WITH YOU IF YOU WERE JUST LIKE YOU ARE IN THESE BOOKS
THAT'S BECAUSE I'M OLDER AND WISER NOW.
JENNIFER'S MORE AWARE OF FEMINIST ISSUES THAN I AM...
IT'S SO INSULTING THAT THEY THINK WOMEN WILL VOTE FOR HER JUST BECAUSE SHE'S A WOMAN...
NOT THAT I'M TOTALLY OBLIVIOUS.
AND WHY DO THEY FOCUS ON HER BEING A "HOCKEY MOM" INSTEAD OF BEING GOVERNOR?
HOWEVER THINGS WERE BETWEEN US, IT ALL CHANGED A COUPLE YEARS AGO.
I'M PREGNANT.
TRUE TO CLICHÉ, A BABY DOES CHANGE EVERYTHING.
THIS MAKES ME QUESTION EVERYTHING...
HOW CAN I LEAVE HIM AND GO BACK TO WORK?
KICK! KICK!
CAN WE AFFORD FOR ME TO STAY HOME?
AND WHAT IF WE NEVER HAVE THIS CHANCE AGAIN? HE'S ONLY A BABY ONCE.
KICK! KICK!

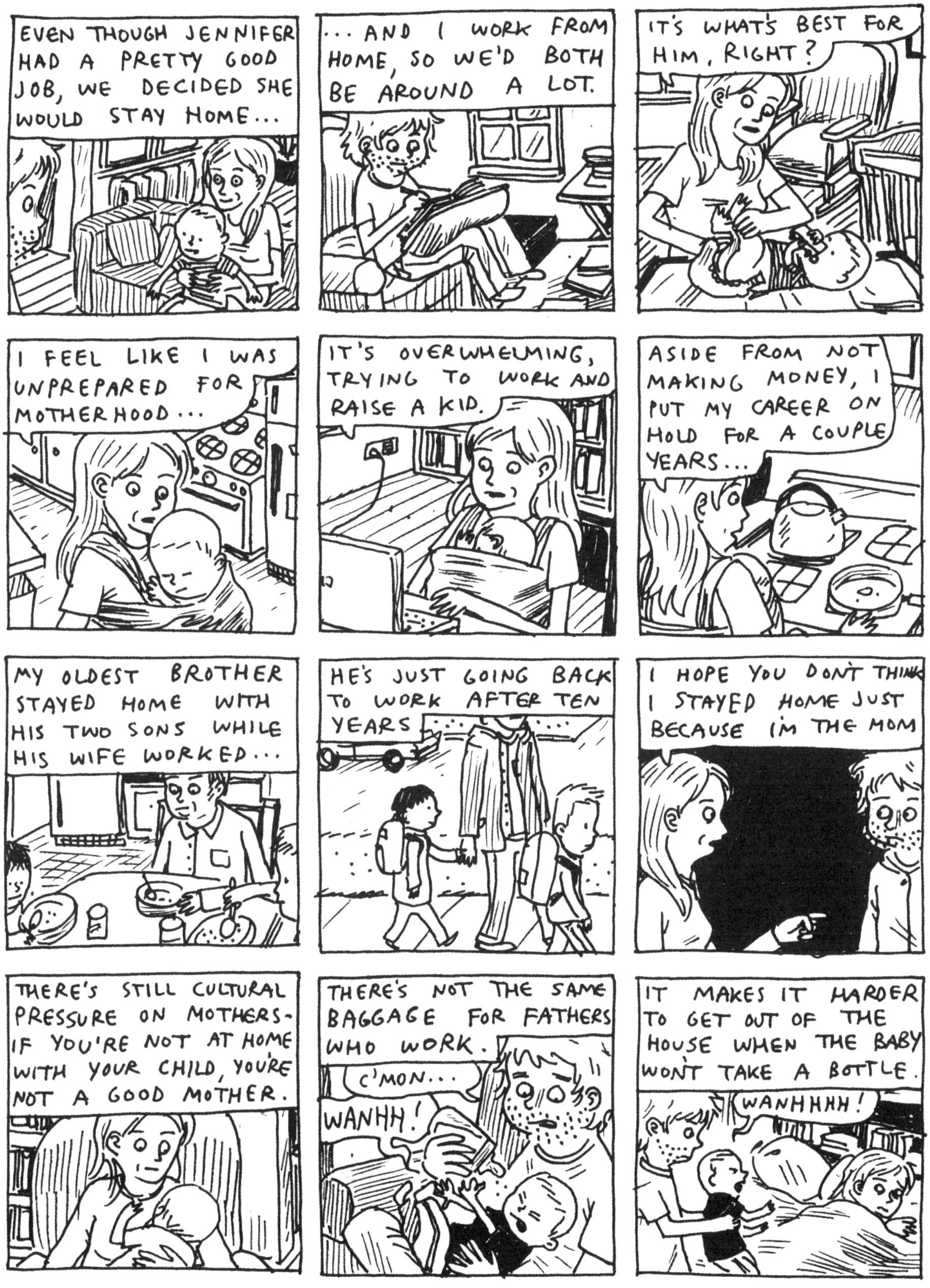
EVEN THOUGH JENNIFER HAD A PRETTY GOOD JOB, WE DECIDED SHE WOULD STAY HOME...
... AND I WORK FROM HOME, SO WE'D BOTH BE AROUND A LOT.
IT'S WHAT'S BEST FOR HIM, RIGHT?
I FEEL LIKE I WAS UNPREPARED FOR MOTHERHOOD...
IT'S OVERWHELMING, TRYING TO WORK AND RAISE A KID.
ASIDE FROM NOT MAKING MONEY, I PUT MY CAREER ON HOLD FOR A COUPLE YEARS...
MY OLDEST BROTHER STAYED HOME WITH HIS TWO SONS WHILE HIS WIFE WORKED...
HE'S JUST GOING BACK TO WORK AFTER TEN YEARS.
I HOPE YOU DON'T THINK I STAYED HOME JUST BECAUSE I'M THE MOM
THERE'S STILL CULTURAL PRESSURE ON MOTHERS - IF YOU'RE NOT AT HOME WITH YOUR CHILD, YOU'RE NOT A GOOD MOTHER.
THERE'S NOT THE SAME BAGGAGE FOR FATHERS WHO WORK.
C'MON...
WANHH!
IT MAKES IT HARDER TO GET OUT OF THE HOUSE WHEN THE BABY WON'T TAKE A BOTTLE.
WANHHHH!

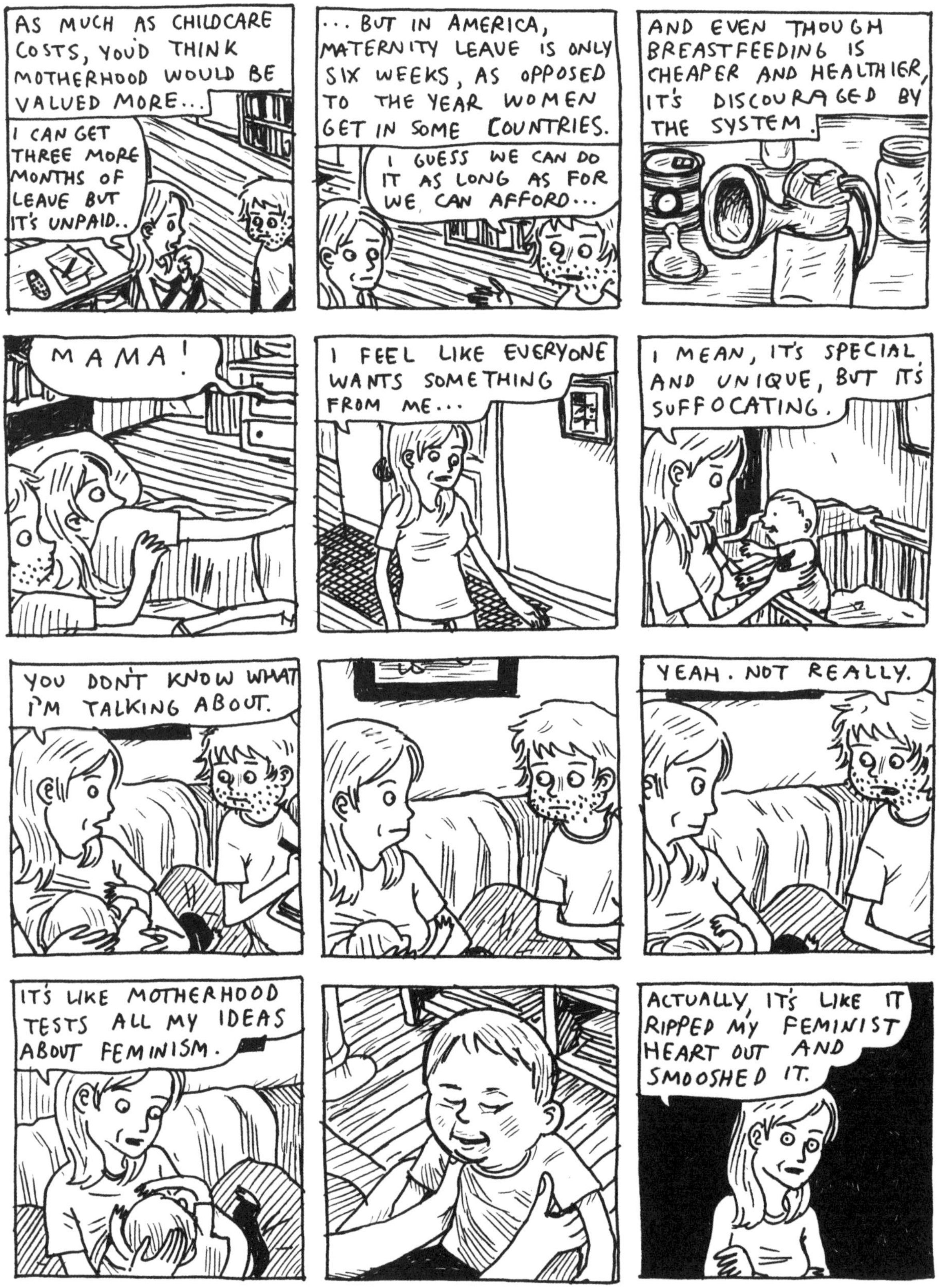

AS MUCH AS CHILDCARE COSTS, YOU'D THINK MOTHERHOOD WOULD BE VALUED MORE...
I CAN GET THREE MORE MONTHS OF LEAVE BUT IT'S UNPAID..
... BUT IN AMERICA, MATERNITY LEAVE IS ONLY SIX WEEKS, AS OPPOSED TO THE YEAR WOMEN GET IN SOME COUNTRIES.
I GUESS WE CAN DO IT AS LONG AS FOR WE CAN AFFORD...
AND EVEN THOUGH BREASTFEEDING IS CHEAPER AND HEALTHIER, IT'S DISCOURAGED BY THE SYSTEM.
MAMA!
I FEEL LIKE EVERYONE WANTS SOMETHING FROM ME...
I MEAN, IT'S SPECIAL AND UNIQUE, BUT IT'S SUFFOCATING.
YOU DON'T KNOW WHAT I'M TALKING ABOUT.
YEAH. NOT REALLY.
IT'S LIKE MOTHERHOOD TESTS ALL MY IDEAS ABOUT FEMINISM.
ACTUALLY, IT'S LIKE IT RIPPED MY FEMINIST HEART OUT AND SMOOSHED IT.

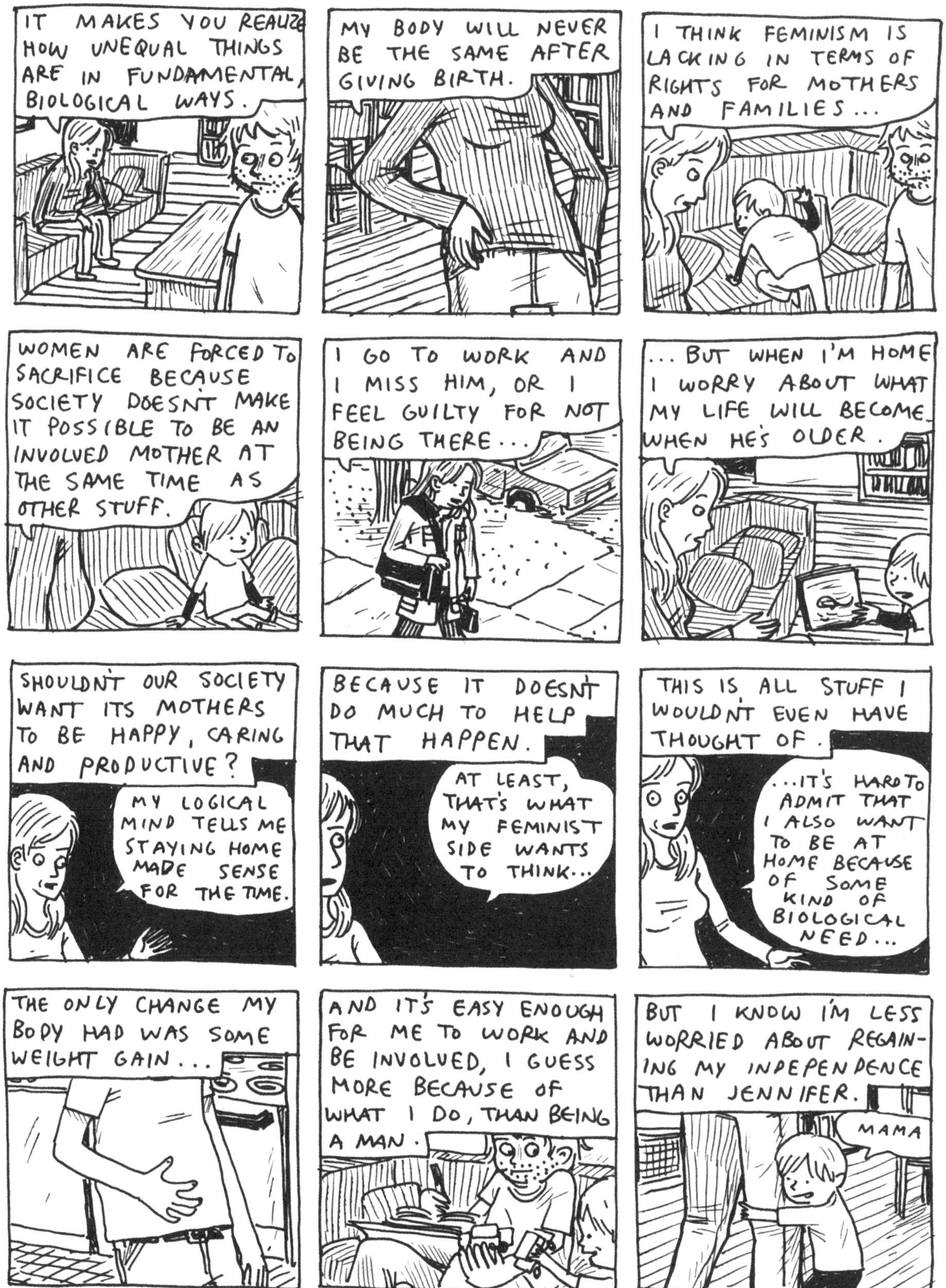
IT MAKES YOU REALIZE HOW UNEQUAL THINGS ARE IN FUNDAMENTAL, BIOLOGICAL WAYS.
MY BODY WILL NEVER BE THE SAME AFTER GIVING BIRTH.
I THINK FEMINISM IS LACKING IN TERMS OF RIGHTS FOR MOTHERS AND FAMILIES...
WOMEN ARE FORCED TO SACRIFICE BECAUSE SOCIETY DOESN'T MAKE IT POSSIBLE TO BE AN INVOLVED MOTHER AT THE SAME TIME AS OTHER STUFF.
I GO TO WORK AND I MISS HIM, OR I FEEL GUILTY FOR NOT BEING THERE...
...BUT WHEN I'M HOME I WORRY ABOUT WHAT MY LIFE WILL BECOME WHEN HE'S OLDER.
SHOULDN'T OUR SOCIETY WANT ITS MOTHERS TO BE HAPPY, CARING AND PRODUCTIVE?
MY LOGICAL MIND TELLS ME STAYING HOME MADE SENSE FOR THE TIME.
BECAUSE IT DOESN'T DO MUCH TO HELP THAT HAPPEN.
AT LEAST, THAT'S WHAT MY FEMINIST SIDE WANTS TO THINK...
THIS IS ALL STUFF I WOULDN'T EVEN HAVE THOUGHT OF.
...IT'S HARD TO ADMIT THAT I ALSO WANT TO BE AT HOME BECAUSE OF SOME KIND OF BIOLOGICAL NEED...
THE ONLY CHANGE MY BODY HAD WAS SOME WEIGHT GAIN...
AND IT'S EASY ENOUGH FOR ME TO WORK AND BE INVOLVED, I GUESS MORE BECAUSE OF WHAT I DO, THAN BEING A MAN.
BUT I KNOW I'M LESS WORRIED ABOUT REGAINING MY INDEPENDENCE THAN JENNIFER.
MAMA

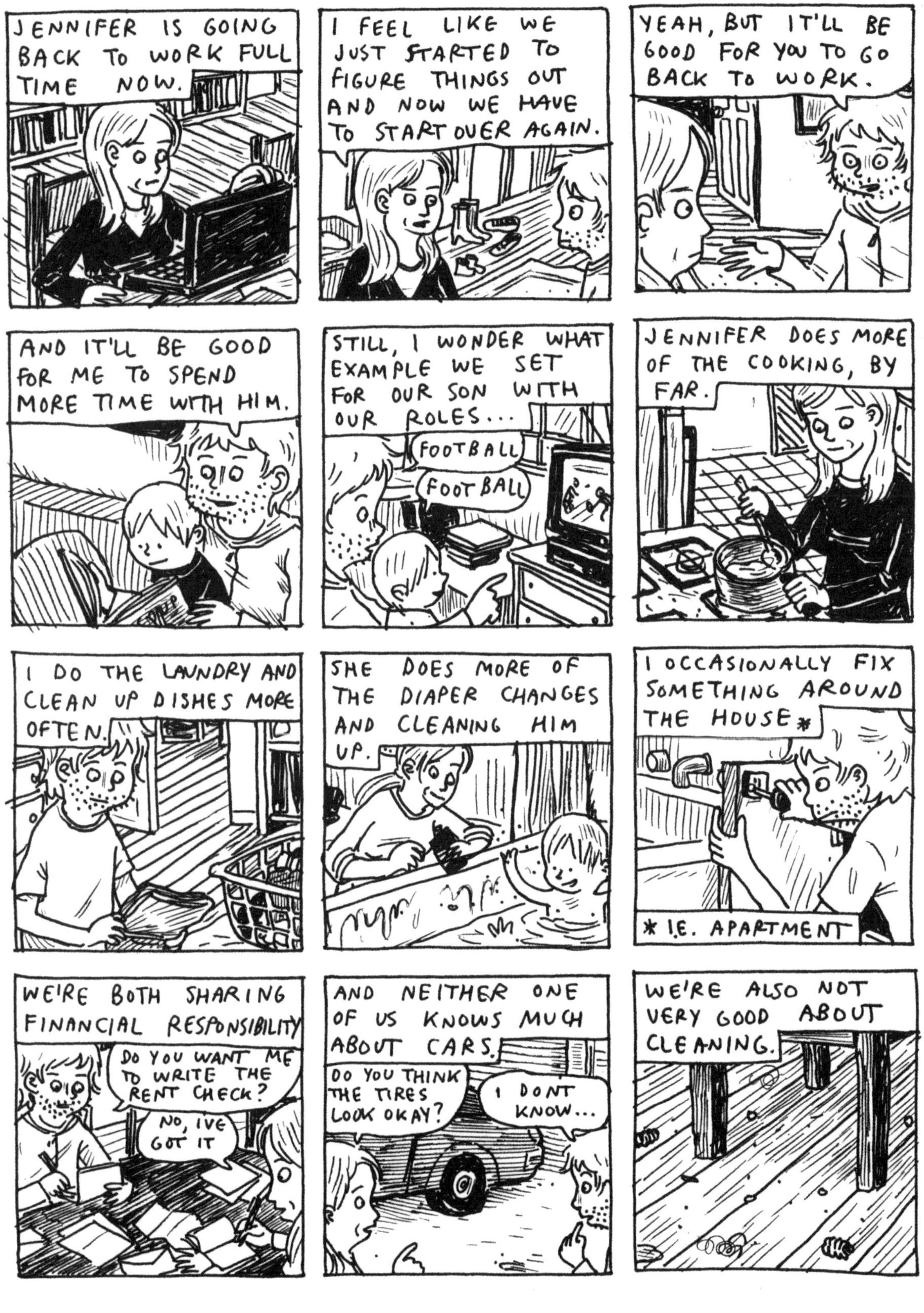
JENNIFER IS GOING BACK TO WORK FULL TIME NOW.
I FEEL LIKE WE JUST STARTED TO FIGURE THINGS OUT AND NOW WE HAVE TO START OVER AGAIN.
YEAH, BUT IT'LL BE GOOD FOR YOU TO GO BACK TO WORK.
AND IT'LL BE GOOD FOR ME TO SPEND MORE TIME WITH HIM.
STILL, I WONDER WHAT EXAMPLE WE SET FOR OUR SON WITH OUR ROLES...
FOOTBALL
FOOTBALL
JENNIFER DOES MORE OF THE COOKING, BY FAR.
I DO THE LAUNDRY AND CLEAN UP DISHES MORE OFTEN.
SHE DOES MORE OF THE DIAPER CHANGES AND CLEANING HIM UP.
I OCCASIONALLY FIX SOMETHING AROUND THE HOUSE*
* I.E. APARTMENT
WE'RE BOTH SHARING FINANCIAL RESPONSIBILITY
DO YOU WANT ME TO WRITE THE RENT CHECK?
NO, IVE GOT IT
AND NEITHER ONE OF US KNOWS MUCH ABOUT CARS.
DO YOU THINK THE TIRES LOOK OKAY?
I DONT KNOW...
WE'RE ALSO NOT VERY GOOD ABOUT CLEANING.

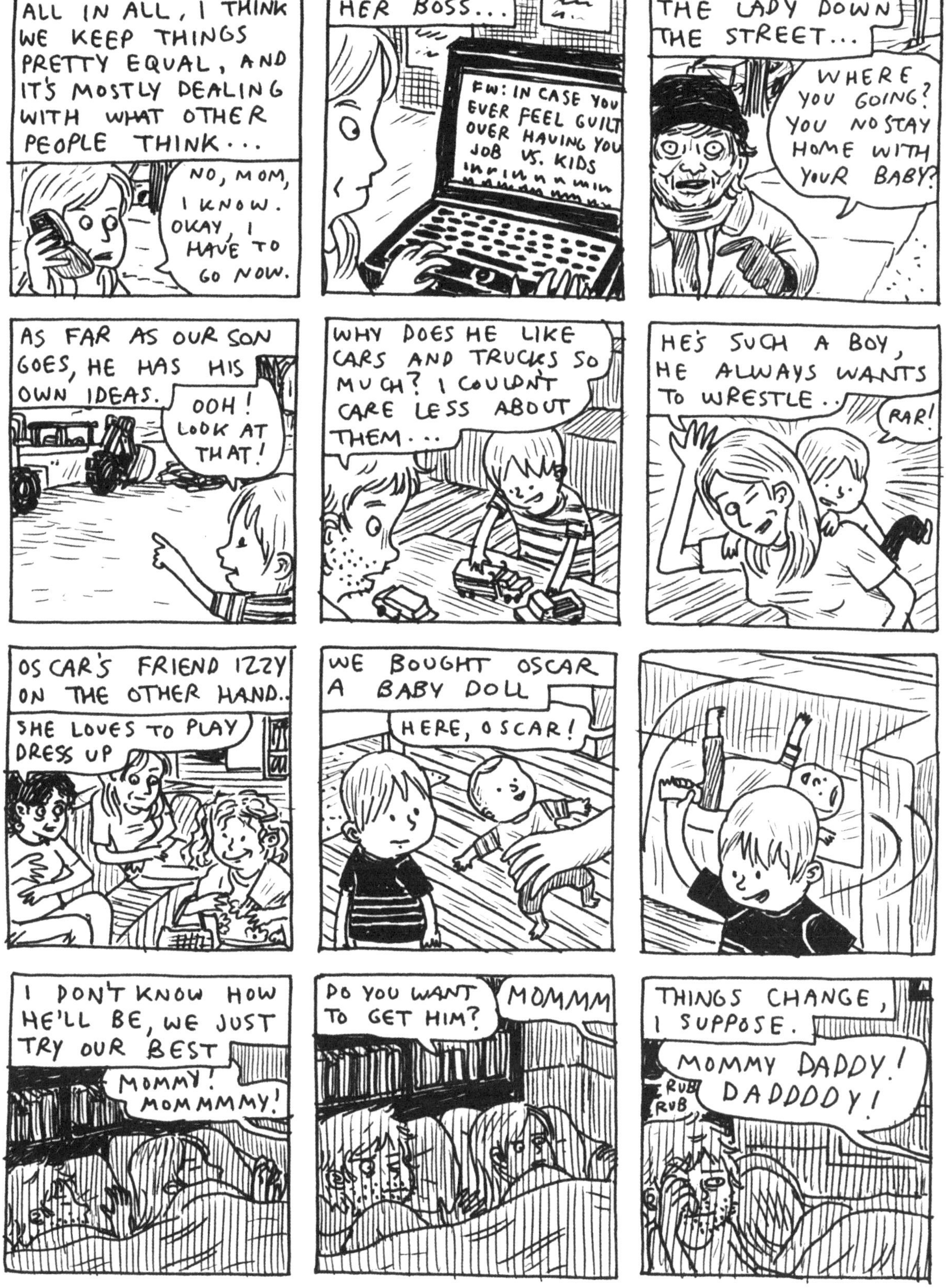
ALL IN ALL, I THINK WE KEEP THINGS PRETTY EQUAL, AND IT'S MOSTLY DEALING WITH WHAT OTHER PEOPLE THINK...
NO, MOM, I KNOW. OKAY, I HAVE TO GO NOW.
HER BOSS...
FW: IN CASE YOU EVER FEEL GUILT OVER HAVING YOU JOB VS. KIDS
THE LADY DOWN THE STREET...
WHERE YOU GOING? YOU NO STAY HOME WITH YOUR BABY?
AS FAR AS OUR SON GOES, HE HAS HIS OWN IDEAS.
OOH! LOOK AT THAT!
WHY DOES HE LIKE CARS AND TRUCKS SO MUCH? I COULDN'T CARE LESS ABOUT THEM...
HE'S SUCH A BOY, HE ALWAYS WANTS TO WRESTLE..
RAR!
OSCAR'S FRIEND IZZY ON THE OTHER HAND..
SHE LOVES TO PLAY DRESS UP
WE BOUGHT OSCAR A BABY DOLL
HERE, OSCAR!
I DON'T KNOW HOW HE'LL BE, WE JUST TRY OUR BEST
MOMMY! MOMMMMY!
DO YOU WANT TO GET HIM?
MOMMM
THINGS CHANGE, I SUPPOSE.
MOMMY DADDY! DADDDDY!
RUB RUB

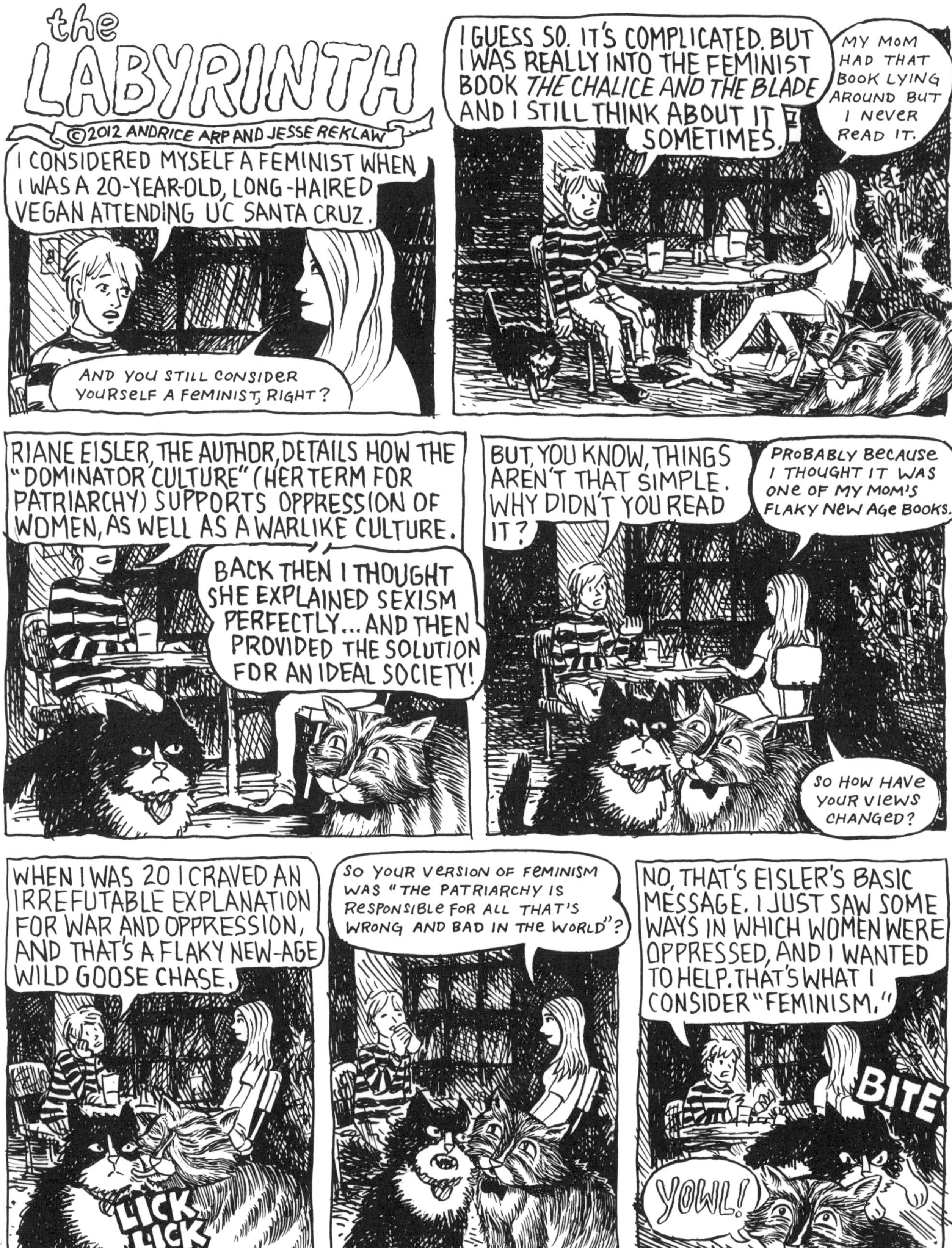
the LABYRINTH
©2012 ANDRICE ARP AND JESSE REKLAW
I CONSIDERED MYSELF A FEMINIST WHEN I WAS A 20-YEAR-OLD, LONG-HAIRED VEGAN ATTENDING UC SANTA CRUZ.
AND YOU STILL CONSIDER YOURSELF A FEMINIST, RIGHT?
I GUESS SO. IT'S COMPLICATED. BUT I WAS REALLY INTO THE FEMINIST BOOK *THE CHALICE AND THE BLADE* AND I STILL THINK ABOUT IT SOMETIMES.
MY MOM HAD THAT BOOK LYING AROUND BUT I NEVER READ IT.
RIANE EISLER, THE AUTHOR, DETAILS HOW THE "DOMINATOR CULTURE" (HER TERM FOR PATRIARCHY) SUPPORTS OPPRESSION OF WOMEN, AS WELL AS A WARLIKE CULTURE.
BACK THEN I THOUGHT SHE EXPLAINED SEXISM PERFECTLY... AND THEN PROVIDED THE SOLUTION FOR AN IDEAL SOCIETY!
BUT, YOU KNOW, THINGS AREN'T THAT SIMPLE. WHY DIDN'T YOU READ IT?
PROBABLY BECAUSE I THOUGHT IT WAS ONE OF MY MOM'S FLAKY NEW AGE BOOKS.
SO HOW HAVE YOUR VIEWS CHANGED?
WHEN I WAS 20 I CRAVED AN IRREFUTABLE EXPLANATION FOR WAR AND OPPRESSION, AND THAT'S A FLAKY NEW-AGE WILD GOOSE CHASE.
LICK LICK
SO YOUR VERSION OF FEMINISM WAS "THE PATRIARCHY IS RESPONSIBLE FOR ALL THAT'S WRONG AND BAD IN THE WORLD"?
NO, THAT'S EISLER'S BASIC MESSAGE. I JUST SAW SOME WAYS IN WHICH WOMEN WERE OPPRESSED, AND I WANTED TO HELP. THAT'S WHAT I CONSIDER "FEMINISM."
BITE
YOWL!

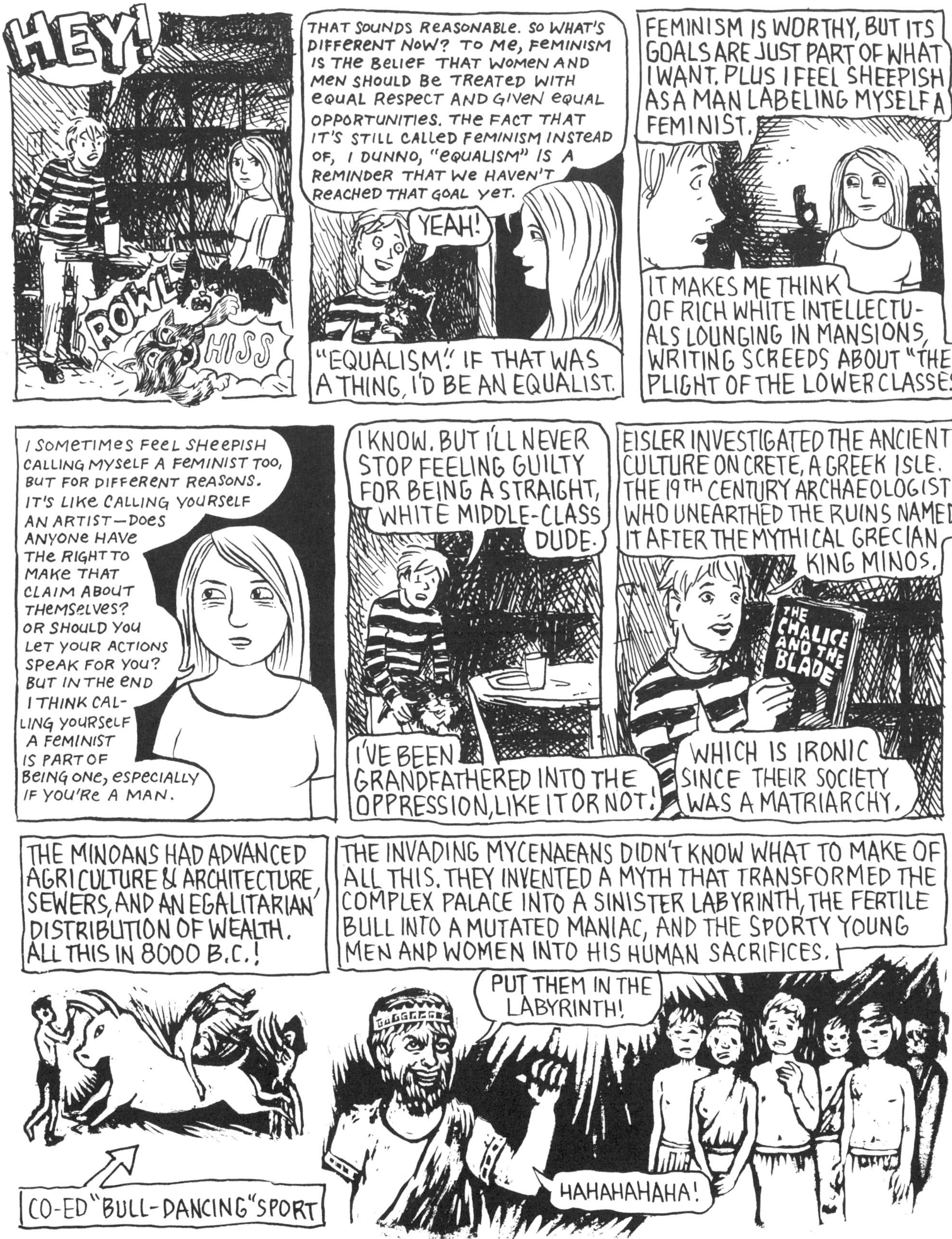
HEY!
ROWL
HISS
THAT SOUNDS REASONABLE. SO WHAT'S DIFFERENT NOW? TO ME, FEMINISM IS THE BELIEF THAT WOMEN AND MEN SHOULD BE TREATED WITH EQUAL RESPECT AND GIVEN EQUAL OPPORTUNITIES. THE FACT THAT IT'S STILL CALLED FEMINISM INSTEAD OF, I DUNNO, "EQUALISM" IS A REMINDER THAT WE HAVEN'T REACHED THAT GOAL YET.
YEAH!
"EQUALISM." IF THAT WAS A THING, I'D BE AN EQUALIST.
FEMINISM IS WORTHY, BUT ITS GOALS ARE JUST PART OF WHAT I WANT. PLUS I FEEL SHEEPISH AS A MAN LABELING MYSELF A FEMINIST.
IT MAKES ME THINK OF RICH WHITE INTELLECTU-ALS LOUNGING IN MANSIONS, WRITING SCREEDS ABOUT "THE PLIGHT OF THE LOWER CLASSES."
I SOMETIMES FEEL SHEEPISH CALLING MYSELF A FEMINIST TOO, BUT FOR DIFFERENT REASONS. IT'S LIKE CALLING YOURSELF AN ARTIST—DOES ANYONE HAVE THE RIGHT TO MAKE THAT CLAIM ABOUT THEMSELVES? OR SHOULD YOU LET YOUR ACTIONS SPEAK FOR YOU? BUT IN THE END I THINK CAL-LING YOURSELF A FEMINIST IS PART OF BEING ONE, ESPECIALLY IF YOU'RE A MAN.
I KNOW. BUT I'LL NEVER STOP FEELING GUILTY FOR BEING A STRAIGHT, WHITE MIDDLE-CLASS DUDE.
I'VE BEEN GRANDFATHERED INTO THE OPPRESSION, LIKE IT OR NOT!
EISLER INVESTIGATED THE ANCIENT CULTURE ON CRETE, A GREEK ISLE. THE 19TH CENTURY ARCHAEOLOGIST WHO UNEARTHED THE RUINS NAMED IT AFTER THE MYTHICAL GRECIAN KING MINOS.
THE CHALICE AND THE BLADE
WHICH IS IRONIC SINCE THEIR SOCIETY WAS A MATRIARCHY.
THE MINOANS HAD ADVANCED AGRICULTURE & ARCHITECTURE, SEWERS, AND AN EGALITARIAN DISTRIBUTION OF WEALTH. ALL THIS IN 8000 B.C.!
THE INVADING MYCENAEANS DIDN'T KNOW WHAT TO MAKE OF ALL THIS. THEY INVENTED A MYTH THAT TRANSFORMED THE COMPLEX PALACE INTO A SINISTER LABYRINTH, THE FERTILE BULL INTO A MUTATED MANIAC, AND THE SPORTY YOUNG MEN AND WOMEN INTO HIS HUMAN SACRIFICES.
PUT THEM IN THE LABYRINTH!
CO-ED "BULL-DANCING" SPORT
HAHAHAHAHA!

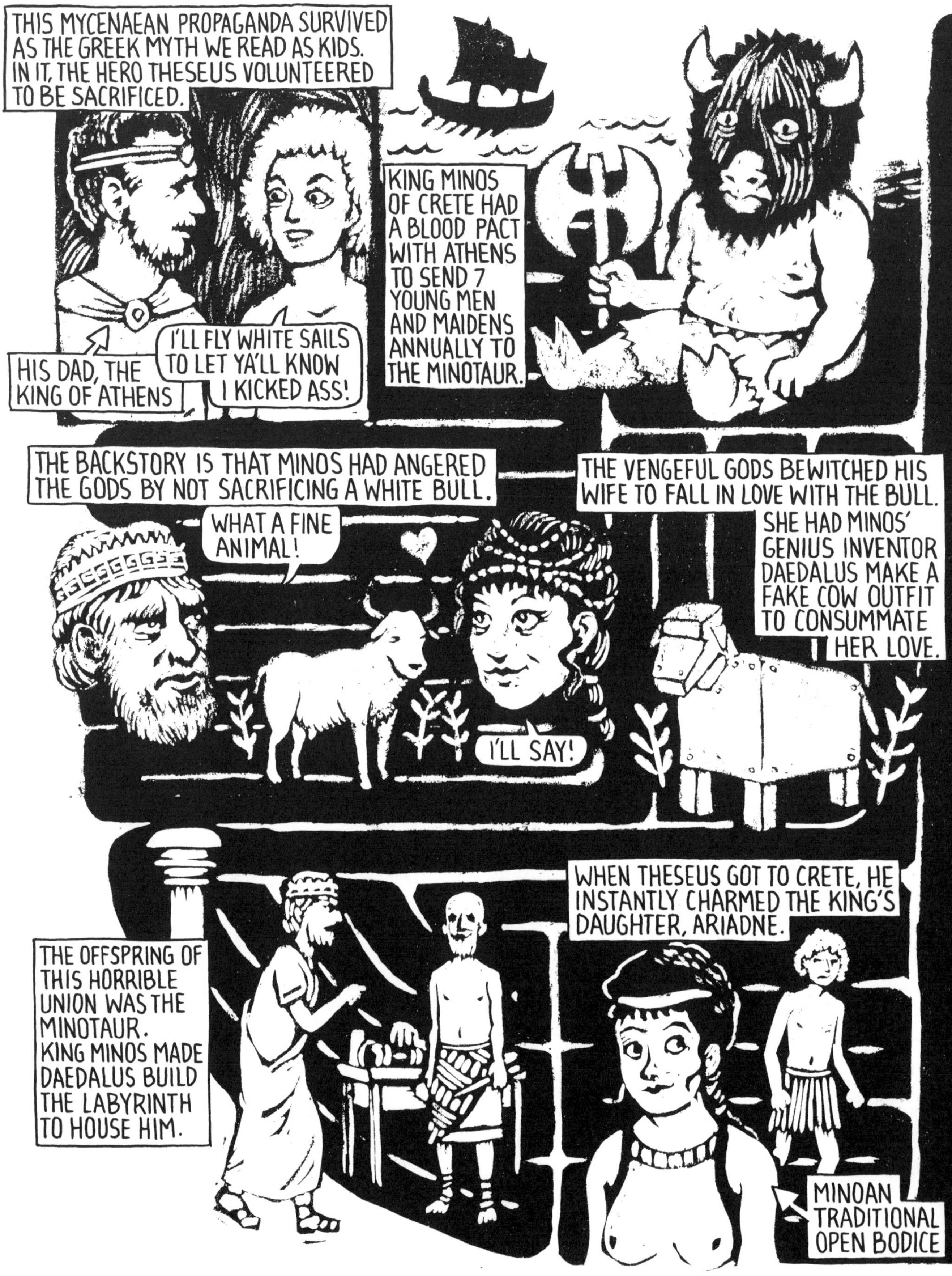
THIS MYCENAEAN PROPAGANDA SURVIVED AS THE GREEK MYTH WE READ AS KIDS. IN IT, THE HERO THESEUS VOLUNTEERED TO BE SACRIFICED.
HIS DAD, THE KING OF ATHENS
I'LL FLY WHITE SAILS TO LET YA'LL KNOW I KICKED ASS!
KING MINOS OF CRETE HAD A BLOOD PACT WITH ATHENS TO SEND 7 YOUNG MEN AND MAIDENS ANNUALLY TO THE MINOTAUR.
THE BACKSTORY IS THAT MINOS HAD ANGERED THE GODS BY NOT SACRIFICING A WHITE BULL.
WHAT A FINE ANIMAL!
I'LL SAY!
THE VENGEFUL GODS BEWITCHED HIS WIFE TO FALL IN LOVE WITH THE BULL.
SHE HAD MINOS' GENIUS INVENTOR DAEDALUS MAKE A FAKE COW OUTFIT TO CONSUMMATE HER LOVE.
THE OFFSPRING OF THIS HORRIBLE UNION WAS THE MINOTAUR. KING MINOS MADE DAEDALUS BUILD THE LABYRINTH TO HOUSE HIM.
WHEN THESEUS GOT TO CRETE, HE INSTANTLY CHARMED THE KING'S DAUGHTER, ARIADNE.
MINOAN TRADITIONAL OPEN BODICE

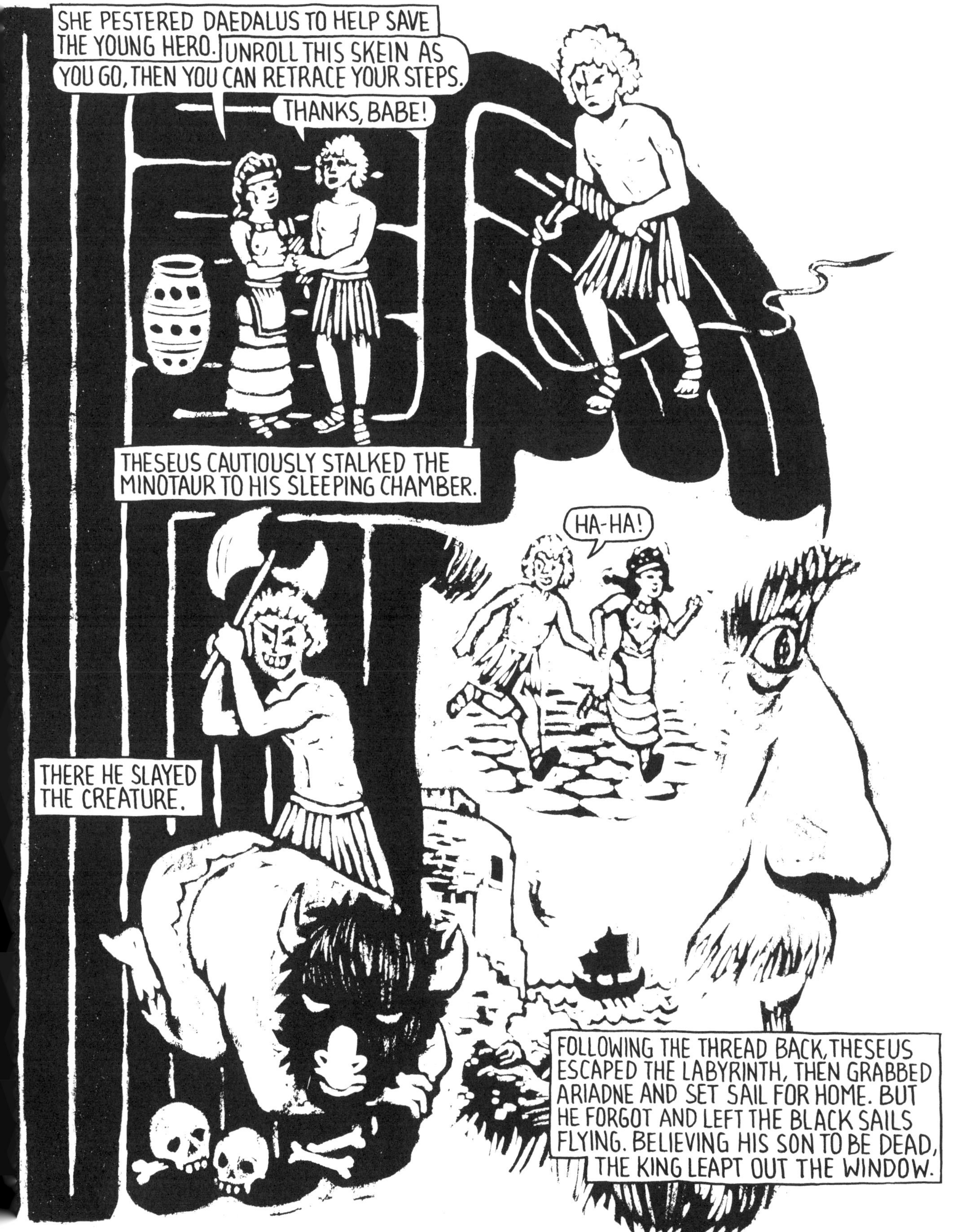

SHE PESTERED DAEDALUS TO HELP SAVE THE YOUNG HERO.
UNROLL THIS SKEIN AS YOU GO, THEN YOU CAN RETRACE YOUR STEPS.
THANKS, BABE!
THESEUS CAUTIOUSLY STALKED THE MINOTAUR TO HIS SLEEPING CHAMBER.
THERE HE SLAYED THE CREATURE.
HA-HA!
FOLLOWING THE THREAD BACK, THESEUS ESCAPED THE LABYRINTH, THEN GRABBED ARIADNE AND SET SAIL FOR HOME. BUT HE FORGOT AND LEFT THE BLACK SAILS FLYING. BELIEVING HIS SON TO BE DEAD, THE KING LEAPT OUT THE WINDOW.

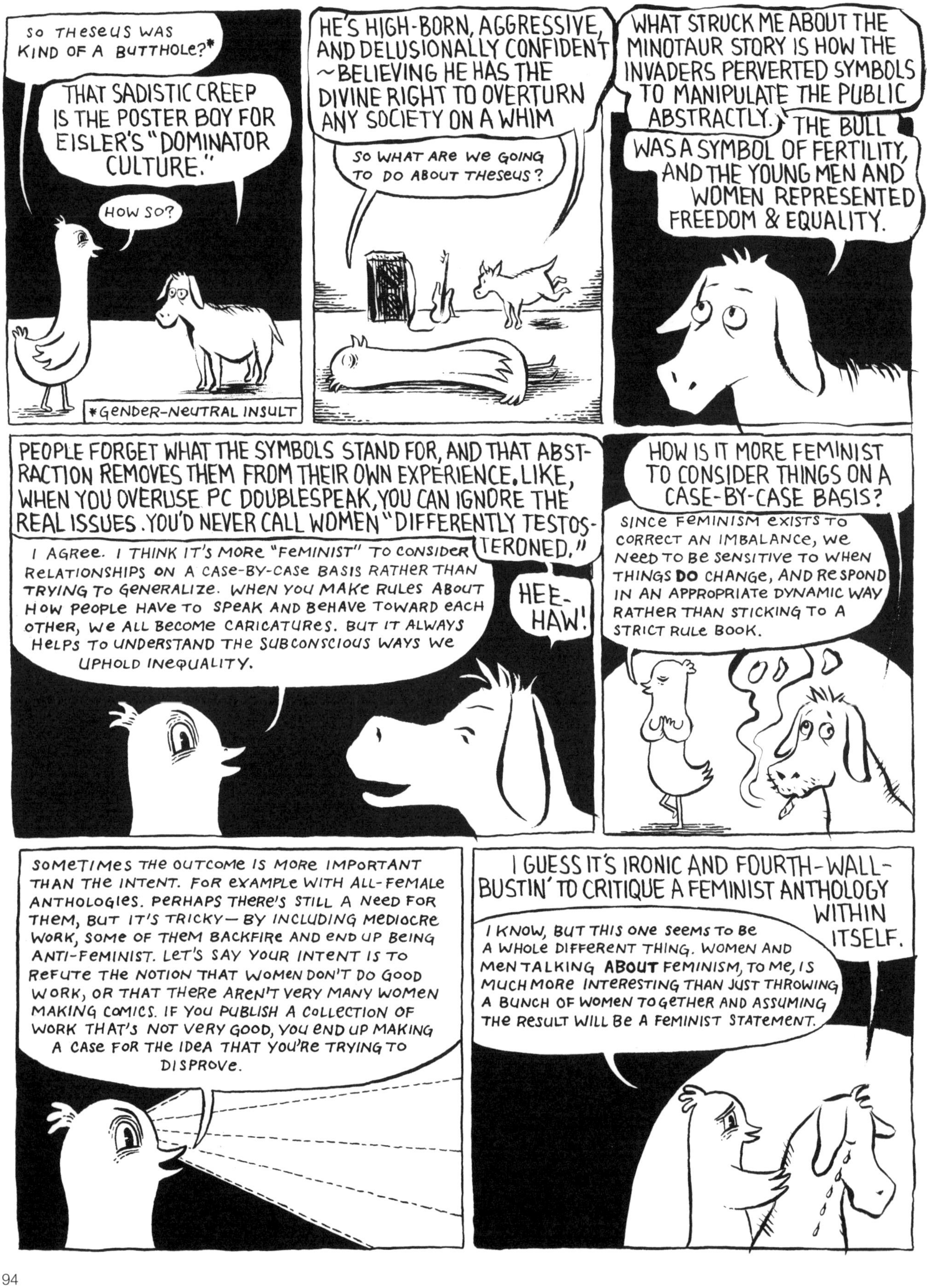

SO THESEUS WAS KIND OF A BUTTHOLE?*
THAT SADISTIC CREEP IS THE POSTER BOY FOR EISLER'S "DOMINATOR CULTURE."
HOW SO?
*GENDER-NEUTRAL INSULT
HE'S HIGH-BORN, AGGRESSIVE, AND DELUSIONALLY CONFIDENT ~ BELIEVING HE HAS THE DIVINE RIGHT TO OVERTURN ANY SOCIETY ON A WHIM
SO WHAT ARE WE GOING TO DO ABOUT THESEUS?
WHAT STRUCK ME ABOUT THE MINOTAUR STORY IS HOW THE INVADERS PERVERTED SYMBOLS TO MANIPULATE THE PUBLIC ABSTRACTLY.
THE BULL WAS A SYMBOL OF FERTILITY, AND THE YOUNG MEN AND WOMEN REPRESENTED FREEDOM & EQUALITY.
PEOPLE FORGET WHAT THE SYMBOLS STAND FOR, AND THAT ABSTRACTION REMOVES THEM FROM THEIR OWN EXPERIENCE. LIKE, WHEN YOU OVERUSE PC DOUBLESPEAK, YOU CAN IGNORE THE REAL ISSUES. YOU'D NEVER CALL WOMEN "DIFFERENTLY TESTOSTERONED."
I AGREE. I THINK IT'S MORE "FEMINIST" TO CONSIDER RELATIONSHIPS ON A CASE-BY-CASE BASIS RATHER THAN TRYING TO GENERALIZE. WHEN YOU MAKE RULES ABOUT HOW PEOPLE HAVE TO SPEAK AND BEHAVE TOWARD EACH OTHER, WE ALL BECOME CARICATURES. BUT IT ALWAYS HELPS TO UNDERSTAND THE SUBCONSCIOUS WAYS WE UPHOLD INEQUALITY.
HEE-HAW!
HOW IS IT MORE FEMINIST TO CONSIDER THINGS ON A CASE-BY-CASE BASIS?
SINCE FEMINISM EXISTS TO CORRECT AN IMBALANCE, WE NEED TO BE SENSITIVE TO WHEN THINGS DO CHANGE, AND RESPOND IN AN APPROPRIATE DYNAMIC WAY RATHER THAN STICKING TO A STRICT RULE BOOK.
SOMETIMES THE OUTCOME IS MORE IMPORTANT THAN THE INTENT. FOR EXAMPLE WITH ALL-FEMALE ANTHOLOGIES. PERHAPS THERE'S STILL A NEED FOR THEM, BUT IT'S TRICKY— BY INCLUDING MEDIOCRE WORK, SOME OF THEM BACKFIRE AND END UP BEING ANTI-FEMINIST. LET'S SAY YOUR INTENT IS TO REFUTE THE NOTION THAT WOMEN DON'T DO GOOD WORK, OR THAT THERE AREN'T VERY MANY WOMEN MAKING COMICS. IF YOU PUBLISH A COLLECTION OF WORK THAT'S NOT VERY GOOD, YOU END UP MAKING A CASE FOR THE IDEA THAT YOU'RE TRYING TO DISPROVE.
I GUESS IT'S IRONIC AND FOURTH-WALL-BUSTIN' TO CRITIQUE A FEMINIST ANTHOLOGY WITHIN ITSELF.
I KNOW, BUT THIS ONE SEEMS TO BE A WHOLE DIFFERENT THING. WOMEN AND MEN TALKING ABOUT FEMINISM, TO ME, IS MUCH MORE INTERESTING THAN JUST THROWING A BUNCH OF WOMEN TOGETHER AND ASSUMING THE RESULT WILL BE A FEMINIST STATEMENT.

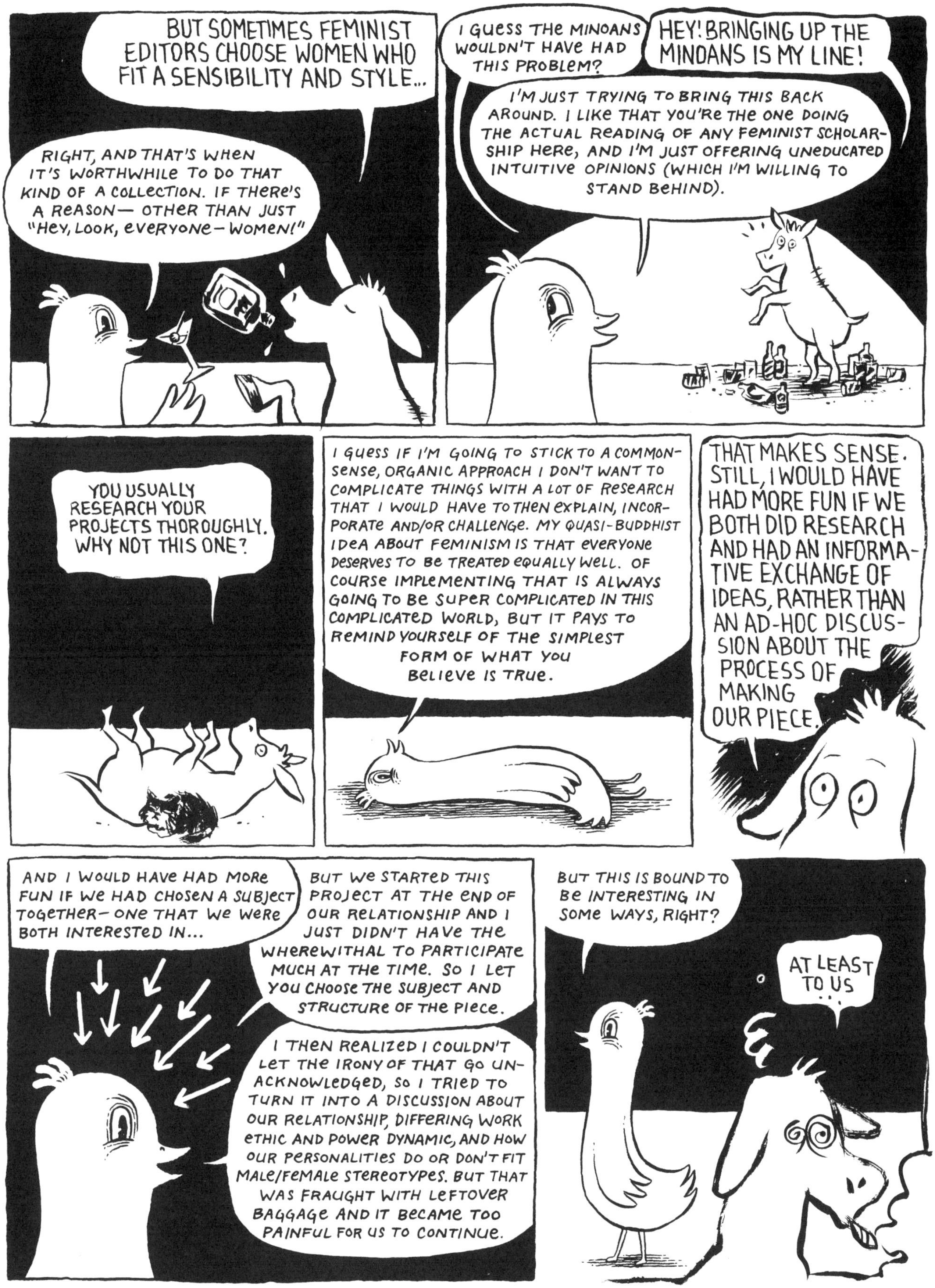
BUT SOMETIMES FEMINIST EDITORS CHOOSE WOMEN WHO FIT A SENSIBILITY AND STYLE...
RIGHT, AND THAT'S WHEN IT'S WORTHWHILE TO DO THAT KIND OF A COLLECTION. IF THERE'S A REASON— OTHER THAN JUST "HEY, LOOK, EVERYONE— WOMEN!"
I GUESS THE MINOANS WOULDN'T HAVE HAD THIS PROBLEM?
HEY! BRINGING UP THE MINOANS IS MY LINE!
I'M JUST TRYING TO BRING THIS BACK AROUND. I LIKE THAT YOU'RE THE ONE DOING THE ACTUAL READING OF ANY FEMINIST SCHOLARSHIP HERE, AND I'M JUST OFFERING UNEDUCATED INTUITIVE OPINIONS (WHICH I'M WILLING TO STAND BEHIND).
YOU USUALLY RESEARCH YOUR PROJECTS THOROUGHLY. WHY NOT THIS ONE?
I GUESS IF I'M GOING TO STICK TO A COMMONSENSE, ORGANIC APPROACH I DON'T WANT TO COMPLICATE THINGS WITH A LOT OF RESEARCH THAT I WOULD HAVE TO THEN EXPLAIN, INCORPORATE AND/OR CHALLENGE. MY QUASI-BUDDHIST IDEA ABOUT FEMINISM IS THAT EVERYONE DESERVES TO BE TREATED EQUALLY WELL. OF COURSE IMPLEMENTING THAT IS ALWAYS GOING TO BE SUPER COMPLICATED IN THIS COMPLICATED WORLD, BUT IT PAYS TO REMIND YOURSELF OF THE SIMPLEST FORM OF WHAT YOU BELIEVE IS TRUE.
THAT MAKES SENSE. STILL, I WOULD HAVE HAD MORE FUN IF WE BOTH DID RESEARCH AND HAD AN INFORMATIVE EXCHANGE OF IDEAS, RATHER THAN AN AD-HOC DISCUSSION ABOUT THE PROCESS OF MAKING OUR PIECE.
AND I WOULD HAVE HAD MORE FUN IF WE HAD CHOSEN A SUBJECT TOGETHER— ONE THAT WE WERE BOTH INTERESTED IN...
BUT WE STARTED THIS PROJECT AT THE END OF OUR RELATIONSHIP AND I JUST DIDN'T HAVE THE WHEREWITHAL TO PARTICIPATE MUCH AT THE TIME. SO I LET YOU CHOOSE THE SUBJECT AND STRUCTURE OF THE PIECE.
I THEN REALIZED I COULDN'T LET THE IRONY OF THAT GO UNACKNOWLEDGED, SO I TRIED TO TURN IT INTO A DISCUSSION ABOUT OUR RELATIONSHIP, DIFFERING WORK ETHIC AND POWER DYNAMIC, AND HOW OUR PERSONALITIES DO OR DON'T FIT MALE/FEMALE STEREOTYPES. BUT THAT WAS FRAUGHT WITH LEFTOVER BAGGAGE AND IT BECAME TOO PAINFUL FOR US TO CONTINUE.
BUT THIS IS BOUND TO BE INTERESTING IN SOME WAYS, RIGHT?
AT LEAST TO US

## About Our Contributors

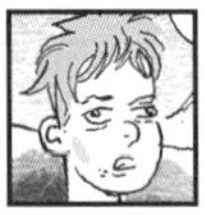
**Trevor Alixopulos** is a cartoonist and illustrator living in California. His graphic novel *The Hot Breath of War* was published by Sparkplug Comic Books and nominated for an Ignatz Award for Outstanding Graphic Novel. His work has appeared in *Studygroup Magazine*, *Playboy*, and *The Graphic Canon*.

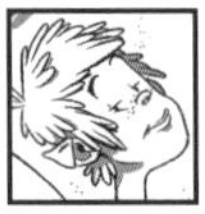
**Charlie Jane Anders**' story "Six Months, Three Days" won a Hugo Award and was shortlisted for the Nebula and Theodore Sturgeon awards. She's the managing editor at io9.com and organizer of Writers With Drinks, a spoken word variety show in San Francisco.

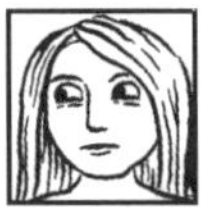
**Andrice Arp** co-founded and co-edited the *Hi-Horse* comic book series from 2001-2004, and was a contributor to the *Mome* anthology series(Fantagraphics) from 2005-2010. Recent and upcoming publications include *The Graphic Canon* Volumes 1 and 3 (Seven Stories Press), *Runner Runner* 2 (Tugboat Press) and *Black Eye 2* (Rotland Press).

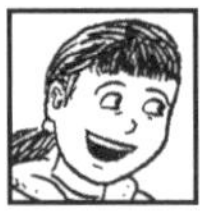
**Liz Baillie** is best known for her comics *My Brain Hurts Volumes 1 & 2* as well as her webcomic, *Freewheel*. She has self-published multitudes of minicomics, and was nominated for both the Maisie Kukoc Award in 2008 and the Kim Yale Award in 2009. She graduated from SVA in 2002 and currently resides in Queens.

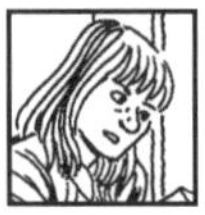
**Gabrielle Bell's** work has been selected for several previous volumes of *Best American Comics* (HMH Books) and featured in the *Yale Anthology of Graphic Fiction*, *McSweeney's*, *The Believer*, and *Vice*. Her story, "Cecil and Jordan In New York," was adapted for the screen by Bell and director Michel Gondry in the film anthology *Tokyo!* Her newest book,*The Voyeurs*, was released from Uncivilized Books in September 2012. She lives in Brooklyn.

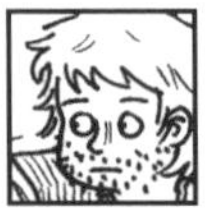
**Jeffrey Brown** has written a half-dozen autobiographical graphic novels, including *Clumsy* and *Funny Misshapen Body*. He also wrote the New York Times bestseller *Darth Vader and son*, co-wrote the film *Save The Date*, and currently teaches comics at The School of the Art Institute of Chicago.

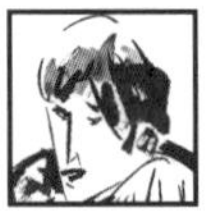
**Ric Carrasquillo** is a cartoonist and illustrator living and working in San Francisco since 1998. His work has appeared in *Not My Small Diary* and *Pet Noir: An Illustrated Anthology of Strange but True Pet Crime Stories*. His webcomic continues to exist at squillostudio.com.

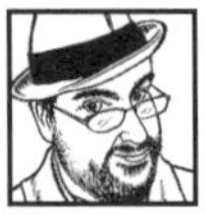
**Rob Clough** has written about comics for The Comics Journal (both the magazine and its online incarnation at tcj.com), Studygroup Magazine, the Poopsheet Foundation, Other, Savant, sequart.com and his own High-Low blog (highlowcomics.blogspot.com). He is married to a whip-smart feminist of a wife and has a young daughter who's not afraid to assert her own sense of agency.

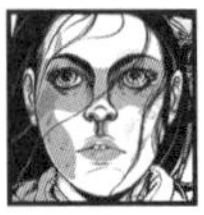
**Kristina Collantes** was born in the Philippines, but now lives and works as a full-time illustrator in sunny Los Angeles, CA. She has contributed editorial drawings to *The New Yorker, The New York Times, GQ Magazine*, and other various publications. Kristina currently works as an inker and colorist for Image Comics.

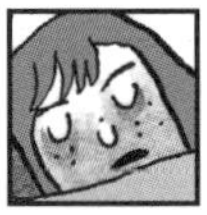
**Vanessa Davis** is the creator of *Spaniel Rage* (Buenaventura Press, 2005) and *Make Me a Woman* (Drawn and Quarterly, 2010). A contributing editor at *Tablet* magazine, her work has also appeared in *The New York Times, Psychology Today*, and *SpongeBob Comics*. She lives in Los Angeles.

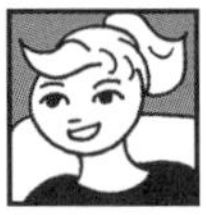
**Abby Denson** is the creator of *Dolltopia*, *Tough Love: High School Confidential*, and *City Sweet Tooth*. She's scripted *Powerpuff Girls*, *Amazing Spider-Man Family,* and other comics for Marvel and DC. Her work has garnered a Lulu Award, an International Manga Award, and a Moonbeam Children's Book Award. See more at http://www.abbycomix.com and citysweettooth.com

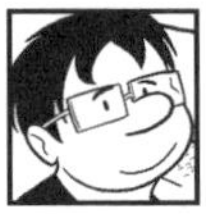
**Barry Deutsch**'s first graphic novel, *Hereville:How Mirka Got Her Sword* won the Sydney Taylor Award (the only time a comic book has won) and was nominated for Eisner, Harvey, Ignatz, and Nebula awards. A second *Hereville* book was published November of 2012, and Barry is currently working on a third.

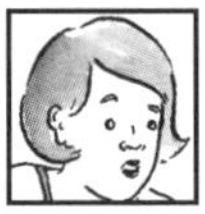
**Emily Flake** is an illustrator and cartoonist. She is the creator of *Lulu Eightball* and a frequent contributor to *The New Yorker*. She wrote a book called *These Things Ain't Gonna Smoke Themselves*. She lives in Brooklyn with her husband, daughter, and a small orange cat. www.eflakeagogo.com

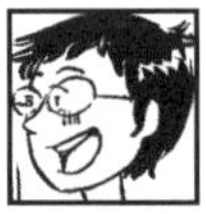
**Hilary Florido** lives in Los Angeles and works for Cartoon Network. She illustrated the graphic novel *Bloody Chester* for FirstSecond Books and has received honorable mention in the *Best American Comics* series in 2009 and 2010. She's really into dogs. You can see more of her work at hilaryflorido.com and hilaryflorido.tumblr.com.

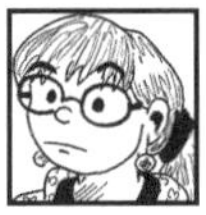
**Shaenon K. Garrity** is an award-winning cartoonist best known for the webcomics *Narbonic, Skin Horse* and *Monster of the Week*. She works as a manga editor for Viz Media and teaches at the Academy of Art in San Francisco. She lives in Berkeley with a cat, two birds and a man.

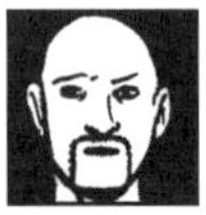
**Justin Hall** is an award-winning cartoonist known for *Glamazonia, True Travel Tales*, and *Hard To Swallow*, plus contributions to Houghton Mifflin's *Best American Comics*, the *S.F. Bay Guardian*, and others. He edited *No Straight Lines: Four Decades of Queer Comics*, and teaches at the California College of the Arts.

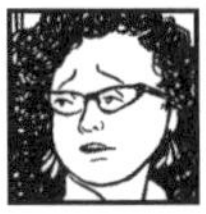
**Suzanne Kleid** lives in San Francisco. Her work has appeared at *The Rumpus, Bitch Magazine, Other Magazine*, and *We Still Like*. She has written reviews for *The Believer* and the blog of KQED, San Francisco's NPR affiliate, and co-edited the book *Created In Darkness By Troubled Americans: Best of McSweeney's Humor Category* in 2004. She is a regular storyteller at the Porchlight Storytelling Series.

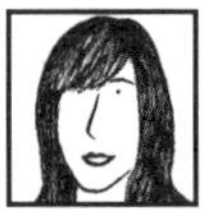
**Beth Lisick**'s books are *Monkey Girl*, *This Too Can Be Yours, Everybody Into the Pool*, and *Helping Me Help Myself*. In 2013 she releases a series of 'zines with Creativity Explored, San Francisco's art studio for developmentally disabled adults, and a collection, *Yokohama Threeway* (City Lights/Sister Spit).

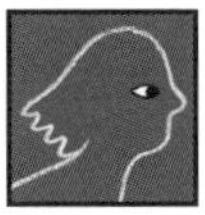
**Stina Löfgren** is working from Stockholm with ideas and esthetics. Recent work includes illustrations for *The New York Times* and Bloomberg, posters for art space Bonniers Konsthall, and a Taiwanese craft project. She has also worked at Galago, Swedens largest publisher of alternative comics.

## About Our Contributors

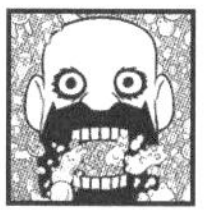

**Ed Luce** is the creator of Wuvable Oaf, an Ignatz nominated series of comics and ever-expanding line of shirts, figures and other schwag. He has also contributed to the infamous *Henry & Glenn Forever & Ever* comic series. Other highlights include pieces in Fantagraphic's *No Straight Lines*, *Maximum RockNRoll* and *BEAR* Magazine. wuvableoaf.com

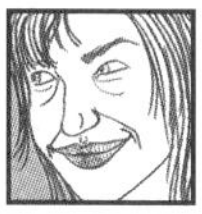

**Ulli Lust** was born in 1967 in Vienna and has lived in Berlin since 1995. She draws comic reports about daily life in Berlin. Her most successful graphic novel *Trop n'est pas assez* won the 2011 Angoulême International Comics Festival *Prix de Revelation* and will be published as *Today is the Last Day of the Rest of Your Life* by Fantagraphics in Spring 2013. Besides drawing comics she runs the screen-comic-publisher www.electrocomics.com.

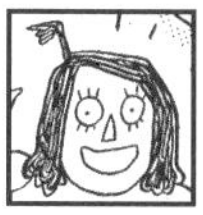

**Corinne Mucha** is a Chicago-based author and illustrator. Her work includes the Xeric-funded *My Alaskan Summer,* the Ignatz Award-winning *The Monkey in the Basement and Other Delusions* (Retrofit Comics), and the YA graphic novel *Freshman: Tales of 9th Grade Obsessions, Revelations and Other Nonsense* (Zest Books). Website: www.maidenhousefly.com

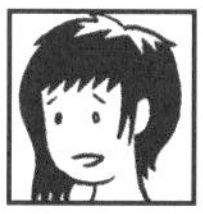

**MariNaomi** is the author and illustrator of the graphic memoir *Kiss & Tell: A Romantic Resume, Ages 0 to 22* (Harper Perennial). She is a regular contributor toTheRumpus.net, SFBay.CA and Tapastic, and is a faculty member at CCA's MFA in Comics program. Learn more at marinaomi.com.

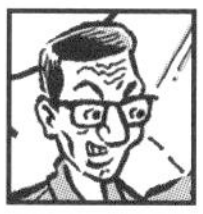

**Josh Neufeld** is the writer/artist of the bestselling nonfiction graphic novel *A.D.: New Orleans After the Deluge*. He is the illustrator of the bestseller *The Influencing Machine: Brooke Gladstone on the Media*. A 2013 Knight-Wallace fellow in journalism at the University of Michigan, he is a Xeric Award-winner and a multiple Eisner and Harvey Award nominee. www.JoshComix.com.

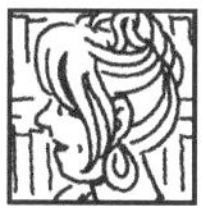

**Shannon O'Leary** is a writer and cartoonist living in Los Angeles, CA. She is a regular contributor to *Publishers Weekly* and a Contributing Editor to *The Beat: The News Blog of Comics and Culture*. She was the Marketing and Publicity Manager for Sparkplug Comic Books from 2007 - 2010 and is the Editor of *Pet Noir: An Illustrated Anthology of True Pet Crime Stories* (Manic D Press, 2007).

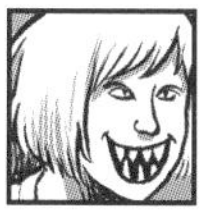

**Sarah Oleksyk** is the creator of the Eisner-nominated graphic novel *Ivy* (Oni Press). Her work has been featured in the *Best American Comics* series, *Papercutter* anthology, and *Dark Horse Presents*. She is currently working as a writer and storyboard artist for Cartoon Network's *Regular Show*.

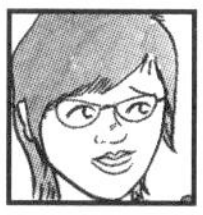

**Virginia Paine** has been self-publishing her zines *Milkyboots* and *Food Stamp Foodie* for many years. Her work has appeared in *Bejeezus, Sadie, Your Secretary,* the *Little Heart* anthology and *Brad Trip*. She lives in Portland, Oregon with her feline life-partner Lyra.

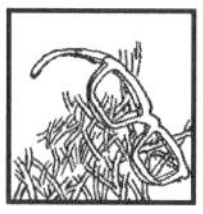

Born 1975 in Berlin, Germany, **Kai Pfeiffer** is the author of *Opérations Esthétiques* (Le Dernier Cri, France, 2000) and other diverse comics projects and publications, including "Radioactive forever", a comics essay on Chernobyl, which appeared in Japanese in the *No Nukes* anthology (Tokyo, 2012). He also edited the anthologies *Plaque* and *flitter* and teaches comics at Kunsthochschule Kassel and is a visiting professor at HBKSaar, Saarbrücken.

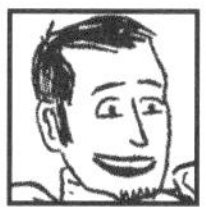

**Mark Pritchard** is the author of two books of short stories, *How I Adore You* and *Too Beautiful and Other Stories*. He is the former co-editor and publisher of *Frighten the Horses*, a sex-and-politics zine that came out from 1990 to 1994. He has lived in San Francisco since 1979.

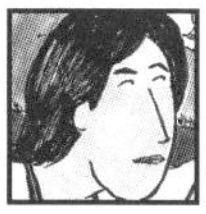

**MK Reed** is the author of *Cross Country* & *Americus* (First Second Books), which received the 2012 Carla Cohen Free Speech Award. She is currently adapting the Irish epic the *Tain Bo Cuailgne*, at aboutabull.com. Her next book, *The Cute Girl Network* (First Second Books), will be released in November 2013. She currently lives in Brooklyn with her fiancee, Peter.

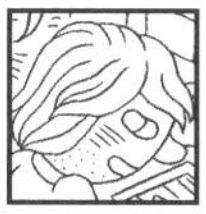

**Ron Regé, Jr.**'s esoteric comics textbook *The Cartoon Utopia* (Fantagraphics) is inspired by various alchemical and new thought texts as well as Maja D'Aoust's Magic Class lectures in Los Angeles, where Regé lives and performs in the band Lavender Diamond.

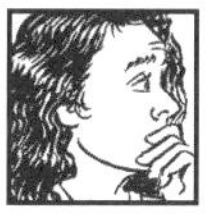

**Joan Reilly**'s comic "Hank & Barbara" for Smithmag.net was listed in *The Best American Comics 2009* under "Notable Comics," and she illustrated a story in *Working: A Graphic Adaptation*, edited by Harvey Pekar. Her cartoons also illustrated the "Ask Marilyn" column in *Parade* magazine for ten years. She was a contributing editor for every issue of the *Hi-Horse* comics anthology, including the *Hi-Horse Omnibus*, published by Alternative Comics.

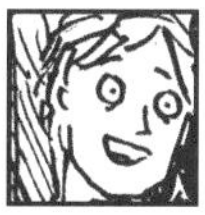

**Jesse Reklaw**'s books with pictures include *Couch Tag, Applicant* and *The Night of Your Life* (Dark Horse Comics). He became a feminist (with help from his sister and girlfriend) in 1988, but finds Deconstruction literature still too wordy.

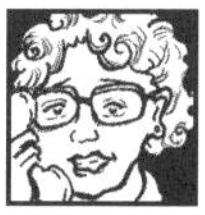

**Kat Roberts** lives in Brooklyn, New York where she divides her time between comics, fashion instruction and general craftiness. http://katroberts.tumblr.com/.

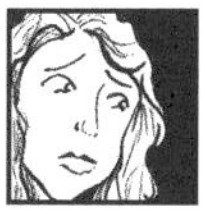

**Lisa Ullmann** is a television and film producer at her independently established company, Root for the Underdog Productions. She was the Executive Producer of the animated series The Ricky Gervais Show, which ran for three seasons on HBO. Originally from Houston TX, Lisa has no visual artistic ability and received an F in handwriting in kindergarten. She lives in Los Angeles, California.

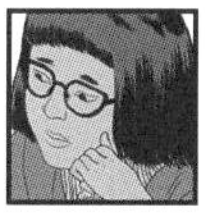

**Angie Wang** is an illustratress and cartoonista currently residing in Los Angeles, CA. She does a mix of editorial illustration, fashion illustration, comics, animation, and solely personal work. She has been published in *The New York Times, Taschen, The New Yorker*, and *The Best American Comics 2011*.

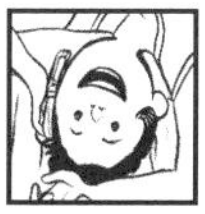

**Jen Wang**'s works have appeared in *Adventure Time* comics and *LA Magazine*. Her graphic novel *Koko Be Good* is available from First Second Books. She lives in Los Angeles, California.

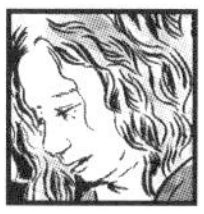

**Lauren R. Weinstein** is a cartoonist who is still recovering from having a baby and moving to the suburbs of New Jersey (it's been three years). Her comic books include *Girl Stories* and *The Goddess of War,* and her work has been published in *Kramer's Ergot, The Ganzfeld, An Anthology of Graphic Fiction*, and *The Best American Comics* of 2007 and 2010. Her work has also appeared in *The New York Times, Glamour*, and *Lucky Peach*. She is currently working on a sequel to *Girl Stories*. Her work can be seen at laurenweinstein.com

## About Our Contributors

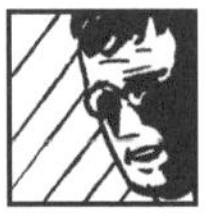

**Dylan Williams** was born in 1970 in Berkeley, CA. He grew up traveling to India, the Middle East, and many other faraway lands. He made hundreds of comics, including the series *Reporter*, and ran Sparkplug Comic Books for nine years. Dylan lost his life to cancer on September 10, 2011.

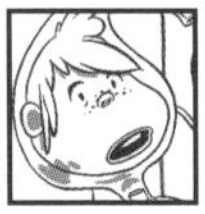

**Britt Wilson** is a cartoonist/illustrator/letterer living in Toronto, Ontario. Her collection of mini-comics and oddities, called *Britt Wilson's Greatest Book on Earth* (Conundrum Press), while not actually the greatest, is still pretty good. More of her work can be found brittwilson.com

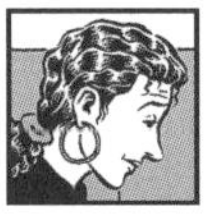

**Sari Wilson**, a former Stegner fellow, is a writer who works in prose and comics. Her writing has appeared in *Agni, Slice*, and *The Oxford American*, and has been anthologized in *From Girls to Grrrlz: A History of Women in Comics.*

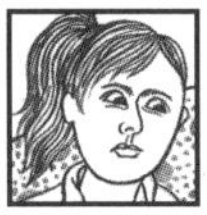

**Andi Zeisler** is the Editorial/Creative Director of Bitch Media and an occasional drawer of comics. She lives, works, and eats in Portland, OR and is working on a book about the legacy of pop culture and the women's movement.

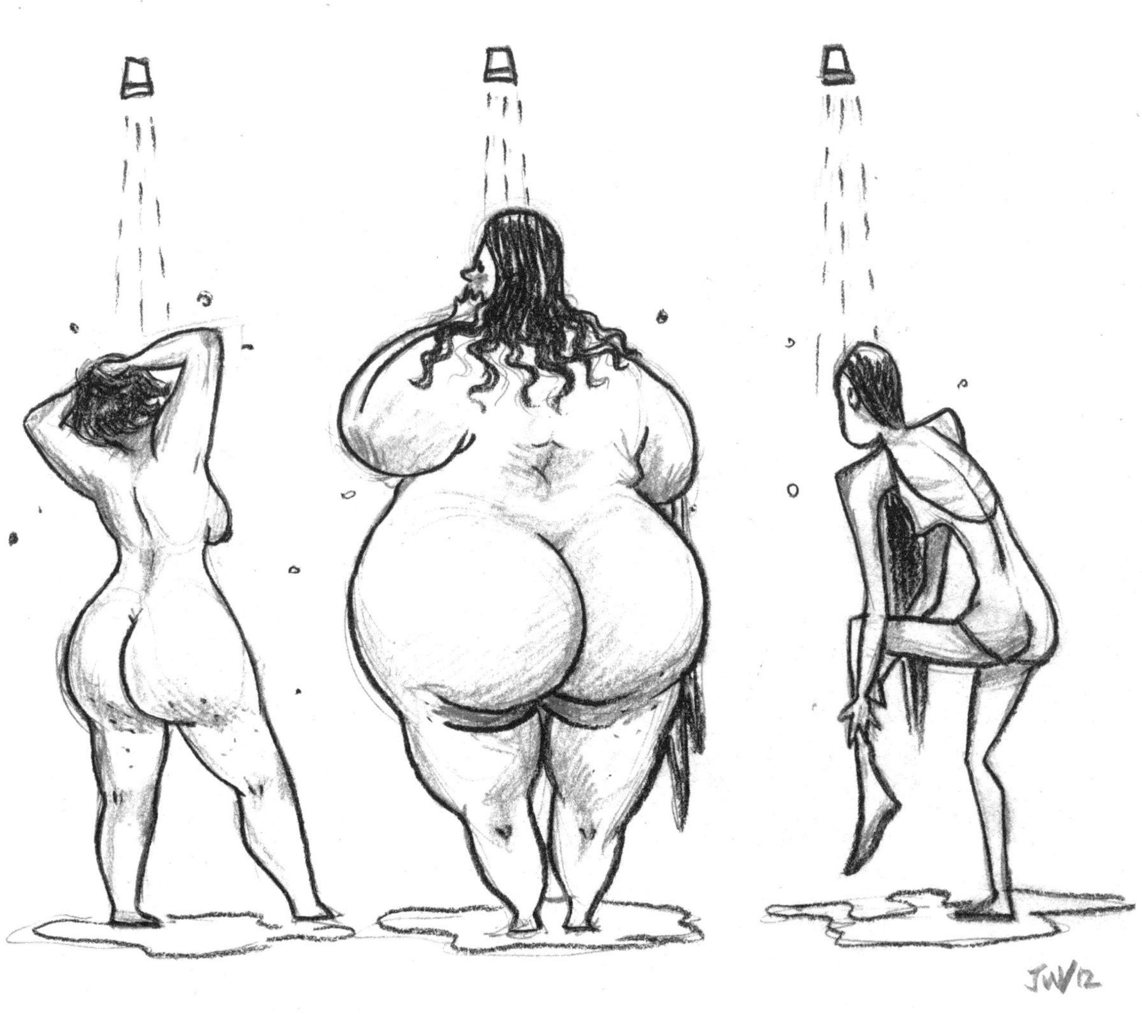
JW/12